To my wife Glyn with all my love

Preface

The primary aim of the text remains to produce a text book which gives a thorough treatment of the subject in a readable and accessible style for students of employment law in higher education. Now in its fourth edition, I have decided to restructure the book by concentrating on principles of individual employment law and remove the chapters on collective employment law which should really be regarded as a separate subject. I have attempted to structure the book in such a way that the subject is a manageable unit of study over a full academic year or a single semester. In my experience of teaching students who are law and business studies undergraduates, the breadth of employment law requires the teacher to make decisions about the input and the degree of emphasis of material from each of the 12 chapters.

The task of explaining this complex and dynamic subject is a challenging one and while I do occasionally comment on my view of the law, in the main I have left it to the law teacher to set the subject in context. A feature of the third edition that I have retained is the inclusion of a series of case study scenarios designed to be used as a vehicle to promote discussion in seminar or tutorial work or to be used as assignment topics. Once again the text relies heavily on case law, and hopefully I have chosen wisely. I am also aware of the fact that many students do not have access to source material and consequently I have included numerous statutory provisions with supporting explanations. It should be a fundamental aim of an employment law course to encourage students to approach source material with confidence and recognise how it is applied in the resolution of conflict. As the sole author I must take responsibility for any errors and resist the temptation to blame them on Monty and Toto who have provided a welcome distraction during the writing of the book

For ease of expression the book adopts the practice of using 'he' for 'he or she' and 'his' for 'his and hers'.

Acknowledgements

I would like to thank Moira Page for her patience and skill in designing and typesetting this book.

All errors and omissions remain the responsibility of the author.

The law is stated as at 1 September 2000

TH
Durham
September 2000

Chapter Assignments

At the end of the chapters of the text dealing with substantive law I thought it would be useful to include a number of scenarios which could be used to promote discussion in seminar work or serve as assignment topics. In the main the legal conflict revealed in the scenarios relates only to the particular chapter but this is not always the case. The scenarios are based on the operation of two organisations and relate mainly to staffing problems which have arisen. Dalton West plc is a large manufacturing company in the private sector and Brinkley Business School is a department of the University of Brinkley, a corporation in the public sector.

Dalton West plc

Dalton West is a large manufacturer of fork lift trucks with depots and retail outlets situated all over Britain. The company employs over two thousand staff at its main factory in Coventry and a further eight hundred at its Birmingham Head Office and the various depots nation-wide. The company recognises the Fitters and General Workers Union (FGWU) for the purposes of collective bargaining on behalf of the manual workers. Melissa Maxwell is the chief personnel officer at Dalton West and she runs a department of twelve staff at the Birmingham headquarters. A number of legal issues relating to staffing are at present unresolved.

Brinkley Business School

It was the end of the Summer Term at Brinkley Business School and it couldn't come soon enough for Miriam Perot, the Director of the Business School. Setting up the Business School at the beginning of the academic year by merging a number of university departments had brought with it numerous benefits and opportunities and certainly business courses and student numbers had increased, but there had also been a dramatic rise in staffing problems due to the reorganisation of the university. Management of the Business School is directly the responsibility of the senior management team consisting of the Director and her two deputies. The management is advised on matters of policy by the Board of Studies of the Business School and made accountable to the Academic Board of the University. It was part of the role of the Academic Board to ratify important decisions relating to staffing including new appointments and termination of contracts of full-time staff. A number of legal issues relating to staffing have arisen during the academic year and are at present unresolved.

Table of Contents

Chapter 5   Equal Opportunities in Recruitment

Chapter 6   Equal Opportunities at the Workplace

Chapter 7   Changing Contractual Arrangements

Chapter 8   Health and Safety at Work

Chapter 9   Statutory Employment Rights at Work and Continuity of Employment

Chapter 10   The Termination of Employment

Table of Cases

E

F

M

Q

R

S

Table of Statutes, Statutory Instruments and Treaties

Chapter 1

Sources of Employment Law

It would be wrong to begin a book of this nature by immediately launching into a discussion of some complex rules of employment law. While the aim of the book is hopefully to promote an appreciation and understanding of aspects of employment law, it is first necessary to set the scene. This requires an exploration of the various sources of employment law, both National and European, and a consideration of the legal framework in which the law is applied. In the first chapter therefore, an attempt is made to identify the main sources of employment law with particular emphasis on the increasing impact of European Community legislation. While the UK legislative process is given only superficial treatment the law making institutions of the European Union with which you may be less familiar are considered in more depth.

The fundamental aim of the book is to explore rights and responsibilities in relation to individual employment law, and exclude the collective position relating to trade union bargaining and industrial action which is now regarded as a distinct legal subject.

Sources of Employment Law

The primary source of law is of course statute, and in the field of employment law there has been an increasing tendency for contemporary governments to legislate. A serious student of employment law must be prepared to recognise that many of the legal rules are to be found within numerous statutory provisions of relatively recent origin. One helpful achievement is the consolidation of collective employment law by statute in 1992. in the Trade Union and Labour Relations (Consolidation) Act 1992. A number of the provisions of this Act are relevant in relation to individual employment rights so reference will be made to its content. More significant is the further consolidating Act passed in relation to individual employment rights, the Employment Rights Act 1996. This Act has subsequently been amended, in particular by the Employment Relation Act 1999. In addition there is widespread legislation on equal opportunity law including sex, race and disability discrimination. As a general introduction to the importance of statutory rights in employment law the table on page 2 identifies some of the main statutes right, their source and the individuals protected.

Table of Key Statutory Employment Rights

Statutory Right	Statutory Source	Individuals Protected
Not to suffer discrimination in recruitment and employment on the grounds of race sex or disability	Sex Discrimination Act 1975 Race Relations Act 1976 Equal Pay Act 1970 Equal Treatment Directive Disability Discrimination Act 1995	Full-time and part-time employees. Contractors providing personal services
To be provided with a safe working environment	The Health and Safety at Work Act 1974 The Health and Safety (Work Place) Regulations 1992	Full-time and part-time employees Contractors providing personal services
To have a written statement of employment terms To have an itemised pay statement Not to suffer unlawful deductions To have maternity leave where appropriate To notice on the termination of employment	The Employment Rights Act 1996	Full-time and part-time employees
To have preferential status against an insolvent employer	Insolvency Act 1986	Full-time and part-time employees
Not to suffer discrimination in recruitment and employment on the grounds of Trade Union Membership or activities	The Trade Union and Labour Relations (Consolidation) Act 1992	Full-time and part-time employees
To be paid a minimum wage and to work a limited number of hours	The National Minimum Wage Act 1998 The Working Time Regulations 1998	Workers
Not to be unfairly dismissed To be paid a redundancy payment where appropriate To receive maternity absence where appropriate To receive a written statement of the reasons for dismissal where appropriate	The Employment Rights Act 1996	Full-time and part-time employees who have one years continuous service with the same employer (subject to exceptions)
Not to suffer a detriment or be dismissed for revealing a protected disclosure	Public Interest (Disclosure) Act 1998	Workers

Delegated Legislation

While primary legislation is a major source of employment law, many statutes contemplate further law making by means of delegated legislation. Numerous Statutory Instruments contain a multitude of regulations which have the force of law, and provide a convenient means of amending previous statutory provisions. Significant changes to the law may be introduced by regulation.

Under the Unfair Dismissal and Statement of Reasons for Dismissal (Variation of Qualifying Period) Order 1999 the qualifying period for unfair dismissal rights was lowered from two years to one year's continuous employment. By this means from June 1999 the number of employees who qualify for unfair dismissal rights was dramatically increased.

The Disability Order 1998 extended the category of employers to which the Disability Discrimination Act 1995 applied from those with twenty or more employees to those with fifteen or more employees.

 The National Minimum Wage Regulations 1999 put the meat on the bone of the National Minimum Wage Act 1998. The Part-Time Workers (Prevention of Less Favourable Treatment) Regulations 2000 confers significant rights on part-time workers in relation to pay, maternity, pensions and time off. Under the umbrella of the Health and Safety at Work etc. Act 1974 the Secretary of State for Employment is given authority on the advice of the Health and Safety Commission to make regulations on a wide range of matters. It is by this means that the previous law on health and safety at work is in the process of being replaced and refined.

It has become an increasingly popular though disconcerting practice for our legislators to pass primary legislation which does little more than provide regulatory powers to the Secretary of State to incorporate the law in Regulations. The Employment Relations Act 1999 is an excellent example of an amending statute which provides that regulation will constitute the primary form of enactment. Even at this point in the text you could appreciate some of the changes introduced by the 1999 Act in particular the raising of the maximum compensatory award for unfair dismissal to £50,000 and the removal of the ability for employers to require employees on fixed term contracts to opt out of unfair dismissal rights.

Later in the chapter we will focus on how Statutory Instruments may be used to incorporate European Community legislation into the domestic law of the United Kingdom. The Transfer of Undertaking (Protection of Employment) Regulations 1981 were passed to give effect to obligations which arose under EC Council Directive 77/187 (the Acquired Rights Directive). Also the Equal Pay (Amendment) Regulations 1983 amended the Equal Pay Act of 1970 to bring it into line with Article 119 of the Treaty of Rome and the Equal Pay Directive of 1975. The

Working Time Regulations 1999 were enacted to give effect to the Working Time Directive.

Statutes and Statutory Instruments are only enacted of course after undergoing a strict parliamentary process. In addition, draft Codes of Practice require the approval of both Houses of Parliament and only come into effect on such date as the Secretary of State appoints. It should not be necessary in a book of this nature to examine the Parliamentary process for the passage of legislation. It would however be a useful exercise to explore the complex process involved in the passage of European Community law and its legal status, with which you may be less familiar.

Codes of Practice have an increasingly important role in the regulation of employment relationships and industrial relations generally. Their primary function is to provide guidance to employers, employers' associations, workers, and trade unions with the aim of improving industrial relations. While a failure to observe the provision of a code of practice does not of itself make a person liable to legal proceedings before a court or tribunal, compliance or non compliance with a code is admissible in evidence. Codes of practice may emanate from the Secretary of State for Employment who has produced codes on picketing, closed shop agreements, and trade union industrial action balloting. In addition, other agencies have authority to issue codes, including the Advisory, Conciliation and Arbitration Service, (ACAS) the Commission for Racial Equality, the Equal Opportunities Commission and the Health and Safety Commission.

A good example of a significant code of practice in employment law is the ACAS Code on Disciplinary Practices and Procedures (under review 2000). An employment tribunal is entitled to use the code as a bench mark when considering the fairness of the employer's conduct in reaching the conclusion to dismiss someone. The EAT held in *Lock v. Cardiff Rail Co Ltd.* 1998 that a train conductor had been unfairly dismissed when his employer relied on a one-off error of judgment . Such a decision to dismiss did not accord with the code of practice which provides for warnings and counselling in such circumstances and was as a consequence found to be unfair.

The Common Law and Statutory Interpretation

While it would be tempting to believe that a broad knowledge of the numerous statutory provisions in relation to employment law is all that is needed to acquire a sound understanding of the subject, such a notion is far from the truth. In the following chapters you will discover that the nature and content of the primary legal instrument that regulates employment relationship, the contract of employment, is determined by applying principles of common law. It is only by applying common law principles in relation to the implication of terms into contracts that the precise nature of a contract of employment can be appreciated. The termination of employment is also largely governed by common law principles as is civil redress in relation to health and safety at work and liability in tort for unlawful industrial action. The common law is continually developed and refined by the courts.

A recent example of this process, which you should be able to appreciate even at this stage in the text, was provided by the Court of Appeal in *Jones v. Tower Book* 1997. The case concerned the potential liability of an employer for a serious act of racial harassment committed by employees under his control. Vicarious or substituted liability, you will discover in Chapter 8, can only be imposed if the employees commit the wrongful act in question during the *"course of employment"*. The phrase course of employment has been the subject of judicial analysis over the years and been held to mean that at the time of the wrongful act the employee in question was carrying out job functions. Obviously this is not usually the case when acts of racial or sexual harassment take place. The Court of Appeal decided that in relation to this type of unlawful act the phrase *"course of employment"* should be given an everyday meaning so that if an employee commits an act of racial harassment at the workplace his employer could be held liable.

The above decision has of course far reaching consequences and should be considered by all employers who wish to assess their potential liability for discriminatory action to their employees.

It is the role of the judiciary to declare the common law but more significantly in employment law the courts and tribunals are called upon to apply and interpret statutory provisions. It is through the process of establishing binding and persuasive precedents in court and tribunal judgments that statutory provisions are given meaning. A student of employment law should appreciate therefore that a thorough understanding of the rules of employment law embodied within statutory provisions can only be achieved by carrying out a study of case-law where the provisions are applied. Even at this stage of the text some examples should help you understand this fundamental role of the courts and tribunals. The examples which have been included will be referred to at various stages of the text and are drawn from health and safety, the use of statutory time limits, unfair dismissal and action short of dismissal.

Health and Safety

The first example is from health and safety law (considered in Chapter 8) and shows that the decision in a case may rest upon the court's interpretation of a word or phrase contained within a statutory provision.

In *Knowles v. Liverpool City Council* 1993 a council flagger sued his employer for damages in negligence when he was injured by a flagstone he was handling which broke because it had not been properly cured by the supplier. Under the Employers' Liability (Defective Equipment) Act 1969 an employer may be deemed to be liable in negligence if an employee is injured as a result of defective equipment supplied by a third party. Equipment is defined in the Act as including *"plant and machinery, vehicles, aircraft and clothing"*. The issue before the Court of Appeal was whether the definition would cover flagstones which were work materials. The court thought that the term equipment should be interpreted broadly to include the *"materials which an employee is given by his employer to use to do his job. Such a broad approach reflects the general purpose of the legislation and is consistent with the ordinary meaning of the word in the context of an employee carrying out his job"*. As consequence the employer was liable under the Act for the injuries sustained to the employee by defective equipment used in the course of employment.

The above case provides us therefore with a precedent as to how the definition of 'equipment' in the Employee's Liability (Defective Equipment) Act 1969 is to be applied. The broad approach to the definition was adopted by the Scottish Court of Session in *Kelly v. First Engineering Ltd 1999* where it was held that a bolt which snapped when a worker was using a spanner could be classified as 'work equipment'

Time Limits

In the Employment Rights Act 1996 you will discover that there are numerous provisions which confer rights on employees. In particular if a qualified employee believes that he has been dismissed without good reason he may under section 111 present a complaint of unfair dismissal against his employer before an employment tribunal (considered in Chapter 11). The Act provides however that there are strict time limits to be complied with, otherwise the right to present a complaint will be lost.

Section 111(2) of the Act states that .... *"an employment tribunal shall not consider a complaint under this section unless it is presented to the tribunal before the end of the period of three months beginning with the effective date of termination or within such further period as the tribunal considers reasonable in a case where it is satisfied that it was not reasonably practicable for the complaint to be presented before the end of the period of three months."*

The legal rule is stating therefore, in relatively straightforward terms, that if a dismissed employee wants to complain of unfair dismissal before an industrial tribunal he must start the proceedings within three months, but if he fails to do so the tribunal still has a discretion to hear the case if it was not reasonably practicable for him to present it within the time limit. If a legal dispute arises over whether an unfair dismissal claim has been presented within the time limits it is the function of the courts and tribunals to attempt to resolve the conflict by applying the exact wording of s.111(2) to the factual situation before it. The subsection requires the industrial tribunal therefore to ask itself one or possibly two questions:

(1) Has the complaint been brought within the three months time limit prescribed in the section?

(2) If not, was it reasonably practicable to present the complaint within the time limit?

If the answer to the first question is no and the answer to the second question is yes then the tribunal should not proceed to hear the complaint of unfair dismissal. If the reverse is true however and either the complaint is within the time limits or it was not reasonably practicable to present it in time then the tribunal does have jurisdiction to proceed.

There are many case decisions which over the years have provided guidance to industrial tribunals as to the approach to be adopted in addressing these questions. To determine the relevant time period it is necessary to know *"the effective date of termination"* which may be difficult to decide particularly if the complainant is dismissed without being given the notice to which he is entitled.

The specific wording of the section was analysed in *University of Cambridge v. Murray* 1993 where an industrial tribunal held that the phrase "beginning with" meant that that date forms part of the time period. If the words *"from"* or *"after"* had been used then the three months would be calculated to the corresponding date of the relevant later month or if no corresponding date the last day of the month. As the expression *"beginning with"* is used in the section however the starting date is a day earlier and so ends with the day before the corresponding date of the later relevant month. If the effective date of termination is the 30th of April therefore the time period expires on the last moment of the 29th July. This case is therefore of great assistance in interpreting the section and provides guidance to future tribunals who are required to apply it.

If a tribunal decide that the complaint was not presented within the time period it would still proceed to hear it if it was not reasonably practicable to present the complaint in time. Parliament has left it to the courts and tribunals therefore to determine the issue of reasonable practicability in any given case. Reasons for late claims brought before tribunals have included postal delays, bad advice from lawyers or civil servants, and obstructive employers. Case decisions made in relation to these reasons provide guidance and in some cases lay down precedents for future cases (see Chapter 11).

To summarise therefore it is possible to say that the law on time limits for presenting a complaint of unfair dismissal is most certainly contained within s.111(2) of the Employment Rights Act 1996 but also as interpreted in the numerous decisions of our courts and tribunals.

Unfair Dismissal

Under s.152(1)(a) of the Trade Union and Labour Relations (Consolidation) Act 1992, the dismissal of an employee by an employer shall be regarded as having been unfair if the reason for it (or if more than one, the principal reason) was that the employee *was, or proposed to become, a member of an independent trade union.* The object of the section is to make it automatically unfair to dismiss an employee because of his trade union membership. In Chapter 11 we will discover that such an individual may present a complaint of unfair dismissal before an employment tribunal in an attempt to secure a legal remedy, without the need to show a period of continuous employment. In relation to s.152 however, there are a number of issues: For instance, when is an individual an employee?; how does a trade union become independent?; and, not least of which, when is a dismissal related to an individual's membership of a trade union?

> In *Discount Tobacco and Confectionery Ltd. v. Armitage* 1990 the complainant was a shop manageress with only a short period of continuous employment who enlisted the help of her trade union official to secure a written contract of employment from her employer. When finally such a contract was issued, and she felt it contained discrepancies, the complainant attempted to raise them with her employer. The employer dismissed her, giving the reason for dismissal as lack of suitability or capability. The dismissal led to the complaint of unfair dismissal, the complainant alleging that by virtue of s.152 her dismissal was automatically unfair because it was by reason of her trade union membership. The task of the industrial tribunal, and then subsequently on appeal, the Employment Appeal Tribunal, was to determine whether the section should apply when the reason for dismissal was the complainant making use of her trade union membership rather than just the fact that she was a member. Both the industrial tribunal and the EAT thought that it should. *"For the purposes of the section there is no genuine distinction between membership of a union on the one hand and making use of the essential services of a union officer on the other. The activity of a trade union officer in elucidating and negotiating terms of employment is an important incident of union membership and the outward and visible manifestation of it. To construe s.152 so narrowly as to apply only to the fact*

that a person was a member of the union, without regard to the consequences of that membership would be to emasculate the provision altogether."

The case above provides us with an example of the judiciary giving a statutory provision a wide interpretation and so extending its application beyond the limits that many commentators would expect.

Action Short of Dismissal

Finally you should appreciate that within the United Kingdom, Parliament is the primary law maker, and if the government disagrees with the interpretation of a statute by the courts, it can through Parliament overrule the case decision by means of an amending statute. An excellent example of how speedily the government can reach to inconvenient judicial decision making is provided below.

A contemporary theme in employment law is the attempt by employers to move employees away from collectively bargained terms of employment to personal contracts, often with financial inducements. The significance of this process is recognised in this text by devoting a full chapter (Chapter 7) to contractual change and its impact.

Two decisions of the Court of Appeal, *Wilson v. Associated Newspapers Ltd.* 1993 and *Palmer v. Associated British Ports* 1993, initially provided some protection to those employees who refused to give up collectively bargained terms and accept a financial inducement to sign personal contracts. In both cases the employer terminated collective agreements and offered new personal contracts which did not involve significant changes except in relation to trade union representation. A pay rise was also offered to staff who accepted the contracts. The issue to be determined by the court was whether this practice infringed s.146 of the Trade Union and Labour Relations (Consolidation) Act 1992 on the grounds that it was action short of dismissal against individuals for the purposes of deterring them from or penalising them for being members of independent trade unions. The Court of Appeal held that the practice was unlawful under s.146 recognising that the employer may have more than one "purpose" in mind when he took the action. The reality of the employer's purpose as *"to penalise those who would not forgo union representation by not conferring on them the benefits bestowed on those who are prepared to do so".*

Within days of the above decisions the government announced its intention to reverse them and amendments to s.146 were hastily introduced into the Trade Union Reform and Employment Rights Bill which was conveniently then before Parliament. Section 13 of the Trade Union Reform and Employment Rights Act 1993 provides that where the employer has the purpose of furthering a change in the relationship with his employees and a purpose also engaging in conduct prohibited by s.146 the industrial tribunal must disregard the latter purpose. That is unless the action was such that *"no reasonable employer would take"*.

The aim of the amendment therefore is to further the government's objective that employers should be free to implement change without fearing legal action from trade unions who refuse to accept it and do not receive financial benefits as a result. Whether the amended section achieves that purpose will depend upon how it is interpreted and applied by the courts and tribunals.

European Community Law

The United Kingdom has been a member of the European Union since January 1st 1973, along with Eire and Denmark. In 1981 Greece became the tenth member state, followed by Spain and Portugal in 1986. In 1990 the unification of Germany had the automatic effect of bringing the territory of the former East Germany into the Community which was further enlarged with the accession of Austria, Finland and Sweden at the beginning of 1995. The fifteen member states, with a population of 370 million, now form a single economic region in which goods, services, people and capital can move almost as freely as they do within national boundaries.

As a Member State of the European Community (EC) since January 1st 1973 the United Kingdom is bound by Community Law. In the field of business this is of enormous significance. This is because the European Community is essentially economic in nature and the community objective of the completion of a single European market is based upon the actual harmonisation of laws relating to business and trade between Member States. Examples can be seen in the fields of:

- company law harmonisation and investor protection;

- consumer rights and consumer protection;

- data protection;

- environmental protection;

- intellectual property rights;

- employment law.

In each of these fields European law has been active in amending and adding to existing UK law, as well as requiring the introduction of new law. For example in employment law the Community has been active in the following areas:

- pregnancy dismissals, maternity leave and parental leave;

- statutory rights for part-time workers and fixed contract workers;

- collective redundancy procedures;

- dismissals and detrimental conduct relating to health and safety;

- acquired rights on a business transfer;

- health and safety at work regulations;

- sex discrimination and equal pay.

The framework of Community law is set out in the Treaty of Rome 1957 as amended by the Single European Act of 1986, the Treaty of European Union signed at Maastricht in 1992 and the Treaty of Amsterdam 1999. The institutions of the European Union must operate within and give effect to these Treaties.

The Treaty on European Union and the Amsterdam Treaty

The Treaty on European Union which was negotiated in Maastricht in November 1991 came into effect at the beginning of November 1993, after completing the difficult process of ratification in each of the member states. It survived a second Danish referendum and challenges to its constitutional validity in the German and UK courts.

The Treaty creates a European Union which has three main elements, often described as *pillars*. The first is the European Community itself, the powers and decision making procedures of which are extended and modified. The second element relates to foreign and security policy, and the third to justice and home affairs. The second and third pillars operate outside of the formal institutional framework of the EC and are based on new inter-governmental arrangements between the member states. As such their decisions do not form part of the body of EC law, which is created by the Council of Ministers acting with the Commission and European Parliament, and are not subject to the jurisdiction of the Court of Justice.

In the present context we are concerned only with the first pillar of the Treaty which provides for closer European integration within the framework of Community law. This part of the Treaty expands the areas of Community activity. Under the Treaty the task of the European Community will be to promote a harmonious and balanced development of economic activities, sustainable and non-inflationary growth respecting the environment, a high degree of convergence of economic performance, a high level of employment and of social protection, the raising of the standard of living and quality of life, and economic and social cohesion and solidarity.

The UK, however originally negotiated to opt out of two important parts of the Treaty, the *Social Chapter* and the third stage of economic and monetary union which is the adoption of a single currency. The remainder of the Treaty applies with full effect to the UK. The Labour government is fully committed to adopting the social chapter and has now done so.

The consequence of adopting the Social Chapter is that the UK government became immediately subject to the European Directives which were previously not binding due to the opt out under the Maarstricht Treaty. A good example is the EU Parental Leave Directive which the UK government was required to implement by 15 December 1999. The rules in relation to parental leave are found in schedule 4 to the Employment Relations Act 1999 which adds a new s.76-80 to the Employment Rights Act 1996 and supported by the Maternity and Parental Leave Regulations 1999. (See Chapter 6).

On the 1 May 1999 the Amsterdam Treaty came into force. Its main significance is the introduction of the revised Social Chapter which formally ends the UK opt out from the Community Social Policy. The most immediate effect of the revised Social Chapter is to abolish the Social Protocol adopted at Maastricht. This means that the Community must act with unanimity in social policy matters and it will no longer be necessary for specific directives to be adopted to bring the UK in line with social policy regimes in other member states.

It also creates a legislative case for the introduction of measures to combat discrimination beyond the spheres of nationality and gender. There are proposed Directives on parental leave, works councils, part-time work, fixed term workers and the burden of proof in sex discrimination cases. The European Commission has more room to manoeuvre in proposing legislation under the new Social Chapter in fields such as working conditions information, consolidation of workers and equal pay. Importantly decision making will be by qualified majority vote for a number of issues. A new Article 13 allows the Council on the European Union to take appropriate action to combat discrimination based on "sex, racial or ethnic origin, religion or belief, disability, age or sexual orientation. The appropriate actions would include encouraging legislation at national level on equal opportunities.

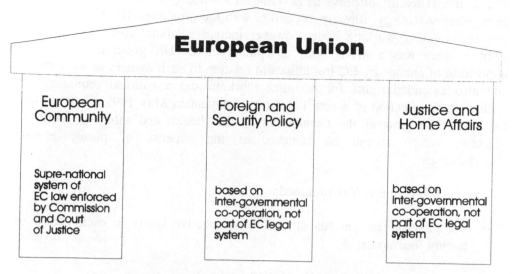

Structure of the European Union

It is clear from an examination of the major EC treaties that the Community has power to legislate over a very broad range of issues which embrace the entire area of employment law. It is in practice by far the most important source of new law in some spheres such as health and safety, maternity rights and equal opportunities. The European Union achieve most of its objectives through the use of legal mechanisms, notably in the field of employment law by directives. Occasionally this has led to direct and well published conflict between the UK government and the European Union. A good example is *United Kingdom of Great Britain and Northern Ireland v. Council of the European Union* 1997 where the UK government challenged the legal validity of the Working Time Directive laying down legal requirements for working time and holidays.

Working Time and the Minimum Wage

The background to the legal action begins with the issue in 1992 of a European Community draft directive related to Working Time. This directive was originally adopted by the European Commission in July 1990 as part of a package of measures concerned with the implementation of the social action programme. The theme of the directive is that physically demanding and socially disruptive working patterns are dangerous to the health, safety and welfare of the workforce.

The UK approach of leaving matters such as the length of the working week and annual leave to be decided by the parties to an employment contract provides, it is argued, insufficient protection to the weaker party, the employee. Legislating on such matters, as part of the Social Action Programme, has been the focus of profound disagreement between the UK government and the European Commission.

The dominant feature of previous government's thinking on employment had been a de-regulatory strategy, directly in conflict with the directive. The government view was that limiting working hours however increases labour costs dramatically. In addition there was a strong body of opinion in the UK government against the imposition of change by EC institutions in relation to such matters as working hours and also extended rights for part-time workers and a national minimum wage. Following the election of a new Labour government in May 1997 this is no longer the case. The view of the Commission is that health and safety at work is an objective which should be achieved at the expense of purely economic considerations.

The revised directive 1/7/91 proposed:

- compulsory rest periods of twelve consecutive hours in each period of twenty four hours;

- one rest day every seven day period;

- a prohibition on overtime by night workers where the work involves special hazards or heavy physical or mental strain;

- regular health checks for night workers;

- maximum working hours;

- minimum periods of annual leave.

In June 1993 the EU's Council of Ministers finalised the most controversial part of the directive, the maximum working week set at forty eight hours per week. The Council of Ministers approved the working time directive by eleven votes to nil with Britain abstaining. The view of the British government, expressed by the then Secretary of State for Employment, was that the directive would be a threat to jobs by having an adverse affect on Europe's international competitiveness. The directive provided for implementation of the mandatory forty eight hour week within ten years but allowed only three years to introduce law to protect workers who are asked to work longer hours and do not wish to do so.

The three year deadline under the directive expired on 23 November 1996, and consequently in advance of the deadline the British government sought to challenge the validity of the directive before the European Court of Justice in Luxembourg. What was sought was a ruling that legislation dealing with working hours could not be validly introduced as a health and safety measure, requiring only a qualified majority vote rather than unanimity. Such a ruling would legitimise the refusal of the government to implement the directive. The European Court delivered the judgment on November 12, less than two weeks before the expiry date. It found against the government. By then it was too late for appropriate legislation to be introduced to implement the directive, leaving the government open to the possibility of action for damages being brought against it. Legislation on working time and of course the minimum wage has now been enacted. The Working Time Regulation and the National Minimum Wage Act 1998 are considered in Chapter 9 on Statutory Employment Rights.

The Community Institutions

The Community Institutions are:

- the Commission

- the Council of Ministers/Council of Europe

- the European Parliament

- the European Court of Justice.

The Commission

The Commission consists of 20 commissioners, two from each of the larger EC states and one from each of the others. They are nominated by their governments and appointed by the unanimous agreements of the governments of the member states for a renewable period of four years. The term of office is increased to five years under the Treaty on European Union which also provides that their appointment shall be subject to the approval of the Parliament. Once appointed they must act with complete independence in the interests of the Community. In the performance of their duties they must neither seek not take instructions from any government or any other body. The main functions of the Commission are to initiate policy and proposals for legislation for ultimate adoption by the Council. It is the executive arm of the EC, with responsibility for ensuring the implementation of agreed policies and managing the community's budget.

As the *guardian of the treaties* it must ensure full compliance by member states with Community obligations in accordance with EC law. The Commission has powers to investigate an alleged infringement of the Treaty by a member state and where it considers that the member state has failed to fulfil an EC obligation, the Commission will issue a reasoned opinion on the matter after giving the member state an opportunity to submit its observations. The member state must comply with the reasoned opinion before the deadline stated in it. Where it fails to do so the Commission may refer the matter to the Court of Justice. This procedure is often used where a member state either fails to implement a directive within the given time limit, or implements it incorrectly.

An important development in discrimination law is the European Union's decision to extend the current requests of Member States to introduce anti discrimination measures. The Amsterdam Treaty 1999 amended the Treaty of Rome by inserting a new Article 6 which gives the Council of Europe power to introduce measures to combat discrimination on the grounds of sex, race, ethnic origin, religion or belief, disability, age and sexual orientation in employment and training.

> In *Commission of the European Communities v. United Kingdom of Great Britain and Northern Ireland* 1994 the European Court of Justice ruled against the UK government in two cases brought by the Commission where it was alleged that the UK had failed to properly transpose Directives on collective redundancies and acquired rights. By failing to ensure worker representation in a workplace where there is no recognised trade union the community law obligation to ensure that worker's representatives are informed and consulted on business transfers and collective redundancies had not been complied with. Most of the criticisms were accepted by the UK government and rectified by specific provisions in the Trade Union Reform and Employment Rights Act 1993.

The work of the Commission is divided into twenty four Directorates General, each D-G dealing with specific aspects of Community activity and policy under the control of an individual Commisioner. Each Commissioner heads a department, and is known as a Director General (DG). For employment matters there is a Commissioner for Employment, Social Affairs and Education.

The Council of Ministers/Council of the European Union

The *Council of Ministers* is the EC's principal decision making body with the final say on most secondary legislation. The Commission initiates proposals for legislation as the Council does not have power to do this itself. It can, however, request the Commission to submit to it proposals on matters which may be desirable in order to achieve the objectives of the Treaty. The Council consists of one government minister from each member state and its membership varies according to the nature of the matter under discussion. The presidency of the Council and therefore of the Community is held by each member state in rotation for a six month term. Towards the end of each term the heads of state will meet for a summit to discuss major current issues and to chart the future course of the Community. When it involves a meeting of the Heads of State the Council is known as the *European Council*.

The Council of Ministers is the one institution which is common both to the European Community and to the Foreign Affairs and Home Affairs pillars of the European Union. Most European Union business is conducted at meetings of the Council of Ministers. Shortly after the coming into force of the Treaty on European Union, the Council of Ministers announced its formal decision to change its name to the Council of the European Union. The other EC institutions, however, have little or no role in the procedures for conducting foreign and home affairs, and it is therefore inaccurate to refer to them as institutions of the European Union. Only the Council has this dual role.

The UK Parliament has the opportunity to assess the legal and political implications of a proposal for EC legislation before the Council votes on it. This is carried out by the *Scrutiny Committees* of the Commons and the Lords who are given copies of the proposals with an explanatory memorandum. The Scrutiny Committees have power to call for written or oral evidence, consult with government departments, call for a debate and if necessary request that amendments to the proposal be negotiated. Once the Scrutiny Committee has cleared a proposal then the minister is free to accept it in the EC Council of Ministers.

The method of voting used in the Council is of particular importance as the Council is the main legislating body in the community. Clearly if all decisions were taken on the basis of a unanimous vote, each member state would have a veto over every Community decision. On the other hand if some form of majority voting system was used, a member state's interests could be overridden and laws introduced against its wishes. The Single European Act introduced qualified majority voting for all measures required to complete the single market, with certain exceptions. These related to approximation of indirect taxes, free movement of persons, and matters affecting the rights of employees, which are still subject to voting by unanimity. Measures related to the health and safety of workers, however, are subject to qualified majority voting procedure. Under the Treaty on European Union qualified majority voting has been extended further, into areas such as consumer protection, health, education and environmental programmes

The European Parliament

Members of the European Parliament, MEPs, are the directly elected representatives of the citizens of the European Union There are a total of 626 MEPs, of which 87 represent British constituencies. The Parliament sits for a five year term and is based partly in Strasbourg and partly in Brussels. Its powers include the right to dismiss the whole of the Commission on a motion of censure by a two-thirds majority. It has no power to dismiss individual commissioners. MEPs can ask oral or written questions of the Council or the Commission, which must be answered. The answers to written questions are published in the Official Journal of the Community. In respect of the Community's budget, the Parliament has a final say over certain items of expenditure, and has the ultimate power to reject the budget as a whole. In terms of law making power, the European Parliament is markedly different from the UK Parliament, having a relatively minor role in the legislative process.

Its powers have been progressively strengthened by the Single European Act and the Treaty on European Union, in response to a fundamental criticism of the lack of democratic accountability of the Community Institutions. This so-called *democratic deficit* has been characterised by a concentration of power in the hands of the unelected Commission, the practice of the Council to take its decisions behind closed doors, the inability of the Parliament to initiate proposals for new legislation, and the limited role of Parliament within the legislative process.

The Treaty on European Union has gone some way towards addressing the democratic deficit, although it may be argued that the criticism remains valid. The increased power of the Parliament is reflected in the three different Community law-making procedures. The *consultation procedure*, under which the Parliament gives its opinion but has little real power, was laid down in the original Treaty of Rome. The *co-operation procedure*, in which it has power to make amendments but not to veto, was introduced by the Single European Act. The *co-decision procedure*, in which it has power to make amendments and a right of veto, is contained in the Treaty on European Union.

The European Court of Justice

The Court of Justice sits in Luxembourg and is composed of 15 judges who are appointed by the mutual agreement of the member states for renewable periods of six years. They must be persons of absolute independence who are qualified to hold the highest judicial office in their own country or who are legal experts of recognised competence. The court is assisted by nine Advocates-General, who must hold similar qualifications to the judges and are appointed on the same basis. It is the duty of the Advocate-General, acting with complete impartiality and independence, to make reasoned submissions in open court as to the application of Community law to the questions posed in the case before the court. The opinion of the Advocate-General is not binding on the court, which may decide the case in a different way, although this is unusual. There is no equivalent to the Advocate-General within the English legal system.

The Court of Justice has power to hear the following types of case:

- *Actions against member states* Where it appears that a member state has failed to fulfil an obligation under Community law the Commission may take infringement proceedings under article 169. Other member states are also able to bring this type of case, under article 170, provided that they first bring the matter to the attention of the Commission. Prior to the Treaty on European Union the powers of the Court of Justice in such cases were limited to making a declaration requiring the defaulting member state to take the necessary measures to comply with its judgment. There was no effective sanction, other than political pressure, to enforce compliance. Under the new Treaty, however, a member state may ultimately be fined if it fails to comply with the court's ruling.

- *Actions against community institutions* The Court of Justice has power to review the legality of acts of Community Institutions, or their failure to act. The court may declare void any illegal action, award damages and review decisions.

- *Employment disputes between the Community and its employees* The Court of Justice acts as an industrial tribunal for the employees of Community institutions. Cases of this type account for just under a quarter of its case load.

- *Preliminary rulings under article 177* Any court or tribunal in a member state may request a preliminary ruling from the Court of Justice as to the meaning or interpretation of an aspect of Community law. Such a request may be made where the ruling is required to enable that court or tribunal to give judgment in a case before it. Where there is no appeal from its decision, the court or tribunal must request a preliminary ruling if it considers this necessary to enable it to give judgment. This procedure provides an important bridge between the legal systems of member states and that of the Community. It is designed to ensure that Community law is applied and interpreted in a uniform manner throughout all member states. The function of the Court of Justice is simply to rule on the interpretation of Community law, in the light of which the domestic court or tribunal will decide the case before it. The House of Lords in *R. v. Secretary of State for Employment ex parte Seymour-Smith and Perez* 1997 referred a number of significant legal questions to the European Court to give preliminary rulings. The decision as to whether the two year qualifying period to qualify for unfair dismissal was indirectly discriminatory rested upon the ruling of the court.

The Single European Act made provision for a *Court of First Instance of the European Community*, to be attached to the Court of Justice in order to deal with certain categories of case. The need for such a court arises as a result of the growth of the number of cases referred to the Court of Justice, and the likelihood of a continued growth in its workload due to the expansion of the Community itself and to a significant increase in Community legislation related to the completion of the

Single Market. It is hoped that the Court of First Instance will reduce the period of time taken to dispose of cases which, before its introduction, averaged 18 months to two years.

The Court of First Instance, established in 1989, has twelve members. They usually act in a judicial capacity, although they are also called upon to undertake the task of Advocate-General. The Court has jurisdiction to hear claims for damages and judicial reviews against Community Institutions, and hear employment cases involving Community employees. There is an appeal on a point of law to the Court of Justice, although a decision of the Court of First Instance on a matter of fact is final. Significantly the Court of First Instance has no jurisdiction to hear cases brought by member states or by Community Institutions, or to deal with references by national courts or tribunals under article 177 for preliminary rulings.

Primacy of Community Law

It is a central feature of Community law that it takes precedence over any conflicting provisions in the national law of member states. This feature has been strongly developed by the Court of Justice in a series of cases as the issue of priority is not addressed directly in the Treaty of Rome. In *VanGend en Loos v Nederlands Administratie der Belastingen* 1963 the Court of Justice described the relationship between Community law and domestic law in the following way: *"By creating a community of unlimited duration, having its own institutions, its own personality, its own legal capacity and capacity of representation on the international plain and, more particularly, real powers stemming from a limitation of sovereignty or a transfer of powers from the states to the community, the member states have limited their sovereign rights albeit within limited fields, and have thus created a body of law which binds both their nationals and themselves."*

The principle of supremacy of Community law was clearly affirmed by the Court of Justice in the case of *Costa v. ENEL* 1964 in which it held that a provision in the EC Treaty took precedence over a rule in a subsequent Italian statute. The Court relied on the statement in Van Gend en Loos, together with the duty imposed by article 5 on each member state to ensure that their obligations under the Treaty are fulfilled, and stated "The law stemming from the Treaty, an independent source of law, could not, because of its special and original nature, be over-ridden by domestic legal provisions, however framed, without being deprived of its character as Community Law and without the legal basis of the Community itself being called into question."

The pervasive nature of Community law was described by Lord Denning MR in *Bulmer Ltd. v. Bolinger SA* 1974 in a famous passage. *"When we come to matters with a European element, the Treaty is like an incoming tide. It flows into the estuaries and up the rivers. It cannot be held back. Parliament has decreed that the Treaty is henceforward to be part of our law. It is equal in force to any statute."*

In *Internationale Handelsgesellachaft mbH* 1970, the Court of Justice, in a case which involved a conflict between an EC regulation and the provisions of the German constitution, decided that the EC rule took precedence. *"The validity of a community instrument or its effect within a member State cannot be affected by allegations that it strikes at either the fundamental rights as formulated in that State's constitution or the principles of a national constitutional structure."*

The significance of these decisions in UK law is underlined by s.3(1) of the European Communities Act 1972, which provides *"For the purposes of all legal proceedings any questions as to the meaning or effect of any of the Treaties, or as to the validity meaning or effect of any community instrument, shall be treated as a question of law and, if not referred to the European Court, be for determination as such in accordance with the principles laid down by and any relevant decision of the European Court."*

This section represents the acceptance by the UK government in the 1972 Act of the principles developed by the Court of Justice in its decisions, including those relating to the supremacy of Community law.

The position of EC law within the English legal system is established by the European Communities Act 1972 which, in s.2(1), gives legal effect to the Community law within the UK. It states *"All such rights, powers, liabilities, obligations and restrictions from time to time created or arising by or under the Treaties, and all such remedies and procedures from time to time provided for by or under the Treaties, as in accordance with the Treaties are without further enactment to be given legal effect or used in the United Kingdom shall be recognised and available in law, and be enforced, allowed and followed accordingly, and the expression "enforceable community right" and similar expressions shall be read as referring to one to which this subsection applies."*

This gives legal force to those provisions in the Treaties and in secondary legislation which are directly applicable. This occurs automatically without the need for further UK legislation. The words from time to time make it clear that future as well as existing Community laws are within the scope of s.2(1). In relation to those Community measures which do not have direct applicability, s.2(2) gives power to make delegated legislation for the purpose of giving them effect within the UK. This power is often used to make Statutory Instruments in order to implement Community directives. The Employment Protection (Part-time Employees) Regulations 1995 were made under s.2(2) to bring the legal position of part-time workers in the UK in line with Europe.

The 1972 Act states that where there is a conflict between domestic law and Community law, the latter will take priority. This is laid down in s.2(4) which provides *"... any enactment passed or to be passed shall be construed and have effect subject to the foregoing provisions of this section."*

The effect of s.2(4) has caused much controversy and debate as to its impact on the unwritten constitution of the UK. This debate centres around the constitutional doctrine of parliamentary supremacy. One of the principal features of this doctrine is that Parliament cannot bind its successors by passing legislation restricting the absolute freedom of a future parliament to repeal or amend existing laws or create new ones. The effect of s.2(4) however is that no future Parliament can validly create legislation which conflicts with Community law.

In *Macarthys Ltd. v. Smith 1979* Lord Denning MR indicated the view of the UK courts on this issue as follows: *"In construing our statute we are entitled to look to the Treaty as an aid to its construction; but not only as an aid but as an overriding force. If on close investigation it should appear that our legislation is deficient or is inconsistent with community law by some oversight of our draughtsmen then it is our bounden duty to give priority to community law. Such is the result of s.2(1) and s.2(4) of the European Communities Act 1972.I pause here, however, to make on observation on a constitutional point. Thus far I have assumed that our Parliament, whenever it passes legislation, intends to fulfil its obligations under the treaty. If the time should come when our Parliament deliberately passes an Act with the intention of repudiating the Treaty or any provision in it or intentionally of acting inconsistently with it and says so in express terms then I should have thought it would be the duty of our Courts to follow the statute of our parliament."*

In *Macarthys Ltd. v. Smith* 1979 the Court of Appeal was faced with a conflict between the literal interpretation of s.1(2) Equal Pay Act 1970 and article 119 of the Treaty of Rome. Mrs Smith was appointed to the position of stockroom manageress on a salary of £50.00 per week four and a half months after the stockroom manager had left the post. He had been paid a weekly wage of £60.00. Section 1(2)(a)(i) of the Equal Pay Act states that a woman is entitled to equal pay where she is employed on like work with a man in the same employment. The employers argued that as she had never been employed with a man she was not entitled to equal pay. Article 119 requires each member state to maintain the application of the principle that men and women should receive equal pay for equal work. It was argued that this is a directly applicable rule of Community law creating an enforceable community right in favour of Mrs Smith, which operates regardless of whether she is employed at the same time as a male comparator. The Court of Appeal recognised that EC law takes priority over conflicting national law, but decided to refer a question to the Court of Justice as to the application of article 119 in the circumstances of the case. The Court of Justice found that article 119 was directly applicable and entitled Mrs Smith to equal pay on the facts of the case; and the Court of Appeal accordingly decided in her favour.

A more contemporary example of the primacy of community law is provided by the important decision of the House of Lords in R v. Secretary of State for Employment ex parte Equal Opportunities Commission 1994. Here their Lordships ruled by a majority of four to one that UK legislation that gives part-time workers (most of whom are women) less protection in relation to unfair dismissal and redundancy than full-time workers (most of whom are men) is indirectly discriminatory and therefore incompatible with European Union Law as to equality between employees.

Types of Community Law

The major sources of Community law are *primary* legislation found in the treaties establishing and developing the EC; *secondary* legislation made on an ongoing basis by the Community institutions; judgments of the Court of Justice and unwritten general principles of law. In relation to treaty provisions and secondary legislation it is useful to distinguish between the concepts of *direct applicability* and *direct effect*.

A Community law is said to be directly applicable when it is of a type which is directly incorporated in its entirety into the laws of the members states without the need for further legislative or administrative action on the part of the member state or the Community institutions. Such rules create immediate rights and obligations as between individuals and or organisations and as against member states. These rights or obligations are directly enforceable in the ordinary courts within the member states. Article 189 states that EC regulations are directly applicable. Certain provisions of the treaties have been held to be directly applicable, although they only come within this category where they are:

- clear and unambiguous;

- unconditional;

- precise;

- self-contained - i.e. requiring no further action to put them into effect.

Directly applicable Community laws will automatically take effect within the UK by virtue of s.2(1) of the 1972 Act.

A Community law which is not directly applicable may nonetheless have direct effects in terms of conferring rights upon individuals which may be enforced in the domestic courts. Such provisions usually will not have direct applicability because they are not self-contained, in the sense that they require some action, usually by the member state, in order to implement them. Typically this will apply where directives have not been implemented in full or at all, and the deadline for implementation has passed. In these circumstances the directive may produce direct effects provided it is sufficiently clear, unconditional and precise. One significant limitation on the doctrine of direct effects is that directives are only directly effective as against the state. This is known as *vertical direct effect* and is examined below in the context of the defective implementation of directives.

It may be seen that whilst all directly applicable provisions will have direct effects, the reverse will not be true so that a rule may be directly effective without being directly applicable. Not surprisingly, the two are often confused and even the courts tend to use them interchangeably.

The Treaties

The primary legislation of the EC consists of the European Treaties and associated documents, agreements and protocols. These include the Treaty of Rome, the Single European Act 1986, the Treaty on European Union 1992 and the Treaty of Amsterdam.

Under the UK constitution each new treaty requires an Act of Parliament to give it effect within the national legal system. This was achieved by the European Communities Act in 1972 in relation to the treaties which pre-dated it. Separate legislation has been introduced for each subsequent treaty so that, for example, the European Communities (Amendment) Act 1993 gives effect to the Treaty on European Union. The European Treaties set out the framework of Community law, create the institutions and lay down the procedures for making secondary legislation on an ongoing basis.

Whilst certain provisions in the treaties lay down broad policies which need to be fleshed out in secondary legislation, the Court of Justice has held that others can be directly applicable. Article 119 of the Treaty of Rome,(now article 141 following the Treaty of Amsterdam) provides that *"Each member state shall ... maintain the application of the principle that men and women receive equal pay for equal work"*. In *Defrenne v. Sabena* 1976 the Court of Justice held that article 141 imposed on member states *"A duty to bring about a specific result to be mandatorily achieved"* and that it could be relied on in an action between an individual and her employer. Defrenne, an air hostess, claimed to be entitled to the same pay as a male steward whose duties were identical to hers. It was held that she could rely on article 141 even though it was addressed to the member state and was not framed as a rule giving rights to individuals. In so far as it relates to direct discrimination and equal work it was held to be directly applicable. The case of *Macarthys v. Smith* 1979, discussed above, is a further example of a direct application of article 141.

In *Barber v. Guardian Royal Exchange* 1990 the Court of Justice applied article 141 in its decision that occupational pension schemes, as opposed to state retirement pension, and the benefits conferred under them on employees, are pay for the purpose of article 141. It is therefore unlawful to discriminate between men and women in relation to them. Mr Barber claimed to be entitled to benefit under his company pension scheme on the same basis as female employees and objected to the fact that he could not receive benefits under the scheme until he reached the age of 65 whereas his female counterparts could benefit at 60. The Court of Justice's decision in his favour caused major changes in many occupational pension schemes to give effect to the equalisation of pension ages and benefits as between men and women.

Secondary Legislation

The Treaties confer significant law making powers on the Institutions of the Community. These powers are limited in that they extend only to areas where the Community has competence to legislate. There are some areas which remain within the exclusive domain of the national sovereignty of the member states. As we have seen, however, the Community's law making competence extents to virtually all aspects of employment law.

Article 189 of the Treaty of Rome states *"In order to carry out their task the Council and the Commission shall, in accordance with the provisions of this Treaty, make regulations, issue directives, take decisions, make recommendations or deliver opinions"*. The article goes on to define each of them.

A *regulation* has general application. It is binding in its entirety and directly applicable in all member states. Regulations are the equivalent of UK statutes on a community scale. They apply to everyone in all fifteen member states and there is no requirement for action at a national level to bring them into effect. This occurs on the 20th day following their publication in the Official Journal where no other date is specified in them.

A *directive* shall be binding, as to the result to be achieved, upon each member state to which it is addressed but shall leave to the national authorities the choice of form and methods. Directives are the major instrument for achieving the harmonisation of national laws as between the member states. They operate by setting out the objectives which the proposed new laws must achieve, giving a time limit within which member state governments must achieve them. The resulting law will be in the form of a domestic law within the member state. In the UK directives are implemented either by a new Act of Parliament or by delegated legislation using the enabling powers in s.2(2) of the 1972 Act. The Treaty gives some discretion as to the manner of implementation, provided that the result is achieved. This allows for a certain degree of flexibility, for example, in relation to the consequences for breach of a particular rules which need not be identical in each member state. Breach of the same substantive rule may, for example, give rise to criminal liability in the UK and civil liability in France. There are many examples of directives in the field of employment law in particular in relation to health and safety, equal opportunities, business transfers and redundancy procedures.

A *decision* is binding in its entirety upon those to whom it is addressed. They may be addressed to a member state, a business or other organisation or an individual. There is no discretion as to the manner of implementation, and decisions take effect upon notification.

Recommendations and opinions are not legally binding or enforceable. They are often addressed to member states and may give a view on a particular matter or set out guidelines to be followed in relation to an issue, sometimes with the implication that if they are not followed proposals for a stronger type of Community law may be made at a later date.

Defective Implementation of Directives

Where a member state has failed to implement a directive within the specified time period, or where implementation has taken place in part only, there are a number of possible consequences:

Infringement proceedings may be taken by the Commission against the member state. This process is outlined above and ultimately results in a ruling against the member state by the Court of Justice. One problem with this process had been the lack of any power to enforce the judgment of the Court of Justice. Since the coming into effect of the Treaty on European Union however, as we have seen, the Court of Justice has power to fine a member state which fails to comply with a judgment against it.

A directive may have direct effects in a case involving the state as defendant. By definition a directive cannot be directly applicable as it requires some action on the part of the member state to give it effect in national law. Where the member state fails to do this, either in whole or in part, the principle of *vertical direct effect* may come into play. This will prevent the member state from using its own wrongful act of failing properly to implement the directive as a defence to a legal action taken by someone who wishes to enforce the rights contained in the directive against it. In order to be directly effective, the rights set out in the directive must be clear, unambiguous, unconditional and precise.

In *Marshall v. Southampton and South West Hampshire Area Health Authority (Teaching)* 1986, the Health Authority operated a retirement policy for employees under which the normal retirement age was 60 for women and 65 for men. This was consistent with s.6(4) of the Sex Discrimination Act 1975, and in line with state retirement pension ages. An employee's retirement could be postponed by mutual agreement and Miss Marshall continued to work until she was dismissed at age 62. The sole reason given for her dismissal was that she had passed the normal retirement age. She claimed that her dismissal was an unlawful discrimination because men could not be dismissed on grounds of retirement at that age. Her claim was based upon the following articles of the Equal Treatment Directive:

"1(1). The purpose of this directive is to put into effect in the member states the principle of equal treatment for men and women as regards access to employment, including promotion, and to vocational training and as regards working conditions...

2(1). The principle of equal treatment shall mean that there shall be no discrimination whatsoever on grounds of sex either directly, or indirectly by reference in particular to marital or family status.

5(1). Application of the principle of equal treatment with regard to working conditions, including those governing dismissal, means that men and women shall be guaranteed the same conditions without discrimination on grounds of sex."

The Court of Appeal sought a preliminary ruling from the Court of Justice as to whether the retirement policy of the Health Authority constituted discrimination on grounds of sex contrary to the directive; and if so, whether article 5(1) could be relied upon as against a state authority acting in its capacity as employer, in order to avoid the application of s.6(4) of the Sex Discrimination Act 1975. The Court of Justice ruled that the difference in compulsory retirement ages as between men and women was discriminatory and that article 5(1) was clear, unconditional and sufficiently precise to be directly effective. As the date for implementation had passed, it could be relied upon so as to avoid the application of s.6(4) as against the Health Authority, a public sector organisation *"Where a person involved in legal proceedings is able to rely upon a directive as against the state, he may do so regardless of the capacity in which the latter is acting, whether employer or public authority. In either case it is necessary to prevent the state from taking advantage of its own failure to comply with Community Law"*.

So the provisions of a directive are capable of direct enforcement against an emanation of the State if there has been a failure to implement the directive into domestic law and it has been written with sufficient precision. The directive will of course have primacy in the event that its provisions conflict with contractual terms.

A good contemporary example of contractual conflict and direct enforceability is provided by *Gibson v. East Riding of Yorkshire Council* 2000 a complaint about the failure to enact Article 7(1) of the Working Time Directive providing that workers are entitled to four weeks annual leave. The EAT had held that during the period the directive had not been implemented it had direct effect and an employee of an emanation of the State was able to take advantage of its protection. The directive was clear and precise with no conditions and *"although it as argued that the complainant expressly contracted on the basis that she would receive no paid annual leave her contractual rights were varied by the directive"*. Parties are not entitled to contract out of the entitlement conferred upon them by European Directives, save to the extent that the directive may permit. The Court of Appeal disagreed with the EAT however and held that the right to paid annual leave is not sufficiently defined in Article 7 to be directly enforceable by an individual in national courts or tribunals. As Article 7 leaves key questions unanswered, such as a precise definition of "working time" it is not possible to decide which workers are entitled to annual leave.

The Court of Justice made it clear that directives can only have vertical direct effects in favour of the individual enforceable against the state. They cannot impose obligations on individuals and therefore are not, without full implementation, capable of horizontal direct effect. The *Marshall* case does not, however, make clear exactly which public bodies or manifestations of the state are subject to the rule of vertical direct effect.

In *Foster v. British Gas plc.* 1990, the factual situation was similar to that in Marshall. The sole issue was whether the British Gas Corporation, a nationalised industry, came within the definition of the state for the purposes of the rule. The Court of Justice formulated a broad definition of the state for these purposes. It ruled that the directive could be relied upon in an action for damages against *"... a body, whatever its legal form, which has been made responsible, pursuant to a measure adopted by the state, for providing a public service under the control of the state and has for that purpose special powers beyond those which result from the normal rules applicable in relations between individuals"*. In the light of this definition, the House of Lords held that British Gas was part of the state, and the directive could be relied upon in an action for damages against it.

In *Marshall v. Southampton and South West Hampshire Area Health Authority (No.2)*1993 a further issue arose as to the amount of compensation recoverable from her employers. The Sex Discrimination Act laid down a statutory maximum award of £6250 under s.65(2). Mrs. Marshall claimed that her full loss amounted to £19,405. Relying on the principles of vertical direct effects developed in the earlier case, she argued that the statutory financial limit was inconsistent with article 6 of the Equal Treatment Directive which in effect requires member states to provide an adequate remedy to a complainant who suffers loss as a result of discriminatory treatment. The House of Lords referred the question to the European Court of Justice for a preliminary ruling under article 177. It ruled that the financial limit conflicted with the requirements of article 6 to provide a real and effective remedy which ensured full compensation for the loss or damage actually sustained. The article had vertical direct effect as against the Health Authority, which as a public body is treated as being part of the State, and which was therefore obliged to pay her compensation in full.

Member state courts have a duty to interpret national law in the light of the wording and purpose of a relevant directive, not only where the national law in question was introduced in order to give effect to the directive, but also where it pre-dates the directive if no further implementing measure has been introduced and the date for implementation has passed.

A member state may be liable in damages to an individual for any loss suffered as a result of the state's failure to implement a directive. This important principle was established by the Court of Justice in the case of *Francovich v. Italian State and Bonifaci 1992*. Liability will arise as against a member state which has failed to implement a directive where the following conditions are met:

(a) the result to be achieved by the directive includes the creation of rights in favour of individuals;

(b) the content of those rights are sufficiently defined in the directive; and

(c) the individual's loss is caused by the failure of the state to implement the directive.

In the *Francovich* case, the Italian government had failed to implement directive 80/987 on the protection of employees in the event of the insolvency of their employer. Under the directive it had been required to ensure that a guarantee institution was in place from which employees could claim payments which could not be met by insolvent employers. Francovich was owed 6 million lire which he was unable to recover from his insolvent employer. He sued the Italian government for damages for its failure to comply with the directive and the Court of Justice gave a preliminary ruling on an article 177 reference that the government was liable in damages for its failure to set up the guarantee institution.

The development of the rule that a member state may be liable to pay damages where it has failed properly to implement a directive is significant in a number of ways. Firstly because the rule of vertical direct effect established in the Marshall case does not provide a remedy against a private sector defendant. As a result of the *Francovich* decision, a plaintiff who is unable to sue such a defendant may now be able to sue his government for its failure to legislate. On a broader front the decision is significant because it demonstrates the ability and willingness of the Court of Justice to develop creatively the principles of Community law and new mechanisms for ensuring its effectiveness in areas where the Treaties provide little or no guidance.

The principle established in the *Francovich* case has now been extended to cover the situation where an individual or organisation suffers loss as a result of national legislation which is contrary to EC law, for example because it is incompatible with a provision of the Treaty of Rome. The member state will be liable in damages where the following conditions are met:

(a)   The provision in community law was intended to create rights in favour of individuals;

(b)   The breach of community law is a serious breach; and

(c)   The loss is directly caused by the member states breach of EC law.

The European Convention on Human Rights and Fundamental Freedoms

The above Convention has emerged as a further source of UK employment law. The Human Rights Art 1998 incorporates the European Convention on Human Rights into UK law from October 2000. A number of Articles in the convention will have impact on employment rights such as article 8, respect for private life, article 10, freedom of expression and article 3 on subjecting an individual to degrading treatment.

The UK ban on homosexuals in the. armed forces has been held to contravene the right to private life under the convention. The European Court of Human Rights also ruled in *Smith and Grady v. United Kingdom 1999* that the investigation into the applicants homosexuality and subsequent discharge from the armed forces were clear breaches of articles 3 and 8 of the Convention. Evidence from the UK Government that the presence of homosexuals in the armed forces would have a substantial and negative effect on morale and operational effectiveness was found by the court to be unconvincing. *"These negative attitudes cannot of themselves be considered by the court to amount to sufficient justification, for the interferences with the applicants rights outlined above any more than similar negative attitudes toward those of a different race, origin or colour".*

The Human Rights Act is directly enforceable against public bodies who should be concerned about any policies that they have which discriminate on the grounds of sexual orientation. While this does not directly extend to private employers, the courts and tribunals are obliged to act compatibly with the convention so that a dismissal on the grounds of sexual orientation such as Saunders v. Scottish National Camps Association 1980 (see Chapter 11) should almost certainly be regarded as unfair.

Conclusion

To sum up, a student of employment law should be aware that the courts will apply law from various sources both national and European in the resolution of conflict. It should also be appreciated that a constructive analysis of an employment dispute will often require an application of employment law from a number of areas of the subject. While it is convenient in a text of this nature to divide the subject into a number of topics dealt with in distinct chapters unfortunately conflict does not usually fall neatly into one topic area and will normally involve a number of legal issues. The case below provides an example.

In *Bass Leisure Ltd. v. Thomas* 1994 the complainant was employed as a collector for the defendants for ten years working from their Coventry depot. Her job involved travelling to a number of public houses to empty fruit machines. In 1991 the defendants decided to close the Coventry depot and the complainant was offered relocation in Erdington, some twenty miles away. The complainant tried the new work location but it soon became obvious that the more onerous travelling made the alternative employment unrealistic and she terminated her employment claiming a redundancy payment. The defendants disputed her claim relying on an express term of her contract which provided that *"the company reserves the right to transfer any employee either temporarily or permanently to a suitable alternative place of work and to change the terms and conditions of employment to meet the needs of the business. Domestic circumstances will be taken into account in reaching a decision if relocation is involved".* As the parties were unable to resolve the conflict a complaint was made to the industrial tribunal and from the tribunal's decision an appeal heard by the Employment Appeal Tribunal. In reaching a decision the tribunal had to analyse the express terms of the contract of employment to determine whether the employer was authorised in requiring the employee to move. Both the tribunal and the EAT thought that in applying the relocation term the employer had not taken account of domestic circumstances or judged objectively offered a suitable alternative place of work. Having decided that the employer was in breach of contract the next issue was whether the breach of contract was so fundamental that it justified the employee leaving and claiming constructive dismissal. This was a constructive dismissal and as it was by reason of redundancy under the definition in the above Act, then the applicant was entitled to a redundancy payment.

In reaching its decision in the above case the tribunal found it necessary to apply a number of legal principles to the conflict. In the text you will find principles of law relating to job relocation and terms of employment in Chapters 4 and 7, constructive dismissal in Chapter 10 and redundancy in Chapter 12.

Chapter 2

Institutions of Employment Law

Having considered the various sources of rules of employment law to complete an introduction to employment law it is also necessary to describe these bodies, judicial and otherwise, which have jurisdiction to interpret the law and have a part to play in the resolution of employment law conflict.

Employment Tribunals

Under the Employment Rights (Disputes Resolutions) Act 1998 industrial tribunals have been renamed as employment tribunals. The vast majority of individual employment law rights and duties are legally enforceable by means of presenting a complaint before an employment tribunal. Originating under the Industrial Training Act 1964 with only a minimal function, the employment tribunal is now the focus for dealing with statutory employment law conflict. Its jurisdiction includes unfair dismissal, redundancy, trade union rights, wage deductions, discrimination at work, balloting and many other employment rights and obligations considered throughout the book. Their original aim remains to provide *"an easily accessible, speedy, informal and inexpensive procedure"* for the settlement of disputes.

One significant employment law limitation on the jurisdiction of tribunals was the fact that claims based on breach of contract were matters to be dealt with in the ordinary courts rather than tribunals. There has been some degree of change in this practice following the Employment Tribunals (Extensions of Jurisdiction) (England and Wales) Order 1994. Now employment tribunals are given jurisdiction over breach of contract claims with certain exceptions, the ordinary courts retaining concurrent jurisdiction. Employees may not make a breach of contract claim in a tribunal until their employment has ended but they do not have to make a concurrent statutory claim. They have three months from the end of employment to commence proceedings for a cause of action which could have arisen in the last six years. Certain claims are excluded including personal injury actions, claims about providing living accommodation, intellectual property, confidentiality and restraint of trade. The maximum award which a tribunal could order in respect of a contract claim is £25,000. In *Sarker v. South Tees Acute Hospitals NHS Trust* 1997 the EAT held that the tribunal had jurisdiction to hear a claim for damages for breach of contract where a contract of employment was terminated by the employer before the employee commenced work.

It should be stressed that an employment tribunal as a body which discharges judicial functions and forms part of the judicial system should be regarded as a "court" rather than an administrative organ of the state. The Divisional Court of the Queen's Bench Division of the High Court held in *Peach Grey & Co. v. Sommers* 1995 that an employment tribunal is an *"inferior court"* and consequently the Divisional Court has power to make an order for committal *"where contempt of court ... is committed in connection with ... proceedings in an inferior court"*. Here the complainant was sentenced to one month's imprisonment as he had attempted to pervert the course of justice by interfering with a witness in employment tribunal proceedings and, therefore, he was guilty of contempt of court.

The constitution of an employment tribunal is laid down in the Industrial Tribunals Act 1996 (now cited as the Employment Tribunals Act 1996) which provides that a tribunal is composed of three members, a legally qualified chairman and two lay members, one of whom is usually a nominee of an employer's organisation, and the other the nominee of a trade union. With the parties consent a tribunal could be composed of a chairman and one other member. Also for a number of proceedings a tribunal could be validly constituted by the chairman sitting alone. Following the Employment Rights (Disputes Resolutions) Act 1998 the Chairman has a discretion to sit alone in matters including the determination of rights on the employer's insolvency, redundancy payments, statements of employment particulars and cases where the parties agree in writing to the chairman sitting alone.

From the outset it is crucial to appreciate the role of the employment tribunal in the resolution of conflict in employment law. It has often been said that the tribunal is an *'industrial jury'* and as such is the final arbiter on questions of fact. There are many occasions, particularly in relation to unfair dismissal, that the tribunal is called on to determine whether in the circumstances of the case the decision taken by the employer is a reasonable one. In making this determination the tribunal must examine the employers decision from a background of sound industrial experience and practice and then decide whether the decision falls within a band of reasonable responses from an employer in similar circumstances. This determination is a core function of the tribunal and should not be disturbed by an appeal court or tribunal other than in exceptional circumstances. (See later the Employment Appeal Tribunal) In *Borders Regional Council v. Maule* 1993 the EAT considered the role of the employment tribunal in decision-making. The EAT said that *"In order to show that they have performed their statutory function it is necessary for the tribunal to explain what considerations have been taken into account and make some attempt to explain how these considerations have been balanced before reaching the conclusion that the employer acted unreasonably."*

While the aim of conferring jurisdiction on tribunals is to encourage decision-making which is both inexpensive and speedy, the reality is that there has been increasing legal complexity introduced into tribunal proceedings. The procedure of tribunals is regulated by the Employment Tribunals (Constitution and Rules of Procedure) Regulations 1993 as amended by the Employment Tribunals (Constitution Rules of Procedure) (Amendment) Regulations 1994. A number of changes were introduced by the 1993 rules in particular an increase in the power of the Chairman to conduct the proceedings prior to the hearing above. The tribunal has more of an inquisitorial role in that it can order the discovery and inspection of documents and the attendance of witnesses on its own initiative. The applicant or respondent can be ordered to answer questions before the hearing to clarify issues or assist in the process of the trial. This enables information to be gathered in advance of the hearing. This is particularly useful where the respondent is a large organisation and it is easy for individuals to deny responsibility.

Submitting the Claim

It is of crucial importance that a complainant to an employment tribunal presents the claim within the appropriate time limits. The law relating to time limits and the discretion of a tribunal to hear a complaint presented out of time is covered in Chapter 5 in relation to discrimination and Chapter 11 in relation to unfair dismissal.

One fundamental principle should be stressed from the outset however. Unlike the ordinary courts the traditionally short time limits in tribunals are jurisdictional. This means that a tribunal is bound to consider the issue of whether or not this is raised by the respondent and the point cannot be waived. The civil courts will only consider whether a claim is presented in time (e.g. three years for personal injuries) if it is raised as a defence by the defendant.

To present a claim it is usual to complete and submit an Employment Tribunal 1 (IT1) form to the Regional Office of Employment Tribunals (ROIT), although the use of that particular form is not a statutory requirement and another form of writing could suffice. The ROIT acknowledges receipt of the IT1 by sending the complainant a form which confirms that copies of the complaint have been sent to the employer and passed on to the Advisory Conciliation and Arbitration Services (ACAS). The form also informs the employee that notice of the hearing will be sent at a future date. The employer (respondent), having received a copy of the IT1 and also a formal notice that the application has been made, has then fourteen days to 'enter an appearance'. It is at this stage that the respondent should attempt to clarify

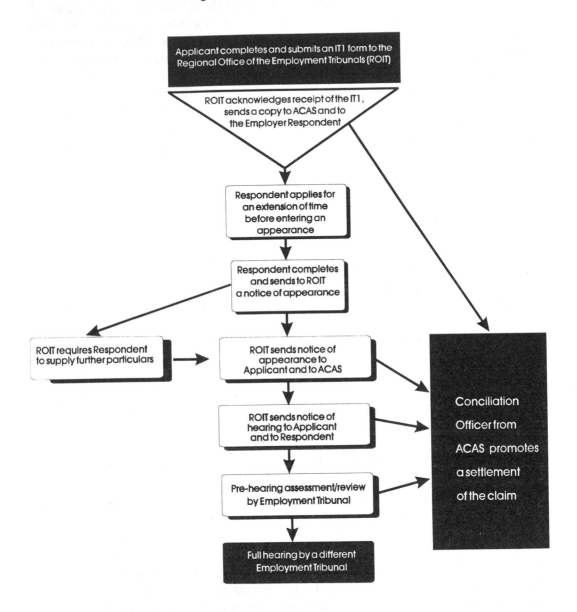

Mains Steps in an Application
brought before an Employment Tribunal

Applicant completes and submits an IT1 form to the
Regional Office of the Employment Tribunals (ROIT)

ROIT acknowledges receipt of the IT1,
sends a copy to ACAS and to
the Employer Respondent

Respondent applies for
an extension of time
before entering an
appearance

Respondent completes
and sends to ROIT
a notice of appearance

ROIT requires Respondent
to supply further particulars

ROIT sends notice of
appearance to
Applicant and to ACAS

ROIT sends notice of
hearing to Applicant
and to Respondent

Pre-hearing assessment/review
by Employment Tribunal

Full hearing by a different
Employment Tribunal

Conciliation
Officer from
ACAS promotes
a settlement
of the claim

the legal position, consider the evidence and, if necessary, apply to the ROIT for an extension of time before entering an appearance. If he requires further clarification of the complainant's grounds for the claim he can make a request for further particulars. Whether or not the respondent wishes to resist the claim, he must complete the notice of appearance and return it to the ROIT. If, in the notice, the respondent fails to provide sufficient particulars of his ground for resisting the claim, he can be required to do so by the tribunal.

A copy of the notice of appearance is sent to the complainant and to ACAS. It is then in the hands of the ROIT to set a date for the hearing but in practice a postponement can be applied for in writing and is normally granted when requested. It may be that the respondent disputes that the applicant is qualified to bring the claim, perhaps on the ground that the employee has insufficient continuous employment for the purposes of a complaint of unfair dismissal. In these circumstances it is usual to request a preliminary hearing to determine the issue.

Conciliation

One of the functions of ACAS (considered later in the chapter) is in relation to conciliation when a complaint is presented alleging that a statutory right has been infringed. The role of a conciliation officer in an unfair dismissal claim is to endeavour to promote a settlement of the complaint without the dispute having to go to an employment tribunal. The officer is required to promote a settlement if requested to do so by either party or if he feels that he could act with a reasonable prospect of success. For this purpose an officer could seek to promote the reinstatement or re-engagement of a dismissed employee on equitable terms or if this is not practicable, attempt to persuade the employer to agree to make the employee a compensation payment. His function is not to negotiate with the parties but rather to act as a channel of communication through which the parties do their bargaining. The conciliation officer will have vast experience of this type of conflict of course, and if asked to do so, he can draw on his experience to give an impartial opinion on the legal position. If a settlement is needed, and this happens in over fifty percent of cases, it is usual for it to be arranged through the conciliation officer. Such a settlement would be enforceable in the same way as an award from an employment tribunal, if necessary by action in the county court.

Compromise Agreements

It is an important feature of employment law that an employee cannot opt out of his statutory rights so that if a private settlement is reached, which is not approved by an ACAS conciliation officer, either party could still present a complaint to an employment tribunal. Any sum of money agreed as compensation in a private settlement would however be taken account of in determining a tribunal award. The relevant statutory provision is contained in s.203(1) of the Employment Rights Act 1996.

> *Under s.203(1) "Any provision in an agreement (whether a contract of employment or not) shall be void in so far as it purports–*
>
> *(a)   to exclude or limit the operation of any provision of this Act; or*
>
> *(b)   to preclude any person from presenting a complaint to, or bringing any proceedings under this Act before, an employment tribunal."*

While there are a number of exceptions to the general rule, for instance fixed term contracts of employment of one year or more which exclude unfair dismissal rights, it would be prudent to call in a conciliation officer to give his stamp of approval to any private settlement. It is now possible for the parties to agree not to institute tribunal proceedings without the need to involve ACAS. The agreement will be valid if it satisfies certain criteria and constitutes under s.203(3) a compromise agreement. The criteria are that the agreement must:

- be in writing

- relate to a specific complaint

- be reached after the complainant has received independent legal advice from a qualified lawyer as to its terms and effect

- identify the adviser who is covered by a policy of insurance.

Under s.9 of the Employment Rights (Disputes Resolution) Act 1998 a compromise agreement will be valid if advice has been received from *a "relevant independent advisor"* rather than a qualified lawyer. Such advisors would of course include lawyers but also trade union officials and advice workers.

A further development under the 1998 Act is provision under s.7 for an arbitration scheme to be drawn up by ACAS (subject to the approval of the Secretary of State). This will initially apply to unfair dismissal claims but other employment rights may be included. Access to the scheme will be by written agreement and in such circumstances the jurisdiction of the Employment Tribunal will be excluded.

If an opinion was reached that a party's case was particularly weak then the tribunal could issue a warning that if the party concerned proceeds to a full trial, an order for costs may be made against him. While the tribunal rarely awards costs, it has a discretion to do so where a party, in bringing the proceedings, has acted frivolously, vexatiously or otherwise unreasonably. By proceeding with a claim after a pre-trial review has decided that it is particularly weak, a party would be regarded as acting unreasonably. An employee who brings a claim without any substance with the aim of harassing the employer, acts frivolously or vexatiously and could have costs awarded against him.

Under s.33 of the Employment Tribunals Act the EAT has power to make a restriction order against a vexatious litigant to bar him from bringing any further proceedings without the leave of the EAT. In *Attorney General v. Wheen 2000* such an order was made against the applicant who had instituted 13 separate discrimination proceedings against various employers all of which were unsuccessful and some of which were regarded as frivolous or vexatious. The aim of this power is to protect respondents from the cost of anxiety of vexatious claims and ensure that the tribunal time is devoted to proceedings where the applicant has a reasonable prospect of success.

Pre-Hearing Review

In 1980 a screening process of pre-hearing assessments was introduced under which either party would apply to the tribunal to examine the papers and rule on the merits of the case and the defence.

The system of pre-hearing assessments has now been replaced by the pre-hearing review. Under this procedure either party to the proceedings can apply to the tribunal to order a pre-hearing review. This can be carried out by a single person (the tribunal chairman) or the full tribunal and significantly, at the review, a party to the proceedings may be required to pay a deposit of up to £150 if he wishes to continue to participate in the proceedings. The aim of course is obvious, to discourage unmeritorious or ill founded claims. The pre-hearing reviews replace the pre-hearing assessment where the present possible warning as to costs, if the tribunal decides that a party has no reasonable prospect of success, has been of limited success in weeding out ill founded complaints. The danger of introducing a system of deposit which may not be returnable and possibly paid over to another party is that it may have the effect of discouraging applicants of limited means from approaching a tribunal at all. It has been called "a tax on justice". The availability of a sum such as £150 to a complainant who has just lost his/her job should not be assumed. Bear in mind also that legal aid does not extend to representation before an employment tribunal despite the obvious need.

The Hearing

An employment tribunal hearing is not conducted with the same degree of formality as a trial in a court of law and the Rules of Procedure makes it clear that a tribunal may conduct a hearing in a manner most suitable to clarify the issues, without the need to comply strictly to the normal rules relating to the admissibility of evidence. This makes it possible for lay representation, often by a trade union official.

> In *Bache v. Essex County Council* 2000 the Court of Appeal considered the statutory right of an applicant to be represented by the person of their choice and ruled that even if the tribunal believes that the representation is incompetent it cannot take away the applicants choice of representation. The tribunal does have power however, under rule 9(1) to regulate the conduct of the representative in the performance of his task.

In tribunal proceedings oral evidence is adduced through the process of witness examination, cross examination and re-examination similar to court proceedings. Tribunals do have power however to control this process and the EAT held in *Zurich Insurance Co. v. Gibson* 1998 that a party does not have an absolute right to cross examination and the tribunal could take the view that it would not be assisted by a particular line of enquiry and so prevent a cross examination. The tribunal may feel that an issue has been sufficiently considered without hearing further evidence.

Legal aid is not available for legal representation which may put the complainant under a disadvantage, particularly if the employer is legally represented. In an attempt to speed up the tribunal proceedings there is no longer a requirement to provide full reasons for a decision except in cases involving discrimination. The reasons must be recorded in a written document signed by the chairman but they could be recorded in a 'full' or 'summary' form. The EAT considered this in *Speciality Care v. Pachela* 1996 and indicated that the mandatory requirement for a tribunal to give reasons for its decision, means that there should be sufficient reasons to show the parties why they won or lost. This particular complaint involved an allegation of dismissal by reason of trade union membership. The EAT stated that *"in practice where a complaint of dismissal by reason of union membership is made, as in this case, it will be for the tribunal to find as a fact whether or not the reason or principal reason for dismissal related to the applicant's trade union membership not only by reference to whether he or she had simply joined a union, but also by reference to whether the introduction of union representation into the employment relationship has led the employer to dismiss the employee. Tribunals should answer that question robustly, based on their findings as to what really caused the dismissal in the mind of the employer."*

In relation to summary reasons, Lord Donaldson MR in the Court of Appeal hearing of *William Hill Organisation Ltd. v. Gavas* 1990 said that *"It is the practice for employment tribunals to give summary reasons and then, if asked, to amplify them as full reasons. It may be convenient to say that, certainly in my experience...we are getting into the position...in which summary reasons have grown and grown until they are scarcely distinguishable from full reasons"*. He went on to suggest that guidance should be given by the EAT to get tribunals *"back to first principles"* so that the applicant and respondent are given no more than in essence what is the reason for the decision when summary reasons are given.

As a general rule a tribunal must not award costs or expenses against a party unless it considers that the party has acted frivolously, vexatiously or otherwise unreasonably in bringing or conducting the case.

> In *Port of London Authority v. Payne (No2)* 1993 it was held that an order for costs is appropriate where one of the parties has been deliberately untruthful in the presentation of the case. Here the employer had been deliberately untruthful in giving reasons for dismissal and was ordered to pay 40% of the complainant costs.

If a tribunal postpones or adjourns a hearing at the request of a party it can order that party to pay costs or expenses incurred.

> In *Cooper and Edwards v. Weatherwise (Roofing & Walling) Ltd.* 1993 a late application for the adjournment of an unfair dismissal claim by the complainant was rejected by the tribunal. Nevertheless, given the complainants non appearance at the hearing, an adjournment was granted and an order made that the complainant should pay the defendant's costs, £4,000, otherwise the application would not proceed. The EAT held that the tribunal had exceeded its powers in granting costs incurred as a result of the adjournment and specifying that the application could only proceed on their payment.

The various remedies that are available to a tribunal will depend upon the nature of the claim but they range from compensation awards to orders requiring a course of action such as reinstatement, declarations and recommendations. An employment tribunal has no power to enforce its own remedies so that if a mandatory order such as reinstatement is not complied with, it can be reduced to a compensation award and if necessary enforced in the county court. If a party wishes to lodge an appeal against a tribunal decision they must do so within 42 days of the document recording the decision being sent to the parties.

The Employment Appeal Tribunal (EAT)

An appeal from an employment tribunal in England, Wales and Scotland on a question of law or a mixed question of law and fact will lie to the Employment Appeal Tribunal. The major part of the case-law referred to throughout this text will be references to judgments of the EAT. First established in 1975, the EAT is regulated by the Employment Tribunals Act 1996. The President of the EAT will be a High Court judge or a Lord Justice of Appeal who will normally sit with two lay members drawn from a panel of persons who have proven industrial relations experience. The procedure of the EAT is regulated by the Employment Appeal Tribunal Rules 1993. The time limit for submitting an appeal from a tribunal decision is 42 days and this involves submitting a notice of appeal together with the reasons for it and a copy of the tribunal decision. Even without the full reasons the EAT can authorise an appeal if it considers that it would lead to the *"more expeditious or economic disposal of any proceedings or would otherwise be desirable in the interests of justice"*. Appeal from the decision of the EAT lies to the ordinary courts, namely the Court of Appeal and from there, in rare cases, an appeal lies to the House of Lords.

We have already said that the tribunal is the final arbiter on questions of fact so you should appreciate that the EAT has only limited jurisdiction to interfere with its decision-making.

In *East Berkshire Health Authority v. Matadeen* 1992, a case which we will consider in relation to unfair dismissal, the Employment Appeal Tribunal, after examining previous case law, stated its own view of its authority to reverse the decision of an employment tribunal. The EAT identified three situations where it can allow an appeal against the decision of a tribunal, if, *"first, there is an error of law on the face of the decision, a misdirection or misapplication of the law; secondly, if there is a material finding of fact relied on by the tribunal in the decision which was unsupported by any evidence or contrary to the evidence before them; and thirdly, if there is a finding of perversity"*. An incorrect application of the law or a misinterpretation of the evidence could justify an intervention by the EAT as could more controversially a finding of perversity. To conclude that a decision is perverse the EAT must decide that in the light of their own experience the decision reached is not a permissible option. A perverse decision is one which is *"a conclusion which offends reason or is one to which no reasonable employment tribunal could come"* or *"so very clearly wrong that it just cannot stand"*. The EAT stressed that *"the occasion upon which the EAT can interfere with the decision of an employment tribunal on the grounds of perversity is likely to be very rare. EAT members should caution themselves against so doing and in particular be careful not merely to substitute their own views for those of the tribunal. They cannot interfere merely because they disagree. They cannot interfere even if they feel strongly that the result is unjust. However, in that latter case, it may be that on careful analysis the decision flies in the face of properly informed logic"*.

If a decision of the EAT conflicts with a higher court then an employment tribunal is bound to follow the higher court's decision. If two EAT decisions conflict then the tribunal has a choice as to which decision to follow. The EAT is not bound to follow its own decisions, which are persuasive, but the EAT will normally try to be consistent. In Chapter 11 on Unfair Dismissal there is a consideration of the *"band of reasonable response, test"* which is applied to determine the fairness or otherwise of an employer's decision to dismiss an employee Despite the fact that this test was approved by the Court of Appeal, the EAT in *Haddon v. Van Den Bergh Foods* 1999 held that it should no longer be applied. In March 2000 a differently constituted EAT held in *Maddon v. Midland Bank* 2000 that the EAT has no authority to disregard a test from the Court of Appeal and that the test should be applied until the Court of Appeal decides otherwise. *"In the light of the doctrine of precedent no court short of the Court of Appeal can disregard the band of reasonable response test as the determinative test in considering whether dismissal was reasonable in the circumstances"*. On July 31 2000 the Court of Appeal ruled that the EAT had indeed departed from previous authorities and reaffirmed the band of reasonable response test. (see Chapter 11)

The Ordinary Courts

In addition to the important appellate jurisdiction of the Court of Appeal and the House of Lords, the ordinary courts of first instance, both civil (the county court and the High Court) and criminal (the Magistrates Court and the Crown Court) have a role to play in the resolution of conflict in employment disputes. In the early chapters of the book the nature of the contract of employment will be explored and like any other contract the mutual obligations of the parties to it are enforceable by legal action in the ordinary courts. An action for breach of contract in the county court or the High Court seeking damages, a declaration or an injunction, as a remedy, will be at the suit of the employer or employee in the event of non-performance or partial performance of contractual obligations. Generally the High Court will hear claims where the damages claimed exceed £50,000.

Previously we stated that following the Trade Union Reform and Employment Rights Act 1993 tribunals now have concurrent jurisdiction over breach of contract claims of up to £25,000, when the contract of employment has terminated. There are some important differences between bringing a claim before a court or a tribunal. In the courts the claimant can represent himself or more usually employ legal representation. In the tribunal however an applicant can be represented by the person of their choice, often a trade union official. Even if the tribunal feels that the representative is unsuitable the applicant has the final discretion as to representation. Representation in courts may be legally aided and costs awarded at the discretion of the court, usually against the unsuccessful party. There is no provision for legally aided representation in tribunals and costs are awarded only in exceptional cases.

In Chapters 4 and 7 you will see that a court order such as a declaration or an injunction may be sought usually in the High Court, where an employer alleges that industrial action is in breach of contract. When we consider health and safety at work, in Chapter 7, you will see that a civil action based on the tort of negligence may be brought against employers in the county court or the High Court alleging primary or vicarious liability. Also breaches of the Health and Safety at Work Act 1974 could lead to criminal prosecutions brought by the Health and Safety Executive in the Magistrates Court or in serious cases, on indictment in the Crown Court. In Chapter 1 the significant role of the European Court of Justice in interpreting Community law was considered. Following the adoption of the European Convention on Human Rights in October 2000 the European Court of Human Rights will have a role to play in the development of employment law.

Advisory Conciliation and Arbitration Service (ACAS)

ACAS has a crucial role to play in the resolution of conflict in employment law both at the individual level between employer and employee and the collective level between the trade union and the employer or employer's organisation . It is charged under s.209 of the Trade Union and Labour Relations (Consolidation) Act 1992 with the general duty of *"promoting the improvement of industrial relations"*. Under the Trade Union Reform and Employment Rights Act 1993 the previous duty of ACAS to encourage the extension of collective bargaining was removed as from the 30th August 1993. Based in London with offices in regional centres, ACAS is managed by a Council consisting of a full-time chairman and nine other members. Its many functions are now contained in the Trade Union and Labour Relations (Consolidation) Act 1992, ranging from conciliation, arbitration, advice, inquiry and the production of codes of practice. In relation to collective employment law the range of matters where ACAS can give advice are contained in s.213.

- *the organisation of workers or employers for the purpose of collective bargaining;*

- *the recognition of trade unions by employers;*

- *machinery for the negotiation of terms and conditions of employment and for joint consultation;*

- *procedure for avoiding and settling disputes and workers' grievances;*

- *questions relating to communication between employee and workers;*

- *facilities for officials of trade unions;*

- *procedures relating to the termination of employment;*

- *disciplinary matters;*

- *manpower planning, labour turnover and absenteeism;*

- *recruitment, retention, promotion and vocational training of workers;*

- *payment systems, including job evaluations and equal pay*

In addition ACAS may if it thinks fit, inquire into any question relating to industrial relations generally or in relation to a particular industry or a particular undertaking. If it appears desirable the findings of the inquiry may be published. Also, the service has power to issue Codes of Practice containing practical guidance for the purpose of promoting the improvement of industrial relations. Furthermore the service is required to issue Codes of Practice providing practical guidance on the disclosure of information for collective bargaining purposes and time off for trade union officials and members.

For the purpose of this text, concentrating on individual employment law, we are more concerned with the role of ACAS in conciliating in individual conflict rather than industrial action. We have already mentioned the significant role played by ACAS in promoting the settlement of tribunal cases and the high rate of success. A further significant development will be the Arbitration scheme for Unfair Dismissal, drawn up by ACAS, which will inevitably ease the burden on tribunals.

The Commission for Racial Equality

The Commission for Racial Equality was established under the Race Relations Act 1976 and is charged with the following duties:

- to work towards the elimination of discrimination;

- to promote equality of opportunity and good relations between persons of different racial groups generally; and

- to help keep under review the working of the Act and when required to do so by the Secretary of State, draw up and submit proposals for amendments.

Power is also conferred on the Commission to grant financial assistance to organisations which appear to be concerned with the promotion of racial harmony and also undertake or assist in research on educational activities for this purpose. Every year the Commission must submit an annual report to the Secretary of State to be laid before Parliament.

The law relating to racial discrimination is examined later in the text. It is found in the Race Relations Act 1976 and its interpretation in numerous reported case-law decisions.

A major role of the Commission is to review the working of the legislation, report and make recommendations. Under its Code of Practice for the elimination of racial discrimination and the promotion of equal opportunity in employment the Commission recommends that employers should monitor the effects of selection decisions and personal practices. The legal status of the Code is that it is admissible in evidence in tribunal proceedings and *"if any provision of such a code appears to be relevant to any question arising in the proceedings it shall be taken into account on determining that question"*.

The present power to conduct formal investigations is that they may be instigated for any purpose in connection with the Commission's duties. On completion of an investigation, the Commission must prepare a report within which it can make recommendations for changes in policies or procedures to individuals or organisations, and recommendations for changes in the law to the Secretary of State. Only the Commission may bring proceedings before the county court in respect of certain unlawful acts, namely discriminatory advertising, unlawful instructions to discriminate and unlawful inducements to discriminate.

As an agency upon which statutory power has been conferred, the Commission is obliged to ensure that it does not misinterpret those powers, otherwise its actions may be declared unlawful.

In *Commission for Racial Equality v. Prestige Group* 1984 the House of Lords considered the power of the Commission to conduct an investigation of a named person, in this case the respondent company. The court held that before such an investigation can commence the Commission must have formed the opinion that an act of unlawful discrimination had occurred (albeit on tenuous evidence). Here the investigation had started without such a belief, or without firstly having given the company an opportunity to make representations. The investigation was therefore unlawful and the non-discrimination notice issued as a result of it was ultra-vires and void.

The Equal Opportunities Commission

In relation to sex discrimination, the Sex Discrimination Act 1975 established the Equal Opportunities Commission charging it with similar duties to those imposed on the Commission for Racial Equality. They include:

- to work towards the elimination of discrimination;

- to promote equality of opportunity between men and women;

- to keep under review the legislation.

The EOC is also obliged to produce and submit an annual report to be laid before Parliament by the Secretary of State. Similar powers are also conferred on the EOC to finance research and educational activities and issue codes of practice. The EOC is empowered to conduct formal investigations in which persons may be required to furnish information or give evidence. The EOC must then report and make recommendations in the light of any of their findings. If in the course of an investigation the EOC is satisfied that discriminatory acts or practices have occurred, then it may issue a non-discrimination notice. Proceedings in respect of discriminatory advertising, discriminatory instructions or inducements can only be brought by the EOC. Both the CRA and EOC have a role to play in assisting an individual who is an actual or prospective complainant. This assistance may be granted if the case in question raises an issue of principle or because of its complexity, it is unreasonable to expect the complainant to deal with it unaided or by reason of any other special considerations. The assistance which both Commissions may offer extends to giving advice, procuring a settlement of the dispute, arranging for legal advice and/or representation and any other appropriate assistance.

When we explore the law relating to gender discrimination you will recognise that there are many areas of conflict between domestic law and European Community Law. The House of Lords has confirmed that part of the role of the EOC, and presumably other similar agencies, is to challenge UK legislation in the courts where there is perceived to be a conflict with EC law. In the momentous decision in *R v. Secretary of State for Employment ex parte EOC* 1994 the House of Lords struck out national limitations on redundancy and unfair dismissal rights for part-time workers as contrary to Article 119 of the Treaty of Rome.(now article 141) Their lordships ruled that in considering the statutory duties of the EOC, in particular to work towards the elimination of discrimination, it was perfectly proper for the EOC to work towards securing amendments to legislation and to attempt to achieve this by means of an application for judicial review in the High Court.

Disability Rights Commission

The Disability Rights Commission Act 1999 established the Disability Rights Commission and from April 2000 it took over the role of the National Disability Council. The new commission has been given powers which mirror the EOC and the CRE but in relation to the Disability Discrimination Act 1995:

- to promote opportunities for disabled people;

- to monitor the Act and eliminate discrimination;

- to inform and assist individuals in bringing claims under the Act;

- to inform and advise employers;

- to conciliate in certain disputes;

- to conduct formal investigations and publish the outcome;

- to issue the code of practice;

- to issue a non discrimination notice when it believes a person is committing or has committed an unlawful act or apply for an injunction.

Disability discrimination law is dealt with in Chapter 4.

Health and Safety Commission/Executive

A further example of where agencies have been created by statute to monitor and enforce an area of employment law is the Health and Safety at Work Act. By this Act the Health and Safety Commission and the Health and Safety Executive were created. The Commission consists of a chairman and a number of commissioners and performs its functions under the direction of the Secretary of State for Employment. Its wide ranging duties include:

- arranging for research and promoting training in health and safety at work;

- submitting proposals for regulation and issuing codes of practice;

- assisting and encouraging the furtherance of the objectives of the 1974 Act;

- acting as an information and advisory service;

The Executive took over the role of the Factory Inspectorate and its essential function is to enforce health and safety law. To this end the Executive through its inspectorate carries out inspections of work places, suggests improvements and has power to issue improvement and prohibition notices and, if necessary, bring prosecutions. The law on health and safety is the subject of Chapter 8

Chapter 3
Employment Relationships

An employment relationship exists where one person, an employer, who may be an individual, partnership, corporate body or unincorporate association, employs another person or persons to perform some work The relationship could be one of employer and employee under a contract of service or that of employer and contractor under a contract for services. Status on an employed or self employed person can have numerous legal and economic consequences. There are in addition further legal consequences if an individual has the legal status of a 'worker' which would normally include an individual who provides personal services as a contractor. Both employees and workers are defined under statute.

Employees

The definition of an employee is contained in s.230 of the Employment Rights Act 1996.

Under s.230(1) *an employee means an individual who has entered into or works under (or worked under) a contract of employment.*

Under s.230(2) *a contract of employment means a contract of service or apprenticeship whether express or implied and if express oral or in writing.*

The same definition appears in s.54(1) of the National Minimum Wage Act 1998.

The definition tells us that to achieve the status of an employee it is necessary to have agreed a contract of employment. Furthermore such a contract could be expressly agreed or implied from the conduct of the parties. An express contract may also be orally agreed and could even consist of written and oral terms. Prior to 1995 there was also an important distinction made between the rights of part-time and full-time employees but this is no longer the case (see Chapter 4).

The above section 230 provides no guidance as to how a contract of employment may be distinguished from other contractual arrangements where individuals are engaged to perform work as self employed contractors. It is to the common law that we must turn to provide us with the tools to tackle the issue of contractual status and this necessarily involves an analysis of the relevant case-law. You should appreciate that the process of identifying a contract of employment has been an employment law issue for many years to which distinguished labour lawyers have applied their minds. Kahn - Freund said that the contract of employment *"is the cornerstone of a modern system of labour law and we should be able to recognise it"*. Lord Wedderburn likened the contract to an elephant when he said that it was *"an animal easy to recognise when you see it but too difficult to define"*.

Workers

A further statutory definition of increasing significance is that of the *'worker'* a status well known in European jurisdictions.

A worker is defined in s.296(1) of the Trade Union and Labour Relations (Consolidation) Act 1992 *as an individual who works or normally works or seeks to work (a) under a contract of employment or (b) under any contract for personal services for another party who is not a professional client*. Workers are also defined in s.54(3) of the National Minimum Wage Act 1998.

It follows therefore that all employees are workers but in addition a self employed contractors would also be included provided they have or seek a contract to provide personal services. Individuals excluded are professional advisors and contractors who reserve the right to sub contract or contract to provide an end product to which others will contribute. There are many self employed tradesmen who will contract to provide there own personal services who as a consequence are classified as workers. The definition also encompasses the numerous casual contract workers previously conceded as self employed.

The classification is important because there is an increasing tendency to confer statutory rights on workers rather than 'employees' for example the minimum wage and working time restrictions. Workers are covered by discrimination legislation and included in the Wages Act (now the ERA) and so protected from unlawful deductions from their pay. Recent legislation which applies to workers rather than just employees includes: The National Minimum Wage Act 1998, The Working Time Regulation 1998, The Public Interest Disclosure Act 1999 and the Part-Time Workers Regulations. More significantly the Employment Relations Act 1999 confers authority on the Secretary of State for Employment to extend existing statutory rights to workers who are not employees. There is no doubt that this is a significant power to extend some or all of the long standing rights to workers leaving outside the statutory protection only the "genuinely self employed". There is a strong belief that the casual workers at the bottom of the employment ladder who are genuinely economically dependent should benefit from statutory employment rights. For many years the distinguished labour lawyer Bob Hepple has advocated replacing the contract of service with a broad definition of employment based upon an employment relationship between the worker and the undertaking where he is employed. By this means the notion of service could be extended to include both the intermittent exchange of work for remuneration and the single continuous contract.

In one of the first cases involving the application of the National Minimum Wage Act 1998 the High Court in *Edmunds v. Lawson* 2000 considered whether a pupil barrister could be classified as a worker and so entitled to the payment of a minimum wage. The High Court held that a pupil barrister does in fact fall within the scope of the legislation because he is employed under a contract of apprenticeship. The employers here denied firstly that there was a contract between themselves and the pupil and secondly that if there was it was invalid as contract of apprenticeship because of the lack of writing.The High Court held all the elements of a legally binding contract were present. Applying an objective test there was a clear intention to contract implied from the nature of the agreement. The offer of professional training had been accepted and was supported by consideration, the promise to work as a pupil. Also the lack of a written agreement did not prevent the existence of a contract which could be purely oral for the purposes of the National Minimum Wage Act.

On appeal the Court of Appeal agreed with the High Court's analysis that the parties had entered into a contract. The offer of 12-month pupillage was intended to have legal consequences, supported by consideration and accepted. The court disagreed however that the contract was one of apprenticeship to which the National Minimum Wage Act applied. The fundamental characteristics of an apprenticeship contract involving mutual duties to educate and train in return for service and work were not present in a pupillage contract. Also the opportunity for the trainee to practice for her own benefit and reward for six months would be anomalous in an employment relationship.

Where full time employment is offered, but only on a temporary basis, perhaps to cover for an employee on maternity leave or secondment, the fact that there is an undertaking as to the temporary nature of the work is important in determining the rights of the parties when the contract is terminated. Certainly the dismissal of a temporary worker eligible to present a claim for unfair dismissal is not automatically 'fair', but it could be regarded as such if the employer has acted reasonably in the circumstances in reaching his decision to dismiss. This would be the same for an employee who is required to serve out a probationary period and is dismissed having worked for the necessary period of continuous employment to qualify to present a claim for unfair dismissal. The use of fixed term contracts is considered in the next Chapter. They are an increasingly popular device giving employers flexibility when they are faced with volatile markets. Such factors are used to attempt to justify the use of zero hours contracts where staff are provided with work, often on a daily basis when there is a demand for their services.

While the presumption is that people on government training schemes are not employees, the Employment Appeal Tribunal has held that participants in a community programme to provide temporary work, are working under a contract of service. A company director is regarded as an office holder rather than as someone having an employment relationship with the company. Increasingly, however, company directors have executive positions in their companies and in such circumstances a contract is likely to be drawn up, which will specify their management role. It is then that an employment relationship will arise under which the director could be regarded as an employee of the company, or in some cases an independent contractor.

Some employees, for instance civil servants, the police, prison officers and health services employees, are regarded as special categories and their legal position tends to differ from employees generally. Also while an apprentice is not regarded strictly as an employee, in practice both the common law and statutory rights available to such a person are very similar to those of any full-time worker under a contract of service. Expiration of the apprenticeship contract however does not carry with it a right to a redundancy payment or the right to claim unfair dismissal in the case where there is no offer of full time employment.

> In *Wallace v. C A Roofing Services Ltd*. 1996 the plaintiff was employed as an "apprentice sheet metal worker" for four years and in his statutory statement it provided that "at the end of your apprenticeship your employer will terminate unless there is a suitable vacancy that we can offer you at the time". When the plaintiff was dismissed prematurely by reason of redundancy he claimed that his apprenticeship contract could not be terminated on that ground and he sued for damages. The High Court held that the oral agreement entered into was a contract of apprenticeship rather than a contract of employment and it could not be terminated by redundancy other than closure of the business or a fundamental change in the character of the work. The plaintiff was therefore entitled to damages for breach of his apprenticeship contract. *"Although modern legislation has assimilated apprenticeships to contract of employment the contract of apprenticeship remain a distinct entity at common law. Its first purpose is training, the execution of work for the employer is secondary. In such a relationship, the ordinary law as to dismissal does not apply. The contract is for a fixed term and is not terminable at will as a contract of employment is at common law."*

It is a fundamental principle of company law that a company is a distinct legal entity with its own legal personality. This principle is supported by case-law such as Lee *v. Lees Air Farming* 1961 which recognise the distinction between a company and its membership even where the sole majority shareholder and director is in unrestricted control of the company. The issue in *Buchan v. Secretary of State for Employment and Ivey v. Secretary of State for Employment* 1997 was whether a person who was the director and majority shareholder in a small private company could also be classified as an employee of the company for the purposes of statutory employment rights. Both companies became insolvent and went into receivership. Mr Buchan as director and full-time employee of his company relied on ss166 and 186 of the Employment Rights Act 1996 and applied to recover arrears of wages, redundancy payments and payments in lieu of notice from the Secretary of State. Mr Ivey the Managing Director and majority shareholder of his company applied to the Secretary of State for a redundancy payment. In both cases the tribunal held that the directors could not be classified as employees for the purposes of statutory employment rights. Even with a written contract of employment the tribunal held that as controllers of the company the directors were in *"every sense the company"*. *"He was a businessman carrying out the functions of a businessman rather than an employee behaving as such"*. The EAT agreed and held that *"there is a distinction, properly recognised by the industrial tribunal between an individual running his own business through the medium of a limited company and an individual employee of a limited company who is subject to the control of the board of directors of that company."*

The Court of Appeal has recently disagreed with the decision of the EAT in *Buchan and Ivey v. Secretary of State for Employment* that an individual who holds the sole or controlling shareholding in a company cannot be regarded as an employee. In *Secretary of State for Trade and Industry v. Bottrill* 1999 the court held that all the facts must be considered to determine an individual's status one of which is the fact that he has a controlling interest in the company and that is likely to be decisive. But other factors include whether the contract of employment is genuine or a sham, whether the individual is in reality answerable only to himself and whether he is able to vote on matters in which he was personally interested such as his own employment. Here it was possible to conclude that there was a genuine contract of employment.

Employees and Contractors

There are an infinite variety of terms and conditions under which one person may do work for another. The requirements of employers will range from the need to engage full-time employees where a long standing relationship with their staff is envisaged, characterised by mutual trust and confidence between the parties, to the use of temporary workers engaged to complete a particular task. It may be that the temporary worker, such as the accountant or solicitor, provides a specialist skill which is required by the employer only on an intermittent basis. Alternatively temporary and casual employment only may be offered, because of economic necessity or the expansion or contraction of the size of the workforce in line with demand. Independent contractors (or self employed workers) are now well established as a substantial proportion of the workforce of some industries, for instance, the media, catering and construction. Of the million or so construction workers, well over half a million are self employed. The changing face of employment patterns in Britain is shown by official figures which reveal that while 62.3% of household income is earned from wages and salaries, over 10% is now derived from self-employment. This form of employment has many advantages for both sides. The employer 'gets the job done' and the contractor is normally well paid in return. A criticism of the system is that it provides no support for the older or infirm worker, no security of employment, and may lead to a general reduction in health and safety standards. The increasing use of the self employed in business to execute work and provide services both in the public and private sectors makes the basic division between the employed and self employed a matter of considerable importance.

A large number of legal and economic consequences stem from the distinction between employed and self employed status. For this reason it is necessary to be able to identify the status of the employment relationship that has been entered into. Employment legislation and the common law both recognise the distinction between employment under a *contract of service* and self employment under a *contract for services*. The distinction is a relatively straightforward one to make in the majority of cases. It is only in a small proportion of cases that difficulties arise, often where employers, or those they employ are seeking to achieve contractor status for economic advantage or in order to evade legal responsibilities. The case law on the following pages demonstrates that it is not only the parties to an employment relationship who have an interest in an individuals employment status but the State may also intervene for such purposes as National Insurance contributions, income tax, and employee rights on an employer's insolvency. An individual may be required to establish employee status to enjoy the benefits of statutory rights in relation to security of employment or health and safety. By asserting a statutory right, such as the right to a statement of employment terms to which an employee is entitled, an individual can bring the issue of status before a tribunal.

The table on the following page provides a summary of the major legal and economic consequences of the employment classification.

Legal and Economic Consequences of Employment Classification

Contract of Service (Employed Persons)	Contract for Services (Self-employed)

Liability

An employer may be made vicariously liable for the wrongful acts of employees committed during the course of their employment.

As a general principle an employer may not be made liable for the wrongful acts of contractors he employs other than in exceptional cases.

Common Law Employment Terms

Numerous terms are implied into a contract of employment by the common law to regulate the relationship of employer and employee e.g. trust and confidence.

The common law is much less likely to intervene in the relationship of employer and contractor.

Health and Safety

A high standard of care is owed by an employer both under statute and the common law with regard to the health and safety of his employees.

While both the common law and statute recognise the existence of a duty of care by an employer in relation to the contractors he employs, at common law it is of a lesser standard than the duty owed to employees.

Statutory Employment Rights

A large number of individual employment rights are conferred on employees by statute which generally arise after a period of service e.g. the right to unfair dismissal protection; to redundancy payments; to belong to a trade union and take part in trade union activities; to protection in the event of the employer's insolvency; to guarantee payments, to security of employment after maternity leave; to statutory maternity pay; to a written statement of the main terms and conditions of employment and the right not to be discriminated against on the grounds of sex, race or marital status.

Contractors are traditionally excluded from the mass of individual employment rights conferred by statute. One notable exception however is the legislation in relation to discrimination, which protects the self-employed when they are providing personal services. Such workers are now more likely to benefit from statutory employment rights e.g.

* the working time rights
* the national minimum wage
* public interest disclosure
* part-time workers regulations
* representation in disciplinary proceedings

Income Tax

The income tax payable by an employee is deducted at source by the employer under the PAYE (pay as you earn) scheme. An employee is referred to as a Schedule E tax payer.

The income tax of a self employed person is payable by the taxpayer and not his employer, on a lump sum basis (Schedule D) on a 'current year basis' of assessment. Schedule D taxpayers retain more favourable treatment in claiming reasonable expenses when assessed for tax. Furthermore an independent sub-contractor may have to charge VAT on services.

Welfare Benefits

Under the Social Security Act 1975 both employer and employee must contribute to the payment of Class 1 National Insurance contributions assessed on an earnings related basis, entitling the employee to claim all the available welfare benefits e.g.Job Seekers Allowance, statutory sick pay, industrial disablement benefit, state retirement pension.

Under the Social Security Act 1975 a self-employed person is individually responsible for the payment of lower Class 2 National Insurance contributions and has only limited rights to claim welfare benefits e.g. statutory sick pay.

Distinguishing between the Employed and Self Employed

Once again while it should be stressed that in the vast majority of cases it is easy to recognise a contract service and a contract for services the distinction between the contracts in borderline cases is not so straightforward.

In the final analysis the determination of whether an individual is an employee or a contractor is a question of law for the courts rather than a question of fact involving placing sole reliance on the description of the contract given by the parties to it. In *Carmichael v. National Power Plc* 2000 the House of Lords confirmed that the decision whether an applicant is employed under a contract of employment is a question of law if the parties to the contract intended all the express terms to be contained in contractual documents. However *"when the intention of the parties, objectively ascertained has to be gathered partly from documents but also from oral exchanges and conduct, the terms of the contract are a question of fact"*. In the absence of perversity questions of fact are of course a matter for the tribunal with which the EAT and appellant courts should not interfere. In this case the House of Lords held that the tribunal was entitled to find that the parties conduct and surrounding circumstances indicated that when the applicants were not working there was no contract of employment and no mutual obligation to work or provide work. This case is considered later in the chapter.

The Common Law Tests

Over the years a number of tests have been formulated by the courts to attempt to determine any given worker's status. Originally the courts would only consider the level of control over a worker by an employer. In *Performing Rights Society Ltd. v. Mitchell and Booker* 1924, McCardie J. said that *"the final test, if there is to be a final test, and certainly the test to be generally applied, lies in the nature and degree of detailed control over the person alleged to be a servant"*. If an employer could tell his workers not only what to do, but also how and when to do it, then the workers would be regarded as employees, employed under a contract of service. Today the courts adopt a much wider approach and take account of all the circumstances to determine a worker's status. This is not to say that control is no longer a significant factor, for it would be difficult to imagine a contract of service where the employer did not have the ultimate authority to control the work performed by the employee.

Control is of course a less obvious feature the more specialised, skilled or trusted the workers become, for example a surgeon. This was why in the 1950s and 60s it was thought necessary to move away from a test based solely on control over the worker. The integration or organisational test favoured by the Court of Appeal at this time was expressed by Denning L J in *Stevenson, Jordan and Harrison v.*

MacDonald and Evans 1952. Here he said that *"under a contract of service a man is employed as part of the business and his work is done as an integral part of the business, whereas, under a contract for service, his work, although done for the business, is not integrated into it, but is only accessory to it"*. Adopting this approach the Court of Appeal was able to determine that medical staff in a hospital were employees and that a trapeze artist in a circus who also helped out with general duties was also an employee. In both cases their work was regarded as an integral part of the organisation.

The present approach of the courts, which involves viewing all of the circumstances of the case to determine status, has been described in various ways as the mixed, multiple or economic reality test. It has its origins in the following case.

In *Ready Mixed Concrete Ltd. v. Ministry of Pensions* 1968 under a peculiar procedure laid down in National Insurance legislation MacKenna J, a single judge of the Queens Bench Division of the High Court, sat as the final appellate court to decide the employment status of a driver for the plaintiff company. This was in order to determine the employer's responsibility in relation to the National Insurance contributions of its drivers. The Ministry of Pensions had rejected the employer's contention that its drivers were self employed, despite the existence of written contracts of employment (30 pages long) which had attempted to create a contract for services rather than contracts of service. The declaration that the driver was self employed was not decisive and all aspects of his job were considered, for instance the fact that the driver purchased the lorry from the company; had to maintain it; that pay was calculated on the basis of the driving work performed. All these factors pointed to the driver being a contractor. Others pointed to his status as an employee. He had to paint the lorry in the company colours, he had to use it exclusively for company business and he was required to obey reasonable orders. McKenna J stated that there is a contract of service if an individual agrees to provide his own work, submits to his employer's control and in addition the majority of the contractual provisions are consistent with a contract of service. This approach has since been referred to as the mixed or multiple test. On the facts the power to delegate work was regarded as a decisive indication that the drivers were self employed under a contract for services.

The status of self employment cannot be achieved simply by including an express provision in a contract. The courts will look to the substance of an employment relationship rather than the label applied by the parties in order to decide a worker's status.

In *Ferguson v. John Dawson Ltd.* 1976 the plaintiff, a builder's labourer agreed to work as a 'self employed labour only sub contractor' an arrangement commonly known as the 'lump'. When working on a flat roof he fell and suffered injuries. No guard rail had been provided, in breach of the duty to employees owed under the Construction (Working Places) Regulations 1966. The High Court decided that the employer was in breach of this statutory duty towards the plaintiff and damages of over £30,000 were awarded. On appeal the employer argued that as the plaintiff was self employed the statutory duty was not owed to him. It was the plaintiff's responsibility to ensure that the guard rail was in place. The Court of Appeal held, by a majority, that the plaintiff was in reality an employee and so entitled to the compensation awarded. The 'lump' was no more than a device to attempt to gain tax advantages and whilst a declaration as to employment status may be relevant, it is not the conclusive factor to determine the true nature of the employment relationship.

A difficult case to reconcile with the decision in *Ferguson* 1976 is *Massey v. Crown Life Insurance Company* 1978. Here a branch manager of an insurance company, who also acted as a general agent, decided to become 'self employed' on his accountant's advice, despite the fact that his duties remained unchanged. The Court of Appeal concluded that a change of employment status had in fact taken place so that he was unable to bring a claim for unfair dismissal. Lord Denning M R stated that if there is ambiguity in the relationship then this can be resolved with a declaration one way or the other.

Whilst there was a degree of ambiguity in the above case in the branch manager's original position as manager/agent, it was significant that here was a 'professional' man, having considered independent advice, making a declaration which he believed would be to his benefit. This is in contrast to the labourer in *Ferguson* 1976 who was unadvised and could not be said to have consciously chosen to be a contractor with the legal consequences that this involved.

Consider also the decision of the Employment Appeal Tribunal in *Thames Television v. Wallis* 1979. Here a researcher, and later a reporter for a TV company, was taxed under Schedule D and treated as self employed. This was despite the fact that there was detailed control over her work over which her employer had exclusive access. On her dismissal she claimed compensation for unfair dismissal alleging that in reality she had been employed under a contract of service. The EAT agreed stating that the original declaration as to status was *"only one consideration that had to be taken into consideration in determining her status"*. It was found possible to distinguish the above decision in *Massey* 1978 on the grounds that in *Massey* here had been a deliberate change in status whereas in Wallis the researchers status was ambiguous from the outset.

Despite the existence of a clear agreement between the employer and the worker that he should be treated as self employed this may nevertheless be regarded by the courts as a false designation and overturned.

In *Young & Wood Ltd. v. West* 1980 the complainant, a sheet metal worker, asked his employer if he could be treated as self employed. This was accepted and despite the fact that there was no difference between his working conditions and those of PAYE workers, he was paid without deductions of tax and was not given holiday entitlement or sick pay. Furthermore the Inland Revenue had accepted the change, resulting in an estimated tax advantage of about £500 over five years because of assessment under Schedule D rather than Schedule E. Stephenson L J seemed to cast doubt on Lord Denning M R's approach in *Massey* 1978 by stating that *"It must be the court's duty to see whether the label correctly represents the true legal relationship between the parties"*. The Court of Appeal found that as it was impossible to regard the complainant as in 'business on his own account' he was not self employed but remained an employee. Consequently the tribunal had jurisdiction to hear his complaint of unfair dismissal.

In *Duke v. Martin Retail Group plc* 1993 a large number of newsagent shop managers called contract managers were employed under an agreement which referred to them as independent contractors. They could employ staff and were paid commission with no holidays sick pay or pension. A tribunal decided that such a manager was self employed and the EAT agreed despite the large degree of control over the company's property the opening hours and the lack of financial investment. Features which pointed to self employed included the freedom on managers to employ staff, insure, delegate managerial work and carry on other business not in close competition with the employer.

Also in *Catamaran Cruisers Ltd. v. Williams* 1994 it was argued that because a worker had provided his services through a limited company he was not an employee and not entitled to present a complaint of unfair dismissal. The EAT held that the worker could still be classified as an employee. *"There is no rule of law that the importation of a limited company into the relationship prevents the continuation of a contract of employment. If the true relationship is that of employer and employee it cannot be changed by putting a different label upon it. Whether or not the contract in question is one of service or one for services is a question of fact. The formation of a company may be strong evidence of a change of status but that fact has to be evaluated in the context of all other facts found"*.

The growth of employment agencies who recruit potential staff and supply them to organisations as temporary workers has led to a debate as to the status of workers when placed with employers.

In *Pertemps Group plc v. Nixon* 1993 the applicant, a fitter machinist, entered into a contract with an employment agency under which he was described as a 'temporary worker' engaged under a contract *'for services'*. The object of the contract was to offer the applicant opportunities to work for clients of the agency. The applicant could refuse such work but if he accepted it, he would be paid an hourly rate by the agency subject to deductions of national insurance and PAYE. Under such an arrangement the applicant worked for three years continuously for a particular client and when this work terminated, and no alternative work was available, the applicant terminated his contract with the agency and claimed a redundancy payment. The tribunal found that he was entitled to such a payment concluding that when he worked for the client a contract of employment existed between himself and the agency. This contract of service existed under the 'umbrella' of the contract for services. On appeal however the EAT disagreed and found that the applicant's contract with the agency was a contract for services and there was no authority to support the implication of a second contract when work with a client was accepted.

By asking the question whether the worker is *'in business on his own account'* or under the control of an employer under a continuing business relationship, the courts have found it possible to conclude that a relationship traditionally regarded as self employment, namely that of a homeworker, was in reality a contract of service. Questions posed in applying this entrepreneurial test would include whether the individual was in business on his own, provides his own equipment, employs other workers and has a financial stake in the business.

In *Airfix Footwear Ltd. v. Cope* 1978 the court held that homeworkers, employed to assemble shoe parts for a company using equipment supplied by them, were not contractors but employees. While the work was provided on a regular basis, the employer argued that there was no obligation to provide work and the worker could also refuse it. In the present case the employment relationship had continued over the seven year period. In reality the employer decided on the things to be done, the manner, means, and the time and place of performance. The homeworker should therefore be regarded as an employee.

In *Nethermere (St. Neots) Ltd. v. Taverna and Another* 1984 the position of homeworkers was once again considered. Here a trouser manufacturer had paid a piece rate to homeworkers over a number of years. Machines for home use had been installed by the employer and work delivered daily. Following a dispute about holiday pay, the arrangement was terminated, and a claim for unfair dismissal brought by the workers. While the Court of Appeal confirmed that the law required mutual obligations for a contract of service in this situation, such mutuality was present in the continuing obligation of the employer to provide and pay for work and the employees' obligation to accept and perform it. Despite the absence of strict legal obligations to carry out the work, by evaluating the practices which reflected the economic realities of the situation (economic and psychological pressures) the majority of the Court of Appeal concluded that the complainant homeworkers were employees.

Mutuality of Obligation

Reliance on a pool of casual workers has long been a tradition in some sectors of business including the catering industry.

The legal status of so called 'regular casuals' was put to the test in *O'Kelly and Others v. Trusthouse Forte plc* 1983. Here a banqueting department run by the employer was staffed in part by full time employees but mainly by so called 'casuals'. Among the casuals were 'regulars' who were given preference when work was available, were often expected to work very long hours and consequently had no other employment. The applicants in this case were 'regulars' but when they became trade union shop stewards they were told by the employer that their services would no longer be required. In a claim for unfair dismissal brought by the applicants, the first issue the industrial tribunal had to deal with was whether they were employed under a contract of service and so protected by the law relating to unfair dismissal. In determining their employment status the tribunal acknowledged that its role was to *"consider all aspects of the relationship, no feature being itself decisive, each of which may vary in weight and direction and, having given such a balance to the factors as seem appropriate determine whether the person was carrying on business on his own account"*. Applying this mixed or multiple test the tribunal isolated factors consistent with a contract of service including the lack of mutual obligations on the part of the employer to provide work and on the part of the worker to offer services (referred to as mutuality of obligation). In addition there was the custom and practice of the catering industry to employ large numbers on a casual basis. By placing most emphasis on the inconsistent factors the tribunal found that the applicants were not employees and therefore not entitled to statutory protection. The Court of Appeal later found it unable to interfere with the tribunal's decision given that the correct legal approach has been adopted.

While there is no doubt that the decision in *O'Kelly* supports the custom and practice of the hotel and catering industry and confirms the fact that a fundamental feature of the contract of employment is the requirement to provide work and offer services, it is nevertheless difficult to reconcile with previous decisions, in particular *Ferguson* 1976. The reality of *O'Kelly* is that the regular casuals were subject to the same control as full time employees. They often worked longer hours than full time staff and a failure to work when required had the dramatic consequences of removal from the regular casual lists. Having no alternative employment, capital equipment or profit sharing, it would be difficult to describe them as business people working on their *"own account"*. The decision has been criticised by eminent labour lawyers. Bob Hepple thought that the approach of the Court of Appeal failed to focus on the purpose of the statute, to confer protection on members of trade unions who are *'workers'*. Gwyneth Pitt asked the question *"can it really be the case that casual workers at the bottom of the employment heap should not receive the protection of the law"*.

The significance of 'mutuality of obligations' for the purpose of identifying a contract of service re-emerged in *Hellyer Brothers Ltd. v. McLeod* 1987. The question faced by the Court of Appeal was whether trawlermen who had sailed exclusively for the same employer for a number of years were entitled to redundancy payments now that their services were no longer required. The difficulty for the crewman was that according to the custom and practice of the industry each voyage was covered by a separate crew agreement which was terminated by mutual consent on completion of each voyage. The crewmen invariably returned to the same employer for the next voyage despite being under no legal obligation to do so. To qualify for redundancy payments however they had to show that they were continuously employed under one overall contract of employment. Due to the lack of mutuality of obligation over the period of employment both the EAT and Court of Appeal held that there was no overall contract of service and so no entitlement to redundancy payments.

The lack of a binding obligation to accept work highlighted in *O'Kelly* was also apparent in *Wickens v. Champion Employment* 1984. Here the EAT examined the employment status of 'agency temporaries'. These are individuals who are employed to provide secretarial services to clients of their agent. On a claim for unfair dismissal the question arose as to the status of their relationship between the agency and the client and the EAT found it to be one of self employment. This was despite the large degree of control over the 'temps', the fact that the documentation referred to them as employees and the growing practices of agencies of giving employment status to temporaries.

It would be wrong to believe that Wickens is authority for a proposition of law that 'agency temporaries' are to be regarded always as self employed workers In *McMeechan v. Secretary of State for Employment* 1997 the complainant worked for an employment agency on a series of temporary contracts. There was a clear statement in his contract with the agency that he would provide his services *"as a self employed worker and not under a contract of service"*. The agency contacted to offer him the opportunity to work on a self employed basis where there was a suitable assignment with a client but there was no obligation to offer work or indeed accept it. When the agency became insolvent the complainant sought to recover money owed to him under a statutory right as an employee of an insolvent business. The tribunal applied *Wickens* above and held that as a temporary, on the books of an employment agency, the complainant was not an employee. The EAT took a different view however deciding that the tribunal had wrongly regarded Wickens as a precedent. *"Where there is a written contract between an employment agency and a worker whose services are provided by the agency to a third party client on a temporary basis, whether the contract is one of employment is a question of law to be determined upon the true construction of the document in its factual matrix. It is necessary to consider all the terms and conditions of the contract. The question is not determined by earlier judicial decisions on different contracts or the label which the parties themselves put on the relationship. The authorities do not lay down a general proposition of law that a worker who renders services under a series of temporary contracts with an employment agency does not have a contract of employment with the agency. The cases go no further than stating the general legal principles applicable to the question of whether a contract of employment exists and then proceeding to decide the individual case on the basis of the actual terms."* Here despite the label of self employed the totality of the written conditions of service between the complainant and the agency indicated that he was an employee of the agency. The Court of Appeal went on to hold that the EAT had adopted the correct approach and effectively overruled the previous decision in Pertemps. A temporary worker can have the status of employee in respect of each assignment actually worked through an employment agency.

In *Costain Building & Civil Engineering Ltd v. Smith* 2000 the EAT considered the status of an agency building worker who had been appointed a safety representative and then dismissed by the agency on the instructions of a builder client. The issue was whether he could claim automatic unfair dismissal as an employee dismissed as a safety representative. The EAT disagreed with tribunal and held that his apparent status as a contractor was genuine supported by factors such as no deduction of tax or national insurance, payment on invoice, no grievance procedure sickness or holiday pay. Certainly the appointment of the applicant as a safety representative could not make him an employee simply because they are required to be so.

In 1990 the Privy Council, which acts as a final appeal court for some Commonwealth countries, was asked to rule the legal status of a worker in Hong Kong.

In *Lee v. 1.Chung and 2.Shun Shing Construction and Engineering Company Ltd.* 1990 the appellant, a mason, claimed compensation when he suffered injury during the course of his work on a construction site in Hong Kong. The accident happened when he was working for a building sub contractor who had been delegated work by the main contractor on the site. Both the District Court and the Court of Appeal of Hong Kong had rejected the claim on the basis that the right to compensation arose in respect of injury caused to a person who worked under a contract of service, and in the circumstances the appellant was employed as an independent contractor. On final appeal, the Privy Council held that as the relevant Ordinance in Hong Kong which dealt with the legal position had been modelled on English Workman's Compensation Acts, then the status of a worker should be determined by applying English common law standards. Confirming that no single test is decisive, the court felt that the standard to be applied was best stated by Cooke J. in *Market Investigations v. Ministry of Social Security* 1969 when he set out the fundamental test as being *"Is the person who has engaged himself to perform these services performing them as a person in business on his own account".* Control is important but not the sole determining factor. *"Other matters which may be of importance are whether the worker provides his own equipment, whether he hires his own helpers, what degree of financial risk he takes, what degree of responsibility he has for investment and management and whether and how far he has an opportunity to profit from sound management in the performance of his task."* The decision will depend upon an evaluation of the facts... *"There will be many borderline cases in which similarly instructed minds may come to different conclusions".* Such a decision should therefore be left to the trial court and changed only by an appellate court in exceptional cases where the trial *court "took a view of the facts which could not reasonably be entertained".* In the present case, their Lordships were entitled to reverse the lower court's decision and find that the worker was in reality an employee. All the indicators pointed to the conclusion that the appellant was an employee. *"The picture that emerged from the facts was that of a skilled artisan earning his living by working for more than one employer as an employee, not as a small businessman venturing into business on his own account as a independent contractor, with all the attendant risks. The appellant ran no risk whatsoever save that of being unable to find employment which is a risk faced by all 'employees'".*

In the final analysis in a borderline case the determination of a worker's status can only be made by asking a number of questions relating to the main features of the relationship such as the extent to which the employee is:

- providing personal services;
- under the employer's control;
- regarded as an integral part of the organisation;
- in business on his own account;

- providing tools and equipment;

- sharing in the profit and contributing towards the losses;

- able to delegate work;

- in agreement as to his status.

The Court of Appeal was faced with the issue of employment status in Hall *(HM Inspector of Taxes) v. Lorimer* 1994. Here the Inland Revenue claimed that a free-lance vision-mixer who worked for a number of production companies should be charged to income tax under Schedule E as an employee rather than Schedule D as a self employed person. The reasoning behind the claim was that the vision-mixer provided no equipment for his work and had no financial status in the programmes upon which he worked. On his behalf it was argued that he took a financial risk in relation to payment for his work, he could also delegate work and had had a large number of different employers. The Court of Appeal agreed with the High Court that he was a self employed person employed under a contract for services. The court stated that *"there is no single path in determining whether or not the contracts from which a person derives his earnings are contracts of service or contracts for services. An approach which suits the facts and arguments of one case may be unhelpful in another".* The earlier decision of the High Court was approved of in particular the approach to this type of analysis that *"it is not a mechanical exercise of running through items on a check list to see whether they are present in, or absent from a given situation. The object of the exercise is to paint a picture from the accumulation of the detail. The overall effect can only be appreciated by standing back from the detailed picture which has been painted, by viewing it from a distance and by making an informed, considered, qualitative appreciation of the whole. It is a matter of evaluation of the overall effect of the detail which is not necessarily the same as the sum total of the individual details. Not all details are of equal weight or importance in any given situation. The details may also vary from one situation to another".*

In *Lane v. Shire Roofing Company (Oxford) Ltd.* 1995, the Court of Appeal considered the issue of employment status in the context of a personal injury scenario. The complainant was Mr Lane a general builder who traded under the name of PJ Building as a one man business. He was categorised as "self employed" for tax purposes working directly for clients and sometimes for other contractors. Shire Roofing was a roofing contractor whose owner Mr Whittaker often hired men for individual jobs.In 1986 Mr Lane was hired by Shire Roofing to work on a large roofing sub-contract. When that work was near completion Mr Whittaker asked Mr Lane to re-roof a porch in a private house. The job was agreed an they both visited the house to decide the fee and the equipment that was necessary to do the work. Because the cost of hiring scaffolding would have made the job unprofitable it was decided that Mr Lane should use his own ladder to do the work. When carrying out the work Mr Lane fell from the ladder and suffered severe head injuries. In an action claiming damages from Shire Roofing the High Court held that as Mr Lane was a contractor he was owed no duty of care. Factors that the court thought were significant in reaching that conclusion included the fact that Mr Lane had his own business, he was recognised as self employed for tax purposes and he was working on a single job without supervision. In addition the court concluded that there was no evidence to support the finding of a breach of duty. The Court of Appeal disagreed with the High Court on both of the main issues and held that Mr Lane as an employee was owed a duty of care by Shire Roofing which they had broken. As a consequence Mr Lane was awarded £102,100 in damages. The court confirmed that in determining whether a worker is an employee or a contractor control is an important factor *"Whose business was it?"* – was the workman carrying on his own business, or was he carrying on that of his employers? The answer to this question may cover much of the same ground as the control test, such as whether he provides his own equipment and hires his own helpers, but may involve looking to see where the financial risk lies, and whether and how far the workman has an opportunity of profiting from sound management in the performance of his task. These questions must be asked in the context of who is responsible for the overall safety of those doing the work in question. The court felt that there are good policy reasons in the safety at work field to ensure that the law properly categorises between employees and independent contractors and recognises the employer/employee relationship when it exists because of the responsibilities that the common law and statutes place on the employer. Despite the fact that Mr Lane was self-employed for tax purposes, his relationship with the employer was much closer to the "lump", where workmen are engaged only for their labour and are clearly employees as in *Ferguson v. John Dawson Ltd*. 1976

The significance of this case is that it illustrates a different approach of the higher courts to the issue of employment status. By emphasising the importance of public policy in deciding a workers' status in the health and safety context, the court found it possible to categorise the worker as an employee and so owed a duty of care by his employer. This was despite the fact that a strict analysis of his contract might have produced a different conclusion. Certainly if the issue had been one of security in employment such as in the *O'Kelly v. Trust House Forte scenario* the result might well have been different. ✗

Contemporary common law and statutory developments have provided further insight into the issue of employment status. The extension of employment rights to workers in new legislation such as minimum wage and working time reflects the belief that individuals providing personal services should have statutory protection. A wide power to extend employment rights to such individuals is contained in the

Employment Relations Act 1999 under s.23 unfair dismissal, redundancy and maternity rights to casual workers providing personal services.

The case-law developments are two major decisions in 1999, one from the Court of Appeal and the other a House of Lords judgment. The Court of Appeals decision in *Express and Echo Newspapers v. Tanton* 1999 is in many ways a further confirmation of the judgment of McKenna J in *Ready Mixed Concrete v. Ministry of Pensions* 1968. Here a driver who had been an ex employee was re engaged as a driver on a self employed basis. His contract contained a provision which stated "in the event that the contractor is unable or unwilling to perform the services personally, he shall arrange at his own expense the services personally. While the driver did not sign the contract he worked in accordance with its terms and on occasion used substitute drivers. Other factors pointed to him being an employee including the requirement to wear a uniform and using the company's vehicles. By requesting a s.1 statement the driver was in essence asking the tribunal to confirm his status. The tribunal's decision that he was an employee giving emphasis to what occurred rather than the documentation was confirmed by the EAT as a permissible conclusion with no arguable point of law. On further appeal however the Court of Appeal held that the right to employ a substitute is inherently inconsistent with status as an employee. A contract of employment must necessarily contain an obligation on the part of the employee to provide services personally. Both the tribunal and the EAT had thought that the substitution clause was not fatal to their being a contract of employment. The Court of Appeal ruled that the right to provide a substitute is inherently inconsistent with employment status. Without such an irreducible minimum of obligation it cannot be said that there is a contract of employment.

The House of Lord's decision in *Carmichael v. National Power* 1999 stresses the need for mutuality of obligation as the core of a contract of employment as a prerequisite for trust and confidence. Here power station guides who were recruited and trained by their employer were employed 'on a casual as required basis'. They often worked for 25 hours a week and were paid net after deductions of income tax and national insurance at the employed persons rate. They could refuse work under their contract and sometimes did. To establish their status a s.1 statement of terms of employment was requested of the employer. All employees are entitled to a s.1 statement. The tribunal thought that the guides were contractors due to the lack of mutuality of obligation and the EAT felt that as the final arbiter on a question of fact that decision should not be interfered with. The Court of Appeal however held that the ordinary meaning of the word 'on a casual as required basis' in these circumstances was that there was an implied term that the employee would provide a reasonable amount of guiding work and subject to the qualification of reasonableness the applicants would accept the work offered. This meant that the contract did impose mutual obligations to offer and to undertake work. Of course this interpretation of mutuality of obligation by the Court of Appeal majority differs significantly from the *O'Kelly v. Trust House Forte* approach which required a legal obligation to offer and accept work as the core of an employment contract. A further appeal to the House of Lords restored the Tribunal's decision.

Relying on evidence which established that there were numerous occasions when the guides were not available for work Lord Irvine drew the objective inference that when work was available the guides were free accept it or not as they chose and they would not be subject to any disciplinary action. This flexibility he felt suited both sides. The tribunal was entitled to decide from the documentation, the circumstances and the parties conduct that they intended their relationship to be governed by a contract when they were not working. The *case "founders on the rock of absence of mutuality".* The words employment on a casual as required basis do not in the opinion of Lord Irvine impose an obligation to undertake guiding work. Ld Hoffmann emphasised that the issue of status is a question of fact for the tribunal when the intention of the parties is to be gathered from documents, oral exchanges and conduct. *"I think that it was open to the industrial tribunal to find as a fact that the parties did not intend their letters to be the sole record of their agreement but intended that it should be contained partly in the letters, partly oral exchanges at the interviews or elsewhere and partly left to evolve by conduct as time went on".* This would not be untypical of agreements by which people are engaged to do work, whether as employees or otherwise. On the basis the ascertainment of the agreement was a question of fact with which the EAT were right not interfere. Having accepted the tribunal's finding as to the lack of mutuality their decision that there was no contract of employment may not be disturbed. The guides could only succeed if their engagement created an employment relationship which subsisted when they were not working.

While the House of Lords in *Carmichael* are saying that there could be no overall global contract of employment subsisting during the period of work inactivity because of the lack of mutuality there still remains the possibility of a services of short term contract of employment during work periods. A continuous period of such contracts could establish sufficient continuity for the purposes of statutory rights.

The fact that there has been such litigation on the employed/self employed distinction suggests that in the borderline cases in particular, decisions are by no means clear cut. The courts are faced with the difficult task of maintaining a balance between the freedom of employers to offer employment on the terms that best suit their interest and the rights of workers, for the most part in an unequal bargaining position, to obtain the benefits of status as an employee. Under European Union employment law rights and duties tend to be conferred and imposed on 'workers' which would include employees or contractors providing personal service. As more rights in the UK are extended to workers the distinction between employees and contractors providing personal services will become less significant.

Case Study

Dalton West plc - The Drivers

Dalton West is a large manufacturer of fork lift trucks with depots and retail outlets situated all over Britain. Alan, Bob and Chris are lorry drivers for Dalton West. They have all been employed for three years. Employees at the company receive both holiday pay and sick pay. The company state in their contracts that lorry drivers are self-employed. All the lorry drivers are employed on different terms.

Alan is paid per delivery, although he is guaranteed a minimum of 20 deliveries a week. His lorry is provided by the company, although he must maintain it. He receives no holiday pay or sick pay. He pays his own tax and national insurance and may substitute another driver if he wishes.

Bob and Chris have similar terms. They are paid a minimum weekly wage (which is the equivalent of 20 deliveries) and after that per delivery. They use company lorries which the company maintain. They may also substitute a driver, but only with written permission from the company. Bob receives no holiday or sick pay and pays his own tax and national insurance. Chris used to receive his wages net, but last year the company told him it would be cheaper for both the company and Chris if he became responsible for his own tax and national insurance. Chris agreed to this and has since received gross wages with no deductions.

Last week Alan suffered a severe burn when he accidentally placed his hand on exposed electrical wiring on the inside wall of Dalton West premises. The next day Bob was injured when his brakes failed when making a delivery. Concerned about safety issues, Chris has requested a copy of his employment contract, but Dalton West have told him that as a contractor he is not entitled to one.

You are required to determine the employment status of the three drivers and to provide some guidance as to Dalton West potential legal liability.

Case Study

Soles plc

Soles plc owns a national chain of shoe shops. For some years now the company has had a policy of recruiting the majority of its largely female sales staff on a casual, part-time basis. After a short probationary period a proportion of sales staff are contracted to work for Soles on an "as and when required" basis. Usually there is almost continuous employment available for these regular casuals. Freda has been employed by Soles as a regular casual for four years. In this time she has had five or six breaks in employment lasting between one and three weeks, usually when she has turned down the offer of work. Freda is paid gross and has no entitlement under her contract to holiday pay or sick pay.

In an attempt to boost the profitability of its shops, Soles has recently introduced a new grade of shop manager called a "contract manager". All new managers are being employed on annual fixed term contracts, with no entitlement to sick pay, holiday pay or pension rights and are being asked to sign clauses waiving their rights to unfair dismissal and redundancy. They can, however, earn high rates of commission on top of their basic salary, which is paid gross. There is an express requirement under the new contract that "contract managers" provide a personal service and cannot delegate their work. Existing Soles managers are offered contract status and Bert, a long standing employee, accepts the offer after being advised by his accountant that there are tax advantages to being self-employed.

Now Soles management has decided to reduce staffing levels due to a fall in demand. Freda is told that she will no longer be required and Bert is informed that his annual contract will not be renewed.

Chapter 4
Establishing the Contract of Employment

Having identified the main employment relationships in Chapter 3 it is now possible to focus attention on the process by which an employer recruits his staff, both full-time and part-time.

A significant trend of employment over the last decade has been the growth of reliance on part-time workers and the self employed. There are approximately six million part-time workers in the UK and significantly the vast majority of them are women. While as a general rule self employed workers tend to work longer hours than employees, there are nevertheless over a half a million (9.5% of the total workforce) self employed part-timers in Britain. As we have already seen many self employed offer personal services and may be classified as *'workers'* with increasing statutory protection.

Full-time, Part-time and Fixed Term Employees

A full-time employee was anyone who worked under a contract of employment for sixteen hours a week or more and as an employee such a person enjoyed the full range of statutory employment rights, generally after a period of continuous employment. In relation to part-time workers the position was that statutory rights could be acquired after five years continuous service for those employed under a contract for between 8 and 16 hours per week. Following the momentous decision of the House of Lords *in R v. Secretary of State for Employment ex parte EOC and Another* 1994 the legal position of part-time workers changed dramatically. Their lordships ruled that UK legislation conferring statutory rights on full-time workers and not part-timers in relation to redundancy and unfair dismissal was indirectly discriminatory against women and incompatible with European Community Law.

The rights of part-time employees have now largely been brought into line with full-time staff by legislation. This was achieved by the Employment Protection (Part-time Employees) Regulations 1995. Under these regulations the hours thresholds are abolished so that all distinctions in statutory employment rights based on the number of hours worked no longer apply. This means that part-time workers can rely on the same amount of continuous service as a full time employee to qualify for rights relating to redundancy pay, unfair dismissal, written reason for dismissal, notice and maternity leave.

All part-time employees are protected by discrimination law, and to comply with European Community law all part-time women are entitled to 18 weeks maternity leave. Now all part-time employees with one years continuous service will also qualify for extended maternity leave.

Significant rights for part-time workers are included in the Part-Time Workers (Prevention of Less Favourable Treatment) Regulations 2000 which are in force from the 1st July 2000. An obvious but significant point is that the regulations apply not only to employees but the broader category of 'workers'. In addition for the regulations to apply there must be a comparable full timer worker employed by the same employer. The one exception is where a full timer goes part time and can make a comparison with his own previous terms.

Some of the main provisions are that part-time workers:

- must not have a lower basic rate of pay than comparable full-timers unless it can be justified on objective grounds;

- will be entitled to receive pay at overtime rates once they have worked the same number of hours as full-timers;

- will be entitled to the same sick pay and maternity rights (pro rata);

- will be entitled to equal access to occupational pension schemes;

- will be entitled to the same training opportunities as full-timers;

- will be entitled to the same annual holidays and potential leave (pro-rata);

- will be treated no less favourably when being selected for redundancy.

The regulations also provide that part-timers can apply to their employers for a written statement of reasons if they believe that they are being treated less favourably than comparable full-timers.

Employers across the full range of occupational categories offer part-time employment but there are particular concentrations of the six million part-time workers in;

- sales and services (check out operators, cleaners, catering assistants, porters)

- teaching and health professionals (school teachers, lecturers, nurses, physiotherapists)

- personal services (cooks, bar staff, hairdressers, domestic staff)

- clerical and secretarial (clerks, typists, computer operators)

Clearly while a number of part-time workers would prefer the opportunity to enter full-time employment a significant proportion of part-time workers choose to work part-time because of the impracticability of full-time hours, given their other responsibilities. An increasingly popular method of recruiting employees is to offer employment on a fixed term contract. In cases where staff are required to cover for long term illness or maternity leave or they are required for a particular project, a fixed term arrangement for six months or a year has obvious benefits for the employer. Many employers believe that by offering fixed term employment they have an opportunity of measuring the employees' capability and it is then possible to exercise options on the expiration of the contract. In these cases the fixed term is almost a probationary period. You will see in Chapter 10 that the expiration of a fixed term contract is a statutory dismissal under s.95(1) ERA 1996. While it is still possible to exclude the right to a redundancy payment in such a contract the Employment Relations Act 1999 provides that unfair dismissal rights can no longer be excluded.

Both full-time and part-time staff are recruited by means of entering into a contract of employment. Despite the unique nature of such a contract the common law rules relating to formation, construction and discharge of contracts are largely applicable. The formation of an employment contract is the culmination of a recruitment process which will normally involve advertising for staff, submission of application forms, job interviews, negotiating terms of employment and selection of staff. Each stage of the recruitment process can be considered culminating in the contract of employment.

The Recruitment Process

The recruitment process will normally begin when the employer places an advertisement indicating that staff are required. Statements of fact in the advertisement may be classified as representations and if they prove to be false and having induced a contract of employment an innocent employee could seek a remedy for misrepresentation. In rare cases statements in the advertisement maybe given the status of contractual terms or at least used as evidence to determine the express terms of employment.

In *Holliday Concrete v. Woods* 1979 the job advertisement indicated that a fifteen month contract was available. This was regarded as the period of employment rather than the employer's view that there was an understanding that the job would last as long on the project continued.

In *Joseph Steinfeld v. Reypert* 1979 the EAT held that the fact that the job advertised "sales manager" bore no relation to the actual job which was mainly clerical, amounted to a repudiatory breach of the contract of employment.

A job advertisement may also place clear obligations on an employee so that if they are not fulfilled this will be a factor in determining the reasonableness of the employer's decision to dismiss as a result.

In *Tayside Regional Council v. McIntosh* 1982 the job advertisement required a car mechanic to have a clean driving licence. Despite the fact that this was not inserted as an express term in an employment contract the subsequent dismissal of a mechanic who lost his licence was held to be fair.

Discriminatory job advertisements are dealt with in Chapter 5.

The Application Form

Advertisements for job applications normally indicate that a prospective employee should complete an application form to assist in the selection process. While a significant feature of the employment contract is that it involves a relationship of trust and confidence it is not a contract uberrimae fidei (utmost good faith) such as partnership or insurance. This means that there is no duty on an applicant to volunteer information which is not requested during the recruitment process, which includes the completion of the application form.

In *Walton v. TAC Construction Materials Ltd.* 1981 the complainant was dismissed after working for thirteen months when the employer discovered that he was a heroin addict. During a medical inspection prior to employment the employee had answered "none" when asked to give details of serious illnesses and failed to reveal that he was injecting himself with heroin. Both the tribunal and the EAT held that it was fair to dismiss the applicant firstly because of his deception and secondly in accordance with their policy not to employ anyone who was addicted to drugs. Although not relevant for the case the EAT considered whether the complainant should have disclosed his addiction for the purposes of employment and decided that *"it could not be said that there is any duty on the employee in the ordinary case, though there may be exceptions, to volunteer information about himself or otherwise than in response to a direct question"*.

If a job applicant is deliberately dishonest on an application form this will normally make any subsequent decision to dismiss fair.

In *Torr v. British Railways Board* 1977 the EAT held that the employers *"were justified in deciding to dismiss the employee as soon as they appreciated that he had obtained employment as a guard by dishonest concealment of a criminal conviction carrying a sentence of three years imprisonment, even though the conviction was as far back as 1958 and the employee had apparently been working satisfactorily as a guard for sixteen months"*. The sentence was of such a duration not to be covered by the Rehabilitation of Offenders Act 1974 (see Chapter 5) and neither could the philosophy behind that Act be extended to render a dismissal in the circumstances unfair *"It is of utmost importance that an employer seeking an employee to hold a position of responsibility and trust should be able to select for employment a candidate in whom he can have confidence. It is fundamental to that confidence that the employee should truthfully disclose his history so far as it is sought by the intending employer"*.

In determining the fairness of an employer's decision to dismiss after discovering an employees mis-statement on an application form all the circumstances must be considered including the significance of the mis-statement, the length of employment and whether the work was satisfactory.

In *Johnson v. Tesco Stores Ltd.* 1976 the application form stated that "a misstatement as to date of birth, previous employment details etc., will render the application and any subsequent contract invalid." When a mis-statement by the complainant as to his employment history was discovered, his job was terminated, despite having worked satisfactorily for eighteen months. The tribunal held that the effect of the clause could not be to make the employment contract void from the outset when the false statement was discovered. When the contract was terminated by the employer there was a dismissal which could be regarded as fair or unfair applying the law relating to unfair dismissal. (See Chapter 11).

Job Interviews

The primary objective of the job interview from the employer's viewpoint is to assist in the selection process. It should be stressed however if a decision to employ an applicant is made it may be at this point that a formal offer is made and accepted and a contract concluded. Even in cases where an understanding is reached, subject to a formal written offer at a later stage, statements or promises made during the interview may be used to interpret the contractual terms or constitute express terms of the contract in themselves. Certainly it makes sense to ensure at the interview stage that a prospective employee is given a realistic picture of the terms and conditions of employment and what the job entails. Even statements such as promotion prospects could be regarded as a term of employment if they later prove to be unrealistic. Certainly a clearly worded job offer will override conflicting statements made in the job advertisement. In the event of conflict between oral statements and writing the writing will normally have primacy but it is the intention of the parties which must be determined.

In *Hawker Siddeley Power Engineering Ltd. v. Rump* 1979 the complainant was employed as a heavy goods vehicle driver in 1973 and signed a contract of employment which stated that he would be liable to travel all over the country. This obligation was confirmed in a later statement of terms of employment issued in 1976 and signed by the employee. In fact the complainant had made it clear when he took the job that because of his wife's illness he would not travel beyond the south of England and that had been orally agreed by a manager when he signed the contract. When finally in 1978 the complainant refused to obey an instruction to travel to Scotland and this led to his dismissal, one issue before the EAT was whether he was contractually obliged to do so. The EAT held that the promise to work only in the south was an oral contractual term. Here *"there was a direct promise by the employers which must have become part of the contract of employment because it was following upon the promise that the employee signed the contract"*. Even the subsequent written statement which included a mobility clause signed by the employer was insufficient to exclude the oral term previously agreed. Here the employee *"had no notice that the oral term he had secured was going to form no part of his new contract. The mere putting in front of him a document and invitation for him to sign it could not be held to be a variation by agreement so as to exclude the important oral term which he had previously secured. Rather if there was a variation at all to the contract, it was a unilateral variation which was not binding upon the employee"*.

Quite often an offer of employment is made conditional, for instance *"subject to the receipt of satisfactory written references"* or the *"passing of a medical examination"*.

In *Wishart v. National Association of Citizens Advice Bureaux Ltd.* 1990 The Court of Appeal considered a case where the plaintiff had been offered the post of information officer *"subject to satisfactory references"* and then when the employer discovered his past attendance record withdrew the job offer.

The issue before the Court of Appeal was whether the employer's decision to treat the references as unsatisfactory could be viewed objectively and tested by the standard of the reasonable person in the position of the employer. In fact the court decided that unlike medical opinion as to the employee's fitness which could be tested objectively, there was no obligation in law on the employer other than to decide in good faith whether the references were satisfactory. *"The natural reading of a communication, the purpose of which is to tell the prospective employee that part of the decision on whether he is firmly offered the post has yet to be made, is that the employer is reserving the right to make up his own mind when the references have been received and studied. "*

If there is a dispute as to whether an appointment has been made or not it is only rarely that a court would grant a temporary injunction to require the employer to allow the employee to remain in the post until the issue is settled at the full trial.

This was the case in *Powell v. London Borough of Brent* 1987 where there was a dispute as to whether the appellant a council officer had been validly promoted. The employer alleged that the decision to promote her was not valid as it had not been confirmed. The Court of Appeal granted an interlocutory injunction requiring the council employer to allow the officer to remain in the promoted post until it was determined at the trial of the action whether she had been validly and effectively appointed to the office in question. *"Although it is a general rule that there cannot be specific performance of a contract of service, part of the basis of which is that mutual confidence is a necessary condition for the contracts satisfactory working, the present case was exceptional. It is unlikely that a plaintiff will be able to satisfy the court that, despite strenuous opposition by her employers to her continuing in the job, nevertheless there subsists the necessary confidence to justify the making of an injunction. Sufficiency of confidence must be judged by reference to the circumstances of the case, including the nature of the work, the people with whom the work must be done and the likely effect upon the employee and the employer's operations if the employer is required by injunction to suffer the plaintiff to continue in the work."* Here the fact that the appellant worked competently in the promoted post for over four months and there was no evidence of any defect in her work relationships enabled the court to grant the injunction pending the trial of the action.

If the acceptance of the job offer is conditional the normal contractual rules apply and it will be taken as a rejection and amount to a counter offer capable of acceptance or rejection. It is in the interests of both the employer and the employee that the express terms of employment are precise and clearly understood. It is then less likely that legal problems will arise in the future when contractual terms are possibly subject to change or it becomes necessary to bring the employment relationship to an end.

Once a contract of employment is concluded there is legal redress available if either party decides to back out of the contract in breach. The unilateral withdrawal by an employer of an offer of employment, once accepted, will constitute a breach of contract, and the damages awarded could in exceptional cases exceed the wages due under the contractual notice period.

In *Gill and Others v. Cape Contracts Ltd*. 1985 the plaintiffs gave up their present employment as insulation engineers in Northern Ireland to take up the offer by the defendants of six months work in the Shetlands on much higher wages. After confirming the arrangement the defendants then withdrew the offer of employment and the plaintiffs sued for damages. The Northern Ireland High Court awarded the men £2,500 damages each holding that *"the plaintiff insulation engineers were entitled to damages for breach of warranty by the defendants in circumstances in which the defendants failed to honour a representation to the plaintiffs forming a collateral contract that if they gave up their existing employment they would be employed by the defendant.... for approximately six months at wages considerably in excess of their existing earnings... those representations formed a collateral contract to the contract of employment"*.

It should be stressed however that the above scenario is rare and damages available against an employer in breach will normally be restricted to the wages due under the notice period Also the courts will not, other than in exceptional cases, order specific performance of a contract of employment the remedy for breach by the employee is damages. In practice unless an employer has incurred substantial recruitment cost the cost of litigation would make an action against an employee in breach unwise. There is no right to bring a potential unfair dismissal claim without two years continuous employment unless the reason for dismissal is shown to be inadmissible such as related to pregnancy, trade union membership, statutory rights or health and safety.

In *Sarker v. South Tees Acute Hospitals NHS Trust* 1997 the employer withdrew a formal letter of appointment before the employee started work. The EAT held that the tribunal had jurisdiction to hear a claim for damages for breach of contract relating to the termination of the contract of employment under the Industrial Tribunals Extension of Jurisdiction Order 1994. An employee is defined as someone who has entered into a contract of employment despite not having started work so that a potential claim for unfair dismissal also arises if the reason for dismissal is shown to be inadmissible such as pregnancy or trade union membership. The EAT rejected the notion that here there was a contract for employment rather than a contract of employment. The employee had entered into a contract of employment to provide future service in consideration of remuneration and no further contract was required to confirm the relationship.

Legal Formalities and the Contract of Employment

Contrary to popular belief, apart from merchant seamen and apprentices, there is no legal requirement that a contract of employment be in writing. While there are problems associated with identifying the terms of an oral agreement, nevertheless given the fluid nature of a contract of employment there is no guarantee that a requirement to reduce the original contract to writing would solve all the problems of interpreting its content.

A contract of employment is unenforceable if it is illegal under statute or its objects are contrary to public policy at common law. Illegality can arise in the formation or during the continuance of the contract. The most common ground for illegality is when the parties agree to commit a fraud on the Inland Revenue by means of tax avoidance.

In *Napier v. National Business Agency* 1951 the plaintiff was employed on a salary of thirteen pounds per week with six pounds a week expenses when both parties were aware that genuine expenses would never exceed one pound. Following her summary dismissal the plaintiff claimed damages for wrongful dismissal. The Court of Appeal held that the contract was unenforceable as contrary to public policy. By contracting as they had *"the parties to it were doing that which they must be taken to know would be liable to defeat the proper claim of the Inland Revenue and to avoid altogether, or at least to postpone, the proper payment of income tax".*

An employer could seek to rely on the fact that a contract of employment is unenforceable on the grounds of illegality as a defence to a complaint of unfair dismissal. This was the case in *Lightfoot v. D & J Sporting Ltd.* 1996 where an employer had arranged to pay part of his gamekeepers wages to his wife so reducing the employee's tax liability and national insurance contributions. Despite the fact that the wife did genuinely assist her husband in his gamekeeping duties the tribunal concluded that the contract of employment was tainted by illegality, for the scheme to reduce tax liability had been adopted after seven years of employment. Accepting the reality of tax avoidance schemes the EAT disagreed with the premis of the tribunal that such schemes are necessarily unlawful. *"A scheme is not necessarily unlawful because its only purpose is to reduce the amount of lawful deductions that ought to be paid to the Inland Revenue or the Department of Social Security. That is the purpose of all legitimate tax avoidance schemes. If the scheme was entered into in good faith and was a proper method of reducing tax, open and above board, which either had been or would be disclosed to the Revenue, there is nothing unlawful about it."*

An illegal contract may not affect an employment claim which does not depend upon its existence for instance the statutory tort of sex discrimination.

> In *Hall v. Woolston Hall Leisure Ltd.* 2000 the Court of Appeal held that despite the fact that an employee knew from her payslips that her employer was defrauding the Inland Revenue and that her contract was therefore tainted with illegality, she was nevertheless entitled to compensation under the Sex Discrimination Act 1975 when she was unlawfully dismissed because of her pregnancy.

Statutory Statement of Terms and Conditions of Employment

On the 14 October 1991 the EC Council of Ministers adopted a directive called 'An Employer's Obligation to Inform Employees of the Conditions of Employment Relationships'. This was the first directive affecting employees' rights at work other than in the field of health and safety under the Commission's Social Charter Action Programme. The UK government responded by including the content of the directive in s.26 and schedule 4 of the Trade Union Reform and Employment Rights Act 1993 which is now included in s.1 of the Employment Rights Act 1996

Under s.1 of the Employment Rights Act 1996 there is a statutory requirement on employers to provide their employees within two months of the commencement of employment with a written statement of the main terms of employment. The section originally applied to full-time employees (those engaged under an employment contract for sixteen hours or more a week) or part-time workers (engaged between eight and sixteen hours) after five years employment. Now under the Employment Protection (Part-time Employees) Regulations 1995 the hours threshold has been removed and s.1 applies to full-time and part-time employees. Certain classes of employees are excluded from s.1 including registered dock workers, Crown employees and employees who work wholly or mainly outside Great Britain. The objective of s.1 is to ensure that employees have written confirmation and a source to scrutinise at least the main terms of their employment contracts. Employers can issue the statement in instalments but within the two months limit and the principal statement should contain certain information prescribed by section 1.

Particulars which must be included in the statutory statement include:

reference to the parties and the dates on which the period of continuous employment began (stating whether a previous period of employment is included as part of continuous employment);

- the scale of remuneration and the method of calculation;

- the intervals at which remuneration is paid (whether weekly or monthly or some other period);

- the terms and conditions relating to hours of work;

- the terms and conditions relating to holidays and holiday pay (sufficient to enable the employee's entitlement to accrued holiday pay on the termination of employment to be precisely calculated);

- the terms and conditions relating to sickness or injury and sickness pay;

- the terms and conditions relating to pension and pension scheme;

- the length of notice which the employee is obliged to give and entitled to receive;

- the title of the job which the employee is employed to do or a brief description of the work;

- a note containing a specification of any disciplinary rules or reference to an accessible document containing such rules;

- the name of the person to whom the employee can apply if he is dissatisfied with any disciplinary decision relating to him;

- the name of the person to whom the employer can apply to seek the redress of any grievance;

- any collective agreement which directly affects terms and conditions of employment.

A section 1 statement may refer to other documents such as a staff handbook or written policy for the purposes of sickness provisions and pensions and a collective agreement for the purposes of notice provisions provided the employee has either a reasonable opportunity of reading such documents during the course of employment or they are readily accessible. It would also be permissible to include a disciplinary and grievance procedure in separate documents provided they are reasonably accessible.

Reference is made several times in s.1 to *"terms and conditions"* of employment and yet there has been no attempt in statute or common law to satisfactorily distinguish between these expressions. The prevalent view seems to be that *"terms"* are those parts of the contract that are mutually agreed, expressly or by implication and are found in the contract, collective agreements and occasionally in statutory provisions. *"Conditions"* on the other hand have a lower status and are unilateral instructions from the employer and will specify how and when employment duties are to be fulfilled. Conditions are usually found in work rules, disciplinary and grievance procedures and job descriptions (see later in the chapter).

To satisfy the requirements of s.1 it is not sufficient simply to be told or shown the above particulars of employment. The employer must present the employee with a document containing the information or at least make such a document available for inspection (e.g. a collective agreement and a rule book). It should be stressed that a statutory statement is not the contract of employment but rather strong prima facie evidence of its terms. Certainly the mere acknowledgement of its receipt does not turn the statement into a contract.

In *System Floors (UK) Ltd. v. Daniel* 1982, Browne-Wilkinson J said in relation to the statement that *"It provides very strong prima facie evidence of what were the terms of the contract between the parties. Nor are the statements of the terms finally conclusive: at most, they place a heavy burden on the employer to show that the actual terms of the contract are different from those which he had set out in the statutory statement"*. This view of the status of the statutory statement was subsequently approved by the Court of Appeal in *Robertson v. British Gas Company* 1983 where it was held that if the written statement does not accurately reflect the agreed terms then the agreed terms prevail.

In *Eagland v. British Telecommunications plc* 1992 the Court of Appeal held that when called upon to scrutinise the accuracy of a s.1 statutory statement the industrial tribunal cannot after all invent terms to cover matters not referred to, such as grievance procedures and holiday pay. LJ Leggatt suggested that he was *"unable to envisage circumstances in which it might become appropriate for an industrial tribunal to invent a term ... in the sense of determining either what term should have been agreed or what term would have been reasonable. If an essential term, such as a written statement must contain, has not been agreed, there will be no agreement. If it has it is the duty of the industrial tribunal where necessary to identify the term as having been agreed, whether expressly or by inference from all the circumstances including the conduct of the parties without recourse to invention."*

Certainly while it is up to the contractual parties to agree the content of the contract of employment it is for the employer to provide the employee with a statutory statement of terms and conditions of employment. All the matters in s.1 should be included in the statement so for instance reference should be made to holidays, holiday pay, and accrued holiday pay rights. In *Morley v. Heritage* 1993 the employee argued that when his employment ceased he was entitled to 13 days accrued holiday pay relying on an implied term of his contract that if his employment terminated with accrued holiday entitlement he would be paid in lieu. The Court of Appeal made the important point that it was not necessary to imply a term into a contract of employment to satisfy the requirements of s.1. While the section does refer to a statement in relation to accrued holiday rights it *"leaves it open to an employer to enter into a contract with an employee which contains no provision at all"*. Applying both the business efficacy test and the presumed intention of the parties the Court of Appeal held that there was no implied term entitling the employee to accrued holiday pay.

While the statutory statement does not constitute the contract of employment the High Court held in *Lee and others v. GEC Plessey Telecommunications* 1993 that there is a heavy burden on a party who claims that the actual contract is different from the statutory statement.

Contractual terms we shall discover, are often the subject of change, in which case an employer is obliged under s.4 to notify the employee of changes in the statement within one month of the change. An employer who fails to comply with obligations in relation to the statutory statement could be the subject of a complaint to the industrial tribunal. With no effective sanction available for employers who fail to comply with s.1, complaints to tribunals are rare, and only arise usually in connection with other complaints, for instance in relation to unfair dismissal. Finally it should be mentioned that those employers who provide their employees with a written contract of employment which covers all the matters which must be referred to in the statutory statement, do not have to supply their employees with a separate statutory statement. The writing should of course reflect what has been orally agreed by the parties.

In *Discount Tobacco and Confectionery Ltd. v. Armitage* 1990 the complainant was a shop manageress with only a short period of continuous employment who enlisted the help of her trade union official to secure a written contract of employment from her employer. When finally such a contract was issued, and she felt that it contained discrepancies, the complainant attempted to raise them with her employer. The response of the employer was to dismiss her, giving the reason for dismissal as lack of suitability or capability. This led to a complaint of unfair dismissal, the complainant alleging that the true reason for dismissal was her trade union membership which was automatically unfair under s.152 of the Trade Union Labour Relations (Consolidation) Act 1992. If trade union membership or activities is the reason for dismissal there is no need to qualify with two years continuous employment for protection against unfair dismissal. Both the industrial tribunal and the Employment Appeal Tribunal thought that there was no genuine distinction between trade union membership and making use of the essential services of a union officer and as a consequence the dismissal in this case was automatically unfair.

The Contents of a Contract of Employment

A contract of employment is composed of its terms, the mutual promises and obligations of the parties to it. Contractual terms may be *express* and become part of the contract through the express agreement of the parties. Usually of course, there is simply agreement by the prospective employee to the standard terms dictated by the prospective employer or terms previously agreed between the employer and a trade union. Alternatively, contractual terms may be *implied* into the contract of employment by an external source. The major sources for implication we shall discover, are the courts and tribunals but occasionally terms are implied into contracts of employment by statutory provisions or through custom. Such mutual obligations have legal significance and a failure to comply with the requirement of a term of the contract could provide the innocent party with the option of securing legal redress. An action for breach of contract may be brought to secure damages against the party in breach of a contractual term. If damages would not suffice to provide a remedy, an injunction could be sought to restrain the breach of contract. In such circumstances an *interlocutory (temporary) injunction* is often sought as a remedy. One rarely used option for an employee who feels that his employer is unreasonably requiring him to do work which is not part of his contractual obligations is to seek an injunction to maintain the status quo at work. A further option for an employee in these circumstances is to apply to the High Court for a declaration as to the legal position.

If a breach of contract is regarded as so serious as to be repudiatory, then the innocent party has the option of accepting the breach and terminating the contract. A repudiatory breach by an employer could, if accepted by the employee, entitle him to regard himself as constructively dismissed if he walks out as a result. Alternatively, a repudiatory breach by the employee could in some circumstances justify summary dismissal by the employer.

A good example of an employer's repudiatory breach of contract is a failure to pay the employees full salary. In *Cantor Fitzgerald International v. Callaghan* 1999 the Court of Appeal distinguishes between an employers failure to pay or delay in paying agreed remuneration and a deliberate refusal to do so. A wilful refusal to pay the agreed salary following perhaps a unilateral reduction in pay will undermine the entire foundation of the contract and constitute a repudiatory breach by the employer. Alternatively a delay or failure to pay due to a mistake or some temporary fault may not constitute a breach which goes to the root of the contract.

In the majority of cases of conflict or dispute between the employer and employee, the true legal position can only be assessed by identifying and analysing the express terms of employment and any implied terms which have become incorporated into the contract.

Express Terms

Earlier in the chapter we saw that the express terms of a contract of employment are those expressly agreed by the employer and employee, and may be in writing or may be purely oral. The statutory statement of the main terms and conditions of employment will normally provide sound evidence of the express terms. Even a job advertisement, an application form or a letter of appointment could contain contractual terms, as well as matters orally agreed in the interview. Express terms relate to matters such as *wages, hours, holidays, sick pay, job description, restraints, etc*. Of course, what has expressly been agreed by the parties may often require interpretation in the courts and employment tribunals. You should also appreciate that express terms will not define the work quality nor the pace of work effort.

It is the ordinary courts that generally but now not exclusively deal with disputes surrounding the interpretation of the terms of a contract of employment based upon an action for breach of contract. The majority of employment disputes however relate to statutory employment rights such as unfair dismissal, redundancy and discrimination and they are heard by employment tribunals and on appeal by the Employment Appeal Tribunal.

A court or tribunal may be called on to determine the rights of the parties by interpreting the exact wording of the express terms of a contract of employment.

In *Cole v. Midland Display Ltd*. 1973 the tribunal was faced with the problem of determining the meaning of the term, *"employed on a staff basis"* when it was applied to a manager. The tribunal held that the phrase meant that the employee was entitled to wages during periods of sickness or no work but in return the employee could be required to work overtime with out pay.

In *McCaffrey v. A E Jeavons & Company Ltd*. 1967 an employee employed expressly as a "travelling man" in the building trade was held to be contractually obliged to move his place of employment anywhere in the country when required to by the employer.

An employee whose job title was described as carrying out *"general duties"* in *Peter Carnie & Son Ltd. v. Paton* 1979 was held to be required to be very flexible in relation to the needs of his employer for the type of work to be carried out.

In *Securicor Ltd. v. Reid and others* 1992 the EAT construed the express term that an employee was *"based at"* a certain location to mean that he could be required to work at any site within the area administered from that location. The employee could be required therefore, under the express terms of his contract to move from one site to another and if the employee refuses to move and is dismissed, he would not be entitled to a redundancy payment.

The fact that an employee has a right to occupational sick pay contained in an express contractual term means that there would be a breach of contract if an employer purported to dismiss an employee who was in receipt of sick benefit unless the dismissal was on the grounds of gross misconduct. *Aspden v. Webb Poultry & Meat Group Ltd.* 1996 indicated that this may be the case even where the employee is served with the appropriate period of notice.

The Court of Session in *Hull v. General Accident, Fire & Life Assurance Co. plc* 1998 approved of the above decision but felt that in these circumstances redundancy could also be a lawful reason for dismissal. The High Court in *Villella v. MFI Furniture Centres Ltd.* 1999 held that there was an implied contractual term that where an employee was entitled to incapacity benefit, the employer would not terminate the contract except for a reason other than ill health, if the effect was to deprive the employee of incapacity benefit.

Contract law dictates that an express term should prevail over an implied term dealing with the same matter however you should appreciate that certain implied terms such as health and safety and trust and confidence will represent an irreducible minimum of obligation in a contract of employment.

There are also circumstances where the courts have recognised that an implied term may take precedence over an express term.

The Court of Appeal decision in *Johnstone v. Bloomsbury Health Authority* 1991. held by a majority that an employer's implied obligation to ensure the health and welfare of his employees could be broken even where the employer was exercising an express option in the contract to require the employee to work a large number of hours overtime. The court felt that if the employer is aware that by requiring a junior doctor to work long hours his health is suffering it would be a breach of contract to impose such long hours on him despite the fact that it was authorised by an express term of the contract.

Work Rules

It is common practice in many spheres of employment for the employer to issue work rules by printing notices or handing out rule books. Such rule books often contain instructions as to time-keeping, meal breaks, disciplinary offences and grievance procedure, sickness and pension rights, job descriptions, and the employer's safety policy. Although there is still some doubt as to the legal status of work rules, the present view is that such documents are unlikely to contain contractual terms. One school of thought is that work rules should be regarded as *conditions* rather than *terms* of employment, hence the expression, *"terms and conditions of employment"* and as such they should be subject to unilateral change by the employer. For example, while the number of hours worked would normally be the subject of express agreement and constitute a contractual term, instructions as to when these hours should be worked will normally be contained in a rule book and as a condition be liable to unilateral change.

In *Cadoux v. Central Regional Council* 1986 the employee's contract of employment was to be subject to the Conditions of Service laid down by the National Joint Council for Local Authorities' Administrative, Technical and Clerical Services, as supplemented by the Authorities Rules, as amended from time to time. The issue in the case was whether, under the Authorities' rules, the employer was entitled to introduce a non-contributory life assurance scheme for staff and then subsequently unilaterally withdraw it. The Court of Session held that here the "Authorities' Rules" were clearly incorporated into contracts of employment. They were however, made unilaterally by the employer, and although introduced after consultation, they were the "Authorities' Rules" and not subject to mutual agreement. Consequently there was *"no limitation on the employer's right to vary, alter or cancel any of the provisions of the Rules. The reference to the Authorities Rules, "as amended from time to time", led to the clear inference that the employer could alter their rules at their own hand"*. In the present case therefore the employer was entitled unilaterally to withdraw the provision of the non-contributory life assurance scheme.

In *Dryden v. Greater Glasgow Health Board* 1992 the EAT held that an employer was entitled to introduce a rule imposing a smoking ban at the workplace and the staff has no implied right to smoke. *"An employer is entitled to make rules for the conduct of employees in their place of work within the scope of the contract and once it was held that there was no implied term in the contract which entitled the employee to facilities for smoking, the rule against smoking was a lawful rule"*.

In *Secretary of State for Employment v. ASLEF (No 2)* 1972 Lord Denning expressed the view that rule books issued to railwaymen by their employers did not contain contractual terms but rather instructions to an employee as to how he was to do his work.

Where, however, a rule book is given or referred to by the employer at the time the contract of employment is formed, the fact that the employee has agreed that it is to be part of the contract and acknowledges that fact by his signature would more than likely give the rule book contractual effect. The EAT held *in Secretary of State for Scotland v. Taylor* 1997 that even a policy may become incorporated into individual contracts of employment. Here the employer's "equal opportunity policy" for the Scottish Prison Service which stated that employees would be afforded opportunities on an equal basis 'regardless of gender, race, religion, sexual preference, disability or age', was part of the contractual rights of individual prison officers and incorporated into contracts of employment.

Implied Terms

A contract of employment is composed of contractual terms which have been expressly agreed or incorporated into the contract by an extraneous source such as a collective agreement, the custom and practice of a particular trade or business, or the common law. To have a full appreciation of the content of a contract of employment you should be aware of the role of the common law in defining rights and duties of employers and employees. In addition to a large number of common law duties relating to such matters as good faith, confidentiality, health and safety, and obedience, which were originally tortious in origin, there is an increased willingness of the courts and tribunals to imply terms into employment contracts to deal with issues such as trust and confidence, mutual respect and sexual harassment. Later when we consider the termination of employment, you will discover that the need to point to a clear repudiatory breach of the contract of employment to establish a constructive dismissal has encouraged judicial ingenuity in incorporating implied terms which the court then declares that the employer has broken.

Statutory Terms

Apart from one notable exception in relation to equal pay, statute is not a major source of implied terms of employment. On the creation of a contract of employment, however, a number of statutory rights arise almost immediately, (for instance the right to a written statement of contractual terms and conditions and maternity leave) Other rights, such as unfair dismissal, attach to the contract after a period of continuous employment. Most of these rights are non excludable and cannot be removed by an express term in the contract of employment. Exceptioally under s.17 of the National Minimum Wage Act 1998 the minimum wage takes effect as a statutory implied term in a worker's contract and is enforceable by legal proceedings for breach of contract.

It has recently been decided by the High Court in *Barber v. RJB Mining (UK) Ltd. 1999* that the maximum forty eight hour working week prescribed for workers in s.4(1) of the Working Time Regulations is a statutory implied term in all contracts of employment. This means that a breach of the regulations will constitute a breach of contract for which the employee could pursue a remedy such as a declaration and/or damages. Mr Justice Gage said that *"It seems to be clear that parliament intended that all contracts of employment should be read so as to provide that the employee should work no more than an average of 48 hours in any week during the reference period"*.

Common Law Tems

The fact that common law implied terms confer rights impose duties on both parties to the employment relationship, suggests that they can be more meaningfully examined by considering each of them in turn in relation to both the employer and the employee. Most of the implied terms can be categorised under broad headings such as the wage/work bargain, health and safety, good faith, confidentiality, fidelity, and trust and confidence.

The courts are careful to stress that terms are implied into contracts of employment by applying one of a number of tests. A term maybe implied if it is either:

- necessary to the functioning of the contract or;

- reflecting the obvious intention of the parties at the time the contract was concluded or;

- an inevitable incidence of the employment relationship.

The fact that a particular policy is regarded as custom and practice is used as a justification for an implied term. In *Duke v. Reliance Systems* 1982 it was held that a policy adopted unilaterally by management cannot become a term of employee's contracts on the ground that it is an established custom and practice, unless it is at least shown that the policy has been drawn to the attention of the employees or has been followed without exception for a substantial period. The issue in *Quinn and Others v. Calder Industrial Materials Ltd* 1996 was whether the employers policy of paying enhanced redundancy payments supported the inference that it should be regarded as an implied term in employee's contracts. The fact that the policy had not been communicated to either the recognised union or the employees helped convince the EAT that it had not been incorporated into individual contracts of employments as an implied term.

It does seem however that the courts and tribunals find it possible to imply a term wherever it is thought necessary.

In *Mears v. Safecar Security* 1983 the Court of Appeal held that if there is no express agreement on a matter, the courts are entitled to consider all the facts and circumstances of the relationship, including the parties' conduct, to determine whether a term should be implied into the contract of employment.

In *Courtaulds Northern Spinning Ltd. v. Sibson* 1988 the Court of Appeal was called on to determine the nature and extent of an implied term in a contract of employment in relation to the place of work. Slade L J said that *"in cases ... where it is essential to imply some term into the contract of employment as to place of work, the court does not have to be satisfied that the parties, if asked, would in fact have agreed the term before entering the contract. The court merely has to be satisfied that the implied term is one which the parties would probably have agreed if they were being reasonable."* Implied terms may be subject to implied qualifications In *Prestwick Circuits Ltd. v. McAndrew* 1990 it was held that *"An implied right to order an employee to transfer from one place of employment to another must be subject to the implied qualification that reasonable notice must be given in all the circumstances of the case. Even where the proposed transfer involves a reasonable distance it is necessary to imply the qualification that the employee be given reasonable notice so as to preclude a contractual right of the employer to transfer the employee to some other place at a moment's notice. Whether the notice given in a particular case was reasonable is a question of fact and degree for the industrial tribunal to determine".*

In *Jones v. Associated Tunnelling Ltd.* 1981 the EAT held that a contract of employment cannot simply be silent on the place of work. If there is no express term, it is necessary to imply some terms into each contract of employment laying down the place of work in order to give the contract business efficacy. The term to be implied in that which in all the circumstances the parties, if reasonable, would probably have agreed if they had directed their minds to the problem.

The role of the courts and tribunals in implying contractual obligations into contracts of employment is a fundamental feature of employment law. Employment conflicts sometime occur in determining whether a particular job function carries the status of a contractual duty even where job descriptions have been agreed by the parties. This conflict often arises during industrial action.

In *Sim v. Rotherham Metropolitan Borough Council* 1986 the High Court had to decide whether the requirement of school teachers to provide cover for absent colleagues during normal school hours was an implied contractual obligation or merely a matter of goodwill. Refusing to provide such cover during a period of industrial action had led the employer to deduct an appropriate sum from the teacher's monthly salary. The High Court recognised that school teachers are a member of a profession and as such you would not expect their contracts to detail the professional obligations under their contracts. *"The contractual obligations of persons employed in a profession are defined largely by the nature of their profession and the obligations incumbent upon those who follow that profession. Teachers have a contractual obligation to discharge their professional obligations towards their pupils and their school. Cover arrangements, the court decided, are part of a teacher's professional obligations and the refusal of teachers to comply with them was a breach of contract".*

In a contract of employment there is an implied duty on the employee to provide personal service for which the employer is obliged to provide a wage. At the appointed time therefore, an employee is required to present himself for work and be ready and willing to perform at the direction of the employer. Absence from work without good reason would clearly constitute a breach of contract which would entitle the employer to adjust the wage accordingly. If the absence is due to industrial action there is an increasing tendency for the courts and tribunals to deal with conflict over entitlement to a wage or a partial wage by applying strict contractual principles.

The principle of 'no work no pay' was reaffirmed by the House of Lords in *Miles v. Wakefield MBC* 1987. Here industrial action taken by Registrars involved them in refusing to carry out a proportion of their work, that of performing marriages, on Saturday mornings. While the Registrars attended for work on Saturdays and performed other duties the employer made it clear that wages would be deducted for Saturday morning hours if the employees were unwilling to perform the full range of their duties. The House of Lords upheld the employer's position that they were entitled to withhold the Saturday wage despite the fact that a substantial part of the work was performed. Lord Templeman said that *"in a contract of employment, wages and work go together, in an action by an employee to recover his pay he must allege and be ready to prove that he worked or was willing to work".*

The Court of Appeal has also expressed the view that limited industrial action which involves non-performance of a part of an employee's contractual duties will prejudice an employee's claim for wages or even partial wages during the relevant period. This is certainly the case where the employer makes it clear that he does not condone part performance of the contract by the employee, so that he can regard any contractual duties performed as purely voluntary. By allowing the employee to come to work and carry out less than his full contractual duties the employer is not accepting a partial performance of the contract, and there is no requirement to prevent the employee working.

In *Wiluszynski v. London Borough of Tower Hamlets* 1989 an estates officer in the Council's Housing Department, as a result of an industrial dispute between NALGO and the Council, took part in limited industrial action which involved boycotting enquiries from council members. While the contractual duty was only a small but important part of the officer's workload, the response of the employer was to warn the officer by letter that if he carried on limited work it would be regarded as unauthorised and purely voluntary and wages would not be paid. The industrial action lasted five weeks, during which the officer was not paid and when it ended it took him two and a half to three hours to deal with the members' enquiries which had built up. The officer's claim for salary during the relevant period was upheld by the High Court on the basis that he had substantially performed his contract and higher management were aware of that, acquiesced in it and took the benefit of the work. On appeal, however, a totally different view was expressed by the Court of Appeal. In these circumstances, the court held, an employee is entitled to dismiss an employer in repudiatory breach of his contract of employment or decline to accept the partial performance of the contract. Here the employer had made it clear that any work undertaken would be voluntary, so that the employee could not reasonably have been confused or misled by this statement. There was no question, therefore of the employer waiving the right not to pay by accepting the services rendered and no obligation to prevent the employee from working, particularly where there is a large workforce. In this case partial performance of the contract had not been condoned by the employer so that no wages were payable.

A unilateral decision by the employer to withhold wages without just cause constitutes a breach of the fundamental obligation under the contract and give the employee the right to accept the repudiatory breach and treat the contract at an end. Such a breach does not however automatically terminate the contract.

In *Rigby v. Ferodo Ltd.* 1987 the employer attempted to impose a lower wage on the employees. On their behalf, the trade union made it clear to the employer that the lower wage was unacceptable and while the employees continued to work they nevertheless regarded the employer as in repudiatory breach of the contract of employment. When an action was brought to recover the unpaid wages, the House of Lords held that the employees were entitled to the full contractual wage from the time that the reduction was unilaterally imposed. (See Chapter 7).

In *Cantor Fitzgerald International v. Callaghan* 1999 the Court of Appeal considered the consequences of an employer failing to pay the contractual wage. Such a failure is of course a breach of contract but the court felt that if it was due to an accounting error or a simple mistake then the breach would not be fundamental. In a case where an employer unilaterally reduces the employee's pay or the value of a salary package however the *"entire foundation of the employment is undermined"* and may be regarded as a repudiatory breach.

Where work is subject to seasonal variations it has become a popular practice to employ staff on *annualised hours*. Usually a standard wage is payable for a notional number of hours per week, taking account of holiday entitlement, and when the annual hours have been worked in a given year, the employee becomes entitled to payment of overtime.

Such a system was adopted by collective agreement in *Ali v. Christian Salvesen Food Services Ltd.* 1997 providing that factory workers worked a notional 40 hour week with total annual hours of 1824. The issue before the Industrial Tribunal and then the EAT was whether in the event of contractual termination by reason of redundancy, an employee who had worked in excess of the notional 40 hour week for part of the given year was entitled to payment for the extra hours on a pro rata basis despite not having worked the 1824 annual hours. The EAT disagreed with the tribunal's decision and found it possible to imply a term into individual contracts of employment providing that an employee whose employment was terminated by the employer before the end of the pay year to be paid for those hours worked in excess of the notional 40 per week. By not making these additional payments for pro rata hours the employers had made unauthorised deductions of wages contrary to the Wages Act 1986. On further appeal to the Court of Appeal the court felt that the EAT was wrong in law to imply a term to that effect and in the absence of express provision for payment, in these circumstances the employees were not entitled to additional payment. The Court of Appeal held that if a collective agreement leaves a topic such as this uncovered, that is not a justification to imply a term into individual contracts to provide for this type of contingency. There may have been a conscious decision by those negotiating the agreement to leave complicated and controversial matters uncovered.

It is suggested that this somewhat surprising decision does seem to ignore the clear basis for implying a sensible term recognising the incomplete nature of the collective agreement and the obvious injustice of non payment for hours worked. Had the parties to the collective agreement, at the time it was negotiated applied their minds to the issue of payment in the event of premature termination for redundancy, their conclusion, it is suggested, would have been inescapable.

While it seems that there is an obligation to pay the contractual wage, this does not carry with it a duty to provide the employees with work. The general proposition was illustrated by Asquith LJ in *Collier v. Sunday Referee Publishing Company Ltd.*

1940 when he said, *"Provided I pay my cook her wages regularly she cannot complain if I choose to take any or all of my meals out."*

If an employee's pay depends upon work being provided, for instance piece work, or commission, the court in *Devonald v. Rosser and Sons* 1906 held that the employer is under an implied obligation to provide sufficient work to enable a reasonable wage to be earned. The obligation to provide work would also apply where the employee's occupation is such that the opportunity to work is an essential feature of the contract because of the possibility of loss of reputation due to inactivity such as an entertainer in *Herbert Clayton v. Oliver* 1930.

Health and Safety

At common law an employer is obliged to provide his workers with a safe system of work. This common law duty encompasses an obligation to ensure that workers are provided with safe plant and appliances, appropriate safety equipment, safe work methods and safe fellow workers.

In *British Aircraft Corporation v. Austin* 1978 the employer was held to be in breach of his implied duty of safety when he failed to investigate a complaint relating to the suitability of protective glasses for an employee. This conduct was held to be a repudiatory breach of the contract of employment sufficient to entitle the employee to terminate the contract and regard himself as constructively dismissed.

Employees themselves are under a duty to co-operate in relation to their own safety and that of their work colleagues. An employee who is unduly negligent in the performance of his work will be in breach of his employment contract and while he is unlikely to be sued by his employer, this could be used as a justifiable reason for dismissal. In *Lister v. Romford Ice and Cold Storage Co. Ltd.* 1957 the House of Lords held that an employee who caused injury by negligently reversing his lorry, was in breach of an implied term of his contract of employment.

In *Walton & Morse v. Dorrington* 1997 the applicant, a non smoker, found that her smoking colleagues created a working environment which constituted a nuisance and a cause of discomfort. This was despite the fact that her employer had implemented a no smoking policy which restricted smoking activities in the building in which she worked. Following an ultimatum by her employer the applicant finally left indicating the smoking issue as the reason and claiming constructive unfair dismissal. The EAT confirmed the tribunal's decision that the employers were in breach of an implied term of the employee's contract of employment in requiring her to work in an environment which was affected by the smoking habits of fellow employees.

"It is an implied term of every contract of employment that the employer will provide and monitor for employees, so far as is reasonably practicable, a working environment which is reasonably suitable for the performance by them of their contractual duties".

The law relating to health and safety at work is examined in Chapter 8.

Good Faith (mutual trust and confidence)

Of all the implied duties, the duty of good faith and mutual respect is the most difficult to define precisely. This is because good faith is such a wide ranging concept and involves an obligation on the employee to respect confidences, obey reasonable instructions, take care of the employer's property, account for money received in the performance of duties and not disrupt the employer's business. An employer on the other hand must treat his workforce with respect, indemnify them for expenses incurred in the performance of their duties and when providing a reference, ensure that it is accurate and fair.

All employees have a duty of faithful service and any attempt by an employee to use his position for undisclosed personal gain, for instance by accepting bribes or making a secret commission, will constitute a breach of the employment contract. The origins of this implied duty can be traced back to nineteenth century case-law.

In *Boston Deep Sea Fishing and Ice Company v. Ansell* 1889 an employee who received secret commissions from other companies for placing orders with them was held to be in breach of this implied duty of his contract of employment.

Reasonable Instructions

Part of the obligation of good faith requires an employee to submit to his employer's control and this involves obeying reasonable orders. What would constitute a reasonable instruction depends upon an objective interpretation of the employee's contractual duties both express and implied.

In *Pepper v. Webb* 1969 the head gardener who responded to his employer's request to plant some flowers with the words, *"I couldn't care less about your bloody greenhouse or your sodding garden"* was held to be in breach of the implied duty to obey reasonable instructions.

The Court of Session established in *Macari v. Celtic Football Athletic Co. Ltd.* 1999 that an employee is in breach of contract if he fails to carry out a lawful and legitimate instruction. The fact that the employer may have some ulterior motive in giving the instruction is irrelevant. Even if an instruction is within the scope of an employee's duties, it may not be reasonable if it involves a risk of serious injury such as *Robson v. Sykes* 1938 or a breach of the criminal law. Certainly the duty of good faith would require an employee to be flexible and move with the times, so that an instruction to adopt work techniques involving new technology, after proper training has been given, would normally be regarded as reasonable. In *Cresswell v. Board of Inland Revenue* 1984, Walton J said that *"there can really be no doubt as to the fact that an employee is expected to adapt himself to new methods and techniques introduced in the course of employment"*.

It is important to distinguish however, between a change in work methods and change in the job itself which if not authorised or agreed to, could not be unilaterally imposed without a possible claim for a redundancy payment or compensation for unfair dismissal. A wilful refusal to obey a reasonable order could lead ultimately to a dismissal so we will return to the problem of reasonable instructions in Chapters 10 and 11.

Employees have an implied obligation to take care of their employer's property. An employee who negligently allows his employer's property to be stolen or causes it wilful damage will be in breach of his employment contract and liable to dismissal.

Industrial Action

Given that the objective of industrial action is normally to cause disruption to the employer's business, an employee who takes part in a strike, go-slow, partial performance or even a 'work to rule' will be in breach of his contract of employment. Industrial action of itself involves a withdrawal of good faith so it is arguable that even an overtime ban, where there is no contractual obligation to work overtime, could be regarded as a breach of contract.

In *Secretary of State for Employment v. ASLEF* 1972, the Court of Appeal held that wilful disruption of the employer's undertaking would amount to breach of this implied duty of good faith. Here the railwaymen were disrupting British Rail services by working to the letter of the British Rail rule book, but nevertheless were held to be in breach of contract.

In *Ticehurst and Thompson v. British Telecommunications Plc* 1992 the Court of Appeal considered the legality of the employer's act of withholding wages during a period of industrial action when staff refused to work normally. The Court held that wages could be withheld if employees are not ready and willing to perform in full their obligations under their contracts of employment and withdraw goodwill. *"There is an implied term to serve the employer faithfully within the requirements of the contract. This term must be implied into the contract if a manager is given charge of the work of other employees and who, therefore, must necessarily be entrusted to exercise her judgment and discretion in giving instructions to others and in supervising their work. Such a direction, if the contract is to work properly, must be exercised faithfully in the interests of the employer. There is a breach of the implied term of faithful service when the employee does an act or omit to do an act, which would be within her contract ... and the employee so acts or omits to do the act not in the honest exercise of choice or discretion for the faithful performance of her work but in order to disrupt the employer's business or to cause the most inconvenience that can be caused."*

One tactic often employed by trade unions is an industrial dispute is to call for members to participate in half day or one day strikes over a period of time. Clearly by taking strike action an employee is in breach of contract and the appropriate sum could be deducted from his wage. If however the employee in question is otherwise working normally during the dispute the employer would not be entitled to refuse to accept work or refuse to pay wages. Again in *Ticehurst and Thompson v. British Telecommunications plc* 1992 the Court of Appeal held that *"the plaintiffs evinced intention to take part in future in a rolling campaign of strike action would not be a sufficient ground, by itself, for the employers to refuse to let her continue to work during the dispute. If the only intention evinced by the plaintiff was to continue to respond to a strike call if and when called upon by the union to strike, then she would, in effect, have been saying to the employers that she was intending to perform the full range of her contractual duties until sometime in the future, which might not happen at all, when she would break her contract by going on strike. If, during the time that her services would be rendered, the employers would receive full value from those services, there was no reason why they should not perform their part of the contract."*

Misconduct

While there is no implied obligation on an employee to reveal to an employer his own misconduct or deficiencies, the relationship of trust and confidence may demand that an employee in a managerial capacity should report the misconduct of others in the organisation. In *Sybron Corporation v. Rochem Ltd. and Others* 1983 the Court of Appeal held that an employee may be so placed in the hierarchy of an organisation so as to have a duty to report either his 'superior's' or 'inferior's' misconduct.

Confidentiality

Good faith most certainly includes respecting confidences so there would be a clear breach of the contract of employment if the employee revealed confidential information relating to any aspect of his employer's business to a competitor, or made use of such information for his own purposes.

Business goodwill revealed in customer lists and accounts or trade secrets such as manufacturing processes or designs, are in the nature of rights in property which the employer is entitled to protect during the employment relationship and to some degree even after its termination. It is a question of fact in each case whether information could be classified or confidential but some guidance was provided in *Marshall Thomas (Exports) Ltd. v. Guinle* 1978 where relevant factors were identified:

- the owner of the information must reasonably believe that its release would benefit a competitor or cause detriment to himself;

- the owner must reasonably believe that the information is confidential and not already public knowledge;

- the information must be judged bearing in mind the practice of the particular trade or industry.

By relying on the duty of fidelity an employer could obtain an injunction to prevent an employee working for a competitor in his spare time or revealing confidential information to a competitor. Breach of confidence could also be a reason relied on by an employer to convince an industrial tribunal that in the circumstances the decision to dismiss an employee was fair.

It has been argued that the implied term not to reveal or make use of confidential information acquired during the course of employment can extend beyond the termination of employment.

Such a duty of confidentiality was alleged by the employer to bind his ex-employee in *Faccenda Chicken Ltd. v. Fowler* 1986. Here the defendant, having previously worked for the plaintiff as a salesman, set up business in competition. The defendant recruited a number of the plaintiff's staff and the majority of his customers were ex-customers of the plaintiff. The plaintiff then claimed damages from the defendant for using confidential sales information relating to prices and customer requirements in breach of his contract of employment. Both the High Court and the Court of Appeal dismissed the claim holding that the use of the information did not in this case involve a breach of contract. The Court of Appeal laid down a number of legal principles to be applied, where in the absence of an express term, an ex-employee makes use of information acquired during the course of employment. The duty of confidentiality in these circumstances is much more restricted in its scope than the general duty of good faith which covers a subsisting employment relationship. Also, such a duty will extend to information which is 'confidential' only in the sense that unauthorised use of it while the contract subsisted would be a breach of the duty of good faith. To determine whether information would fall within the implied term and be capable of protection beyond the termination of employment, it is necessary to consider the following:

- the nature of the employment;

- the nature of the information;

- whether the information can be easily isolated from other information which the employee is free to use; and

- whether the employer impressed upon the employee the need for confidentiality.

A number of issues including confidentiality were considered by the High Court in *Nottingham University v. Fishel* 2000. The case concerned the head of a University's infertility clinic who had carried out private work at clinics abroad without his employers knowledge or consent. The High Court held that while he had broken his contract by not seeking permission there was no contractual loss from the breach. In addition here was no fiduciary duty on an employee to reveal such outside work in the absence of express provision in his contract. By using other university employees to pursue the work the doctor was in breach of contract.

It seems then that only genuine trade secrets are capable of protection by an implied term relating to confidentiality following the termination of employment. To achieve a greater degree of protection therefore, a prudent employer should ensure that an express restraint clause is inserted into the employment contract. Such a clause is of course an example of an express term in a contract of employment. Restraint clauses are given special treatment under the common law and were considered earlier in the chapter.

Further guidance in relation to the implied duty on an employee to respect confidential information even on the termination of employment was provided in *Universal Thermosensors Ltd. v. Hibben* 1992. The court concluded that *"The contracts of employment between the plaintiff and the three defendants did not include any provision restraining their activities after their employment had ended. So when they left they were free to set up at once a directly competing business in the same locality. Further, they were entitled to approach the plaintiff's customers and seek and accept orders from them. Still further they were entitled to use for their own purposes any information they carried in their heads regarding the identity of the plaintiff's customers or pricing policies, provided they had acquired the information honestly in the course of their employment and had not for instance, deliberately sought to memorise lists of names for the purposes of their own business. What the defendants were not entitled to do was to steal documents belonging to the plaintiff, or to use for their own purposes confidential information contained in such documents regarding the plaintiff's customers or customer contacts or customer requirements or the prices charged. Nor were they entitled to copy such information onto scraps of paper and take these away and use the information in their own business".*

It is only relatively recently that the courts and tribunals have recognised that an employee's duty to trust and respect his employer is in fact a mutual obligation in an employment relationship.

Trust and Confidence

Leading labour law commentators have welcomed the development of the implied term in relation to maintaining trust and confidence unreservedly. It exemplifies the core of the employment contract and was confirmed by the House of Lords as a term *"now established in employment law"*. Trust and confidence sets the contract of employment apart from commercial contracts for goods and services by recognising that an employment relationship involves more than simply a transfer of work for payment. In *Wallace v. United Grass Growers* the court stated that *"work is one of the most fundamental aspects of a persons life, proving the individual with a means of financial support and as importantly a contributing role in society. A persons employment is an essential component of his or her sense of identity, self worth and emotional well being."*

The development of the implied term of trust and confidence can be traced back to case law from the 1970's.

In *Robinson v. Crompton Parkinson Ltd.* 1978 the EAT considered the contract of an employee who had been dismissed for theft from his employers for which he was prosecuted and then subsequently acquitted by the Magistrates Court. When no apology was forthcoming from his employer he resigned claiming constructive dismissal. The EAT held that a false accusation of theft without an apology constituted a breach of confidence and trust such as to amount to a repudiation of the contract of employment. *"In a contract of employment, there has to be mutual trust and confidence and if either party is in breach of that mutuality of confidence there may be a breach of contract."*

Mutual respect has always been an important feature of an employment relationship.

In *Isle of Wight Tourist Board v. Coombes 1976* a personal secretary walked out of her job when she heard her manager declare in front of other staff that she is *"an intolerable bitch on a Monday morning"*. Such a statement destroyed the relationship of mutual trust and respect and constituted a repudiatory breach of her contract of employment.

The definition of trust and confidence which is most usually quoted today has its origins in the following case.

In *Woods v. W H Car Services (Peterborough) Ltd.* 1982 the EAT recognised that in every employment contract there is an implied term of great importance, that of trust and confidence between the parties. Such a term requires that employers *"will not, without reasonable and proper cause, conduct themselves in a manner calculated or likely to destroy or damage the relationship of trust and confidence between employer and employee"*.

The House of Lords in the landmark judgment in *Malik v. Bank of Credit and Commerce International SA* 1997 considered the significance of the implied term of trust and confidence in a contract of employment. The case arose from a claim by ex employees of the BCCI for stigma damages for pecuniary loss allegedly caused by the bank's breach of an implied contractual obligation of mutual trust and confidence. The employees claimed that the fraudulent practices of the bank ultimately leading to its dissolution, put them, as innocent employees, at a severe disadvantage in the job market. A unanimous decision of the House of Lords reversed the Court of Appeal and held that *"if conduct by the employer in breach of the implied term of trust and confidence prejudicially affects an employees future prospects so as to give rise to continuing financial losses, and it was reasonably foreseeable that such a loss was a serious possibility, in principle damages in respect of the loss should be recoverable"*. Also there is no requirement that the employee should while employed, be aware of the trust destroying conduct or that it should be directed at the employee in question.

The House of Lords confirmed that stigma damages may be recoverable by employees who had suffered a disadvantage in the labour market when the highly publicised dishonest conduct of their ex-employer placed them under a cloud. For a claim of damages to succeed it must be established:

(a) that the employer conducted a dishonest or corrupt business and this was capable of constituting a breach of the implied term of trust and confidence; and

(b) financial loss was suffered by employees as a consequence which was not too remote from the breach.

The possibility of damages being awarded in such circumstances was then tested by a number of ex employees of the bank in *BCCI SA v. Ali* 1999. Here the High Court accepted that the employer had as a bank been guilty of systematic fraudulent activities over a long period and this amounted to a breach of the term of trust and confidence implied into the employee's contracts. However while there was a stigma attached to the employees as a result of the employer's conduct the employees had failed to establish that the publicity given to the bank's wrongdoing blighted their prospects of obtaining fresh employment and caused them financial loss. *"Where an employee claims that the employer's breach of trust and confidence term created a stigma which resulted in his being under a handicap in the labour market, damages are only recoverable if the "stigma in the market place" results in financial loss. Damages are not recoverable for the stigma itself. The onus is on the employee to establish on the balance of probabilities that the stigma was a cause of a job application not succeeding or the loss of an opportunity of obtaining a job or the loss of a job or a particular level of remuneration. It must not be merely the occasion for the loss."*

The House of Lords in Malik (above) provides a clear justification for the incorporation of a trust and confidence term. *"An employment contract creates a close personal relationship where there is often a disparity of power between the parties. Frequently the employee is vulnerable. Although the underlying purpose of the trust and confidence terms is to protect the employment relationship, there can be nothing unfairly onerous or unreasonable in requiring an employer who breaches the trust and confidence term to be liable if he thereby causes continuing financial loss of a nature that was reasonably foreseeable."* The court emphasised that the trust and confidence term is a useful tool, *"well established now in employment law"*. In his judgment Lord Steyn gave full support to the term. He said that the evolution of the implied term of trust and confidence is a fact. *"It has not yet been endorsed by your Lordships House. It has proved a workable principle in practice. It has not been the subject of adverse criticism in any decided cases and it has been welcomed in academic writings. I regard the emergence of the implied obligation of mutual trust and confidence as a sound development."*

Employers who have been guilty of conduct such as verbal or physical abuse of their employees or unilateral attempts to impose unreasonable changes in employment terms have found themselves in breach of this implied term.

In *Hilton International Hotels (UK) Ltd. v. Protopapa* 1990 the complainant resigned from her job as a telephone supervisor in one of her employer's hotels when she was severely reprimanded by her manager. The reason for the reprimand was her failure to obtain permission before making a dental appointment and the fact that it was *"officious and insensitive"* constituted a repudiatory breach of her contract of employment. The EAT confirmed that she was *"humiliated, intimidated and degraded to such an extent that there was a breach of trust and confidence which went to the root of the contract"*.

Later in Chapter 10 when we consider the termination of employment, you will discover that the development of this particular implied term is tied to the doctrine of constructive dismissal, and the need for an employee to establish a repudiatory breach of the contract of employment by the employer to justify the contractual termination.

> In *Lewis v. Motorworld Garages Ltd.* 1985 over a long period the employer was guilty of consistently repudiating his employee's contract of employment by insisting on unilateral variations of it. These changes were in fact accepted by the employee so that they could not be raised to support an allegation of constructive dismissal. The Court of Appeal held that such imposed variations did, however, establish a course of conduct so that if an employee did not waive a subsequent breach he could also raise this previous conduct to show that the employer was in breach of the implied term of trust and confidence.

The notion that an employee is under the control of his employer carries with it an obligation to indemnify the employee for expenses incurred in the performance of his duties. Furthermore we will see in Chapter 8 that an employer may be made vicariously liable for the wrongs committed by an employee during the course of his employment.

The Right to Information

The right to information is another aspect of the requirement to maintain trust and confidence in an employment relationship.

> In *Scally v. Southern Health and Social Services Board* 1991 the House of Lords held that there is an implied term in a contract of employment imposing a duty on the employer to take reasonable steps to provide an employee with certain information. Here the information in question related to pension rights which had been negotiated on the employee's behalf but they had not been informed of the benefits they conferred. Four junior doctors sued their employer for loss sustained by them because of the failure of their employer to give them notice of the right to purchase added years of pension entitlement. *"It is necessary to imply an obligation on the employer to take reasonable steps to bring a term of the contract of employment to the employee's attention so that he may be in a position to enjoy its benefit where the terms of the contract have not been negotiated with the individual employee but result from negotiation with a representative body".*

The obligation to inform does not extend to requiring an employer to guide an employee in the direction of the most beneficial pension

In *University of Nottingham v. (1) Eyett (2) The Pensions Ombudsman* 1999 the right for an employee to be given pension information by his employer so as to secure the most beneficial entitlement was tested in the High Court. Earlier the pension ombudsman had upheld a complaint that the employer was in breach of the implied term of trust and confidence by not alerting the employee as to the most beneficial course of action. On appeal the High Court held that the implied duty of mutual trust and confidence in a contract of employment does not include a positive obligation on the employer to warn an employee who is proposing to exercise important rights in connection with the contract of employment that the way in proposing to exercise them may not be the most financially advantageous.

The obligation to inform does not extend to requiring an employer to guide an employee in the direction of the most beneficial pension.

To suggest that to give an employment contract business effect it is necessary to imply an obligation on an employer to give his employees an annual pay rise would not be acceptable.

In *Murco Petroleum v. Forge* 1987 the complainant, having had pay increases for the past ten years resigned when one year she did not receive a pay rise. She was the only employee not to receive a pay increase, her employer stating that her work was not satisfactory. The tribunal found there to be an implied term in her contract that she would receive an annual pay rise and failing to give her one without warning or criticism of her work, constituted a breach so as to justify constructive dismissal. This finding the EAT held was totally unreasonable. It was impossible to say that there is an implied term in a contract of employment that there will always be a pay rise. It *"is not part of the industrial structure and neither employer or unions would wish it to be so"*.

The Right to a Reference

While there is no duty to provide one, if an employee decides to supply his employee with a reference the employer should ensure that it is a fair and accurate assessment of the employee in question. If it is alleged that the reference supplied contains a defamatory statement, the employee is entitled to raise the defence of qualified privilege which is effective, provided that the employer can show that the statements were made without malicious intent.

Recently the Court of Appeal in *Bartholemew v. London Borough of Hackney* 1999 ruled that an employer who provides a reference is under a duty to ensure that it is in substance *"true, accurate and fair"*. While it does not have to be full and comprehensive it must not give an unfair or misleading impression overall even if it is factually correct. A reference could be misleading although factually accurate, if it gives a false impression of the employee. Also *TSB Bank v. Harris* 2000 is the first reported case to hold that an employee was entitled to walk out of his job and claim constructive unfair dismissal because a reference provided by her employer was in breach of the implied term of trust and confidence. Here a reference was neither fair nor reasonable.

In *Spring v. Guardian Assurance Plc* 1994 the Court of Appeal held that the giver of a reference owes no duty of care in negligence to the person who is the subject of the reference or in obtaining the information upon which it is based. On appeal to the House of Lords however in 1994 their Lordships took a different view. The case surrounded a reference which had been supplied for the plaintiff in which he was described as a man of "little or no integrity and could not be regarded as honest" and that there was evidence of negligence in his work. Not surprisingly the plaintiff found it difficult to find employment and claimed damages against his ex-employer for the economic loss he had suffered as a result of the bad reference. His claim based on malicious falsehood failed because of the lack of malice and the failure to establish a contractual term which required references to be supplied with reasonable care. His claim in negligence succeeded in the High Court however and despite being reversed in the Court of Appeal has now been affirmed on final appeal to the House of Lords. By a majority of four to one their Lordships held that an employer giving a reference is under a duty to the subject of the reference to take reasonable care in compiling it or in obtaining the information on which it was based. If the subject of the reference suffers economic loss as a result of an employer's failure to meet this duty he can claim damages. Liability based on negligent misstatement could be established if:

1. the damage was foreseeable and it occurred. An employer who gives a careless reference can foresee economic loss;

2. there was a certain proximity between the nature of the misstatement and the subject so as to create a duty situation. The relationship of employer and employee was sufficiently closer to give rise to a duty; and

3. the situation was one where it was fair just and reasonable to impose a duty of care. This was the case with the giver of a reference who should take reasonable care in compiling it.

In *Kidd v. Axa Equity and Law Life Assurance Society plc* 2000 an employee made a claim against his ex-employer for damages on the ground that they had a duty of care to provide him with a reference making full and frank disclosure of all relevant matters and to ensure that the reference was fair and not misleading and that they were in breach of such a duty. The High Court rejected this claim and found that there was no duty to provide the claimant with a reference which was fair, full and comprehensive " *The duty owed by the giver of a reference to the subject of that reference, whether arising in tort or from contract, is a duty to take reasonable care not to give misleading information about him, whether as a result of the unfairly selective provision of information, or by the inclusion of facts or opinions in such a manner as to give rise to a false or misleading inference in the mind of a reasonable recipient. The giver of a reference owes no additional duty to the subject to take reasonable care to give a full and comprehensive reference, or to include in a reference all material facts.* " The court considered the proof necessary to establish a breach of the duty to take care not to provide misleading information in a reference. The claimant must establish: that the information was misleading; that this information was likely to have a material effect on the mind of the reasonable recipient to the claimant's detriment; and that the defendants were negligent in providing such a reference.

It has been known for employers to retaliate against former employees who have made legal claims against them by refusing to provide a reference or labeling the employee as a troublemaker in the reference.

In *Coote v. Granada Hospitality (No 2)* 2000 the EAT gave effect to a European Court of Justice ruling and held that under the Sex Discrimination Act it would be possible to make a complaint of victimisation in respect of events which occurred after the employment relationship has terminated. This would include failing to provide a reference because the complainant had brought earlier proceedings against the employer. Here the tribunal found that Ms Coote's former employers wrote a tardy and misleading reference because they bore a grudge in relation to her earlier sex discrimination claim.

Collective Agreements and the Contract of Employment

In practice, the process of negotiating and varying terms and conditions of employment is not carried on by employees individually bargaining with their employers but by employers and trade unions engaging in collective bargaining on their behalf. The product of collective bargaining is called a collective agreement which will normally contain, along with a number of other matters, specific reference to individual terms and conditions of employment. In Adams *v. British Airways* 1996 the Master of Rolls was called upon to interpret a collective agreement and made the following comment. *"A collective agreement has special characteristics, being made between an employer or employer's organisation on one side and a trade union or trade unions representatives of employees on the other, usually following a negotiation. Thus it represents an industrial bargain, and probably represents a compromise between the conflicting aims of the parties, or 'sides' as in this context they are revealingly called. But despite these special characteristics, a collective agreement must be construed giving a fair meaning to the words used in the factual context which gave rise to the agreement".*

Over seventy five percent of workers are still covered by collective agreements so that it is crucial to appreciate their legal standing and those parts of a collective agreement that are suitable for incorporation into individual contracts of employment. The legal status of collective agreements is referred to in the Trade Union and Labour Relations (Consolidation) Act 1992 which provides that such agreements are conclusively presumed not to be legally enforceable unless in writing and expressed to be so. As between the parties to a collective agreement therefore, (the trade union or unions and the employer or employer's association), collective agreements while in writing are not usually expressed to be legally enforceable and are consequently not legally binding. Those parts of the collective agreement that are incorporated into individual contracts of employment will become legally enforceable however between the employer and employee.

Doubt was cast on this fundamental principle of employment law in *Marley v. Forward Trust* 1986. Despite the fact that collective agreements are conclusively presumed not to be legally enforceable, here because of custom and practice, an express provision in a collective agreement stated that the agreement *is "binding in honour only and is not intended to give rise to any legal obligation"*. On the basis of this express provision both the industrial tribunal and the EAT somewhat surprisingly found that the effect of the clause was to take the whole of the agreement's terms out of the sphere of legal enforceability. Accordingly, any provision of the collective agreement which had been implied into an individual contract of employment was binding in honour only. As a result, in a particular case the applicant failed in his claim that he had been constructively dismissed despite the fact that the employer did not honour redundancy terms in the collective agreement. Such terms although incorporated into the individual contract were not, said the EAT, intended to be legally binding. Thankfully, a different approach was adopted by the Court of Appeal who, in deciding that the EAT was wholly wrong, restored the law to the position that was generally understood. The terms of an unenforceable collective agreement if incorporated into an individual contract of employment are legally enforceable. An honour clause in the collective agreement refers to the parties to it, the employer and the union, who cannot therefore enforce it. Here, since the terms of the redundancy agreement were incorporated into the applicant's contract of employment, they were legally enforceable.

The Process of Incorporation

The usual method of incorporation is by the individual contract of employment making express reference to the collective agreement or agreements. Statements such as *union conditions or subject to a national agreement* either in the contract of employment or even the statutory statements of the main terms and conditions of employment would normally suffice for the purpose of incorporation. It should be stressed however, that the agreed terms of employment prevail over the statutory statement.

> In *Robertson and Jackson v. British Gas Corporation* 1983 the Court of Appeal held that an express reference in the contract of employment to the effect that "incentive bonus conditions apply to the work carried on" made the payment of an incentive bonus a contractual obligation, the terms of which were to be found in the collective agreement which existed at the time of appointment. A conflicting reference in the statutory statement of particulars of employment to the effect that the bonus scheme could be unilaterally withdrawn by the employer had no significance.

The suggestion is, therefore, that collective agreements can only be varied by the parties to them rather than some unilateral act of the employer. Of course the employer is free to seek an individual's agreement that collectively agreed terms should no longer apply but to attempt to achieve that result unilaterally would result in a repudiatory breach of the contract of employment.

> In *Edinburgh Council v. Brown* 1999 the employer had agreed a policy on re-grading with the Unions and on express terms in individual contracts of employment incorporated that policy into the employee's contracts. As a consequence the unilateral withdrawal from that policy by the employer had no impact on individual employees who could still rely on contractual rights conferred under it. This meant that the employee was entitled to have his re-grading back dated to the date of his original application and the employers decision to unilaterally do away with retrospective on re-grading had no impact on individual contracts of employment.

Part of the process of identifying the terms of a contract of employment must involve discovering those parts of a collective agreement which have been incorporated into individual contracts of employment. This is by no means an easy task, for it is a question of sorting out those parts of the agreement that deal with employer/trade union matters, for instance the machinery for collective bargaining, and those parts which have significance for individual employees, such as wage negotiations.

In *British Leyland (UK) Ltd. v. McQuilken* 1978 a collectively agreed redundancy scheme was negotiated between the employer and a trade union to deal with a massive reorganisation which involved employees in retraining and possible transfer to other work locations. When the employer failed to implement the agreed scheme in relation to the complainant, he resigned due to uncertainty about his future. To succeed in a claim for unfair dismissal it was necessary for the complainant to show that he had been constructively dismissed. Constructive dismissal is established by proving that the employer has been guilty of a significant breach of the employment contract. One issue in the case therefore, was whether by failing to implement the scheme the employer had been guilty of such a breach. The EAT thought not. The redundancy scheme was a long term plan dealing with policy rather than individual employment rights and was not therefore capable of incorporation into individual contracts of employment.

In *Lee and others v. GEC Plessey Telecommunications* 1993 the High Court agreed that in appropriate circumstances the terms of a collective agreement relating to redundancy matters could be incorporated into individual contracts of employment. In order to decide whether this had occurred in a particular case, a court had to look for the "necessary contractual intent on both sides of the bargain and also look at the content and character of the relevant parts of the collective agreements." The court held that an employer has no right to withdraw unilaterally its employee's contractual entitlement to generous enhanced redundancy payments and that those entitlements were not extinguished by a later collective agreement because the terms of that agreement were not incorporated into individual contracts.

Further support for this approach was provided by *Anderson v. Pringle of Scotland Ltd.* 1998 where it was held that an employer was obliged to comply with the terms of a redundancy procedure which had been incorporated into the employee's contract of employment. Despite the fact that there was no express reference in the employee's contract to the redundancy procedure there was a reference to the fact that employment was in accordance with the collective agreement. This reference, the Court of Session held, was sufficient to incorporate the *"last in first out"* selection criterion into the employee's contract and ensure that the employee in question was secure in employment.

Subject to the approval of the Secretary of State for Employment, a collective agreement can replace certain of the statutory rights, for example, to a redundancy payment or guaranteed payment. In cases where approval is granted the statutory right is substituted by the right under the collective agreement which becomes legally enforceable as a term of the individual contract of employment to which it relates. Once identified as terms of individual contracts of employment it may still be necessary to interpret their nature and the scope of their application.

In *Brigden v. Lancashire County Council* 1987 the Court of Appeal considered a term inserted into a lecturer's contract by a relevant collective agreement which provided *that "where a teacher is appointed under a Principal to take charge of adult education work in a particular centre or area where the unit total is 75, the teacher shall be graded not less than Lecturer Grade II"*. The complainant having been initially appointed at a lower grade argued that she should have been immediately upgraded when her work reached the appropriate level. She claimed that the employer was in breach of this provision and she was justified in claiming constructive dismissal which was unfair. The Court of Appeal however confirmed the decision of the EAT that the employer's were not in breach of contract. The relevant provision should be interpreted as *"applying only to an initial appointment"* and the *"fact that the work increases to the prescribed level does not create a new appointment"*.

In *Davies v. Hotpoint Ltd.* 1994 the contracts of employment of factory workers employed by the respondents had the terms of a 1984 collective agreement incorporated within them. One term provided for guaranteed wages stating *"All hourly rated manual workers employed by the company for not less than four weeks shall be guaranteed employment for five days in each normal week. In the event of work not being available for the whole or part of the five days, employees covered by the guarantee will be assured earnings equivalent to their time rate for thirty nine hours"* subject to the condition that *"where approved short time is worked as an alternative to redundancy... the guarantee shall be reduced accordingly."* Despite union objections there were a number of occasions where the employer put workers on short-time, paying them less than the guaranteed minimum wage. The employees complained that the employers were in breach of the Wages Act in paying them less than the guaranteed wage without the approval of the union. The issue before the EAT therefore was whether the term *"approved short-time working"* meant that the employer could not unilaterally introduce it but needed the consent of the union. The EAT held that *"the use of the word "approved" indicated a requirement of the consent or agreement of someone other than the person making the decision to be approved. The word would be redundant if it meant "approved by the employer". Moreover since the context of the collective agreement was a guaranteed minimum wage negotiated between management and the union on behalf of the workforce, if the guarantee were to have any substance it could not have been the intention of the parties that it should depend solely on the unilateral decision of the employer to abandon the guarantee by deciding on short-time working."*

The Court of Appeal considered the interpretation of a collective agreement in relation to the status of employees on the merger of two large organisations in th following case.

In *Adams and Others v. British Airways* 1996 a number of British Airways pilots as plaintiffs sought a ruling from the High Court that BA had wrongly interpreted a collective agreement that applied to them. Following BA's takeover of British Caledonian, 300 hundred of British Caledonian pilots joined BA and were given seniority above the plaintiffs. This was significant for the plaintiffs as seniority is important in determining promotion and choice of route. By giving the new pilots seniority based upon their experience the plaintiffs claimed that constituted a breach of their own contractual seniority rights. The clause of the collective agreement in dispute stated that in relation to *"new entrants"*, *"on initial appointment all pilots will enter service in the grade of first officer on point 000"*. For the plaintiffs it was argued that this clause was entirely unambiguous and meant that BA should install the new British Caledonian pilots as new entrants at the bottom of the ladder. The alternative argument was that the British Caledonian pilots were *not "new entrants"* and the intention of the merger could not have been to rank senior British Caledonian pilots below junior pilots of BA. This argument was rejected by the High Court which held that the relevant clause was unambiguous and as new entrants by giving the British Caledonian pilots seniority BA were in breach of the plaintiff's contracts of employment. The Court of Appeal disagreed and held that the High Court had wrongly applied the literal working of the collective agreement to a merger situation. While the British Caledonian pilots were new entrants to BA as new employees, they were not *"new entrants"* to the Gatwick based airline undertaking of British Caledonian which BA had taken over. To regard the British Caledonian pilots as simply *"new entrants"* in the sense of new recruits of BA was absurd, they were in fact experienced employees of an airline which had been merged with another. There was nothing in the language of the collective agreement to indicate that it was intended to apply to the merger of two airlines. Accordingly the British Caledonian pilots should be entitled to seniority according to their years of service.

Earlier in the chapter the case of *Ali v. Christian Salvesen Food Services Ltd.* 1997 was considered. The contemporary view of the court in relation to the interpretation of collective agreements is instructive. *"Where a collective agreement negotiated across a broad front for a substantial labour force leaves any topic uncovered, the inference is not that there has been an omission so obvious as to require judicial correction, but that the topic was omitted advisedly from the terms of the agreement on the ground that it was seen as too controversial or complicated to justify any variation of the main terms of the agreement to take account of it."*.

Case Studies

Brinkley Business School - The Security Rota

Brinkley Business School was set up last year by merging a number of departments in the University of Brinkley. The Director of the School is Miriam Perot who, with her two deputies, comprise the senior management team of the School. The senior management team is the final arbiter on staffing issues in the School, subject to formal ratification by the academic board of the University.

As one response to the problem of theft in the Business School, the Senior Management Team resolved that Resource Directors should draw up a rota by which each member of staff would spend one hour per week patrolling the corridors in their part of the Business School to check security. In the main the lecturing staff co-operated with the rota system other than a number of accountancy lecturers who refused to patrol saying *"it was beneath their dignity as professional people"*. Two marketing lecturers refused to comply saying that as academics *"such a task could not possibly be part of their job function"*.

Miriam and the Senior Management Team saw this minority response as a direct challenge to their credibility and prerogative to manage and ordered that those staff boycotting the system should have their salaries reduced by *"one hour's wages per week"*. The rota was terminated in May but it will be reintroduced in the next academic year. Miriam said at the Academic Board in June that if some staff still refuse to participate *"their work will be regarded as voluntary and no salaries will be paid"*.

Dalton West plc - The Trade Union Activist

Dalton West is a large manufacturer of fork lift trucks with depots and retail outlets situated all over Britain.

Recently Dalton West interviewed for the full-time post of works manager at the Coventry factory. After the interviews one of the interviewees, Roger Shields, was invited back before the interview panel and formally offered the post subject to the receipt of appropriate references. Roger immediately accepted the offer. Some days later the company contacted Roger and informed him that they were no longer willing to proceed with his post having received an unsatisfactory reference from his last employer. Angry and upset, Roger telephoned the Personnel Manager of his ex-employer. He was told that the reference given described him as *"conscientious and efficient employee who had been an active union member"*.

Chapter 5
Equal Opportunities in Recruitment

This chapter is devoted to a consideration of equal opportunity law as it applies to the recruitment process. Discrimination law is examined further in Chapter 6 in relation to the workplace and on the termination of employment.

As a general principle, employers are free to pick and choose to whom they offer employment and can reject an applicant for all manner of reasons including qualifications, attitude, references or suitability. A limitation on the freedom to employ is embodied within the Disabled Persons (Employment) Act 1958 which provides that an employer with twenty or more employees must in the absence of an exemption certificate, have a minimum of three percent of the workforce registered as disabled persons. Indeed in certain jobs, disabled persons must be given priority and anti discrimination law in relation to the disabled was finally introduced in 1995 (see later).

Rather than stigmatising an individual for life because of his past conduct, the Rehabilitation of Offenders Act 1974 allows past offenders who have criminal convictions to regard them as *'spent'* in certain circumstances. Imprisonment for 30 months or more can never be spent and in a number of professions even spent offences must be disclosed for instance medicine, the law, teaching and local authority employment in connection with the provision of social services. In *Wood v. Coverage Care Ltd.* 1996 the EAT held that the social service exception applied not only to social workers but to a range of employment opportunities relating to social service functions. Accordingly it was lawful to take account of spent convictions when deciding the suitability of an applicant for the posts of manager or bursar at a residential care home for persons over the age of 65. If the offence is spent then on a job application the past conviction need not be mentioned and the failure to disclose it is no ground for an employer to discriminate against individuals by refusing to employ them or by dismissing them for past offences. It is reasonable of course for an employer to expect full disclosure of information on a job application and this would most certainly include a prospective employee providing details of criminal convictions which were not spent. A failure to fully disclose details of previous employment or trade union activities however may not be regarded as fatal to the validity of the contract of employment.

In *Fitzpatrick v. British Railways Board* 1991 the complainant obtained a job with British Railways Board and deliberately failed to provide full details of her previous employment and participation in trade union activities. When it became obvious to the employer that the complainant was, and had been a union activist, they dismissed her on the ground that she had obtained the job by deceit. The complainant then claimed that her dismissal was unfair as it was on the ground of trade union activities contrary to s.58 EPCA 1978 (now s.152 of the Trade Union and Labour Relations (Consolidation) Act 1992). If the reason for a dismissal is trade union membership or activities then the requirement of two years continuous employment to qualify for protection does not apply. The Court of Appeal held that the true reason for the complainant's dismissal was her union activities in previous employment and the fear that these activities will be repeated in her present employment. *"An employer is in clear breach of the section if he dismisses an employee on the basis of previous trade union activities, when the only rational basis for doing so is the fear that those activities will be repeated in the present employment. Although the trade union activities referred to in the section are activities in the employment from which the employee alleges that he has been unfairly dismissed, what happened in the employee's previous employment may form the reason for dismissal in subsequent employment and therefore can be highly relevant to the question which an industrial tribunal has to answer under the section..... in order to fall within the section the activity need not be sufficiently precise to be identifiable. The purpose is to protect those who engage in trade union activities and there is no reason why that should not apply irrespective of whether the precise activities can be identified"*. Here the Court of Appeal felt that the reason for dismissal here was a fear of a repetition of the same conduct and in the circumstances it fell within the section and was therefore unfair.

Under the Trade Union and Labour Relations (Consolidation) Act 1992 s.137 it is unlawful to refuse employment because a person is or is not a trade union member. Also under the Act if a job advertisement indicates that trade union membership is a requirement and, then employment is refused it will be presumed to be for that reason if the applicant is not a trade union member.

Unfortunately you should appreciate that despite the superficial emphasis given to equal opportunities in business, industry and the professions, numerous studies have shown that discriminatory practices are still widespread in staff recruitment in the UK. Prospective employees are discriminated against for various reasons including racial origin, sex, sexuality, religion, age and disability. In an attempt to reduce and hopefully eradicate these practices, legislation has been passed in the UK to make sex, race and disability discrimination unlawful in employment.

As a consequence of discriminatory recruitment practices we have a workforce in the UK divided by sex and race. Members of racial and ethnic minority groups generally occupy a low position in the occupational structure, concentrated in unskilled manual jobs and unrepresented in skilled manual jobs, managerial and professional occupations. They are found mainly in low paying industries such as clothing and textiles, in service sector jobs and in hospitals, shops and catering. Furthermore male black workers earn considerably less than male white workers and suffer a much higher rate of unemployment. Female workers are similarly concentrated in low paid unskilled jobs in a relatively small number of occupations including mainly clerical and related jobs and industries such as cleaning, catering and manufacturing. Because of child care responsibilities many women take part-time or casual work, often unskilled with poor pay and conditions. Economic trends in the labour market indicate an increase in the use of wage payment systems which encourage overtime, shift work and bonus payments, which necessarily discriminate against women. In addition to UK legislation on discrimination there is also European Community law which is directly applicable in UK Courts and also incorporated into United Kingdom law by Statute and by Statutory Instruments.

The right not to be discriminated against on the grounds of sex, race or marital status is one of the few individual employment rights that has not been weakened but rather strengthened over recent years. This has been mainly due to the impact of Community law and judgments of the European Court of Justice particularly in relation to gender.

The tendency to stereotype sexes and races and also perceive jobs to have male or female characteristics means that discrimination in Britain is still widespread. Nevertheless there are still relatively few complaints brought and success rates are consistently low. Studies have shown that there are numerous reasons for this, ranging from ignorance as to legal rights, insufficient support for complainants, difficulties of proof, low levels of compensation, and fear of victimisation. On the positive side however, there have been some notable successes recently which have caused change in employment practices. Unlawful discrimination has been found in a number of important equal pay cases, in employment practices in relation to part-time workers, in unnecessary demands for British qualifications, in maximum age limits and in stringent language tests. There is no doubt that there is a change in attitude, for there is increasing evidence that employers in the public and also in the private sector of the economy are adopting equal opportunity employment practices. Equal opportunity is an important issue in industrial relations, and the law can act as an important stimulus to both employers and trade unions to ensure that organisations adopt employment practices designed to combat discrimination. Bear in mind also, that there is increasing pressure in Britain to extend the law to protect those in our society who are less favourably treated in employment because of their age, religion and sexual orientation.

In May 1999 the Amsterdam Treaty came into force and Article 141 strengthens the sex equality provisions to ensure equal opportunity and equal treatment. In addition a new Article 13 (inserted as Article 6 of the Treaty of Rome) empowers the Council on the European Union to take appropriate action to combat discrimination based on sex, racial ethnic origin religion or belief, disability, age or sexual orientation in employment and vocational training.

While European Union Law has yet to provide protection from discrimination on the grounds of sexual orientation following *Smith and Grady v. United Kingdom* 1999 it does seem that homosexuals may have rights under the European Convention on Human Rights. Here the European Court of Human Rights held that the Ministry of Defence had violated the private lives of members of the armed forces by carrying out investigations into their homosexuality and their subsequent discharge from the services. Following this case the government is now preparing a code of practice on discrimination on the grounds of sexual orientation. (See Chapter 1 Human Rights Act 1998).

On May 1 1999 the Sex Discrimination (Gender Reassignment) Regulations 1999 came into force to confer protection on individuals who suffer less favourable treatment because of their change in gender. The regulations protect individuals against less favourable treatments at recruitment and in employment due to the fact that the person intends to change, is undergoing, or has undergone gender reassignment. The regulations also prevent disparity of pay and benefits on these grounds.

Sex and Race Discrimination

The Race Relations Act 1976 and the Sex Discrimination Act 1975 as amended, identify similar categories of unlawful acts in relation to discrimination, namely direct discrimination, indirect discrimination, and victimisation. It is convenient to set out these unlawful acts of discrimination in tabular form as a means of comparison.

The fact that both pieces of legislation were drafted in a largely similar fashion means that case-law involving the Sex Discrimination Act will also serve as an aid to the interpretation of the provision of The Race Relations Act. It is proposed therefore to consider the provisions of both Acts in unison.

Race Relations Act, 1976	Sex Discrimination Act, 1975

Direct Discrimination

This occurs where one person: Treats another less favourably on racial grounds e.g. by segregating workers by race. s.1(1)(a)	This occurs when one person: Treats another less favourably on the grounds of sex or marital status e.g. by providing women with different working conditions or selecting married women first for redundancy. s.1(1)(a) s.3(1)(b)

Indirect Discrimination

This occurs where one person: Requires another to meet a condition which as a member of a racial group is less easily satisfied because:	This occurs where one person: Requires another to meet a condition which as a member of a particular sex or as a married person is less easily satisfied because:
(a) the proportion of that group who can comply with it is smaller; and	(a) the proportion of that sex or married persons who can comply with it is smaller; and
(b) the condition is to the complainant's detriment and is not justified.	(b) the condition is to the complainant's detriment and is not justified.
There would therefore be indirect discrimination if an employer required young job applicants to have been educated only in Britain. s.1(1)(b)	There would therefore be indirect discrimination if an employer advertised for a clerk who is at least six feet tall. s.1(1)(b) s.3(1)(b)

Victimisation

This occurs where one person: Treats another less favourably because the other has given evidence or information in connection with, brought proceedings under, or made allegations under the Act against the discriminator. s.2	This occurs where one person: Treats another less favourably because the other has given evidence or information in connection with, brought proceedings under, or made allegations under the Act or the Equal Pay Act, 1970, against the discriminator. s.4

The Sex Discrimination Act 1975 is concerned with discrimination on grounds of gender either by males against females, or vice versa, and on grounds of marital status by treating a married person less favourably than an unmarried person. In *Nemes v. Allen* 1977 an employer in an attempt to cope with a redundancy situation dismissed female workers when they married. This was held to be unlawful direct discrimination on the grounds of sex and marital status.

The Race Relations Act 1976 is more complex in relation to those it protects and under s.3 is concerned with discrimination on racial grounds which, is based upon colour, race, nationality, or ethnic or national origin. In Race *Relations Board v. Mecca* 1976 an individual telephoned to apply for a job but when the employer discovered the applicant was black, he put the telephone down. This was held to be unlawful direct discrimination as the applicant had been denied the opportunity to apply for a job on racial grounds.

While the definition of racial grounds is wide there is no reference to discrimination based on religion. It does seem however that some religions would normally be covered by the definition colour, race, nationality, or ethnic or national origins. In *Seide v. Gillette Industries* 1980 the EAT held that the term "Jewish" can mean membership of a particular race or ethnic group as well as a religion. Also in *Mandla v. Dowell Lee* 1983 the House of Lords held that Sikhs were a racial group within the meaning of the Act.

In *Northern Joint Police Board v. Power* 1997 the EAT held that discrimination against an English person or a Scottish person based on national origins is discrimination on racial grounds within the meaning of the Race Relations Act. National origins in the definition has a different meaning from nationality, which points to citizenship.

Wakeman v. Quick Corporation 1999 was an unusual case where British employees of a Japanese company in the UK claimed that they had been discriminated against on the grounds of race when the redundancy pay package they received was substantially less than that paid to Japanese secondees in comparable roles. The EAT dismissed the complaint on the grounds that local recruits were very different from secondees who were in the UK temporarily. Locally hired Japanese would be paid on the same scale as locally hired UK nationals. The Court of Appeal agreed and held that the higher level of pay was not attributable to nationality but rather the status of the staff as secondees

Certainly to share a common language would not on its own be sufficient to establish a racial group.

In *Commission for Racial Equality v. Dutton* 1989 the Court of Appeal was required to determine whether the display of a sign at a public house saying "sorry no travellers" unlawfully discriminated against gypsies on racial grounds contrary to the Race Relations Act 1976. The court held that gypsies could come within the definition of "racial group" as an identifiable group defined by reference to ethnic origins, having a long shared history, customs, and unique dialect. There remains a discernible minority who have not merged wholly in the population and have not lost their separateness and self awareness as being gypsies.

In *Crown Supplies PGA v. Dawkins* 1993 the Court of Appeal held that Rastafarianism is no more than a religious sect and not an ethnic group for the purposes of the Race Relations Act. As a consequence when a Rastafarian is refused employment because of the way in which he wears his hair that does not amount to discrimination under the 1976 Act.

In relation to employment, any discriminatory practice which comes within any of the three categories (direct, indirect or victimisation) is unlawful. Section 6 of the Sex Discrimination Act and section 4 of the Race Relations Act are similar in format and relate to discrimination by employers in the recruitment process, at the workplace and in relation to the termination of employment.

Under s.6 (1) It is unlawful for a person, in relation to employment by him at an establishment in Great Britain, to discriminate against a woman:

    (a) in the arrangements he makes for the purpose of determining who should be offered that employment, or

    (b) in the terms on which he offers her that employment, or

    (c) by refusing or deliberately omitting to offer her that employment.

(2) It is unlawful for a person, in the case of a woman employed by him at an establishment in Great Britain, to discriminate against her:

    (a) in the way he affords her access to opportunities for promotion, transfer or training, or to any other benefits, facilities or services, or by refusing or deliberately omitting to afford her access to them, or

    (b) by dismissing her, or subjecting her to any other detriment.

Under s.4(1) of the Race Relations Act It is unlawful for a person, in relation to employment by him at an establishment in Great Britain, to discriminate against another:

> (a)   *in the arrangements he makes for the purpose of determining who should be offered that employment; or*

> (b)   *in the terms on which he offers him that employment, or*

> (c)   *by refusing or deliberately omitting to offer him that employment.*

(2)   *It is unlawful for a person, in the case of a person employed by him at an establishment in Great Britain, to discriminate against that employee:*

> (a)   *in the terms of employment which he affords him; or*

> (b)   *in the way he affords him access to opportunities for promotion, transfer or training, or to any other benefits, facilities or services, or by refusing or deliberately omitting to afford him access to them, or*

> (c)   *by dismissing him, or subjecting him to any other detriment.*

It is therefore unlawful for a person in relation to employment by him to discriminate in the arrangements he makes for the purposes of deciding whom should be offered employment, the terms on which it is offered or by refusing to offer employment. Also where there is an existing employment relationship it is unlawful for an employer to discriminate in the way he gives access to opportunities for promotion, transfer, training or any other benefits, or refuses to afford such access. Furthermore, it is unlawful to discriminate by dismissing the complainant or subject him to any other detriment.

In *Blaik v. The Post Office* 1994 the complaint was based on the fact that postwomen were not required to wear a tie and this it was alleged discriminated against men who were required to wear a tie as part of their dress code. Applying *Schmidt v. Austicks Bookshops* 1977 it was held that the requirement to wear a tie was not to be regarded as 'serious' so as to amount to a detriment. In Schmidt *"the employers treated both female and male staff alike in that there were in force rules restricting wearing apparel and governing appearance which applied to women, although the rule in the two cases were not the same given the differences in sex".*

It should be noted however, that originally unlawful sex discrimination practices in employment did not apply to employment for the purposes of a private household or where the number of employees was less than five. In a number of cases in the 1980s the European Commission criticised the United Kingdom sex discrimination law as being out of step with the Equal Treatment Directive. The law did not cover internal work rules, rules governing independent professions, private households or undertakings where five or fewer were employed. Furthermore in *Marshall v. Southampton and South West Hampshire Area Health Authority (Teaching)* 1986 it was held that in public sector employment, the difference in retirement age of men and women also contravened the Directive.

The result of these criticisms was that the UK Parliament passed the Sex Discrimination Act 1986. The 1986 Act applies the discrimination law to undertakings with five or fewer employees, removes the private household exemption and extends the law to collective agreements, work rules and professional associations. The Equal Treatment Directive has had considerable impact on UK discrimination law and in *Johnston v. Chief Constable of the RUC* 1987 it was confirmed that the Directive was unconditional and sufficiently precise to be used by an individual against a member state or in a national court. An individual could not enforce the Directive against a private employer however.

While it is clear that UK domestic law, particularly the Sex Discrimination Act, provides no redress to a person who suffers discrimination in employment because of sexual orientation there is a possibility that European Union law may provide a remedy.

In *P v. S* 1996 the European Court of Justice considered whether the Equal Treatment Directive applied to the case where a transsexual had been dismissed for a reason related to a sex change. Following the complainant's announcement that he intended to undertake gender reassignment, and the commencement of initial surgery, he had been dismissed. The European Court held that the Directive's principle of equal treatment required no discrimination on the grounds of sex and its scope should not be confined to a person's gender status but also to gender reassignment. A comparison should be drawn in such a case with the treatment the applicant received before undergoing the reassignment and after.

In *R. v. Secretary of State for Defence ex parte Perkins* 1997 the High Court has requested the European Court of Justice to give a preliminary ruling on whether the Equal Treatment Directive outlaws discrimination against homosexuals.

The anti-discrimination legislation provides redress for those who "contract personally to execute any work or labour". In *Quinnen v. Hovells* 1984 the EAT confirmed that the legislation was not confined to employees therefore and would also protect the self employed provided they are supplying personal services.

The EAT in *Hill Samuel Investment Services Group Ltd. v. Nwauzu* 1994 held that an insurance agent employed on a commission only basis as a self employed person offering personal services was protected by the Race Relations legislation. The employer was found to be guilty of discrimination when the issue of the complainant's race influenced the decision to terminate his contract.

In *Daley v. Allied Suppliers Ltd.* 1983 an allegation of racial discrimination could not be entertained because it was felt that working as a YOP trainee created relationships which were neither ones of employment or personally executing work. Now however, trainees have been brought within the discrimination legislation by departmental order.

Disability Discrimination

Disability discrimination legislation was introduced in 1995 in the form of the Disability Discrimination Act in force from December 1996 in relation to employment.

The extent of the Act has been the subject of much criticism particularly from groups representing the disabled. The Act applies to employers who have 15 or more employees,making it unlawful to discriminate against someone who has or who had a disability in recruitment or at the workplace. The original threshold was reduced from 20 employees to 15 to bring more small businesses within the framework of disability discrimination legislation. It does seem that further reductions are likely in the future. Most discrimination claims are against employers but the Act, allows under s.12, for claims brought by contract workers against their 'principles'. This covers the situation where workers are supplied by their employers to perform work for another organisation and it is the organisation which discriminates.

In *Abbey Life Assurance Co. Ltd. v. Tansell* 2000 the Court of Appeal gave a positive and liberal interpretation of the provision in favour of the disabled applicant. As an employee of a company which had supplied him to an agency which in turn had supplied him to an end-user, the applicant was a contract worker and could place a claim against the end-user as being a principal. This was despite the fact that there was no direct contractual relationship between the employer and the principal who made the work available Lord Justice Mummery stated that *"it is more probable that parliament intended to confer than to deny protection from discrimination in cases where the supply of the employee was made by his company to the principal through an employment agency rather than direct to the principal."*

Disability is defined *as "a physical or mental impairment which has a substantial and long term adverse affect on the persons ability to carry out normal day to day activities"*. The unlawful forms of discrimination created under the legislation are *less favourable treatment* and *failure to make adjustments* both of which are potentially justifiable. Less favourable treatment is equivalent to direct discrimination with which is considered later in the chapter.

An employer discriminates against a disabled person under s.5(1)

For a reason which relates to the disabled person's disability;

- *the employer treats that person less favourably than he treats or would treat others to whom that reason does not or would not apply; and*

- *if, and only if, the employer cannot justify the less favourable treatment.*

An employer also discriminates against a disabled person if:

- *the employer fails to comply with any duty to make adjustments imposed by the 1995 Act; and*

- *if, and only if, the employer cannot justify the failure to comply with the duty*

In *O'Neill v. Symm & Co Ltd* 1998 the EAT held that s5(1) only applied when the employer knew that the worker had a disability. However in *Heinz Co Ltd v. Kenrick* 2000 the employee was dismissed after a long period of illness later diagnosed as chronic fatigue syndrome of which the employer was unaware. The EAT felt that nevertheless the dismissal was related to his disability and as the employer had not adequately considered possible alternative employment the discrimination was unjustified.

A significant feature of both forms of unlawful discrimination under s5(1) is that they may be justified. Justification must however be by reference to a reason which is both substantial and material to the circumstances of the particular case. *In Baynton v. Saurus General Engineering Ltd* 1999 the EAT held that " *the cicumstances of the case related to both the employer and the disabled employee and the tribunal must carry out a balancing exercise between the two.*"

In *Goodwin v. The Patents Office* 1999 the EAT reversed the tribunals decision and found that a paranoid schizophrenic who was dismissed because of his behaviour was a disabled person under the Disability Discrimination Act 1995. The EAT rejected the approach of the tribunal in determining disability and laid down helpful guidelines stressing the need to interpret the legislation with its object in mind and relying on non statutory sources such as Codes of Practice issued by the Secretary of State the evidence should be examined in the light of four different conditions.

1. Does the applicant have an impairment which is either mental or physical. Mental impairment includes one which results from mental illness which is "clinically well-recognised".

2. Does the impairment affect the applicant's ability to carry out normal day to day activities focusing on the things that the applicant cannot do or only do with difficulty.

3. Is the adverse effect substantial taking account of how the applicants 'manage' and considering the impact of taking medication.

4. Is the adverse affect long term?

In Schedule 1 of the Act the expression *"long term effect"* means a period of at least 12 months but even where the impairment has ceased it should be treated as having a long term effect if it is likely to recur. The issue in *Greenwood v. British Airways plc* 1999 was whether the complainant who suffered from depression and had periods off work had been discriminated against because he did not get the position he sought.

In *Kapadia v. London Borough of Lambeth* 2000 the EAT held that *"treatment"* within the meaning of the Act would include counselling sessions as a response to clinical depression. While supporting the discretion of a tribunal to reject uncontested medical opinion the EAT felt in this case the medical evidence justified a finding that the applicant was disabled and it was wrong for the tribunal to disregard the *"deduced effects"* of the impairment.

In *Vicary v. British Telecommunications plc* 1999 the EAT held that tribunals should use their own judgment when making an assessment of the effect of an impairment, and should not rely on the opinion of medical experts. *"In deciding whether someone has a disability a tribunal should focus on what the worker cannot do, not on what he can do. The fact that someone can mitigate a disability does not mean that he is not disabled."*

The Court of Appeal in *Clark v. TDG Ltd.* 1999 ruled that in the case of an employee dismissed because of excessive absence a comparison should be made with a non disabled employee.

There would be a prima facie case of failure to make adjustments when an employer makes arrangements or his premises have a feature which places the disabled person at a substantial disadvantage in comparison with non-disabled persons. In such circumstances the employer is under a duty to take such steps as are reasonable to stop the arrangements or remove the feature, for instance adjust the premises or alter terms and conditions of employment. In deciding whether it is reasonable for the employer to make the adjustments all the circumstances including cost and disruption should be taken account of.

A good example of a failure to make reasonable adjustments is provided by *London Borough of Hillingdon v. Morgan* 1998 where the employer failed to allow an employee to work from home until she readjusted to work following a period of sick leave. The size and resources of the employer were such that a staged return to work should not be out of the question.

In *Kenny v. Hampshire Constabularly* 1998 the EAT felt that reasonable adjustments did not extend to providing a carer to assist a disabled person when using the toilet notwitrhstanding that without that help the disabled person was deprived of the opportunity to be employed by the employer.

Time Limits

Complaints of unlawful discrimination are made to the industrial tribunal and the time limit for presenting a complaint is three months from the act or last act of discrimination. The tribunal has power to permit a claim presented out of time if it is just and equitable in the circumstances. While time begins to run from the date of the last act complained of, the statutes also provide that *"any act extending over a period shall be treated as done at the end of the period"*.

In *Calder v. James Finlay Corporation* 1989 the employers operated a subsidised mortgage scheme which had an unwritten rule excluding women. An employee lodged a complaint of unlawful discrimination five months after she was refused a mortgage subsidy but within three months of leaving employment. The EAT held that as long as the complainant was an employee, and the scheme operated, it constituted discrimination against her in the way she was *afforded access to the scheme*. The last *act* of discrimination was when her employment terminated so that she was within the three month time limit for lodging a complaint.

In *Barclays Bank v. Kapur* 1991 an employer's refusal to give its Asian employees the same favourable pension terms as its European employees was held to be a continuing discriminatory act extending over the period of employment until the employment terminated.

In considering the meaning of the phrase *"continuing act"* under the Race Relations Act the EAT held in *Sougrin v. Haringey Health Authority* 1991 the loss of wages resulting from an alleged discriminatory grading of a black nurse did not qualify A *"continuing act" is a rule or regulatory scheme which during its currency continues to have a discriminatory effect on the grounds of sex or race. In the present case, the industrial tribunal had not erred in distinguishing between the decision not to change the appellant's grade and the failure to pay the appellant the same as her comparator. The "rule" was that the appellant was paid according to her grade and her complaint was that he was not up graded when her appeal was heard. The fact that he continued to be paid less than her comparator was a consequence of the decision on appeal and was not of itself a continuing act of discrimination. "*

Even in cases where there is no 'continuing act', the time should not begin to run until it is clear that an act of discrimination has occurred and the course of action has crystallised.

In *Clarke v. Hampshire Electro-Plating Co Ltd.* 1991 the complainant, a metal polisher who had seventeen years employment with the defendants enquired about a supervisors post within the company. On the 25th April he was told by a director that he was not the person he was seeking for that particular appointment. On the 4th September a white man was appointed to the post and after consulting with his union the complainant, a black man, brought proceedings for racial discrimination. The tribunal held that it did not have jurisdiction to hear the complaint as it was out of time. The act of discrimination occurred on the 25th April and when proceedings were commenced the three month time limit had expired. On appeal the EAT disagreed however stressing the obvious point that the cause of action depended upon the employer's decision to appoint someone of a different racial group to the post. *"In determining when the act complained of was done, the question is whether the cause of action had crystallised on the relevant date, not whether the complainant felt that he had suffered discrimination on that date. The phrase "the act complained of was done" indicates that there was at that time an act of discrimination and that the cause of action could properly be said to be complete at that time, because otherwise there would be no point in bringing proceedings. Every case must depend upon its own facts as to the clarity of the crystallisation of any cause of action! In the present case, if the appellant's cause of action had not crystallised on the date when his promotion application was rejected, then the date a white man was appointed would have crystallised the cause of action by providing the comparison. "*

In *Cast v. Croydon College* 1997 the complainant, an information centre manager, made a request to her employers for job sharing or part-time work when her maternity leave expired. The request was refused on the 26th March

1992 and following further requests was given written reasons for the employer's decision on the 14th May 1993. The complainant resigned in early June and complained of unlawful sex discrimination on the 13th of August. Both the tribunal and the EAT felt that the claim was out of time as the act of discrimination occurred on the first refusal of the complainant's request which was nearly a year and half before she made the claim. *"It could not be held that time began to run when the complainant resigned because she could not work part-time and claimed constructive dismissal on the basis that the act of discrimination complained of was the dismissal. The proper analysis was that there was a detriment at the date the request to work part-time was refused and the later resignation was a result of that detriment. The resignation did not create a fresh cause of action."*

If the complainant is out of time the tribunal still has jurisdiction to hear the complaint if it is *"just and equitable in the circumstances"*.

In *Forster v. South Glamorgan Health Authority* 1988 the failure to present the complaint within the time limits was found to be understandable as it was due to a change in the law. In such circumstances the EAT held that whether or not it is *"suitable"* to hear a complaint out of time is a *"question of fact and degree for the tribunal to determine in each case"*. In Hawkins v. Ball 1996 the EAT held that a tribunal was entitled to find that it could be just and equitable to extend the three month limitation period on the grounds that the complainant received incorrect legal advice.

In *Hawkins v. Ball & Barclays Bank Plc* 1996 the EAT confirmed that the tribunal has a wider discretion to allow claims out of time under discrimination legislation than unfair dismissal law. A tribunal could take account of the fact that the complainant was badly advised and this caused the delay.

In *Aniagwu v. London Borough of Hackney* 1999 the EAT was prepared to extend the three month time limit in a race discrimination case where the applicant had delayed presenting the claim because he hoped that an internal appeal procedure would resolve the matter

A copy of a complaint of unlawful discrimination must be sent to ACAS who will pass it on to a conciliation officer. It is the duty of the conciliation officer to attempt to resolve the conflict between the parties, if requested by them to do so, or if he feels that he has a reasonable prospect of success. If there is no settlement and the tribunal finds that there has been discrimination it can declare the rights of the parties, award compensation up to the unfair discrimination limits, and recommend action to be taken by the guilty party to reduce the adverse affects of the discrimination. A failure to respond to a recommendation without good reason could lead to an award of increased compensation. Enforcement and redress are considered later in the chapter along with the role of the Commissions. You should appreciate that the Commission for Racial Equality and the Equal Opportunities Commission have a role to play in encouraging, advising and providing financial assistance to prospective litigants. Furthermore only the Commissions may bring proceedings in respect of certain unlawful acts including discriminatory advertising, unlawful instruction to discriminate and unlawful inducements to discriminate.

Direct Discrimination in Recruitment

Direct discrimination occurs where one person treats another less favourably on the grounds of sex, race or marital status. In an allegation of direct discrimination in recruitment the formal burden of proof is on the complainant. The difficulty is of course that often direct evidence of discrimination is not available and consequently it is sufficient if the complainant can establish primary facts from which inferences of discrimination can be drawn. Evidence is necessary therefore to draw comparison with some person, actual or hypothetical who falls outside the relevant racial group or gender who was or would be treated differently by the employer.

A good example of this approach is provided by *Humphreys v. St. Georges School* 1978. Here a complainant woman teacher established the following primary facts. As an experienced teacher along with two less experienced and less well qualified male applicants, she had applied for two vacant posts within a school. These facts, along with the fact that both male applicants were appointed, were sufficient to raise a prima facie (on the face of it) case of sex discrimination. The Court of Appeal stressed that it is only in an *"exceptional or frivolous case."* that the complainant will fail to establish a prima facie case.In identifying primary facts for the purposes of establishing a prima facie case it is imortant to consider the evidence as a whole. This is particularly so for alleged cases of racial or sexual harassment (see Chapter 6).

The EAT said in *Qureshi v. Victoria Univerity of Manchester* 1996 that in deciding whether or not to infer discrimination tribunals should not consider each incident in isolation to assess whether it occurred on racial or sexual grounds as this would *" inevitably have the effect of diminishing any eloquence that the cumulative effect that the primary facts might have"*.

Once the primary facts indicate a prima facie case of discrimination therefore *"the employer is called on to give an explanation and, failing a clear and specific explanation being given by the employer to the satisfaction of the industrial tribunal, an inference of unlawful discrimination from the primary facts will mean the complaint succeeds"*.

This approach of drawing inferences from primary facts has since been approved in *Noone v. North West Thames Regional Health Authority* 1988. Here the complainant, Dr. Noone, who was born and obtained her initial qualification in Sri Lanka, had unsuccessfully applied for the post of consultant microbiologist with the Health Authority despite superior qualifications, experience and publications than the successful candidate. Her complaint of unlawful discrimination on the grounds of race, was upheld by the industrial tribunal and she was awarded £5,000 for injury of feelings. The tribunal found that the interview procedure was *"little more than a sham"* and had been driven to the conclusion that the interviews had treated the applicant less favourably than they would have treated an indigenous applicant of the same experience. The health authority successfully appealed to the Employment Appeal Tribunal however who concluded that while the decision not to select Dr. Noone was unsatisfactory and unreasonable there was no evidence to justify a finding of discrimination on racial grounds. Recognising that there is rarely direct evidence of discrimination the Court of Appeal reversed the EAT's decision and found that there was sufficient material to entitle the industrial tribunal to drawn an inference of discrimination on racial grounds in this case. The court did feel however that the award of damages was on the high side and reduced it to £3,000.

Certainly there is no burden on an employer to disprove discrimination but once a prime facie case has been made out a tribunal is entitled to turn to an employer for an explanation of the facts.

In *King v. The Great Britain–China Centre* 1991 the applicant who was Chinese and educated in Britain, failed to secure the post of deputy director of the China Centre despite her obvious qualifications for the job. She was not one of the eight candidates short-listed who were all white and no other ethnic Chinese person had ever been employed at the Centre. The Court of Appeal held that the tribunal was entitled to conclude that it was legitimate for them to draw an inference of discrimination on racial grounds in the absence of a satisfactory explanation by the employer.

The Court of Appeal in the above case produced some helpful guidelines in determining a claim of unlawful race discrimination.

- It is for the applicant to make out a case of race discrimination on the balance of probabilities;

- Direct evidence of race discrimination is rare, it is rarely admitted and is often based on an assumption that the applicant may not fit in rather than be ill-intentioned;

- Outcomes will often depend upon inferences drawn from primary facts and these can include evasive or equivocal replies to a questionnaire;

- If there are primary facts which point to a finding of a difference in race and the possibility of discrimination, in the absence of a satisfactory and adequate explanation by the employer it is legitimate for a tribunal to infer that the discrimination was on racial grounds;

- At the conclusion of all the evidence the tribunal should make findings as to the primary facts and draw such inferences as they consider proper. They should then reach a conclusion on the balance of probabilities bearing in mind both the difficulties which face a person who complains of unlawful discrimination and the fact that it is for the complainant to prove his or her case.

While there is no legal obligation as a employer to give reasons for not selecting a candidate for a job the discrimination legislation provides that following a complaint an employer could be required to complete a questionnaire in which reason for decision making are asked. The questionnaire is admissible in evidence and evasive responses by the employer in the questionnaire will influence the tribunal's findings.

In *Brighton Borough Council and Bishop v. Richards* 1993 the fact that the employer had delayed for two and half months in completing the questionnaire without good reason was thought to be significant by the EAT. In looking to the council for an answer to a prima facie case of discrimination the tribunal was entitled to take account of the delay with the questionnaire, the failure to provide an explanation as to why the successful candidate had been selected, the fact that no notes had been made of the significant stages of the selection process and the failure to monitor the equal opportunities policy.

Direct discrimination extends not only to acts based on sex but also decisions made on gender-based criteria. The intention of the alleged discriminator is immaterial and tribunals should focus simply on whether the act or decision satisfies the *"but for"* test. Would the complainant have received the same treatment but for his or her sex?

Where discrimination is alleged to have occurred as a result of the cumulative effect of a number of incidents, for instance in cases of sexual or racial harassment, it would be tempting to consider each incident in isolation to determine whether it was discriminatory. This approach to raising an inference of discrimination is the wrong one said the EAT in *Driskel v. Peninsula Business Services Ltd.* 2000 The EAT approved of an earlier decision where it was held that in *"deciding whether or not to infer race discrimination, tribunals should not look at each incident separately to assess whether it occurred on racial grounds as this would inevitably have the effect of diminishing any eloquence that the cumulative effect of the primary fact may have"*. In cases of harassment the EAT said that the tribunal should find all the facts and then decide the totality of the successive incidents.

In *Ace Mini Cars Ltd. and Loy v. Albertie* 1990 the EAT held that there was unlawful direct discrimination by an employer who refused to employ a black female minicab driver because he believed that she would be the subject of racial attacks.

If the employer puts forward a number of reasons for his conduct, some valid and some discriminatory, then provided the discriminatory reason was an important factor, there is unlawful discrimination.

In *Owen & Briggs v. James* 1982 a case involving race discrimination, the complainant was a young black girl who had applied for a job as a shorthand typist with a firm of solicitors. She was interviewed for the job but rejected. When the post was re-advertised some months later she re-applied, but when she arrived for her interview the employer refused to see her. The same day a young white girl was appointed to the post despite the fact that her shorthand speed (35 words per minute) was far inferior to the complainant's (80 words per minute). It was also established that one of the partners of the firm had said to the successful *candidate "why take on a coloured girl when English girls were available"*. The applicant's unlawful direct discrimination on the grounds of race was upheld in the industrial tribunal and on appeal in the Employment Appeal Tribunal. On further appeal to the Court of Appeal by the employer, it was argued that there could be no unlawful discrimination unless the sole reason for the conduct was the racial factor. This argument was rejected, the court deciding that it is sufficient if race is an important factor in the employer's decision and accordingly the appeal was unsuccessful.

One major difficulty facing a complainant is that proving discrimination may be impossible without access to documents which the employer holds. Since they may be confidential the applicant cannot have access to them unless the industrial tribunal chairman believes that they are relevant.

The Court of Appeal in *Nassè v. SRC* 1979 held that an industrial tribunal should not order or permit the disclosure of a report or reference, given and received in confidence, except in rare cases where, after inspection of the document, the chairman decides that it is essential in the interests of justice that the confidence should be overridden.

The words *'on the grounds of'* sex, race or marital status in the statutes would cover the situation where the reason for discrimination was a generalised assumption that men, women, married persons, or persons of a particular race, possess or lack certain characteristics. In *Skyrail Oceanic Ltd. v. Coleman* 1981 two rival firms employed a man and woman who were subsequently married and for reasons of confidentiality, the woman was dismissed. The Court of Appeal held by a majority that, as the reason for dismissing the woman rather than the man was based on a general assumption that the man in a marriage is the breadwinner, and this is an assumption based on sex, this amounted to unlawful discrimination. In *Cockroft v. Restus Ltd.* 1989 the complainant was not selected for an interview as a warehouse assistant as the employer required someone that had physical strength and the work was therefore unsuitable for a *"young lady"*. The presumption that only a *"big strong lad"* would be qualified for the job was held to be unlawful discrimination on the grounds of sex. In fact the complainant whose hobbies included weight lifting clearly demonstrated that physical strength was not an exclusively male characteristic.

A useful tool to attack the credibility of the employer's denial of discrimination is statistical evidence. This is particularly so when the management decisions on matters such as promotion or access to benefits are based upon subjective criteria such as *excellence, potential* or *efficiency*. In *Owen & Briggs v. James* 1982 if the firm of solicitors could have shown that they had other black employees, this could have gone a long way towards enabling the tribunal to reach a contrary decision. In *West Midlands Passenger Transport Executive v. Singh* 1988 the Court of Appeal ruled that statistical evidence of the employer's record of appointing ethnic minority applicants in the past, is material as to whether he has discriminated on racial grounds against a particular complainant. This enables a tribunal to scrutinise the employer's stated reason for rejecting the complainant and test it against comparative evidence of the employer's overall record.

The types of questions asked in interviews may be of relevance to determine whether there has been discrimination.

In *Saunders v. Richmond on Thames LBC* 1978 the EAT confirmed that it is not in itself unlawful to ask a question of a woman which would not be asked of a man. Here in an interview for a job as a golf professional, the female applicant was asked whether there were other female golf professionals and whether she thought that men would respond as well to a woman golf professional as to a man. Her claim of unlawful discrimination when she was not appointed did not succeed. The existence of direct discrimination depended upon whether she was treated less favourably on the grounds of sex than a man. Here, while the questions demonstrated an out of date attitude, the industrial tribunal was entitled to find that they were not asked with the intention of discriminating.

Asking questions about domestic circumstances would not necessarily be discriminating particularly when they could be asked of both male and female candidates.

In *Adams v. Strathclyde Regional Council* 1989 an applicant for a post as senior lecturer was asked at her interview how many children she had and their ages. This question was held not to constitute unlawful discrimination given that it could have equally have been asked of a male candidate and had been asked simply to help put her at her ease in the interview despite having the very opposite affect.

It is also unlawful to show an intention to commit an act of discrimination in relation to employment. Therefore the publication of an advertisement which invites applicants for the post of salesman or barmaids would constitute unlawful discrimination. (see later).

Under the EC "Equal Treatment Directive" the UK is required to implement the principle of *"equal treatment for men and women as regards access to employment". The directive also provides that "there shall be no discrimination whatsoever on grounds of sex in the conditions, including selection criteria, for access to all jobs or posts".*

In *Dekker v. Stichting Vormingscentrum voor Jonge Volwassenen Plus* 1991 the European Court of Justice held that it is a breach of the directive to refuse to employ a woman because she is pregnant despite the fact that this could mean grave financial consequences for the employer. If a woman receives less favourable treatment because she is pregnant this is direct discrimination and there is no need to establish that a man in comparable circumstances would not have been treated better. Pregnancy dismissals are considered in Chapter 6.

In *Webb v. EMO Air Cargo (UK) Ltd. (No 2)* (1996) the European Court of Justice held that it amounts to sex discrimination to refuse to employ a woman who due to her pregnancy cannot immediately perform the job. This was the case in *Mahiburg v. Land Mecklenbury Vorpommen* 2000 where a nurse was refused a permanent post in a heart clinic because being eight weeks pregnant she could not work in an operating theatre for health and safety reasons. The European Court of Justice held that this was unlawful sex discrimination

EC law does not refer specifically to race discrimination but does provide that there should be no discrimination based on nationality within the Community in Article 48 of the Treaty of Rome. Nationality is under the Race Relations Act 1976 included within the protection against discrimination on racial grounds.

Indirect Discrimination

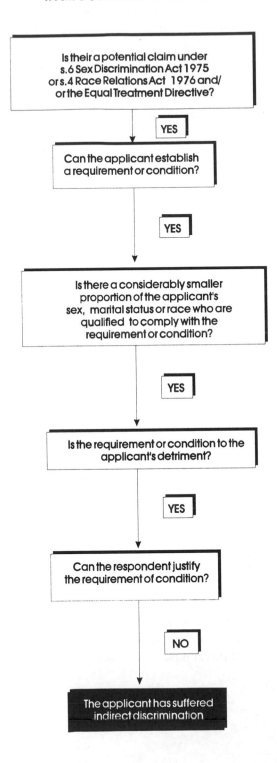

Indirect Discrimination in Recruitment

Indirect discrimination, a more subtle form of discrimination than direct discrimination, is designed to cover overt yet not blatant acts of discrimination. A complaint of indirect discrimination could be brought under the UK legislation or the Equal Treatment Directive if applicable. Indirect discrimination occurs where a person requires another to meet a requirement or condition which as a member of a particular sex, race or marital status is less easily satisfied. This is because the proportion of those of that type who can comply with the requirement or condition is smaller, and it is to the complainant's detriment and not justifiable. It was held in *Perera v. Civil Service Commission* 1981 that in an allegation of indirect discrimination it is necessary to show that the requirement or condition is mandatory rather than one of a number of criteria which the employer would take into account.

> In *Meer v. London Borough of Tower Hamlets* 1988 the requirement was alleged to be job selection criteria, one of which was to have experience working in Tower Hamlets. The fact that this particular criteria was not mandatory meant that it could not constitute a requirement for the purposes of indirect discrimination.

For the purposes of showing that the proportion of the complainant's type who can comply with the condition is smaller there is no need to produce elaborate statistical evidence, but rather a common sense approach is to be encouraged. Nevertheless to succeed it is necessary to show that the proportion who can comply is considerably smaller.

> In *Price v. Civil Service Commission* 1978 the complainant alleged indirect discrimination on the grounds of sex because far fewer women than men could comply with the age limits of seventeen and a half to twenty eight to qualify as an eligible candidate for the executive officer grade. By comparing the proportion of qualified women with the proportion of qualified men, it is obvious that as a larger number of women of that age group will be likely to be having or bringing up children, then the proportion who can comply with the age requirement is less. The EAT held that as the proportion who can comply in practice is less and the requirement was not justifiable, there was unlawful indirect discrimination.

Even where indirect discrimination is established there are no damages payable if it is shown to be unintentional. Where the fundamental purpose of the claim is to secure compensation for the victim there is little point in presenting a complaint where there was no intention to discriminate.

> In *Tickle v. Governors of Riverview CE School and Surrey County Council* 1994 the tribunal held that damages are available for unintentional indirect

discrimination if the claim is brought under the Equal Treatment Directive. Here as the teacher involved was employed by a local authority, an emanation of the state, the Directive was applicable.

Although no damages are payable for unintentional indirect discrimination in practice under the statute it is the employer who must satisfy the burden of establishing that the requirement or condition was not applied with the intention of treating the claimant less favourably. In *J H Walker Ltd. v. Hussain* 1996 the EAT held that an employer had indirectly discriminated against Muslim employees by refusing to allow staff to take holidays during the busy season and so preventing the claimants from taking a day off work to celebrate a religious holiday. The EAT supported the tribunal's award of £1000 for injury to feelings having taken account of the nature of the detriment, the claimants length of service, work record, upset and distress caused and the imposition of final written warning when they took the day off. Stressing the burden of proof on the employer under the statute the EAT held that an act of indirect discrimination is applied intentionally at the time of the act if the person (a) wants to bring about the state of affairs which constitute the unfavourable treatment and (b) knows the prohibited result will follow from his acts. It is permissible for a tribunal to infer that an employer wants to produce certain consequences from his acts if he knows what those consequences will be.

The approach to be adopted by a tribunal in a complaint of indirect race discrimination was laid down in *Tower Hamlets LBC v. Qayyum* 1987. The tribunal should:

- identify the applicant's race, colour, nationality or ethnic origin;

- ascertain whether there is a racial group similar;

- see whether the requirement or condition is imposed generally;

- decide whether the proportion is considerably smaller than a comparable proportion of the indigenous group.

It is a question of fact in each case to determine the proportion of the complainant's group who can comply with the requirement or condition in practice. By deciding what proportion of the complainant's group can comply and comparing that figure with the proportion of qualified persons who can comply but fall outside the group, it is possible to decide whether it is considerably smaller.

In *Fulton v. Strathclyde Regional Council* 1986 the employer decided that certain social work posts should be exclusively for full-time staff. Of the basic grade social workers the statistics showed that 90% of the women could comply with the full-time requirement and all of the men. It was held on a complaint of indirect discrimination that 90% is not *"considerably smaller"* than 100% and so the claim must fail.

In *London Underground Ltd. v. Edwards* 1998 the Court of Appeal provided further guidance as to the purpose of the phrase *"considerably smaller"* and how it is to be interpreted. The phrase the court held has a dual statutory purpose *"the first is to prescribe as the threshold for intervention a situation in which there exists a substantial and not merely marginal discriminatory effect as between men and women, or that it can be clearly demonstrated that a prima facie case of indirect discrimination exists, sufficient to require the employer to justify the application of the condition or requirement in question. The second is to ensure that a tribunal charged with deciding whether or not the request is discriminatory may be application of the requirement or condition"*. The court also said it is not possible to lay down a rule of law for *"considerably smaller"* to apply to all employment situations. In the case before the court, involving train operators, the introduction of a flexible shift system was held to be indirectly discriminatory in relation to female single parents despite the fact that she was the only woman, in a minority of female operators adversely affected.

The success of an indirect discrimination claim will turn on the choice of the pool for comparison.

In *Pearse v. Bradford MC* 1988 one 'requirement' of eligibility to apply for a post as a senior lecturer in a college was that the applicant was presently a full-time employee of the local authority in the college. This 'requirement' was claimed to be indirectly discriminatory, the complainant alleging that the proportion of women who could comply with it, 21.8% of the academic staff, was considerably smaller than the proportion of men, 46.7% of the academic staff. The EAT held that the correct pool for comparison was not all of the full-time academic staff but rather those academic staff who had appropriate qualifications for the post. Consequently the statistical evidence put forward by the complainant was inappropriate and she had failed to show that the requirement of being employed full-time had a disproportionate impact on the qualified women. The argument that the pool for comparison must be extended to those eligible to apply, could not be accepted, for it would be irrational to ignore the fact that appropriate qualifications were a pre-requisite to apply for the post.

In *Jones v. University of Manchester* 1993 the Court of Appeal held that the appropriate pool in a recruitment case was all those who could comply with the selection criteria other than the requirement which was alleged to be discriminatory, in this case the age limit of (27-35).

The definition of indirect discrimination also requires the complainant to have suffered a detriment and the requirement or condition must not be justifiable. The fact that the complainant has been adversely affected by the condition is sufficient to establish a detriment. It is open however for the defendant to show as a question of fact that in all the circumstances the requirement is justifiable.

In *Singh v. Rowntree Mackintosh* 1979 the complainant objected to a 'no beard rule' operated by confectioners, which was alleged to be indirectly discriminatory against Sikhs. Here the EAT held that while the rule was discriminatory, it was a justifiable requirement on the grounds of hygiene, supported by medical advice, and therefore not unlawful. The burden of proof was on the employer to justify the requirement or condition and here the tribunal recognised that in adopting standards *the employer must be allowed that independence of judgment as to what he believes is a common expedient in the conduct of his business. Certainly the requirement must be more than convenient but need not be necessarily essential.*

If a person produces reasons for doing something which would be acceptable to right thinking people as sound and tolerable reasons for so doing, then he has justified his conduct.

In *Hampson v. Department of Education and Science* 1989 Balcombe L J held that to determine whether a condition is justifiable or not, an objective standard is required in each case. *'Justifiable' "requires an objective balance to be struck between the discriminatory effect of the condition and the reasonable needs of the party who applies that condition".*

In *Cobb v. Secretary of State for Employment and Manpower Services Commission* 1989 on a complaint of unlawful indirect discrimination, the tribunal held that the eligibility criteria for admission to the Community Programme, which included receipt of the appropriate social security benefit, had a disproportionate impact on women in general and married women in particular. Nevertheless the EAT confirmed that the tribunal is entitled to find that such a criterion is justifiable in the circumstances without reliance on a mass of statistical or sociological evidence but rather by taking a broad and rational view of the circumstances. *"In a case of indirect discrimination it is for the respondent to satisfy the tribunal that the decisions which he took were objectively justified for economic, administrative or other reasons. It is for the tribunal to decide what facts it found proved and to carry out the balancing exercise involved, taking into account all the surrounding circumstances and giving due emphasis to the degree of discrimination caused against the object or aim to be achieved, the principle of proportionality".*

The fact that a claim of indirect sex discrimination may also be founded upon Article 141 of the *Treaty of Rome* and the Equal Treatment Directive is no better illustrated than by a direct challenge to national legislation brought by the Equal Opportunities Commission in 1994. In a momentous judgment in 1994 the House of Lords ruled by a majority of four to one that UK legislation that gives part-time workers, predominantly women, less protection than full-time workers, predominantly men, is incompatible with European Union law as to equality between employees.

In *R v. Secretary of State for Employment, ex parte the Equal Opportunities Commission* 1994 the House of Lords considered the Employment Protection (Consolidation) Act 1978 which confers statutory rights relating to unfair dismissal and redundancy on full-time employees who have been continuously employed for two years. When compared with the position of part-time employees (employed between eight and sixteen hours) who qualify for such statutory rights after five years employment, the Lords held that such provisions indirectly discriminate against women. This case is examined in more depth in Chapter 11.

Both the Equal Opportunities Commission and the Commission for Racial Equality have issued Codes of Practice to provide guidance to employers as to how to avoid sex and race discrimination particularly in recruitment. While the Codes are not law they are admissible in evidence in any proceedings under the legislation. An employer who complies with the Codes is more likely to avoid liability. One recommendation that employers should adopt is to monitor their recruitment processes, for resultant statistics could be used to overturn an inference of discrimination. Certainly this would be useful information to enable an employer to comply with the questionnaire procedures available to an individual considering or having brought proceedings under the discrimination legislation.

It is of course much more difficult to challenge recruitment decisions as discriminatory when informal recruitment methods are used because of the secrecy attached to them. Quite often jobs are filled without advertising or interviewing with staff appointed on the basis of personal recommendations. In these circumstances if ethnic minorities or a particular gender do not have access to these informal networks then they will continue to be under represented. In 1990 an enquiry by the Commission for Racial Equality into the London Underground revealed that following a reorganisation none of the numerous managers appointed were from the organisation's substantial ethnic minority staff.

Lawful Discrimination in Recruitment

Both the Sex Discrimination Act 1975 and the Race Relations Act 1976 identify circumstances where it is lawful to discriminate in the recruitment of staff. They are referred to as instances of genuine occupational qualification (goq). It should be stressed from the outset that goq defence only applies to the making of a job offer or access to promotional, training or other benefits. It does not apply to subjecting to a detriment or dismissal

> In *Timex v. Hodgson* 1981 however, the EAT took a broad view of goq and applied it to a situation where a man had been selected for redundancy rather than a woman of shorter service. The employer's reason for selection was that the remaining job had been revised to come within the goq relating to considerations of decency. The EAT held that the goq applied because the discrimination was not attached to the dismissal but failure to offer the man the revised job.

If a job applicant shows on the balance of probabilities that an act of direct or indirect discrimination has occurred it is open to an employer to establish as a defence that being of a particular sex or racial group is a genuine occupational requirement. To do this the employer must establish that the job falls within a number of identified categories. It would not be sufficient to argue that the employer was simply motivated to recruit from a particular sex or race to achieve a more balanced workforce.

Previously in Chapter 1 we mentioned the ruling of the European Court of Justice in *Marleasing SA v. La Comercial International de Alimentacion SA* 1992 which stated that courts and tribunals of member states should construe domestic legislation in accordance with EC law wherever possible. The defence of goq in the Sex and Race Discrimination legislation is alluded to in the Equal Treatment Directive which while prohibiting sex discrimination provides that *"this Directive shall be without prejudice to the rights of Member States to exclude from its field of application those occupational activities and, where appropriate, the training leading thereto, for which, by reason of their nature or context in which they are carried out, the sex of the worker constitutes a determining factor"*. It seems that if any of the duties of the job fall within the goq then the defence will apply. However if the employer has staff already employed who could easily carry out the goq duties then the position may be different.

> In *Etam plc v. Rowan* 1989 the complainant was refused a job as a sales assistant because the employer argued he could not carry out all the duties of the post because as a man he could not enter the fitting rooms in a shop which sold female clothing. The EAT agreed with the tribunal's finding that the complainant could have performed the majority of the job functions and there were plenty of female sales assistants who could enter the fitting rooms should that prove necessary. The complainant had suffered sex discrimination and the goq provided no defence.

The categories of genuine occupation requirements under the Sex Discrimination Act s.7(2) are as follows.

s.7 (2) Being a man is a genuine occupational qualification for a job only where:

(a)   *the essential nature of the job calls for a man for reasons of physiology (excluding physical strength or stamina) or, in dramatic performances or other entertainment, for reasons of authenticity, so that the essential nature of the job would be materially different if carried out by a woman; or*

(b)   *the job needs to be held by a man to preserve decency or privacy because:*

   (i)   *it is likely to involve physical contact with men in circumstances where they might reasonably object to its being carried out by a woman, or*

   (ii)   *the holder of the job is likely to do his work in circumstances where men might reasonably object to the presence of a woman because they are in a state of undress or are using sanitary facilities; or*

(ba) *the job is likely to involve the holder of the job doing his work, or living, in a private home and needs to be held by a man because objection might reasonably be taken to allowing to a woman:*

   (i)   *the degree of physical or social contact with a person living in the home, or*

   (ii)   *the knowledge of intimate details of such a person's life, which is likely, because of the nature or circumstances of the job or of the home, to be allowed to, or available to, the holder of the job; or*

(c)   *the nature or location of the establishment makes it impracticable for the holder of the job to live elsewhere than in premises provided by the employer, and:*

   (i)   *the only such premises which are available for persons holding that kind of job are lived in, or normally lived in, by men and are not equipped with separate sleeping accommodation for women and sanitary facilities which could be used by women in privacy from men, and*

(ii) *it is not reasonable to expect the employer either to equip those premises with such accommodation and facilities or to provide other premises for women; or*

(d) *the nature of the establishment, or of the part of it within which the work is done, requires the job to be held by a man because:*

(i) *it is, or is part of, a hospital, prison or other establishment for persons requiring special care, supervision or attention, and*

(ii) *those persons are all men (disregarding any woman whose presence is exceptional), and*

(iii) *it is reasonable, having regard to the essential character of the establishment or that part, that the job should not be held by a woman; or*

(e) *the holder of the job provides individuals with personal services promoting their welfare or education, or similar personal services, and those services can most effectively be provided by a man, or*

(f) *the job needs to be held by a man because it is likely to involve the performance of duties outside the United Kingdom in a country whose laws or customs are such that the duties could not, or could not effectively, be performed by a woman, or*

(g) *the job is one of two to be held by a married couple.*

(3) *Subsection (2) applies where some only of the duties of the job fall within paragraphs (a) to (g) as well as where all of them do.*

The goq under s.7(2)(a) would not apply if it is shown that the employer has a stereotyped assumption about the physical abilities of men and women. It would be permissible under this subsection to recruit a female actor or male model or a female for a chat line.

The decency or privacy goq under s.7(2)(b) can only be raised if in the circumstances it is not practical to employ a man or a woman.

In *Wylie v. Dee & Co (Menswear) Ltd.* 1978 the tribunal rejected the goq defence under s.7(2)(b) on the basis of physical contact between the sexes raised by a menswear shop manageress who argued that a female applicant would be prevented from taking customer's inside leg measurements. The tribunal thought that such measurements were often known, could be estimated or easily taken by a male colleague.

One feature of this goq is that *"reasonable objection might be taken if the job holder were of a different sex."*

In *Secretary of State for Scotland v. Henley* 1983 the decency or privacy goq was raised as a defence to recruit a male as a hall governor in a men's prison on the grounds that the job holder might have to be present in the toilet areas or where the men might be in a state of undress. The fact that no objection had been raised by the men helped the tribunal decide that the goq did not apply.

In *Neal v. Watts* 1989 the tribunal held that there was no unlawful discrimination when the complainant was refused a job as a nanny. Here the goq under s.7(2)(ba) applied because of the likely contact between the male applicant and the child's mother when the baby was bathed in the bathroom. Being a woman was a goq for the job.

In *Sisley v. Britannia Security Systems Ltd.* 1983 the EAT provided guidelines as to what is meant by "living in" premises for the purposes of s.7(2)(c) and disagreeing with the tribunal felt that twelve hour shift workers who were provided with beds for rest periods did not qualify. *"The words 'to live in' involve the concept of residence either permanent or temporary and do not cover the cases where an employee is obliged to remain on the premises for a limited period of time. We think that whether there is the necessary feature of residence is a question of fact and degree in every case".*

The categories of genuine occupational requirement in race discrimination are set out in s.5(2) of the Race Relations Act 1976.

s.5 (2) Being of a particular racial group is a genuine occupational qualification for a job only where:

(a) *the job involves participation in a dramatic performance or other entertainment in a capacity for which a person of that racial group is required for reasons of authenticity; or*

(b) *the job involves participation as an artist's or photographic model in the production of a work of art, visual image or sequence of visual images for which a person of that racial group is required for reasons of authenticity; or*

> (c) *the job involves working in a place where food or drink is (for payment or not) provided to and consumed by members of the public or a section of the public in a particular setting for which, in that job, a person of that racial group is required for reasons of authenticity; or*

> (d) *the holder of the job provides persons of that racial group with personal services promoting their welfare, and those services can most effectively be provided by a person of that racial group.*

> (3) *Subsection (2) applies where some only of the duties of the job fall within paragraph (a), (b), (c) or (d) as well as where all of them do.*

In *London Borough of Lambeth v. Commission for Racial Equality* 1990 the EAT held that the goq defence under s.5(2)(d) exception provides a defence only if the post advertised is for the provision of personal services, and the particular racial groups of the holder of the post and persons to whom the services are provided are sufficiently identified so as to establish that they are both of the same racial group. Here the fact that the local authority's advertisement related to posts which were of a managerial and administrative nature which involved very little contact with the public meant that they should not be confined to applicants of Afro-Caribbean or Asian origin. The intention of this exception under the 1976 Act *"envisaged circumstances where there was direct contact, mainly face to face or where there could be physical contact, and where language, cultural understanding and religious backgrounds were of material importance"*. Subsequently the Court of Appeal agreed with the EAT that the holders of the jobs advertised, being managerial positions, did not provide personal services promoting the welfare of persons of a particular racial group.

In *Tottenham Green Under Fives Centre v. Marshall (No2)* 1991 the scope of the goq defence under s.5(2)(d) relating to personal services was further examined. The case arose out of the complainant's application for the post of nursery worker which was rejected on the grounds that the employer wished to recruit an Afro-Caribbean worker and a white person he was not suitable. The employer raised the goq defence to the complaint of unlawful discrimination claiming that *'personal services'* applied. The personal services involved in the job were maintaining a cultural background link for the children of Afro-Caribbean background who attended the centre; dealing with these children's parents; reading and talking to the children in a West Indian dialect and having an awareness of their skin and healthcare needs. The industrial tribunal rejected the defence deciding that there was no evidence that a nursery worker of any ethnic origin could not render the required services. An appeal was upheld by the EAT however which laid down number of guidelines:

- the question for the tribunal in deciding whether the goq applied was not whether the personal services promoting the child's welfare could not be provided by a person of another racial group but by which group could the service be most effectively provided;

- in answering that question the tribunal had to carry out a delicate balancing exercise bearing in mind the need to guard against discrimination and promoting racial integration;

- if the tribunal accepted a conscious decision of a responsible employer to commit an act of discrimination and rely on a goq and that decision was based on a genuinely held and reasonably based opinion that applying a goq would best promote the welfare of the recipient of the personal services, then the tribunal should give considerable weight to the employer's decision.

Positive Action

In addition to these specific instances where the sex or race of an employee is regarded as a genuine occupational requirement there are provisions in the Sex Discrimination Act and the Race Relations Act which enable employers and others (trade unions, employer's organisations and professional bodies) to achieve a more balanced work force. Employers are authorised to take positive action to encourage females or members of a particular racial group to apply for positions in their organisations where they are under-represented in those jobs. The requirement for positive encouragement to do certain work under the Sex Discrimination Act is that during the previous twelve months there were no or comparatively few women doing that type of work. Under the Race Relations Act it must be shown that either no members of the racial group are doing the work in question at the organisation or that the proportion of that group who do that work is small among those employed, or among the population of the area from which recruitment normally takes place. Of course it is one thing positively to encourage applicants from under-represented groups by stating in a job advertisement that applications from ethnic minorities or women will be particularly welcomed. If it is shown however than an employer is attempting to limit recruitment exclusively to the members of a racial group, where there is no genuine occupational requirement, then this will be unlawful.

In *Hughes and Others v. L B Hackney* 1986 the defendant council advertised for gardeners stating that applicants from ethnic minority people would be warmly welcomed. Subsequently three white applicants for the jobs were told that the posts were only open to applicants who were ethnic minority members. The tribunal found that to limit job recruitment in this way was not authorised by the legislation, and in fact in this particular case neither was the criterion for encouraging applicants from a particular racial group satisfied. The defendant council had argued that the proportion of ethnic minorities doing work of this kind was small in comparison with the population of the recruitment area. This argument was rejected by the tribunal who found that the population area should not be restricted to Hackney for a substantial number of workers were recruited from outside the borough.

In *Kalanke v. Freie Hansestadt* 1995 the European Court of Justice confirmed that the Equal Treatment Directive does not permit affirmative action.

Enforcement and Remedies

Discrimination law in employment may be enforced by individual complaint to an industrial tribunal. Also both the Commission for Racial Equality and the Equal Opportunities Commission have a role to play in the enforcement of the law and where certain unlawful acts are alleged, their role is an exclusive one. The process and time limits relating to the presentation of a complaint were considered earlier.

If despite the attempts at conciliation the complainant decides to go ahead, there is a special pre-tribunal procedure to assist in the effective presentation of the complaint and access to information.

The remedies available to a tribunal who felt that a complaint has been made out are:

- an order declaring the rights of the parties;

- an order requiring the respondent to pay the complainant damages subject to the upper limit for unlawful dismissal claims;

- a recommendation of action to be taken by the respondent to reduce the adverse effect of discrimination.

A failure by the respondent without reasonable justification to comply with a recommendation may lead to an award of increased compensation. In the case of indirect discrimination if the respondent proves that the requirement or condition was applied without any intention to discriminate then no compensation will be awarded.

In *Noone v. North West Thames Regional Health Authority* 1988 the Court of Appeal confirmed that awards for incidents of racial discrimination were subject to the same rules as awards for damages for personal injury in respect of any other breach of statutory duty. Here the complainant was 'devastated' by the discriminatory act and suffered a severe injury to feelings which should be acknowledged by the award of damages. Nevertheless bearing in mind that she suffered no actual loss, the award of £5,000 was too high and should be reduced to £3,000.

Marshall v. Southampton and South West Hampshire Area Health Authority (No 2) 1993 held that the maximum compensation under the Sex Discrimination Act does not provide an adequate remedy as required by Article 6 of the EC Equal Treatment Directive. The European Court of Justice held that an employee of the State is entitled to rely on Article 6 to challenge the employer's discriminatory retirement policy successfully and compensation payable is not restricted to the statutory limit under the Sex Discrimination Act of £11,000. Here the complainant's total loss was assessed at £19,405, well in excess of the statutory limit. The award was made for discrimination on the grounds of sex contrary to the Equal Treatment Directive when the complainant was dismissed at the age of 62 because she had passed the respondent's normal retirement age for women when men could go on working until 65. The European Court of Justice answered three questions referred to it by the House of Lords.

- Whether the limit of compensation for sex discrimination under UK legislation meant that there was a failure to implement Article 6 of the Equal Treatment Directive.

- Whether it is essential for proper implementation of the Directive that compensation should not be less than the total loss and should include interest from the date of discrimination.

- Whether Article 6 could be used by an individual against an employer that constituted an emanation of the State to overrule the compensation limits.

On all three questions the ruling was in Mrs Marshall's favour. The court said that compensation must be *"adequate in that it must enable the loss or damage actually sustained as a result of the discrimination dismissal to be made good in full accordance with the application of the rules"*.

The effect of this important decision is that employees of public bodies can rely directly on community law to set aside a national provision such as the Sex Discrimination Act which imposes limits on compensation recoverable.

The Sex Discrimination and Equal Pay (Remedies) Regulations 1993, formally removed the ceiling on compensation for unlawful sex discrimination and set out the method of calculating the interest. In 1993 it was also recognised that thousands of women who had been dismissed from the armed forces because they were pregnant can claim sex discrimination. The fact that the ceiling on compensation was lifted dramatically increased the significance of the potential claims and tens of thousands of pounds have been awarded. Tribunals have recognised that injury to feelings in such cases can include the emotional effect of discharge from the services evidenced by feelings of humiliation, isolation, loss of status and career aspirations and personal hurt. The notion that a higher level post should carry with it a higher award of compensation was recognised in *Sharifi v. Strathclyde Regional Council* 1992.

The guidelines to be applied by tribunals also the principles to be applied in assessing compensation for servicewomen who were dismissed contrary to European Community Law because of their pregnancy, were laid down by the EAT in *Ministry of Defence v. Cannock and others* 1994. Those women dismissed from the services by reason of pregnancy between 1978 and 1990 have a valid claim for sex discrimination under the Equal Treatment Directive. Following the decision in Marshall 1993, where the European Court of Justice held that the upper limit of the compensatory award for sex discrimination was also contrary to the Directive, the potential awards for such discrimination took on a new significance. *Compensatory awards well over a £100,000 were made, which led to the call for guidance. In Cannock the EAT confirmed that unlawful acts of discrimination are statutory torts and the relevant principle for redress was to put applicants in the position they would have been but for the unlawful conduct of the Ministry of Defence in dismissing them by reason of their pregnancy. Damages should be evaluated on a percentage basis as the loss of the chance of continued employment. This involves assessing the chances that the applicant would have returned to work had maternity leave been granted, the length of service hypothetically lost and career advancement. Tribunals were advised to keep a sense of proportion so that "the total seems a sensible and just reflection of the chances which have been assessed." An award should not be made which would be more* appropriate to someone who lost a career due to a continuing disability *"A woman who has been unlawfully dismissed while pregnant is not incapacitated from alternative work or from pursing an alternative career. The hypothesis on which she may recover anything at all from loss of earnings is that she could have been ready, willing and able to resume her onerous duties six months after the child was born. If the tribunal assesses the chances of her being in that position as very small, she will recover only a nominal sum for the loss of a remote chance".*

The statutory ceiling of £11,000 on a compensatory award for race discrimination has also been lifted under the Race Relations (Remedies) Act 1994. If a complaint is well founded then the tribunal must decide whether it is "just and equitable" to award damages. The damages should reflect a sum of injury to feelings and the pecuniary loss subject to the ceiling. Damages for injury to feelings should compensate the complainant for the insult and humiliation suffered. In *Browne v. Cassell* 1972 Ld Diplock said that *"where salt is rubbed into the wound by high handed malicious insulting or offensive conduct additional compensation may be awarded by way of aggravated damages"*.

In *Alexander v. Home Office* 1988 the Court of Appeal considered an appeal against an award of compensation for injury to feelings where a complaint of race discrimination had been established. Increasing the award from £50 to £500 the Court of Appeal gave some indication as to the principles to be applied in assessing damages in race discrimination cases. LJ May said that *"The objective of an award for unlawful racial discrimination, as with any other awards of damages, is restitution. Where the discrimination has caused actual pecuniary loss, such as the refusal of a job, then the damages referable to this can be readily calculated. Damages for unlawful discrimination, however, are not limited to the pecuniary loss that can be specifically proved and it is impossible to say what is restitution for the injury to feelings, humiliation, and insult. The answer must depend on the experience and good sense of the judge and assessors. Awards should not be minimal, because this would tend to trivialise or diminish respect for the public policy to which the Act gives effect. on the other hand, just because it is impossible to assess the monetary value of injured feelings awards should be restrained. To award sums which are generally felt to be excessive does almost as much harm to the policy and the results which it seeks to achieve as do nominal awards. Moreover injury to feelings, which is likely to be of a relatively short duration, is less serious than physical injury to the body or the mind which may persist for months or for life. The injury to feelings for which compensation is sought must have resulted from knowledge of the discrimination. Although damages for discrimination will in many cases be analogous to those for defamation, they are not necessarily the same. In the latter, the principal injury to be compensated is that to the plaintiff's reputation and it is doubtful whether this will play a large part in discrimination cases. On the other hand, if the plaintiff knows of the racial discrimination and that he has thereby been held up to "hatred, ridicule or contempt", then the injury to his feelings will be an important element in the damages. In the substantial majority of discrimination cases the unlawful conduct will cause personal hurt, in the sense of injury to feelings, or of preventing the plaintiff from working in more congenial conditions, or of preventing the plaintiff from obtaining a better, more remunerative job. However, unless the court can and feels it right to draw an inference that the discrimination will cause a plaintiff "hurt" of a particular kind, the mere fact that a defendant is guilty of racial discrimination is not in itself a factor affecting damages."*

In *Orlando v. Didcot Power Station Sports and Social Club* 1996 the EAT held that in a sex discrimination case in assessing injury to feelings, the willingness of the employer to admit that it has acted in breach of the discrimination legislation may help to reduce the hurt which is felt, in that it can spare the complainant the indignity and further hurt of having to rehearse the nature of her treatment. Such a reduction in *"hurt"* can of course be reflected in the level of damages awarded.

The decision in *Armitage Marsden and the Prison Service v. Johnson* 1997 provides an indication of the level of compensation payable in cases or race discrimination. The complainant was a prison officer who had been subjected *to "appalling treatment"* by two work colleagues including racist remarks, false accusations and biased treatment. The EAT upheld the tribunal's award of £20,000 for injury to feelings with an additional £7,500 aggravated damages for the malicious nature of his employers attitude. A further award of £500 was made against each of the officers in question on the grounds that they had victimised the complainant and aided the employer to discriminate. The EAT summarised the relevant principles for assessing awards for injury to feelings.

(1) Awards for injury to feelings are compensatory. They should be just to both parties. They should compensate fully without punishing the tortfeasor. Feelings of indignation at the tortfeasor's conduct should not be allowed to inflate the award.

(2) Awards should not be too low, as that would diminish respect for the policy of the anti-discrimination legislation. Society has condemned discrimination and awards must ensure that it is seen to be wrong. On the other hand, awards should be restrained, as excessive awards could be seen as the way to untaxed riches.

(3) Awards should bear some broad general similarity to the range of awards in personal injury cases. This should be done by reference to the whole range of such awards, rather than to any particular type of award.

(4) In exercising their discretion in assessing a sum, tribunals should remind themselves of the value in everyday life of the sum they have in mind. This may be done by reference to purchasing power or by reference to earnings.

(5) Tribunals should bear in mind the need for public respect for the level of awards made.

In *Sheriff v. Klyne Tugs (Lowestoft) Ltd.* 1999 the Court of Appeal held that a claimant may recover compensation for any injury caused by discrimination both mental and physical from the Employment Tribunal. The Court also noted that in negligence proceedings for personal injury a claimant would have to show that the injury was reasonably foreseeable. In discrimination statutes there is no such requirement and it is sufficient if it is shown that the act of discrimination caused the injury.

Pecuniary loss which is quantifiable includes the loss of wages, the loss of opportunity to work and the loss of advantage on the labour market. Exemplary damages were thought to be available where a public employer was guilty of offensive conduct or a private employer discriminates for profit.

In *Gibbon v. South West Water Services Ltd.* 1992 the Court of Appeal indicated that exemplary damages are not available for all civil wrongs. The court held that an award of exemplary damages could only be made for torts which existed prior to 1964 when *Rookes v. Barnard* established the right to exemplary damages in defined circumstances.

As the statutory torts of discrimination were not created until the mid 1970s it seems that exemplary damages are not therefore available.

In *Deane v. London Borough of Ealing* 1993 the EAT held that it was bound by the above decision and found that the statutory tort of race discrimination under the Race Relations Act 1976 does not carry with it the possibility of an award of exemplary damages.

In *Ministry of Defence v. Meredith* 1995 the EAT held that exemplary damages are not available for breach of the Equal Treatment Directive. Punitive damages are not usually available for tortious liability and the Directive is a tort *"comparable ... with statutory tort of discrimination under the Sex Discrimination Act"* for which exemplary damages are not available.

In *British Gas Plc v. Shama* 1991 the Employment Appeal Tribunal confirmed that there are limits to the extent that tribunals have power to make recommendations to reduce the adverse affects of unlawful discrimination. While the tribunal had found that the complainant had been the victim of direct racial discrimination when she was not promoted, the tribunal had no power to recommend that she should be promoted to the next suitable vacancy.

Enforcement of the legislation is also the role of the Commissions who having instituted a formal investigation and, being satisfied that unlawful discriminatory acts or practices have taken place, may issue a non-discrimination notice on any person. Such a notice will require the person on whom it is served not to commit the acts complained of and also comply with any required changes in conduct. The

Commissions may seek an injunction to prevent repeated discrimination within five years of the non-discrimination notice becoming final.

Only the CRC or EOC can initiate proceedings under the legislation alleging discriminatory advertising which indicates an intention to discriminate. A job advertisement which indicates a racial or sexual preference such as "steward" or "waitress" would contravene the legislation without further explanation. Both the publisher and the advertiser could be made liable for a discriminatory advertisement but the publisher would have a defence if he can establish that he reasonably relied on a statement by the advertiser that the advertisement was not unlawful.

> In *Cardiff Women's Aid v. Hartup* 1994 it was confirmed that only the Commission for Racial Equality can bring proceedings for racially discriminating advertising. The important point was made however that it is still possible for an individual complainant to use a discriminatory advertisement as evidence of direct discrimination in the recruitment process.

The present power to conduct formal investigations is that they may be instigated for any purpose in connection with the Commission's duties. The terms of reference for an investigation must be drawn up by the Commission and general notice of the holding of an investigation served. To assist the investigatory process, power to require a person to furnish written information or to give oral evidence and produce documents is also conferred. On completion of an investigation the Commission must prepare a report within which it can make recommendations for changes in policies or procedures to individuals or organisations, and recommendations for changes in the law to the Secretary of State. Such investigations may also lead to the issue by the Commission of a non-discrimination notice on any person. This would be the case where the individual is committing or has committed an unlawful discriminatory act or has applied or operated an unlawful discriminatory practice. Only the Commission may bring proceedings before the county court in respect of certain unlawful acts, namely discriminatory advertising, unlawful instructions to discriminate and unlawful inducements to discriminate under ss.30 and 31 of the Race Relations Act 1976.

> The meaning of ss.30 and 31 were considered by the EAT in C.R.E. v. *Imperial Society of Teachers of Dancing* 1983. Here there had been a request by an employer to a school's head of careers that no coloured students should be sent to fill a job. The EAT held that there had been no instruction to discriminate under s.30 because the instructor had no authority over the instructed. Nevertheless there had been a contravention of s.31, for the request was an attempt to induce an infringement of the Race Relations Act.

Where an unlawful act is committed by an employee in the course of his employment, the principles of vicarious liability apply and the employer is also made liable for the act whether or not it is done with his approval. It is a defence for an employer to prove that he took such steps as were reasonably practicable to prevent the employees from doing that act or from doing, in the course of his employment, acts of that description. Such steps would certainly include full implementation of the Commission for Racial Equality Code of Practice on discrimination. Furthermore an employer is not liable unless the discriminatory act is done in the course of employment. Vicarious liability for discrimination in the workplace is considered in more detail in Chapter 6.

In *Irving & Irving v. Post Office* 1987 the complaint of race discrimination was based on the conduct of an employee of the post office who when sorting the mail had written a racially insulting comment on a letter addressed to his neighbours who were of Jamaican origin. The issue before the Court of Appeal was whether the employee was acting in the course of his employment so that the Post Office could be made vicariously liable for the discriminatory act. The employee's act of writing on the mail was clearly unauthorised so the question was whether the act was an unauthorised mode of doing an authorised act. Here the misconduct formed no part of the postman's duties and could not be regarded as an unauthorised way of performing his work. *"An employer is not to be held liable merely because the opportunity to commit the wrongful act had been created by the employee's employment, or because the act in question had been committed during the period of that particular employment."*

The decision of the Court of Appeal in *Jones v. Tower Boot* 1997 casts doubt on the approach adopted in *Irving* and provides a more realistic analysis of *"course of employment"* in cases involving discrimination. Here the complainant has been subjected to serious racist attacks at the workplace and yet the employer escaped liability on the grounds that the actions of the employees in question fell outside the course of their employment. The Court of Appeal dramatically adopted a novel view if the interpretation of course of employment for the purposes of statutory torts such as race and sex discrimination. The court held that unlike common law torts, for the purposes of statutory torts the expression "course of employment" should be given an everyday meaning so as to include acts committed during working hours. On this basis the employer was held to be vicariously liable for the racist attack.

If it does little else, discrimination law should stimulate equality of opportunity and act as a framework within which to identify barriers facing women and ethnic minority workers at work. As was suggested earlier, there is a view that there should be similar laws to protect people who are discriminated against because of their disability, sexuality or age. Ethically, job applicants should be judged on the basis of their ability rather than their gender or racial origin. Having considered the fundamental principles of equal opportunity law applied to the recruitment process the next Chapter explores discrimination at the workplace including equal pay.

Proof of Discrimination

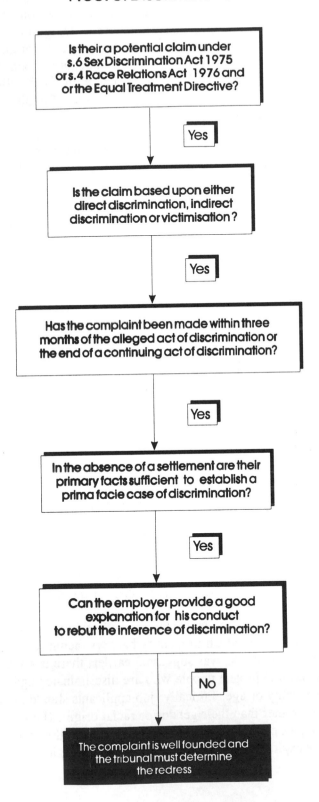

Case Study

Brinkley Business School - Mary's Radical Background

Brinkley Business School was set up last year by merging a number of departments in the University of Brinkley. The Director of the School is Miriam Perot who, with her two deputies, comprise the senior management team of the School. The senior management team is the final arbiter on staffing issues in the School, subject to formal ratification by the academic board of the University. A legal issue has arisen over the dismissal two months ago of Mary Boyde, an Information Technology lecturer in the Business School, who had been serving her probationary year. She had been appointed in the previous September and in the words of her resource director had immediately adopted an *"aggressive attitude towards him"*. Of major concern to her was the job description issued to her which conflicted, she claimed, dramatically with what had been agreed upon when she was appointed in July. When called to a *"clear the air"* meeting with the Resource Director and the Director of the Business School, Mary insisted on having a union official with her. That meeting did not have a successful outcome, Mary claiming that she felt she was the victim of discrimination. After checking her background more thoroughly, Miriam discovered that in her previous employment Mary had been regarded as a *"left wing feminist"* heavily involved in the union and having an *"anti-management"* attitude. Miriam's recommendation that Mary should be given notice was approved by Senior Management Team and ratified by Academic Board of the University.

Case Study

Dalton West plc -The Drivers Gender

Dalton West is a large manufacturer of fork lift trucks with depots and retail outlets situated all over Britain. Life has not been very kind to Mary Hutchinson. Having three young children her husband is partially disabled following a factory accident and will never work again. Subsequently the family received a lump sum payment and now an invalidity pension so that they will not suffer financially. Perhaps it was that fact that her husband's working life was prematurely ended that promoted Mary into paying for and attending a training course which eventually led to her acquiring a HGV licence. With her husband at home and some assistance from relatives Mary felt that she could now hold down a full-time HGV driver's job so that when Dalton West advertised for drivers at their Manchester depot she applied immediately. Receiving no reply to her application, Mary decided to contact the company by phone and was promised an interview by the Transport Manager in Manchester for a possible driver's job. Mary was interviewed and turned down as 'unsuitable'. She has now written to the company claiming that the interview conducted by the Transport Manager and his assistant was no more than a sham. They asked her whether she would have difficulty fitting in with the other male drivers and also how she could possibly cope with full-time work and a young family. They pointed to the fact that although she held an HGV licence she was totally inexperienced and would find the heavy work too difficult to manage.

Chapter 6
Equal Opportunities at the Workplace

In the previous chapter we considered discrimination law relating to staff recruitment, in particular s.6 of the Sex Discrimination Act 1975 and s.4 of the Race Relations Act 1976 which make it unlawful for a person in relation to employment by him to discriminate in the arrangements he makes for the purpose of deciding who should be offered employment, the terms on which it is offered or by refusing to offer employment. Here we are concerned with subsisting employment relationships which are also covered by s.6 and s.4 making it unlawful for an employer to discriminate in the way he gives access to opportunities for promotion, transfer, training or other benefits, or refuses to afford such access. They further provide that it is unlawful to discriminate by dismissing an individual or subjecting him to any other detriment. Once again an allegation of discrimination at work must be categorised as either direct discrimination, indirect discrimination or victimisation.

A complaint of sex or race discrimination at the workplace is not dependent on the existence of an enforceable contract of employment. In *Leighton v. Michael and Charalambous* 1996 the EAT held that despite having an illegal contract the complainant could still claim unlawful sex discrimination based upon sexual harassment.

Victimisation

Protection from victimisation at the workplace is a fundamental right for potential equal opportunity claimants and has been greatly enhanced by a recent House of Lords decision. Victimisation you will remember from the last chapter is less favourable treatment because the claimant has given evidence or brought proceedings under the legislation. The Court of Appeal has long held that for a victimisation claim to succeed the claimant must establish a conscious motive on the part of the discriminator. In *Nagarajan v. London Regional Transport* 1999 the House of Lords found no justification from the language of the legislation to interpret victimisation in this way. To establish discrimination by way of victimisation it is necessary to establish that the less favourable treatment suffered was *"significantly influenced"* or an *"important cause"* of the fact that the claimant had brought proceedings against the employer. Here the applicant had been victimised in respect of an unsuccessful application for a vacancy because the interviewers were consciously or subconsciously influenced by the fact that he had brought proceedings. The House of Lords recognised that unconscious prejudice may be just as prevalent as deliberate discrimination *"All human beings have preconceptions, beliefs, attitudes and prejudices on many subjects. It is part of our make-up. Moreover, we do not often recognise our own prejudices. Many people are unable or unwilling, to admit even to themselves that actions of theirs may be racially motivated. An employer may genuinely believe that the reason why he rejected an applicant had nothing to do with the applicant's race. After careful and thorough investigation of the claim, members of an ET may decide that the proper inference to be drawn from this evidence is that whether the employer realised it at the time or not, race was the reason why he acted as he did... Members of racial groups need protection from conduct driven by unconscious prejudice as much as from conscious and deliberate discrimination".*

A further development in the law of victimisation is provided by the case of *Coote v. Granada Hospitality Ltd.* (No 2) 2000. Here the complaint was brought by an ex employee who claimed that her employers reluctance to provide her with a reference was a reaction to her previous claim for unlawful discrimination. The EAT ruled that as the Sex Discrimination Act only applies to discrimination during the course of the employment relationship it did not have jurisdiction to hear the complaint. Following a reference to the European Court of Justice however the EAT decided that the Sex Discrimination Act 1975 could be interpreted as protecting ex employees against victimisation. Unfortunately this contrasts with the position under the Race Relations Act.

Unlawful discrimination in this form is rarely alleged but is intended to protect employees at the work place who are given less favourable treatment by the employer for bringing a complaint under the legislation or giving evidence on behalf of a complainant. It is of course the fear of victimisation that often prevents employees from taking or supporting legal action against an employer. Possible victimisation and sensational reporting are reasons why many employees who suffer sexual harassment from a superior decide not to seek legal redress.

In *Northampton County Council v. Dattani* 1994 the complainant's employers promised to investigate a complaint that she has not been selected for a period of paid study leave. When the employer received notification of her claim under the Race Relations Act the investigation was dropped. The EAT upheld the tribunal's ruling of unlawful victimisation.

Direct and Indirect Discrimination at Work

For the purposes of direct discrimination the intention of the alleged discriminator is immaterial, rather tribunals should focus simply on whether the act or decision satisfies the "but for" test. Would the complainant have received the same treatment but for his or her sex or race. In *Horsey v. Dyfed CC* 1982 the act complained of was a refusal by the employer to recommend a married female social worker for secondment in London. The reason for the refusal was the fact that the wife's husband was already working in London and the employer believed that on completion of her secondment she would not return. This assumption the EAT held was one based on sex and in the circumstances constituted direct discrimination.

If the reason for dismissal is based upon a general assumption about a particular gender which is discriminatory, this will normally amount to unlawful discrimination. In *Skyrail Oceanic Ltd. v. Coleman* 1981 two rival travel companies employed a man and a woman who were subsequently married. For reasons of confidentiality the two companies decided that one of them should be dismissed and the woman was chosen. The Court of Appeal held that as the reason for dismissing the woman rather than the man was based on a general assumption that the man in a marriage is the breadwinner, and this is an assumption based on sex, this amounted to unlawful discrimination.

It is still necessary to establish for a successful claim of sex discrimination that the complainant was subjected to a detriment on the grounds of his or gender. It is entirely permissible for a tribunal to decided that while the act complained of may be offensive and a detriment it may be equally so for a man or woman.

> This was the decision of the EAT in *Stewart v. Cleveland Guest (Engineering) Ltd.* 1994 when the substance of a female worker's complaint was the practice of the male dominated workforce in a factory displaying pin ups and calendars featuring naked and semi naked women. The management of the factory thought the complaint trivial and it was only following union intervention that the pictures were removed. Nevertheless when the complainant suffered hostility from fellow workers for her action she resigned and complained of unlawful sex discrimination. The EAT agreed with the tribunal that even though it was possible to find that the complainant suffered a detriment there may be no sex discrimination. The display of the pictures could be equally offensive to men so that there was no less favourable treatment on the grounds of sex for the purpose of direct discrimination. The tribunal, as the industrial jury, was best placed to decide whether the employer had discriminated against the complainant.

In *Smith v. Safeways plc* 1996 the Court of Appeal provided guidance as to the circumstances in which an employer's dress and appearance code would constitute sex discrimination. Here the employer had adopted an appearance code which applied to delicatessen staff but which operated differently for men and women particularly in relation to length of hair. The complainant was dismissed for refusing to have his ponytail shortened claiming that a woman in a comparable position would surely be required to keep her hair clipped back. The majority of the EAT thought that the hair length rule was discriminatory and unlike a dress code it was a rule which extended beyond working hours. In an important judgment the Court of Appeal disagreed with EAT and emphasised that *"there is an important distinction between discrimination between the sexes and discrimination against one or the other of the sexes. Discrimination is not failing to treat men and women the same. If discrimination is to be established, it is necessary to show not merely that the sexes are treated differently, but that the treatment accorded to one is less favourable than the treatment accorded to another"*. Appearance codes should be even handed and will not be discriminatory if their content is different *"if they enforce a common principle of smartness or conventionality, and takes as a whole and not garment for garment or item by item, neither gender is treated less favourably in enforcing that principle."* The guide provided by the court therefore is that there should be a package approach to the effect of an appearance code in deciding whether it is discriminatory.

Equal opportunity cases involving dress codes are often given notoriety through the press. Such was the case in a claim brought by Judy Owen, a training manager, against her employer the Professional Golf Association. She maintained that she left her job after only three weeks when she was required to wear a dress rather than the trouser suits that she favoured. A tribunal in Birmingham in January 2000 found that the PGA had discriminated against Mrs Owen by applying standards of dress to women that it did not apply equally to men.

A racial insult, even though overheard by the employee cannot of itself amount to a detriment for the purposes of s.4 of the Race Relations Act, even if it causes the employee distress.

In *De Souza v. Automobile Association* 1986 the Court of Appeal held that before an employee can be said to have been subjected to a 'detriment' it must be found that by reason of the act complained of, *"a reasonable worker would or might take the view that he had been thereby disadvantaged in the circumstances in which he had thereafter to work"*. It is not necessary however to have to show that the result of the discrimination complained of was either dismissal, disciplinary action or the employee leaving or seeking a transfer if *"the discrimination was such that the putative reasonable employee could justifiably complain about his or her working conditions or environment, then whether or not these were so bad as to be able to amount to constructive dismissal or even if the employee was prepared to work on and put up with the harassment. I think this too could contravene the subsection."* Even though the insult here indicated that the applicant may have been thought of less favourably, there was no evidence to suggest that she had been treated less favourably for the purposes of direct discrimination.

An important issue is whether it is possible to be the victim of unlawful discrimination when any employee suffers less favourable treatment for failing to implement an employer's racist policy.

In *Weathersfield Ltd. t/a Van and Truck Rental v. Sargent* 1999 the applicant had obtained a job as a receptionist for a van rental company and was told during her induction that she was to effectively discriminate against potential clients who were from ethnic minorities. Refusing to implement what she felt was a racist policy she left claiming constructive dismissal constituting unlawful discrimination. When she succeeded before the tribunal and the EAT the employer finally appealed to the Court of Appeal claiming firstly that there was no dismissal and secondly if there was less favourable treatment it was not on racial grounds. The court held that an employee is unfavourably treated on racial grounds if they are required to carry out a racially discriminatory policy even though the instruction concerned a different racial group to the complainants. The employee was entitled to leave because of the repudiatory conduct of the employer without notifying the employer of the reason. *"For many employees the more outrageous or embarrassing are the instructions given to them, or suggestions made to them, the less likely they may be to argue the point there and then. They may reasonably wish to remove themselves at the first opportunity and with a minimum of discussion. Leaving the employment without notifying the reason does not preclude a finding of constructive dismissal though it will usually make it more difficult to obtain such a finding."*

A useful tool to attack the credibility of the employer's denial of discrimination is statistical evidence. This is particularly so when the management decisions on matters such as promotion or access to benefits are based upon subjective criteria such as 'excellence', 'potential' or 'efficiency'. In *West Midlands PTE v. Singh* 1988 the Court of Appeal ordered that the employee was entitled to discovery of statistical material relevant to assist the complainant in establishing that the treatment of coloured employees was on racial grounds. Ethnic monitoring is recommended by the Race Relations Code of Practice and *"unless the monitoring was to be merely an academic exercise, there could be no purpose in the Code of Practice encouraging the production of statistics save to use them as some indication of whether racial discrimination was being practised or not".*

In *Clymo v. Wandsworth LBC* 1989 the issue before the EAT was whether the failure to extend job sharing to managerial positions within the respondent council constituted indirect sex discrimination. Both the complainant and her husband were employed as librarians by the defendant council. The complainant had a more senior position with managerial responsibilities and following maternity leave she applied to share her job with her husband so that they could share child care between them. The council's job sharing policy covered non-managerial positions. Her request was consequently refused, and she resigned and presented a claim for unlawful indirect discrimination. Both the industrial tribunal and the EAT rejected the claim. The EAT held that the unavailability of job sharing was not a denial of access to a *'facility'* since no such facility was currently available. Neither was the complainant subjected to a detriment by being refused access to a facility which was not available and the provision of an advantage which is not available to others is not a detriment.

A different attitude was expressed in April 1995 by the Court of Appeal in a claim brought on behalf of Mrs Meade-Hill against her employer the British Council. The court ruled that a mobility clause in her contract was indirectly discriminatory in that a higher proportion of women than men are secondary earners and so find it more difficult in practice to comply with a direction to move house.

Sexual and Racial Harassment

Racial harassment would amount to discrimination on racial grounds and constitute unlawful direct discrimination under the Race Relations Act. Sexual harassment while not referred to specifically in the Sex Discrimination Act has been held to constitute unlawful direct discrimination for which an employer could be made vicariously responsible. The EC Resolution on the Protection of the Dignity of Men and Women at Work defines sexual harassment as conduct of a sexual nature, or other conduct based on sex affecting the dignity of men and women at work which is

- unwanted, unreasonable and offensive to the recipient;

- used as a basis for employment decisions; or

- such as to create an intimidating, hostile or humiliating work environment for the recipient.

The code recommends that employers should facilitate a climate of opinion at work which inhibits sexual harassment. This could involve the issuing of a policy statement which is communicated and promoted through training. Also employers should adopt clear and precise procedures for dealing with complaints including sympathetic counsellors and incorporating independent and objective investigations. A range of conduct which could constitute sexual harassment emerges from the case-law including:

- physical attacks;

- brushing against the victim;

- making suggestive statements or telephone calls;

- pressurising the victim to enter into a sexual relationship;

- sending the victim suggestive material.

Reed and Bull Information Systems Ltd. v. Stedman 1999 was considered in Chapter 4 as an illustration of how the failure of an employer to investigate alleged incidents of sexual harassment constituted a breach of the implied term of trust and confidence. The bullying behaviour of the manager with sexual overtones amounted to harassment as a course of unacceptable and unwelcome conduct which pervaded sexual innuendo and a sexist stance. This was despite the fact that there was no single incident capable of constituting sexual harassment. The view of Mr. Justice Morison the retiring President of the EAT provides helpful guidance to tribunals to identify unlawful sexual harassment. *"The essential characteristic of sexual harassment is that it is words or conduct which are unwelcome to the recipient and it is for the recipient to decide for themselves what is acceptable to them and what they regard as offensive. Because it is for each individual to determine what they find unwelcome or offensive, there may be a gap between what a tribunal would regard as acceptable and what the individual in question was prepared to tolerate. It does not follow that the complaint must be dismissed because the tribunal would not have regarded the acts complained of as unacceptable. It is particularly important that the tribunal should not carve up the case into a series of specific incidents and try and measure the harm or detriment in relation to each. Once unwelcome sexual interest has been shown by a man to a woman, she may feel bothered about his attentions which, in a different context would appear quite unobjectionable. There may be difficult factual issues to resolve as to whether conduct is unwelcome. Some conduct, if not expressly invited, could be described as unwelcome. A woman does not have to make it clear in advance that she does not want to be touched in a sexual manner. At the lower end of the scale, a woman may appear, objectively, to be unduly sensitive to what might otherwise be regarded as unexceptional behaviour. But because it is for each person to define their own levels of acceptance, the question would then be whether by words or conduct she made it clear that she found such conduct unwelcome. Provided that any reasonable person would understand her to be rejecting the conduct of which she was complaining, continuation of the conduct would, generally, be regarded as harassment."*

An employer may be made vicariously liable for the action of his employees committed during the course of employment and this would include sexual or racial harassment constituting unlawful discrimination. In fact if sexual harassment constitutes less favourable treatment under s.1(1)(a) for the purpose of direct discrimination it could also amount to a breach of s.6(2)(b) by *"subjecting her to any other detriment."* Liability for sexual harassment is imposed vicariously on the employer.

Under s.41(1) Anything done by a person in the course of his employment shall be treated for the purposes of this Act as done by his employer as well as by him, whether or not it was done with the employer's knowledge or approval.

(2)   *Anything done by a person as agent for another person with the authority (whether express or implied, and whether precedent or subsequent) of that other person shall be treated for the purposes of this Act as done by that other person as well as by him.*

(3)   *In proceedings brought under this Act against any person in respect of an act alleged to have been done by an employee of his it shall be a defence for that person to prove that he took such steps as were reasonably practicable to prevent the employee from doing that act, or from doing in the course of his employment acts of that description.*

In *Conniffe v. East Riding of Yorkshire Council* 2000 the complainant brought a sex discrimination case against her employer based upon a set of serious acts of sexual harassment by a work colleague. The employer accepted that they were vicariously liable under s.41(1) but sought to establish a s.41(3) defence. They argued that better implementation of policies about sex discrimination and harassment would have had no effect on the criminal assault carried out by the perpetrator and the tribunal agreed. On appeal however the EAT did not believe that the employer had established a s.41(3) defence. *"The proper approach is first to identify whether the respondents took any steps at all to prevent the employee from doing the act or acts complained of in the course of employment and secondly, having identified the steps, to consider whether there were any further acts that they could have taken which were reasonably practicable".*

An action against the harasser could of course be brought in tort and if his conduct constitutes a criminal offence there could be a prosecution. Under the Sex Discrimination Act however he may only be made liable as a secondary party.

This means that if the harasser is acting outside the course of employment the victim could not claim against him under the Sex Discrimination Act. Alternative actions in tort for the victim include assault and battery and more significantly the increasing recognition of a separate tort of harassment. In *Burnett v. George* 1992 the Court of Appeal recognised a separate tort of impairment of health caused by the intentional molestation of another. Here, and in *Khorasandjian v. Bush* 1993 an injunction was granted to restrain threats made by telephone. In the later case the Court of Appeal went some way to recognising a tort of personal injury by molestation.

Under s.42(1) A person who knowingly aids another person to do an act made unlawful by this Act shall be treated for the purposes of this Act as himself doing an unlawful act of the like description.

    (2) For the purposes of subsection (1) an employee or agent for whose act the employer or principal is liable under section 41 (or would be so liable but for section 41(3) shall be deemed to aid the doing of the act by the employer or principal.

Usually the harasser will escape liability under the Act if the employer rebuts the allegation of vicarious liability. However if the employer establishes a s.41(3) defence by showing he has taken reasonably practicable steps to prevent harassment it seems that the harasser could still be liable under s.42(2). So despite the employer's defence, if vicarious liability is established the employee who committed the unlawful act of sex discrimination is liable for it. So held the EAT in *AM v. LWC 2. SPV* 1999 where a police officer was held to be liable for his own discriminatory act.

For the purposes of vicarious liability employment has an extended meaning in s.82(1) so that an employer would be responsible for the actions of self employed workers who were personally executing work or labour such as sales representatives or building workers. The need to establish *"course of employment"* seems to be less onerous in sexual harassment cases and it seems to be sufficient to show that the misconduct occurs during the normal interaction of employees at the workplace. This approach is necessary if women are to be protected at the workplace. It is difficult however to reconcile with the decision in *Irving & Irving v. The Post Office* 1987 (examined in Chapter 5) where a distinction was drawn between the employee who acts in the course of his employment and the employee who takes advantage of the opportunity provided by his employment in order to commit the wrongful act. Now however, as a result of the important decision of the Court of Appeal in *Jones v. Tower Boot* 1997 it seems that in race discrimination cases also the expression *"course of employment"* should be given its *"everyday meaning"* and extend to acts committed during working hours.

In *Chief Constable of the Lincolnshire Police v. Stubbs* 1999 the EAT upheld the tribunal's decision that a police officer was acting in the course of his employment when he subjected a fellow officer to sexual harassment contrary to the Sex Discrimination Act 1975. The EAT found the employer vicariously liable despite the fact that the conduct complained of occurred at social events outside the police station. The tribunal had decided that such gatherings were extensions of the working day and so within the course of employment for purposes of liability.

The victim of sexual harassment at the workplace has a potential claim for unlawful direct sex discrimination, victimisation or even unfair dismissal where appropriate. Under the Trade Union Reform and Employment Rights Act 1993 tribunals can now make restricted reporting orders in cases involving sexual misconduct, to protect the identity of those making or affected by the allegations. Breaking such an order is a criminal offence punishable by a fine of up to £5,000.

To succeed in such a claim the complainant would need to establish that she suffered less favourable treatment on the grounds of her sex which in the words of s.6 caused her a detriment.

In *Porcelli v. Strathclyde Council* 1985 the complainant, a science laboratory technician working in a school claimed that she was sexually harassed by two male technicians. The men's conduct, which was clearly sexual harassment, actually led to her request for a transfer to another school. Nevertheless her complaint of sexual discrimination was rejected by the tribunal on the ground that the men's treatment of her was not related to her sex, but they would have acted in a similar unpleasant way to any male colleague that they had disliked. This surprising decision was thankfully reversed by the EAT who found that the men's conduct, having sexual overtones, constituted to unlawful direct discrimination for which their employer, Strathclyde Regional Council, could be made vicariously liable. The Appeal tribunal stressed however that sexual harassment at work does not of itself amount to unlawful discrimination and it is necessary that the victim should point to a detriment related to her employment such as dismissal, non promotion, or access to training, etc. Here the fact that the complainant was obliged to seek a transfer was a sufficient employment detriment for the purpose of the Act.

Following *Snowball v. Gardner* 1987 the tribunals are more willing to accept that suffering sexual harassment is of itself detrimental to the person concerned and capable of constituting unlawful direct discrimination. The *Porcelli* case also illustrates the fact that where the unlawful act of discrimination is committed by an employee in the course of his employment, the employer is vicariously liable under s.41(1) whether or not the act is done with his approval. It is a defence of course for an employer to show under s.41(3) that he took such steps as were reasonably practicable to prevent the employee from committing the act of discrimination. By implementing the provisions of the EC Code of Practice the employer is more likely to establish a defence. If an individual knowingly aids another to commit an unlawful act of discrimination then that person will be treated as doing the unlawful act himself.

In *Bracebridge Engineering Ltd. v. Derby* 1990 the EAT held that a single act of sexual harassment was a 'detriment' to the complainant within the meaning of s.6 of the Sex Discrimination Act. *"A single incident of sexual harassment, provided it is sufficiently serious, clearly falls within the proper intention and meaning of the statute as it is an act of discrimination against a woman because she is a woman"*. When the act of sexual harassment took place the perpetrators were supposedly engaged in exercising their disciplinary and supervisory function and were consequently within the course of their employment for the purpose of vicarious liability. Here when the employee had left her job because of the treatment she received and her employers failure to treat her allegations seriously, this also amounted to a constructive dismissal which was unfair.

In *Insitu Cleaning Co Ltd. v. Heads* 1995 the EAT considered whether a single act of verbal sexual harassment is sufficient to found a complaint of direct sex discrimination. Here the complaint related to a derogatory remark made by a young male manager in a meeting and directed at the complainant, a female area supervisor. Despite the fact that the remark referred to complainant's breasts the employer argued that it was not sex related and therefore could not amount to direct discrimination. The EAT agreed with the tribunal that the employer was vicariously liable for the sexual harassment which constituted direct sex discrimination. *"The appellant's argument that the remark was not sex-related in that a similar remark could have been made to a man, for example, in relation to a balding head or beard, was absurd. A remark by a man about a woman's breasts cannot sensibly be equated with a remark by a woman about a bald head or a beard. One is sexual, the other is not. The industrial tribunal was entitled to find that the respondent suffered a detriment as a result of the remark. Detriment means no more than disadvantage. For the boss's son to make a sexual remark causing distress to a female employee nearly twice his age was a form of bullying and not acceptable in the workplace in any circumstances. As the European Commission Code of Practice on measures to combat sexual harassment makes clear, such conduct is likely to create an intimidating, hostile and humiliating work environment for the victim."* The EAT confirmed that one incident of verbal sexual harassment can constitute direct discrimination depending on its seriousness.

Unfortunately this eminently sensible view of gender specific words being inherently discriminatory against a female, and different from the abuse of a male, was not followed in *Pearce v. Governing Body of Mayfield Secondary School* 2000. Here a teacher had been driven out of her job by a campaign of homophobic abuse from her pupils. Applying the male comparator test the EAT held that there was no evidence that a male homosexual would have been treated less favourably so that there was no discrimination. This is a view which is disappointing given that many labour theorists would suggest that sexist language or gender specific abuse is inherently or automatically discriminatory.

Normally sex and race discrimination cases require a comparative approach but in harassment scenarios the courts have established an exceptional category where conduct is regarded as *sex or race specific*. (e.g Porcelli, Insitu, Bracebridge). Both the EAT and the Court of Appeal held in *Sidur v. Aeorospace Composite Technology Ltd* 2000 that when the applicant was racially abused and assaulted on a works outing the conduct of the harasser was race specific. The Court of Appeal felt however that when the employer dismissed the applicant as well as the harasser for being violent and so contravened company policy , this was not race specific conduct. This harsh interpretation of the policy however did lead to a finding of unfair dismissal.

It is inevitable that in a claim for sexual harassment the employment tribunal will award compensation for hurt feelings and decide the level that is appropriate whether or not compensation is payable under any other head. In *Sharifi v. Strathclyde DC* 1992 the EAT held that £500 was at or near the minimum for hurt feelings. Certainly conduct which causes distress should be reflected in the level of compensation and substantial awards should be made if the harassment leads to depression, resignation or transfer. In *Cobbold v. Sawyer t/a Immigrants Advisory Bureau* 1993 the complainant was a seventeen year old who walked out of her first job as a result of sexual harassment by her manager. Her claim off sex discrimination was upheld and the meagre award of £150 for hurt feelings was increased by the EAT on appeal to £750.

Increasingly the tribunals are recognising that injury to feelings should be more substantially compensated and that awards should also be made against individually named harassers.

In *Whitehead v. Isle of Wight NHS Trust and Others* 1999 a female paramedic was awarded £67,337 including £37,500 for injury to feelings when she was subjected to sexual harassment and her employers had failed to deal with the problem. She suffered stress and ill health as a result and was awarded £2,500 personally against the harasser.

In *Burton and Rhule v. De Vere Hotels* 1996 the EAT held that two black waitresses who were employees at a hotel had suffered sexual and racial harassment when they were required to work in a banqueting hall during Bernard Manning's performance as guest speaker. Their employer, the hotel, could be held vicariously liable for subjecting the staff to racial abuse and sexual harassment by a third party if the employer had sufficient control to minimise the harm by adopting good employment practice. *"An employer subjects an employee to the detriment of racial harassment if he causes or permits harassment serious enough to amount to a detriment to occur in circumstances in which he can control whether it happens or not. A persons subjects another to something if he causes or allows that thing to happen in circumstances where he can control whether it happens or not. Foresight of the events, or the lack of it, is not determinative of whether the events were under the employer's control."*

Applying this principle the EAT held in *Bennett v. Essex CC* 2000 that a school was responsible for race discrimination in its failure to take reasonable steps to prevent the racial harassment of a black teacher by its pupils.

Unfortunately this was not the case in relation to a lesbian teacher who had regularly suffered homophobic taunts and abuse by pupils. The EAT in *Pearce v. Governing Body of Mayfield Secondary School* 2000 (above) rejected her claim of sex discrimination because there was no evidence that a hypothetical male homosexual teacher would have been treated any differently. The EAT also gave a narrow view of the responsibility of the school for the conduct of its pupils. *"Before finding a school or any similar body to have subjected an employee to discrimination, not only must the steps be identified which the school failed to take and could have taken, but also there must be a conclusion that taking those steps would have prevented or reduced discrimination, so as to hold that the school was guilty of subjecting its employee to discrimination by the absence of those steps being taken".*

Equal Pay

Equal opportunity legislation relating to the sexes was originally contained in the Sex Discrimination Act 1975 and the Equal Pay Act 1970 and while both Acts have been considerably amended, not least because of the UK's membership of the European Community, they still remain the corner stones of equal opportunity law. While the Equal Pay Act is concerned with pay and related matters arising from the contract of employment, as we have seen the sex discrimination legislation covers non financial matters from the contract or any other matter not dealt with in the contract of employment. In cases of doubt a decision as to the relevant legislation must be left to the industrial tribunal.

At present there is still widespread inequality in the way men and women are financially rewarded for the work that they do and general agreement that the status of women must be improved. A conservative interpretation of the equal pay legislation in the courts and a tendency to employ women exclusively in low paid jobs so that comparisons are difficult to make, has meant that the law has provided little assistance in redressing the balance. By restricting the right to equal pay under the Equal Pay Act 1970 to cases where *'like work'* or *'work rated as equivalent'* can be shown, many women in low paid jobs were effectively excluded from a remedy. Despite the introduction of the Equal Pay Amendment Regulations 1983 applicants have still found it necessary to turn to European Community law to maintain a successful claim. Certainly the Treaty of Rome and various European Community Directives have had considerable impact in the field of equal pay.

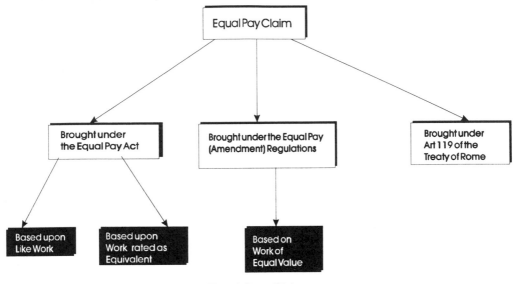

Equal Pay Claims

European Community Law

Article 119 of the Treaty of Rome imposes a requirement of equal pay for equal work and by virtue of the European Communities Act 1972 this Article is directly applicable to the UK. Following the Treaty of Amsterdam this Article is now Article 141. As early as 1976 the European Court of Justice in *Defrenne v. Sabena* ruled that Article 141, which lays down the principle of equal pay for equal work, is directly enforceable by every employee and against every employer throughout the Member States. *Macarthys v. Smith* 1981 also confirmed that Article 141 is directly enforceable in domestic courts who in theory should apply the law of the national state first. In *Pickstone v. Freemans plc* 1988 the House of Lords held that a complainant could rely on domestic or European law in attempting to secure a remedy. There is no doubt that a wide interpretation of equal pay rights is achievable by applying Article 141 rather than the Equal Pay Act (see later in the chapter).

In addition to the Treaty of Rome each member state of the European Community is required to bring its domestic law into line with Community law. As we saw in

Chapter 1 this is achieved mainly by Directives from the European Community outlining the law which member states should then adopt. An example is the Equal Pay Directive which expands the principle of equal pay in Article 141. A failure to incorporate a Directive into domestic law could be pointed out by the European Court of Justice.

In *Commission for the European Communities v. The United Kingdom* 1982 the Commission successfully argued that UK law had not *adopted "the necessary measures"* to adopt the Equal Pay Directive. Under existing British law a worker's claim that work is of equal value would have to be dropped if the employer refused to cooperate by not introducing a job classification system. This decision led to an amendment in UK Equal Pay law by the 1983 Equal Pay Amendment Regulations.

This whole process of effecting change on a reluctant member state by means of EC Directives laying down the law and the state being left with the form and method of implementation can be very drawn out. Attempts have been made therefore to enforce European Directives directly in national courts. The European Court of Justice has ruled that a Directive may be relied on by an individual before a national court where the Directive is *"sufficiently precise and unconditional"*. Such actions however are limited to where the respondent is a government authority acting *"as an employer"*. The rationale for restricting the direct enforcement of European law to government authorities is that it is the member states' responsibility to bring its own domestic law into line and private employers should not be made responsible for that failure.

A Member State of the European Community may not take advantage of its own failure to comply with Community law.

So held the European Court of Justice when asked by the House of Lords to give a preliminary ruling in *Foster and Others v. British Gas plc* 1990. British Gas, a statutory corporation governed by the Gas Act 1972, was privatised by the Gas Act 1986 and its rights and liabilities were transferred to British Gas plc with effect from August 1986. British Gas followed a policy of requiring its employees to retire at an age when under UK law they were entitled to a state pension, 60 for women and 65 for men. The complainants were female employees of British Gas who were required to retire at the earlier age when they wished to continue working. They claimed that their compulsory retirement was contrary to the Equal Treatment Directive on the implementation of the principle of equal treatment without discrimination on the grounds of sex in employment, vocational training and promotion and working conditions. While the dismissals contravened the directive they did not offend UK law, so the issue was whether the Directive could be relied on directly against British Gas. The European Court held that while it had jurisdiction to give a ruling determining the categories of persons against whom the Directive could be relied on it was for the national court to decide whether a party to the proceedings fell within one of those categories. Relying on *Marshall v. Southampton and South-West Area Health Authority* 1986 where it was held that a person could rely on a Directive against the state, the court ruled that *"whenever the provisions of a Directive appeared to be unconditional and sufficiently precise about their subject matter, but implementing measures were not adopted within the prescribed period, the provisions of the Directive could be relied upon as against national provisions which are incompatible with the Directive provisions, or insofar as they defined rights which individuals could assert against the state ... It followed that a body, whatever its legal form, which had been made responsible pursuant to a measure adopted by the state, for providing a public service under the state's control and for that purpose had special powers beyond those which resulted from the normal rules applicable in relations between individuals, was included among the bodies against which the provisions of a Directive having direct effect might be relied upon."*

This directive has been held to be unconditional and sufficiently precise to be relied upon by an individual and applied by the national courts against such a body.

In *Worringham v. Lloyds Bank* 1982 the European Court of Justice ruled that a contribution to a retirement benefits scheme paid by the employer in the name of the employee by addition to his gross salary is pay under Article 141 of the Treaty. This meant that women were to be treated the same as men in relation to the repayment of pension contributions on the termination of employment.

The Equal Pay legislation is not just concerned with pay discrimination but covers discrimination in all aspects of an employees' contract of employment including holiday entitlement and sick leave provision. The definition of *"pay"* under Article 141 is even wider and covers *"the ordinary basic or minimum wage or salary and any other consideration whether in cash or kind, which the worker receives."*

In an extremely important decision the European Court of Justice in *Barber v. Guardian Royal Exchange Assurance Group* 1990 held that pensions are pay within the meaning of the directly enforceable provisions of Article 141 of the Treaty of Rome. This means that an occupational pensions scheme that discriminates on the grounds of sex and offends Article 141 may be declared unlawful.

The dramatic impact of the above ruling therefore is that pension benefits cannot discriminate on the grounds of sex, and any condition differing according to sex contravenes Article 141. Pensions must now be equated with pay and if rates are determined by gender criteria they are now unlawful. People must be treated as individuals rather than members of gender groupings so that in determining pay and pensions the fact that statistically women live longer, or take more sick leave than men, should be disregarded in determining levels of sick pay or pension benefits. Also despite the present difference in the State pension age, as a result of this case, pension ages under occupational schemes must be equalised. The court further confirmed that the Treaty takes precedence over Directives so that Social Security Directives which permitted the implementation of equal treatment in occupational pension schemes to be deferred, are consequently overridden by the decision. Finally the court has decided that the principle of equal pay applies to each element of remuneration and is not satisfied by a comprehensive assessment of overall pay. This means that differences in contractual terms between men and women employed on equal work cannot be offset against each other. Applying the equality clause therefore, each aspect of the contract of employment must be equalised.

Equal Pay Act Claims

The main objective of the Equal Pay Act 1970 is to secure equal treatment for men and women in the same employment in relation to terms and conditions of employment. Originally certain terms were excluded from the operation of the Act including those affected by laws relating to the employment of women. In fact such laws are gradually being removed for example by the Sex Discrimination Act 1986 and the Employment Act 1989. Terms *"affording special treatment to women in connection with pregnancy or childbirth"* are still outside the province of the Act and so a man has no right to paternity leave (other than unpaid parental leave) in circumstances where a woman is entitled to maternity leave. Also, terms *"related to death or retirement, or to any provision made in connection with death or retirement"* are also excluded. This would not cover terms related to the *"membership of an occupational pension scheme"*.

The mechanism by which the Equal Pay Act attempts to achieve its objectives is the *'equality clause'*. The Equal Pay Act is one of the few employment law statutes that actually implies a term into a contract of employment. Under the Act *if the terms of a contract under which a woman is employed at an establishment in Great Britain do not include (directly or by reference to a collective agreement or otherwise) an equality clause they shall be deemed to include one.*

Under the equality clause a woman has the right to equal pay with a man if either:

- she is employed on *'like work'* with a man in the same employment;

- she is employed doing *'work rated as equivalent'* with a man following a job evaluation study; or

- she is employed to do work of *'equal value'* with a man in the same employment in terms of the demand placed upon her.

There are therefore three avenues upon which a claim could be based, *'like work'*, *'work related or equivalent'* or *'equal value'*. Equal value was introduced by the Equal Pay Amendment Regulations 1983. A claim based on equal value can only be considered where there is no basis for a claim on *'like work'* or *'work rated as equivalent'*. The starting point for a claimant under the Equal Pay Act is to identify an individual male 'comparator' with whom she wishes to claim equal pay. This man must be employed on work which is the same or broadly similar to her own (like work or work rated as equivalent).

Like Work

The problem of using the concept 'like work' as a criterion for achieving fair treatment for women at the workplace, is that in fact large numbers of women workers are often at establishments where there are no male employees upon which to draw comparisons. Accordingly, the definition of 'like work' has been given a 'broad brush approach' interpretation by courts and tribunals.

Section 1(4) provides that a *"woman is to be regarded as employed in like work with men if, but only if, her work and theirs is of the same or a broadly similar nature and the differences (if any) between the things she does and the things they do are not of practical importance in relation to terms and conditions of employment: and accordingly in comparing her work and theirs regard shall be had to the frequency or otherwise with which any such differences occur in practice as well as to the nature and extent of the differences"*.

Insignificant differences in work and vague or unrealistic responsibilities are to be ignored therefore, in deciding whether individuals are engaged in like work.

In *Electrolux v. Hutchinson* 1977 female workers engaged in broadly similar work to their male counterparts were held to be entitled to equal pay, despite that the men alone would be required to work overtime, at weekends or at night. The fact that the men were rarely called on to do extra work was a major consideration.

The decision as to whether similar work is being carried on demands not a comparison between the contractual obligations of the parties, but rather a consideration of the things actually done and the frequency with which they are done.

In *Coomes (Holdings) Ltd. v. Shields* 1978 the female counter clerks in bookmakers shops were paid a lesser rate of pay than their male counterparts. The employers sought to justify the differences on the grounds that the male employees had extra duties, including acting as a deterrent to unruly customers and transporting cash between branches. The Court of Appeal held that, in deciding the question as to *'like work'*, it was necessary to consider the differences between the things the men and women were required to do. Furthermore, it was necessary to consider the frequency with which such differences occur in practice. Finally, the court must consider whether the differences are of any practical importance. This approach should enable the court to place a value on each job in terms of demands placed upon the worker, and if the value of the man's job is higher he should be paid an increased rate for the job. In the present case the differences were not of sufficient importance to justify a different rate of pay.

In *Thomas v. National Coal Board* 1987 the EAT held that for the purposes of determining 'like work' there was no implicit requirement that a selected male comparator should be representative of a group. It was possible therefore to compare the terms and conditions of female canteen assistants with the only male canteen attendant. The EAT also held however that the tribunal was entitled to find that the additional responsibility of the male attendant in working permanently at night alone, and without supervision, was a *"difference of practical importance in relation to terms and conditions of employment"* and so not *'like work'* for the purposes of the Act.

Work Rated as Equivalent

The second means by which an equality clause will operate is if the employer has carried out a job evaluation study or work rating exercise and the women's work is rated as equivalent to that of a man employed at the same establishment. The study must be carried out in accordance with the Act which provides in s.1(5) that *"a woman is to be regarded as employed on work rated as equivalent with that of any men, if but only if, her job and their job have been given an equal value in terms of the demands made on a worker under various headings (effort, skill, decision making etc.) on a study undertaken with a view to evaluating in those terms the jobs to be done by all or any of the employees in an undertaking or group of undertakings"*.

To maintain an equal pay claim based upon job evaluation therefore it is necessary that a valid study has been carried out adopting one of the principal job evaluation methods laid down by ACAS. The fact that both trade unions generally and a number of employers are wary of job evaluation studies and there is still doubt as to whether an employer is bound to implement a scheme which has been carried out, means that equal pay claims based on work rated as equivalent are relatively rare.

The Comparison

For both *'like work'* and *'work rated as equivalent'* it is left to the woman rather than her employer, to choose the male comparator but such a person must be typical and cannot be a hypothetical person. The comparison could even be with the man whom the woman replaced provided there was only a short break between this occurring. Both the applicant and the comparator must be employed which includes employees and contractors providing personal services.

A further requirement is that the comparison must be between the applicant and another in the *'same employment'* which would include the same establishment. Comparison with an individual employed by the same or associated employer at a different establishment is also permissible provided common terms and conditions of employment are observed at both establishments.

> In *Leverton v. Clwyd County Council* 1988 the complainant, a nursery nurse, sought to compare herself with higher paid clerical staff employed at different establishments by the council. To prevent a comparison the employers argued that common terms and conditions of employment were not observed for the relevant employees despite the fact that they were covered by the same collective agreement. In particular the nurses worked a 32.5 hour week and had 70 days annual holiday compared with the comparator's 37 hour week and 20 days basic holiday. Both the tribunal and the EAT felt that these differences were sufficient to defeat the contention that there were common terms of employment observed at the different establishments and so the claim failed. By a majority the Court of Appeal agreed. *"Although common terms and conditions of employment does not mean 'identical' terms and conditions, as that would defeat the whole purpose of the legislation, there must be a sufficient element of common identity to enable a proper comparison to be made".*

The above case gives considerable support to the notion of cross establishment comparison where the applicant and the comparator are covered by the same collective agreement. This is particularly significant in the public sector where national agreements prevail and even in the private sector where employers have multi-site operations and employees with standard terms and conditions of employment.

> In *British Coal Corporation v. Smith* 1996 the House of Lords considered s.1(6) in relation to a claim by female canteen workers and cleaners for equal

pay for work of equal value where the comparators were surface mineworkers or clerical workers employed at different establishments. The court found that the cleaners were in the "same employment" as their male comparators because they were "common terms and conditions of employment" despite minor differences. It is sufficient, the court stated *"for the applicant to show that her comparators at another establishment and at her establishment were or would be employed on broadly similar terms. Whether any differences between the woman and the man selected as the comparators are justified depends on s.1(3), where the onus is on the employer. It would be far too restrictive a test to exclude the inquiry under s.1(3) unless the terms and conditions of the men at the relevant establishments were common in the sense of identical"*.

Earlier we said that an equal pay claim based on Article 141 may be easier to establish then relying on the Equal Pay Act. Certainly a claim based on the Act relies heavily on the complainant identifying an appropriate male comparator. A claim under Article 141 can have a broader basis however and the European Court in *Handels-og Kontorfunktion-aerenes Forbund i Danmark v. Dansk Arbejdsgiverforening (acting for Danfoss)* 1989 said that the complainant must establish a prima facie case of discrimination and usually reliable statistical evidence of average pay differences will suffice. It is then left to the employer to explain the differences on non discriminatory grounds. It is the industrial tribunal which must determine the validity and reliability of the statistical evidence and whether a good explanation is put forward by the employer. The onus under Article 141 falls on the employer to provide employees with as much information as possible about their pay systems showing how pay increments are obtained and how job evaluation and performance related pay schemes operate. In *Diocese of Hallam Trustee v. Connaughton* 1996 the EAT held that under Article 141 it was possible for a woman to compare her pay with her male successor.

Equal Value

In cases where the provisions of *'like work'* and *'work rated as equivalent'* do not apply, a further option is to rely on an equality clause based on work of equal value added by the Equal Pay (Amendment) Regulations 1983. The equal value route is crucial in achieving the goal of equal pay for there are numerous areas of work even of a professional nature, which tend to be female dominated with relatively low rates of pay. Under the regulations a woman is employed on work, which is, in terms of the demands made on her (for instance under such headings as effort, skill and decision making), of equal value to that of a man in the same employment. In such circumstances the equality clause has the effect of modifying less favourable terms in the woman's contract to bring them in line with the man's contract and inserting any beneficial terms in a man's contract into the woman's contract of employment.

If a complaint is presented, the tribunal has no jurisdiction to hear the case unless it is satisfied either that there are no reasonable grounds for determining that the work is of equal value or it has required a member of the panel of independent experts to prepare a report with respect to that question and has received that report. The panel is designated by the Advisory, Conciliation and Arbitration Service (ACAS) but must not comprise officers or members of that body.

There would be no reasonable grounds for determining that the work is of equal value if different values have been given to the work and that of the male comparator following a study and there is no evidence that the evaluation was made on a system which discriminated on the grounds of sex.

In *Bromley v. H J Quick Ltd.* 1987 the employer had commissioned an independent job evaluation study under which grading boundaries were decided. Despite a different ranking under the study, a number of female clerical workers brought an equal value complaint comparing their work to male managers. The tribunal decided that because of the job evaluation study there were no reasonable grounds for determining that the work was of equal value. On appeal on behalf of the women it was argued that the job evaluation did not fall within the requirement of the regulations because the study in question was non analytical and the regulation demanded an analysis of the characteristics of each job. It was also argued that if there was any ground for alleging discrimination which cannot be dismissed, the tribunal must refer the case to an independent expert. Both arguments were rejected by the EAT. Stressing that it was necessary for a tribunal to examine carefully the job evaluation scheme upon which the employer relies, the EAT felt that the study in question, although having blemishes, was valid. *"Although systems which are not analytical and which are based on a 'felt fair' hierarchy or a paired comparison on a 'whole job' basis are much more vulnerable to sex discrimination, the proposition that any job evaluation study which is not analytical is thereby invalid , could not be accepted".*

In *Springboard Sunderland Trust v. Robson* 1992 the EAT held that where a job evaluation scheme has been used as a basis for a grading structure then jobs which fall within the same grade should attract the same pay. This is despite the fact there may be wide variations within the grade and yet minimal differences at the boundaries of the grades.

An important equal value claim considered by the House of Lords was the decision in *Hayward v. Cammell Laird Shipbuilders Ltd.* 1988. Here a female canteen assistant, employed at a shipyard, claimed that she was doing work of equal value to male comparators, who were shipyard workers paid at the higher rate for skilled tradesmen in the yard. An independent evaluation convinced the tribunal that the women's work was of equal value. However when comparing all her terms and conditions of employment with the male comparator which revealed a free canteen lunches and two additional days holiday, the tribunal found that she was not entitled to a higher rate of pay. The approach was upheld by the EAT and the Court of Appeal but on final appeal to the House of Lords, the decision was reversed. The Lords suggested that individual contractual terms should be compared with similar provisions in the comparator's contract and a decision reached as to their respective merits. One such term related to pay, and a comparison could be drawn between the complainant's basic pay and the male comparator's. Despite the fact that when looked at as a whole, the complainant's contract was no less favourable.

The above ruling suggests therefore that if a woman can point to a term of her contract which is less favourable than a term of a similar one in the man's contract she is entitled to have that term made not less favourable irrespective of whether she is less favourably treated as a whole.

The important decision of the European Court of Justice in *Enderby v. Frenchay Health Authority* 1993 has gone some way to remove some of the obstacles facing women seeking equal pay for equal value. The claim was brought by the complainant, a NHS speech therapist, a profession dominated by women, who sought pay comparable with NHS clinical psychologists and principal pharmacists, professions which were male dominated. The EAT struck out the claim finding no direct discrimination and holding that the level of pay was dictated by collective bargaining arrangements. The European Court rejected this view however and proposed a more realistic burden of proof for those attempting to establish equal value claims. The complainant is required to establish a prima facie case and can do this by showing that the work is of equal value, that there is a significant pay differential, and that the lower paid workers are almost exclusively women and the higher paid are men. The burden then shifts to the employer to show that the pay differential is based on objectively justified factors unrelated to sex discrimination.

In *Enderby v. Frenchay Health Authority and Secretary of State for Health* 2000 the Court of Appeal made an important policy on the consequences of making an equal value finding. The issue in dispute was whether an equality clause under s.1(2) should operate so that the relevant term of the woman's contract of employment "should be treated as so modified as to be no less favourable" than her male comparator so that her salary should mirror the comparator on the incremental pay scale. The alternative argument was that having decided that the speech therapist should be put on the higher incremental scale, then they should be placed at the incremental point commensurate with their years of service. The Court of Appeal agreed that the claimant should mirror her comparator on the incremental pay scale and therefore enter the scale at the lower point rather than at a more favourable point. The fact that the speech therapist had greater length of service and experience played a significant part in her establishing that she was doing work of equal value to her comparator and was entitled to equal pay.

Defence

At this point it is convenient to consider the main defence to an equal pay claim. An equality clause shall not operate in relation to a variation between the woman's contract if the employer proves that the variation is genuinely due to a material factor which is not the difference of sex. If the claim is based on an equality clause relying on *'like work'* or *'work rated as equivalent'* then there must be a material difference between the woman's case and the man's for the defence to operate. For claims based on equal value however, it is slightly different and the factor may be a material difference.

In *Snoxell and Davies v. Vauxhall Motors* 1977 the EAT held that an employer cannot establish a defence, that the variation between the woman's contract and the man's contract was genuinely due to a material difference between her case and his, when it can be seen that past discrimination has contributed to the variation. Even if the original discrimination occurred before the effective date of the Act *"it cannot have been the intention of the legislation to permit the perpetuation of the effect of the earlier discrimination".*

Genuine material differences would include a consideration of factors such as the place of employment or academic qualifications of the individual involved.

In *Rainey v. Greater Glasgow Health Board* 1987 the House of Lords held that the word 'material' means 'significant and relevant' and the difference had to be between the woman's case and the man's. The decision involves a consideration of all the relevant circumstances and they might go beyond personal qualifications, skill, experience or training. It could be that the difference was reasonably necessary to achieve some result such as economic necessity or administrative efficiency and was not directly related to the personal characteristics of the individual involved.

In *R v. Secretary of State for Social Services and Others ex parte Clarke and Others* 1988 speech therapists sought to compare their work to that of clinical psychologists and pharmacists. The response of their employer, the Health Authority was to point to the National Health Service (Remuneration and Conditions of Service) Regulations 1974 which provide that officers' remuneration which has been negotiated and approved by the appropriate body is the sum payable and the employer was bound to pay the salary in accordance with the Regulations. Even if their work was of equal value, the pay variation was *"genuinely due to a material factor which is not the difference of sex"*, the material factor being the requirement that the employers comply with the Regulations. On a judicial review of the tribunal's decision, the Divisional Court of the Queen's Bench Division held that the mere fact that the applicants' pay had been approved under Regulation did not provide a defence to an equal pay claim. Whether an employer had satisfied the defence required evidence and the simple assertion that the employers were bound by law to pay the salaries was not enough.

A complaint in relation to equal pay may be presented to a tribunal by an individual, an employer and in certain circumstances, by the Secretary of State for Employment. If the tribunal finds that a claim has been established, it can make a declaration to that effect and award up to two years' back pay to the successful applicant. The burden of proof rests with the complainant and it is for the employer to an establish a defence.

The two year limit on arrears of remuneration under the Equal Pay Act was held by the EAT in *Levez v. T H Jennings (Harlow Pools) Ltd.* (No 2) 1999 to be in breach of Article 141 and therefore unenforceable. Individuals who are successful in equal pay claims may therefore be able to claim up to six years back pay in accordance with the general limitation period.

Maternity Rights

A pregnant employee has a number of statutory rights:

- the right not to be dismissed for pregnancy or a reason connected with it or to suffer a detriment;

- the right to maternity pay;

- the right to return to work after her pregnancy or childbirth;

- the right to time off for ante-natal care.

Since the mid 1970s pregnant employees have had security of employment rights. In the UK while we have the longest maternity leave period in the European Union our Statutory Maternity Pay Scheme is one of the least generous. There is now some provision for paternity rights introduced by the Employment Relations Act 1999. In addition under the 1999 Act a new right not to suffer a detriment on the grounds of pregnancy, childbirth or maternity has been inserted as s.47C of the Employment

Rights Act 1996. The rights provide an alternative to claim for sex discrimination and should provide wider protection covering detrimental treatment.

The right to maternity leave and pay was first introduced in the Employment Protection Act 1975 as amended by the Employment Act 1980. The law is now contained in the Employment Rights Act 1996.

Despite the very basic nature of the right to maternity pay and leave, legislative provisions governing the right are difficult to interpret and were described by Browne-Wilkinson J as of *"inordinate complexity, exceeding the worst excesses of a taxing statute"*. He further observed that this was especially regrettable bearing in mind that they are regulating the rights of ordinary employers and employees.

The ERA 1996 provides that if a woman has a contractual right to maternity leave in addition to the statutory right, then it is the most favourable right that should be exercised.

Pregnancy Dismissal

If an employee is dismissed because of her pregnancy then this will constitute unlawful sex discrimination under s.6(2) of the Sex Discrimination Act 1975.

A dismissal because of the employee's pregnancy or because of a reason connected with the employee's pregnancy would also constitute automatically unfair dismissal under s.99 of the Employment Rights Act 1996 and this applies regardless of the length of service of the employee

A dismissal is automatically unfair if the reason for it is either:

- that she is pregnant or a reason connected with pregnancy such as a miscarriage;

- that she has given birth or a reason connected with the birth and she was dismissed during maternity leave;

- that she took maternity leave;

- that she gave the employer a medical certificate stating she was incapable of work after the end of the maternity period and her contract was terminated within four weeks of the end of maternity leave;

- that she is suspended from work on maternity grounds;

- that she was made redundant during maternity leave and without an offer of suitable alternative employment.

The expression *'any reason connected with pregnancy'* was given a wide interpretation by the House of Lords in a judgment on earlier legislation which emphasises the importance of this statutory right.

In *Brown v. Stockton on Tees* BC 1988, the complainant was a care supervisor who, along with three others, was told that her employment would terminate on a given date. All four staff were given the opportunity of applying for three posts, each of one years duration, and they all applied. The complainant who was pregnant at the time of her interview was the unsuccessful candidate and so the only one made redundant. This was despite the fact that there was no criticism of her work and one of the successful candidates had less service with the council. While she successfully claimed unfair dismissal before the industrial tribunal the decision was reversed by the EAT and the Court of Appeal. Both appellate bodies upheld the decision to dismiss on the grounds that the employer had acted reasonably and fairly for the purpose of s.57(3) and this was the appropriate section where the principal reason for dismissal was redundancy. The House of Lords disagreed, however. Their Lordships held that the dismissal contravened the Act as automatically unfair where the reason for dismissal is that the complainant is pregnant or in any other reason connected with her pregnancy. Ld Griffiths in reviewing the history of equal opportunities legislation said *that "it must be seen as a part of social legislation passed for the specific protection of women and to put them on an equal footing with men".* While recognising the inconvenience caused to employers in coping with maternity leave and security of employment, he said that *"it is part of the price that has to be paid as a part of the social and legal recognition of the equal status of women in the work place. If an employer dismisses a woman because she is pregnant and he is not prepared to make arrangements to cover her temporary absence form work he is deemed to have dismissed her unfairly. There is no reason why the same principle should not apply if in a redundancy situation an employer selects the pregnant woman as the victim of redundancy in order to avoid the inconvenience of covering her absence from work in the new employment he is able to offer others who are threatened with redundancy".*

In *Intelligent Applications v. Wilson* 1992 the applicant's absence during maternity leave revealed a genuine redundancy situation when it became obvious that her work could be carried out by existing staff. She claimed unfair dismissal when she was notified that she was being dismissed for redundancy because of over capacity. The EAT agreed with the tribunal that this dismissal was automatically unfair because the reason for dismissal was connected with her pregnancy. The connection arose because the redundancy originally occurred as a result of the reallocation of duties and this came about because of the maternity leave which of course was granted due to her pregnancy.

Failure to consult in a redundancy situation where the redundant employee was on maternity leave was a feature in *McGuigan v. T A Baynes & Sons* 1997. Following a selection exercise a female solicitor was chosen for redundancy while on maternity leave and the EAT held that the dismissal was both unfair and constituted direct sex discrimination. But for her pregnancy the employer would have consulted her and less favourable treatment on the grounds of pregnancy did not require a male comparator.

In *Caledonia Bureau Investment and Property v. Caffrey* 1998 the complainant failed to return to work at the end of her 14 week maternity leave because of post-natal depression and submitted a medical certificate. When her illness ran to six weeks her employer dismissed her on the grounds of ill health with pay in lieu of notice. She complained of unfair dismissal and sex discrimination and succeeded on both counts in the employment tribunal. On appeal the EAT held that her dismissal for failing to return to work on the expiration of her maternity leave due to post-natal depression was for a reason connected with her pregnancy within the meaning of the ERA s.99 and automatically unfair. The EAT confirmed that the section is not limited to dismissals during the pregnancy and maternity leave but also where the contract of employment has been expressly extended. Such a dismissal was also held to be unlawful sex discrimination. *"Where a woman is dismissed by reason of an illness which is related to being pregnant, or having given birth, which illness arises or emerges during the course of the maternity leave period, the dismissal is still discriminatory even though it takes place after the expiry of that period, on the basis that at the time of dismissal she suffered from an illness from which a man could not suffer and thus was treated differently from her male counterparts".*

A dismissal by reason of pregnancy is unlawful under the Sex Discrimination Act 1975 and would also infringe the Equal Treatment directive.

In *Shomer v. B & R Residential Lettings Ltd.* 1992 the Court of Appeal considered a complaint of sex discrimination by a complainant who claimed that she had been dismissed on account of her pregnancy. Employed as a negotiator the complainant had been provided with a company car but she disobeyed a clear instruction by the managing director to deliver up the car for her employer's use while she was aboard on holiday. When she returned from holiday she found she had received a notice of dismissal. Her complaint of sex discrimination was based on the fact that prior to the holiday the complainant had informed the managing director that she was pregnant and this she alleged was the true reason for the dismissal. The Court of Appeal disagreed with the majority finding of the industrial tribunal that there was unlawful discrimination The Court confirmed that the for determining sex discrimination was to ask *"whether the woman would have received the same treatment as a man but for her sex. A tribunal is entitled to find discrimination even if there is not direct evidence, if there is some evidence from which they can properly draw an inference that a woman has been dismissed because of her pregnancy, whereas she would not be dismissed were she not pregnant and a man in comparable circumstances would not have been dismissed".* All the circumstances should be taken into account in drawing the hypothetical comparison including in a case such as this the fact that there was serious misconduct. If a hypothetical man would have been dismissed for such misconduct there was no discrimination and the tribunal's decision could be regarded as perverse.

The European Court of Justice has now cast doubt on this approach and it now seems that despite the fact that pregnancy is unique to one sex, unfavourable treatment on the grounds of pregnancy is automatically discrimination on the grounds of sex. There is no longer any need to compare the treatment of a pregnant woman with that of a hypothetical male. Such a ruling greatly strengthens the position of women so that a refusal to employ a woman because of the financial costs of the pregnancy can no longer be justified. This decision was reached in a Dutch case called *Dekker v. Stichting Vormingscentrum Voor Jonge Volwassenen (VJV Centrum)* 1991 (mentioned previously) and this interpretation of the Equal Treatment Directive should be followed by national courts in Britain.

In *Webb v. EMO Air Cargo* 1994 the European Court of Justice was called upon to give a ruling on the issue. The complainant had been employed by a small firm to replace an employee who was due to take maternity leave in six months time. It was envisaged that the complainant could become a permanent employee but when three months after starting work she also became pregnant the employer decided to dismiss her. The English domestic courts including the House of Lords had held that if a comparable man had been recruited in similar circumstances and became unavailable for work for a similar period due to some medical reason he would also have been dismissed. On that basis there was no unlawful discrimination under the 1975 Act. The European Court however held that there could be no question of comparing the situation with that of a man. Pregnancy was not in any way comparable with a pathological condition there being a clear distinction between pregnancy and illness. The termination of the complainant's employment contract on the grounds of her pregnancy could not be justified by the fact that she was prevented on a purely temporary basis from performing the work for which she had been engaged. It is unlawful therefore for an employer to recruit an employee for an indefinite period and then dismiss her when she becomes pregnant, even if she was initially employed to replace another pregnant employee.

In the light of this ruling by the European Court however the House of Lords finally decided in her favour in *Webb v. EMO Air Cargo (UK) Ltd. (No 2)* 1995. A decision to dismiss by reason of pregnancy therefore will constitute direct discrimination and given that the maximum level of compensation has been removed in sex discrimination cases it could provide a more significant remedy than unfair dismissal.

The EAT in *O'Neill v. Governors of St Thomas More RCVA Upper School* 1996 upheld a complaint of unfair discrimination against a school which had dismissed a religious instruction teacher during her maternity leave when it became known that the father of her child was the local Roman Catholic priest. The EAT rejected the contention that the motive for the dismissal was the paternity of the child and the applicants position at the school. These reasons it was held were all related to the pregnancy which was the dominant reason for the dismissal.

The EAT also held in *Caruana v. Manchester Airport* 1996 that the failure to renew a fixed term contract on the grounds that the applicant would not be available for work due to her pregnancy constituted sex discrimination. Here the new contract was an extension of a continuing employment relationship and to disqualify it from the protection of discrimination law *"would be a positive encouragement to employers to impose a series of short term contracts to avoid the impact of discrimination law, rather than offer a continuous and stable employment relationship"*. The applicant in this case was self employed and did not therefore qualify for protection under unfair dismissal law.

If the underlying cause of the dismissal is the fact that the employee is absent on maternity leave that will constitute unlawful sex discrimination. In *Rees v. Apollo Watch Repairs Plc* 1996 the complainant secretary was dismissed while on maternity leave because her employer found that her temporary replacement was more efficient. The EAT applied the decision of the House of Lords in *Webb (No 2)* and rejecting the test of the comparable male found the dismissal constituted discrimination on the grounds of sex. *"The protection afforded to women on maternity leave would be drastically curtailed if an employer was able to defeat a complaint of direct discrimination by a woman who, during such absence, discovers that her employer prefers her replacement, a state of affairs which has arisen solely as a result of her pregnancy and therefore of her sex"*.

If the tribunal finds reasons for dismissal other than pregnancy then it could decide there has been no discrimination.

In *Berrisford v. Woodward Schools Ltd.* 1991 the complainant, a matron at a girls boarding school run by a Church, was dismissed when she informed the headmaster that she was pregnant but had no plans to marry. The decision to dismiss was taken, it was agreed not because the matron was pregnant, but because her pregnancy demonstrated extra-marital sex. As male employees at the school were subject to the same code of conduct a majority of the EAT held that the tribunal was entitled to find that the dismissal was not discriminatory. There was no less favourable treatment as *"evidence of extra-marital sexual activity would have been treated as a ground for dismissal just as much in a man as in a woman."* Furthermore as the dismissal was not for pregnancy, without more it was not in breach of the EC Equal Treatment Directive.

Maternity Leave

The right to secure employment for a pregnant employee has been embodied within legislation for a quarter of a century. Numerous amendments to the maternity rule have added to their complexity but recently under the Employment Relations Act 1999 an attempt has been made to simplify the rules and the procedure. As the new rules relating to maternity leave are being introduced during the year 2000 it is proposed to consider maternity leave in the light of the change that they introduce. For the present maternity rights are conferred on employees and not the self employed or workers, and under the Employment Protection (Part-Time Employees) Regulations 1995 the right to maternity leave now extends to part-time employees also. If an employee had a contractual right to maternity leave which is more beneficial than the statutory rights then the employee can take advantage of the most beneficial right.

In schedule 4 of the Employment Relations Act 1999 an attempt has been made to strengthen and simplify maternity rights. The new rules are inserted into the Employment Rights Act 1996 as Part VIII replacing ss71-75 and supplemented by the Maternity and Parental Leave Regulations 1999. It is the regulations that contain the details of the new rules. Those employees whose expected childbirth is 30 April 2000 or later should benefit from the new rules. As yet maternity rights are limited to employees but the Secretary of State does have power under the 1999 Act to extend such rights to workers.

A distinction is made in the new rules between ordinary maternity leave and additional maternity leave. All pregnant employees have the right to 18 weeks ordinary maternity leave (previously 14) in line with the Statutory Maternity Pay period of 18 weeks. With one year's continuous service at the 11th week before the expected date of childbirth a pregnant employee is entitled to take maternity leave of up to 29 weeks after the birth of the child (additional maternity leave).

There remain procedural rules relating to claiming maternity leave but there has been some relaxation of the formality. To trigger ordinary or additional leave the employee must give at least 21 days notice to her employer:

- that she is pregnant;

- of the expected week of childbirth;

- the date she intends to start her maternity leave.

If requested the employee should also produce a medical certificate.

There is no requirement that the 21 day notice should be in writing unless requested but it still makes sense to rely on written notice. The leave period cannot begin earlier than the 11th week before the expected week of childbirth. At this stage there is no longer a requirement that the woman has to give notice that she intends to take additional maternity leave. It is assumed that she will take leave until she notifies her employer of the date she intends to return to work.

Under regulation 5 of the Maternity and Parental Leave Regulations 1999 the leave may start:

- by notification (as above);

- on the first day after the beginning of the sixth week before the expected week of childbirth where the employee is absent wholly or partially because of pregnancy;

- with the birth of the child.

Under s.71 the ordinary leave period is 18 weeks but for those qualified for additional leave it will run for 29 weeks.

It should be stressed that failure to give proper notice in no longer fatal but without it absence would be regarded as unauthorised and this could constitute a disciplinary matter.

Under s.72 it is an offence for an employer to permit an employee to work during a compulsory maternity leave period which is a minimum of two weeks prior to the birth.

During the ordinary maternity leave period, other than remuneration the employee is entitled to the full benefit of all terms and conditions of employment with the exception of remuneration as if she had not been absent. The regulations clarify that the term remuneration is limited to *"sums payable by way of wages or salary"*. This means that a woman on maternity leave would still be entitled to receive a performance bonus which is not salary and retain other benefits such as a company car or a mobile phone. Significantly the contract of employment continues into the additional leave period for the purposes of good faith and express obligations of confidentiallity and exclusivity. During the ordinary leave period employees are entitled to statutory maternity pay subject to the qualifying conditions.

The Right to Return to Work

The position is straightforward in relation to ordinary maternity leave for there is an assumption that the employee will return to her original job and no notice is required. If a woman wishes to return to work either before the end of the ordinary or additional maternity leave periods she must give the employer 21 days notice. Once the date of birth is known then the 29 additional leave weeks can be calculated if it is relevant. There are notification provisions in relation to additional leave bearing in mind that the mother may have a change of heart and employers need to plan ahead. Not earlier than 21 days before the end of the ordinary leave period the employer may request written notification of:

1. the date of birth; and

2. whether she intends to return to work after the additional maternity leave.

There is a request to reply with 21 days but failure to do so will not result in a loss of rights but could constitute a disciplinary matter.

Previously a woman who suffered a detriment because she took maternity leave would have had to present a complaint of sex discrimination. Now the regulations extend the right to complain to a tribunal because of detrimental treatment by an employer because a woman:

- is pregnant or has given birth;

- has taken the benefit of ordinary or extended maternity leave;

- has taken time off for ante-natal care;

- is subject to a relevant statutory recommendation (e.g. a risk assessment).

The right to return from ordinary leave is to the original job on terms and conditions which are less favourable. The right to return after additional leave is to a job of a *'prescribed kind'* which will be the subject of regulations.

Parental Leave

In Chapter 1 the EU Parental Leave Directive was used as an example of the impact of signing up to the Social Chapter in 1997. The right to parental leave was inserted into the Employment Rights Act 1996 by the Employment Relations Act 1999 and the detail is contained in the Maternity and Parental Leave Regulations. The regulations contain the key elements of parental leave which will apply to all qualifying employees with the aim of encouraging employers to draw up their own schemes to suit the needs of their organisations. A contractual scheme that is in force prior to the regulations will continue to be binding in so far as it is equivalent to or more favourable than the statutory scheme. The model scheme in the regulations will apply as a default scheme is the employer fails to produce their own.

The right extends to employees with one years continuous employment who have responsibility for a child and the leave is for the purpose of "caring for that child". The birth certificate will normally provide evidence of the employees responsibility for children born or adopted after 15 December 1999. The key age is up to five years from birth or adoption and the amount of leave is 13 weeks for each child. Under the regulations employees may take a minimum of one week at a time up to four weeks in one year. A minimum of four weeks notice of intention to take two weeks parental leave must be given and longer notice for longer periods of leave. Because the leave is an entitlement granted in respect of the child an employee who changes employer without having taken the full leave entitlement may transfer any remaining leave to the new employer. Before taking that leave however the employee would have to requalify by working for a full year for the new employer.

Employers cannot refuse to grant leave but may postpone it for up to six months if the operation of the business would be substantially prejudiced if the employee took leave during the period identified in the notice. The contract of employment continues during the period of the leave in particular implied terms relating to trust and confidence and confidential information continue to apply but there is no right to be paid. The employee is entitled to the benefit of terms and conditions which would have applied had not he not been absent. There is a right not to suffer a detriment or be dismissed for taking parental leave.

Obviously the right to parental leave is an excellent example of a family friendly provision in employment law its major weakness is the fact that the leave is unpaid and a reduction in the earning capacity of a parent at the time of childbirth necessarily decreases its value.

Maternity Pay

In the case of maternity pay, it is also necessary for the woman to notify the employer, in writing if requested, at least twenty one days before the absence begins or as soon as is reasonably practicable that she will be absent from work because of the pregnancy. The same notice could be used to inform the employer that she intends to return to work after the birth of the child. A further requirement for the woman is that if requested by her employer she must produce a certificate from a registered medical practitioner or a certified midwife indicating the expected number of weeks of her confinement.

Statutory maternity pay is paid by the employer at the moment at two levels depending on the length of service, the lower rate and the higher rate. The lower rate for those qualified under the Social Security Contributions and Benefits Act 1992 is a fixed amount (£59.55) whereas the higher rate, for those with two years continuous employment, depends on the claimant's average weeks pay. The maximum pay period is eighteen weeks so that a qualifying employee with less than two years service is entitled to the lower rate for that period. Employees with two years service will receive six weeks at the higher rate (9/10 of a weeks pay) and twelve weeks at the lower rate. It is necessary to offset any payments of SMP against contractual maternity pay. Also any wages to which the claimant is entitled are set off against the statutory payment. If an employer fails to meet his obligation to make the payment, then an employee can present a complaint to a tribunal within three months and they can order that the payment is made. An employer who fulfils the statutory obligation in relation to maternity pay is entitled to recover the full amount paid as a rebate from the Maternity Fund financed by National Insurance Contributions.

Time Off for Ante Natal Care

Under s.55(1) Employment Rights Act 1996 an employee who is pregnant and on medical advice who makes an appointment to attend at a place for ante-natal care has the right not to be unreasonably refused paid time off to enable her to keep the appointment. If challenged, the employee should be prepared to verify that she is pregnant by producing a medical certificate to that effect and producing an appointment card. This does not apply when the employee's appointment is the first during her pregnancy. Once again, an employee who feels that the employer is infringing her right, may complain to an industrial tribunal within three months and the tribunal has power to make a declaration and award compensation.

Case Studies

Dalton West plc - Sexual Allegations

Dalton West is a large manufacturer of fork lift trucks with depots and retail outlets situated all over Britain.

Katy Longmore is an administrative assistant who has had many years service with the company at its Birmingham headquarters. In an interview with Melissa Maxwell, the Chief Personnel Officer at the Birmingham head office, Katy made some serious allegations against David Charnley, her office manager. The interview was held at the request of Miss Longmore following her disappointment at not obtaining promotion to the post of senior administrative officer six weeks ago.

Her allegations are firstly that Mr. Charnley, who effectively has the last word on promotions in the department, is biased in favour of men, and that explains his decision to promote a relatively junior and less experienced administrative officer to the post of senior administrative officer. Secondly, Katy claims that Mr. Charnley is hostile to her in any event because she keeps refusing his amorous advances towards her. At last years Christmas party she alleges that he followed her into the ladies toilet and she had to fight him off. Katy says that *"unless he is moved to another department I'm going to take him to the Tribunal."* When the allegations are raised with Mr. Charnley he denies them absolutely calling Katy a *"vindictive bitch who lives in a fantasy world"*.

Brinkley Business School - Jean's Grievance

Brinkley Business School was set up last year by merging a number of departments in the University of Brinkley. The Director of the School is Miriam Perot who, with her two deputies, comprise the senior management team of the School. The senior management team is the final arbiter on staffing issues in the School, subject to formal ratification by the academic board of the University. Due to the retirement of David Henthorn, the post of Resource Director of Management becomes vacant from the end of the academic year. The college was authorised to advertise the post initially to internal staff with the proviso that if a suitable candidate could not be found then external candidates would be invited to apply.

Following internal applications a short list of six candidates was drawn up, one of whom was Jean Davison, a senior lecturer in management. Jean holds the post of section leader in the department and is a highly qualified member of staff widely respected throughout the University. Interviews were held in early May by the

Senior Management Team and eventually the post was offered and accepted by Bill Robinson, also a senior lecturer in management. Bill had less teaching experience than Jean, is less well qualified and has no experience of managing staff.

Jean felt aggrieved and subsequently was given the opportunity of a post appointment interview with the Director of the Business School to air her grievances. At that meeting she alleged that her gender must have been a factor in deciding not to appoint her, given her background in relation to the successful candidate. Two questions she was asked at the interview which were not asked of the male candidates indicated, she claims, that there was evidence of gender bias. One asked by the Director was whether she felt that she could gain the respect of a department essentially dominated by men. Another question asked by a Deputy Director was whether she wanted to add to her present family of young children in the near future. At the end of the post appointment interview Jean said that she was contemplating legal action.

Brinkley Business School - Laura's Secondment

Brinkley Business School was set up last year by merging a number of departments in the University of Brinkley. The Director of the School is Miriam Perot who, with her two deputies, comprise the senior management team of the School. The senior management team is the final arbiter on staffing issues in the School, subject to formal ratification by the academic board of the University.

One of the functions of the Board of Studies of the Business School is to make recommendations to the Director in relation to staff development, having been advised by the relevant University Committee. One such recommendation had been that Laura Davison, a Senior Lecturer in Management, should be given a one year secondment by the University to read for a Masters Degree in Management at University College London. The Director confirmed the offer two months later. Laura was informed and she accepted the offer conditional on the requirement that she would serve the University for a minimum of two years on completion of the course.

Subsequently it transpired that the Davisons have sold their house in Brinkley and Laura's husband David has moved to London and obtained a permanent post as a senior social worker in the London borough of Camden. After interviewing Laura, the Director told her that the offer of secondment was withdrawn forthwith. Laura has indicated to her resource director that she feels that she has been the victim of discrimination and intends to persue a legal claim against the University.

Chapter 7
Changing Contractual Arrangements

In the first part of the book we considered the legal process under which a business organisation recruits its staff. Chapters 6, 7, 8 and 9 consider the rights and responsibilities of employers and employees during the substance of the employment relationship. This will involve a consideration of the legal position relating to changing contractual arrangements, equal opportunities, health and safety and the numerous statutory rights and responsibilities which apply to the parties to a subsisting contract of employment.

It is inevitable that the success and in some cases the survival of any business organisation in the public or private sector will depend on its ability to respond positively to legal, economic or social change. Here we will consider the legal position relating to changing contractual arrangements. Human nature dictates that there will be a degree of opposition to change so it makes sense for an employer to attempt to manage the change process sensitively. This will involve supplying affected employees with information, engaging in consultation and seeking their acceptance of the proposed change. A contemporary feature of present day employment is the attempt by employers to introduce new contracts which in some spheres of employment represent a move away from collectively bargained terms and conditions of employment to individual or 'personal' contracts. The legal position relating to changing contractual arrangements is the subject matter of this chapter.

One point should be stressed from the outset. Despite the contrary view of numerous employers, contracts of employment contain terms which cannot be unilaterally varied but depend upon mutual agreement to change. In *WPM Retail Ltd. v. Lang* 1978 the complainant was promoted to area manager in 1974 with the right to earn an additional bonus based upon performance. After one bonus payment the employer sought to withdraw the right to a bonus unilaterally. The EAT held that the obligation to pay the bonus was a contractual term and remained in force until the employment was terminated. There was no question of the employee waiving his rights by remaining in employment. *"For as long as the employee goes on working in the same job, each time the employer does not pay the correct amount the employer incurs a liability which he will ultimately have to meet if the employee asserts his right to be paid the agreed amount."*

In *Miller v. Hamworthy Engineering Ltd.* 1986 the plaintiff, a salaried fireman, made a claim for the net loss of wages which he suffered during periods of short-time working which was not agreed to by him or his union. While the County Court rejected his claim the Court of Appeal held that the employer was liable for the net loss of pay which he suffered as a result of being put on to short-time without the agreement of either himself or his union *"where there is an admitted contract of employment under which a salary is payable, if the provision as to payment of salary in that contract is to be displaced, the employers must show some agreed variation of the contractual term binding upon the employee".*

Unilateral Change

In Chapter 4 we considered the expression "terms and conditions of employment" and said that conditions of employment cover numerous matters under the control of the employer such as disciplinary procedures, safety policy, meal breaks which are ultimately subject to unilateral change.

In *Dryden v. Greater Glasgow Health Board* 1992 the EAT held that an employer was entitled to introduce a rule imposing a smoking ban at the workplace and the staff had no implied right to smoke *"An employer is entitled to make rules for the conduct of employees in their place of work within the scope of the contract and once it was held that there was no implied term in the contract which entitled the employee to facilities for smoking, the rule against smoking was a lawful rule".*

Also in *Hussmen Manufacturing Ltd. v. Weir* 1998 an employee objected to the employer's unilateral change in the shift systems under which he was required to move from night shift and suffer a consequential reduction in shift allowance payments. His claim of an unauthorised reduction in wages was rejected however on the grounds that the employers were unilaterally entitled to vary his conditions of employment and move him from one shift to another.

While it would be prudent to consult before changing working rules obviously substantial alterations to the working environment can nevertheless be achieved unilaterally by an employer in this way.

Usually an employer will except that a code of practice will be unlikely to contain contractual terms and be subject to unilateral variation. A code of practice on staff sickness which contains procedures for monitoring and reviewing different categories of absence may be amended by the employer.

So held the Court of Appeal in *Wandsworth London Borough Council v. D'Silva 1998* disagreeing with the tribunal and the EAT's decision that the code contained contractual terms subject to change through mutual agreement. The Court of Appeal held that *"whether a particular provision in an employer's code of practice is contractually binding depends upon whether it should properly be regarded as conferring a right on employees or as setting out no more than good practice which managers were intended to follow. In the present case the language of the provision in question did not provide an appropriate foundation on which to base contractual rights."* The code could be unilaterally changed by the employer.

Authorised Change

More significantly as a result of a change process in any organisation, an employer may wish that members of the workforce should accept an increase or decrease in hours or pay, different contractual duties or responsibilities, a change in job location or different job functions or work practices. A sensitive employer would usually seek their consent even where the workforce may be legally required to accept the change within their terms of employment. If express terms of employment authorise the employer to implement the change, then an employee is legally obliged to accept it provided the term is interpreted reasonably.

In *McCaffery v. A.E. Jeavons Ltd.* 1967 an employee employed expressly as a 'travelling man' in the building trade was held to be bound to move anywhere in the country.

It seems that it would be perfectly proper for an employer to expressly authorise the right to change a contractual term by reserving such a right in the contract. So for example an express mobility clause in a contract could authorise the employer to move the employees place of employment from one part of the UK to another. If the clause is triggered and the employee is required to move, there as a consequence the contract of employment has changed because the employer has a new place of employment. In this way a unilateral change is authorised by the contract. Notice that the clause has authorised the change to widen the scope of the mobility clause to from for instance *"the UK"* to *"the world"* rather than the clause itself being changed

This process was alluded to by the Court of Appeal in *Wandsworth London Borough Council v. D'Silva 1998.* (above) In obiter the court stated that "although contracts of employment generally can only be varied by agreement, either party can reserve the ability to change a particular aspect of the contract unilaterally by notifying the other party as part of the contract that this is the situation. However, clear language is required to reserve to one party an unusual power of this sort. In addition the court is unlikely to favour an interpretation which does more than enable a party to vary contractual provisions with which that party is required to comply. To apply a power of unilateral variation to the rights which an employer is given could produce an unreasonable result, which the courts in construing a contract of employment will seek to avoid".

The guidance from the Court of Appeal is that while a well drafted mobility clause can authorise unilateral contractual change the courts will not enforce a clause purporting to confer on the employer an absolute power of unilateral variation of employee rights.

Even where there is a well drafted mobility clause in a contract of employment, for example, *'the bank may from time to time require an employee to be transferred temporarily or permanently to any place of business which the bank may have in the UK for which a relocation or other allowance may be payable at the discretion of the bank',* an employer must act reasonably when relying upon it. It is perfectly proper for a tribunal to imply a term into a contract which has the effect of controlling the exercise of a discretion expressly conferred in the contract.

In *United Bank Ltd. v. Akhtar* 1989 the employer was in repudiatory breach of an implied term of the contract of employment requiring reasonable notice when he sought to rely on the above mobility clause to require a junior bank employee to move from the Leeds branch to Birmingham after giving only six days notice. As a consequence the employee who refused to move without more notice could regard himself as being constructively dismissed. The EAT held that *"the tribunal were entitled therefore to imply a term that the employer's discretion under the mobility clause was one which they were bound to exercise in such a way as not to render it impossible for an employee to comply with his contractual obligation to move. It was necessary to imply that requirement into the contract in order to avoid impossibility of performance".* Furthermore the employer's conduct in relation to the transfer could also be said to be in breach of the general implied contractual duty of trust and confidence.

In *White v. Reflecting Roadstuds Ltd.* 1991 the complainant worked for a number of years for the employer in the dispatch department of the company and then asked for a transfer to more highly paid but onerous work in the rubber mixing department. When he found the new work too demanding the employer eventually transferred the complainant to lighter work in the pressing department at a reduced wage. The complainant resigned claiming constructive dismissal, despite a clear flexibility clause in his contract of employment *"The company reserves the right when determined by requirements of operational efficiency, to transfer employees to alternative work and it is a condition of employment that they are willing to do so when requested".* The industrial tribunal held that the transfer amounted to a repudiatory breach of contract. The flexibility clause, the tribunal held, was subject to further implied terms, that firstly it would be exercised reasonably and secondly that there would be no reduction in pay if it was relied on. The EAT disagreed and held that there were no grounds to imply a term that requires that express terms in a contract are subject to a test of reasonableness when exercised or that a change in job functions that produces a wage reduction automatically constitutes a breach of contract. *"Where organisation and reorganisation are concerned, it is for management to reach decisions, provided they do so responsibly. This principle can be given effect within the legal framework of a clear contractual term on mobility or job transfer."*

Even with express authority to impose change there is an overriding requirement to maintain trust and confidence in the relationship.

In *St Budeaux Royal British Legion Club Ltd. v. Cropper* 1995 there was an express clause in the contract of employment authorising the employer to change working hours on reasonable notice. On economic grounds the employer reduced working hours by five, giving employees six weeks notice of the change. The Tribunal and the EAT held that the reduction in hours was a fundamental breach of the implied terms in relation to trust and confidence and the resulting constructive dismissal was unfair.

Implied Terms

In Chapter 4 we saw that courts and tribunals have a wide discretion to imply terms into contracts of employment to give effect to the parties' intentions by more fully expressing the contractual bargain.

In *Jones v. Associated Tunnelling Co. Ltd.* 1981, the EAT held that, in the absence of express terms to the contrary, there is an implied term in a contract of employment that the employer has the right to transfer the employee to a different place of work within reasonable daily commuting distance of his home.

By implying a term into employment contracts that employees should be flexible and adaptable and react positively to change, an employer is authorised to implement quite sweeping changes in job functions provided staff are given sufficient training to enable them to cope with the different demands placed upon them.

In *Cresswell v. Board of Inland Revenue* 1984, employees sought a legal declaration that their employers had broken the terms of their contract of employment by introducing new technology and expecting them to adapt to it. The High Court declared, however, that, provided they received adequate training, employees were expected to adapt to new methods and new techniques. There is a general contractual duty on employees to adapt to changing working methods. There was also a right for the employer to withhold pay for those employees who refused to conform to the new methods, for they are in breach of their contractual obligations.

The legal position is much more complex if the changing contractual arrangements are not expressly or impliedly authorised by the contract of employment. An obvious example would be the situation where an employer requires his staff to move from full-time to part-time work or accept a reduction in wages. Here the employer must seek the express or implied assent of his workforce or their trade union to the change and he cannot legally impose the change unilaterally.

Certainly by continuing to work under protest the employee is demonstrating his unwillingness to accept a proposed contractual change and is entitled to a period of grace during which he can assess his legal position.

In *Marriott v. Oxford District Co-operative Society Ltd.* 1969 a foreman supervisor was told by his employer that the position of foreman was no longer required and that his wages were to be reduced by £1 per week to reflect his loss of status. The employee continued to work under protest for three weeks before terminating his contract of employment by notice and claiming a redundancy payment. The Court of Appeal held, reversing the Divisional Court's judgment, that as there was no implied assent to the contractual change, it amounted to a repudiation of the contract of employment. The employee's reaction of continuing to work for a short period under protest was understandable and in no way constituted implied assent to the contractual change.

In *Hayes v. Securities and Facilities Division* 2000 a number of employees brought a contract action in the county court alleging that their employer had unilaterally attempted to reduce their subsistence allowances. The court upheld the claim and on appeal the Court of Appeal rejected the employer's claim that the contract provided for unilateral alteration. The court confirmed that it would be unlikely that a contract of employment would impliedly give an employer unrestricted access to change terms.

One option for an employee who feels that his employer is unreasonably requiring him to do work which is not part of his contractual obligations is to seek an interlocutory (temporary) injunction to maintain the status quo at work.

Changing Contractual Arrangements

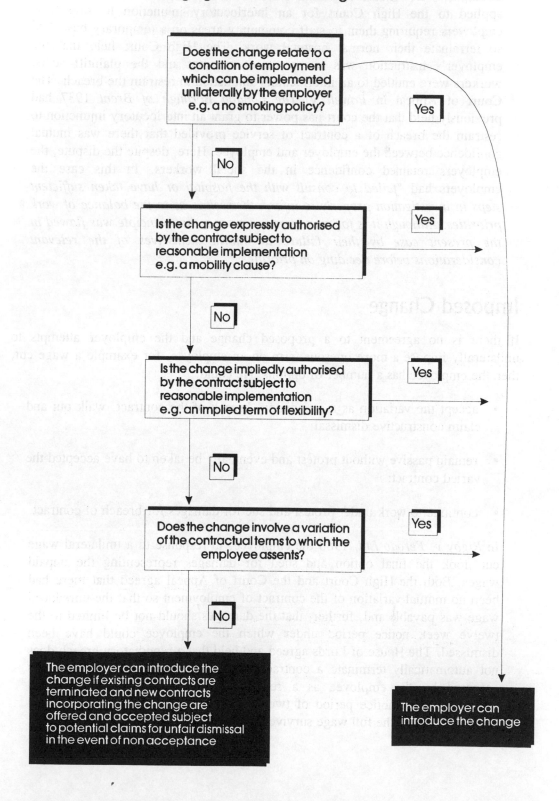

Does the change relate to a condition of employment which can be implemented unilaterally by the employer e.g. a no smoking policy?

Yes

No

Is the change expressly authorised by the contract subject to reasonable implementation e.g. a mobility clause?

Yes

No

Is the change impliedly authorised by the contract subject to reasonable implementation e.g. an implied term of flexibility?

Yes

No

Does the change involve a variation of the contractual terms to which the employee assents?

Yes

No

The employer can introduce the change if existing contracts are terminated and new contracts incorporating the change are offered and accepted subject to potential claims for unfair dismissal in the event of non acceptance

The employer can introduce the change

In *Hughs v. London Borough of Southwark* 1988 a number of social workers applied to the High Court for an interlocutory injunction to stop their employers requiring them to staff community areas on a temporary basis and so terminate their normal hospital work. The High Court held that the employer's instruction was in breach of contract and the plaintiff social workers were entitled to an interlocutory injunction to restrain the breach. The Court of Appeal in *Powell v. The London Borough of Brent* 1987 had previously held that the court has power to grant an interlocutory injunction to restrain the breach of a contract of service provided that there was mutual confidence between the employer and employee. Here, despite the dispute, the employers retained confidence in the social workers. In this case the employers had *"failed to consult with the hospital or have taken sufficient steps in investigation properly to inform themselves as to the balance of work priorities. Although it is for managers to manage, that principle was flawed in the present case by their failure to inform themselves of the relevant considerations before deciding on priorities."*

Imposed Change

If there is no agreement to a proposed change and the employer attempts to unilaterally impose a more onerous term on an employee, for example a wage cut, then the employee has a number of options. He could:

* accept the variation as a repudiatory breach of the contract, walk out and claim constructive dismissal;

* remain passive without protest and eventually be taken to have accepted the varied contract;

* continue to work under protest and sue for damages for breach of contract.

In *Rigby v. Ferodo Ltd.* 1988 the employee, in response to a unilateral wage cut, took the final option and sued for damages representing the unpaid wages. Both the High Court and the Court of Appeal agreed that there had been no mutual variation of the contract of employment so that the unreduced wage was payable and, further, that the damages should not be limited to the twelve week notice period under which the employee could have been dismissed. The House of Lords agreed and held that a repudiatory breach does not automatically terminate a contract of employment unless the breach is accepted by the employee as a repudiation. Damages were not limited therefore to the notice period of twelve weeks and the primary contractual obligation to pay the full wage survived.

The EAT has suggested that tribunals should be very cautious in reaching the conclusion that an employee had accepted a variation to his or her contract merely because he or she had continued working without any overt objection to the new terms.

In *Aparau v. Iceland Frozen Foods plc* 1996 new employers had issued new contracts to existing staff containing an express mobility clause. The complainant did not sign the new contract and continued working for twelve months so that when she objected to a mandatory transfer there was an issue as to whether the mobility clause was part of her contract. The decision of the EAT in *Jones v. Associated Tunnelling* was approved where it was stated that *"where there is a unilateral alteration by the employer of the terms of employment which has no immediate practical effect, there is a need for great caution before implying that the employee had consented to the variation by continuing to work without objecting to it."* In the circumstances of this case there was no express mobility clause and no justification for implying a term. *"Although there must necessarily be some term as to place of employment in a contract of employment, there was no necessity to have any clause about mobility in the employee's contract. The nature of her work did not make such a clause necessary, nor was it needed in order to give the contract business efficacy."*

The legal position relating to contractual variation was examined by the High Court in *Alexander v. Standard Telephones and Cables Ltd.* (no 2) 1991. Mr. Justice Hobhouse stated that *"Although an employer is not entitled unilaterally to vary a contract, it is always open to an employer, as a matter of contract, to say to his employee that after the expiry of the contractual notice period the employer will only continue the contract of employment on different terms. Such a notice is equivalent to giving notice to terminate the existing contract and offering a revised contract in continuation of and substitution for the existing contract. The period of notice has to be the notice that is required to terminate the existing contract. It is then up to the employee to decide whether he is willing to accept the revised terms"*. It seems therefore that provided the correct notice is given, an employee could be contractually bound to accept a change in terms of employment. There must be an unequivocal termination of existing contracts however by the employer for the courts would be unlikely to imply a dismissal from a notice of variation. An attempt by an employer to vary existing contracts unilaterally could be restrained by court action.

In *Burdett-Coutts v. Hertfordshire County Council* 1984 the council employer attempted to vary the contracts of employment of a number of "dinner ladies" by sending them a letter of "amendment of contract of service", detailing the changes with a notice of when they were to take effect. The plaintiff employees made it clear that they were not prepared to accept the changes and brought proceedings for breach of contract. The High Court held that the employer's letter amounted to a repudiatory breach of contract. *"The plaintiffs were entitled to a declaration that the defendants were not entitled in law to vary unilaterally the terms of the plaintiffs' contracts of employment and to damages in the form of arrears of wages".* The court was not prepared to construe the letter as a notice of termination. *"Nor could it be held that the plaintiffs, by subsequently staying at their posts and taking the lower sums which were paid to them, by implication had waived their right to treat their contract as having been brought to an end and by implication had entered into a fresh contract".*

Termination of Employment

In the absence of agreement therefore it seems that an employer who wishes to impose change must proceed by way of notice of termination with the offer of a new contract. An employee who is faced with a dismissal notice however, if qualified to do so, having one years continuous employment, would have the right to pursue a claim for unfair dismissal. This type of economic dismissal is potentially fair under the category "some other substantial reason for dismissal contained in s.98(1) Employment Rights Act 1996". Economic dismissals are explored in Chapter 11 on Unfair Dismissal but some of the issues can be dealt with here.

By requiring such an employee to accept more onerous terms of employment an employer will be in repudiatory breach and if accepted by the employee this could constitute constructive dismissal and potentially an unfair dismissal.

In *Hill Ltd. v. Mooney* 1981 the EAT held that an attempt by an employer to unilaterally alter his obligation to pay the agreed remuneration was a breach which went to the root of the contract and consequently constituted a repudiation of it. The complainant was entitled therefore to regard himself as constructively dismissed when he resigned following the employer's decision to unilaterally change the basis upon which sales commission was payable to him. *"Although a mere alteration in the contractual provisions does not necessarily amount to a fundamental breach constituting repudiation, if an employer seeks to alter that contractual obligation in a fundamental way such attempt is a breach going to the very root of the contract and is necessarily a repudiation. The obligation on the employer is to pay the contractual wages, and he is not entitled to alter the formula whereby those wages are calculated".*

In *Greenaway Harrison Ltd. v. Wiles* 1994 a telephonist who worked a split shift to fit in with her child care responsibilities was told to work a new shift pattern which was not compatible. Her employer warned her that unless she accepted the new shift pattern she would be dismissed with one month's notice. The complainant left claiming constructive dismissal which was unfair. The EAT upheld the finding that the case fell within a constructive dismissal because the decision to dismiss had already been taken before she left and this was a fundamental breach of contract.

The imposition of a radical change in job functions could indicate a breakdown in trust and confidence. The EAT held in *Brown v. Ministry of Defence* 1992 that to move the applicant after eighteen years service from his work as a boatman to work in a paint shop at a different work location would constitute a breach of the implied term of trust and confidence. The applicant was entitled to regard himself as constructively dismissed when he left as a result.

In the present employment climate the potential redress for a successful complaint of unfair dismissal will hardly compensate for the loss of secure employment. Rights in relation to unfair dismissal are considered later in Chapter 11 but the following cases provide an illustration of the approach to be adopted by tribunals.

In *St. John of God (Care Services) Ltd. v. Brooks* 1992 following a reduction in State funding the response of the hospital employer was to attempt to reduce costs, and to assist in the process the staff were offered less favourable terms of employment. Such terms included a reduction in holidays, the abolition of overtime rates and the generous sick pay scheme and a freeze on pay levels. Employees were told they had a reasonable time to accept the new terms, but failure to do so would lead to dismissal. As a consequence three employees were dismissed, a further employee having walked out in response to the changes, claiming a repudiatory breach and constructive dismissal. In the event 140 out of 170 staff accepted the new terms of employment. The claim of unfair dismissal was upheld by an industrial tribunal who in determining the fairness of the employer's conduct asked the question whether the terms offered were those which a reasonable employer could offer and decided that they were not. On appeal however the EAT took a different view and held that the question as to fairness should also be considered in the light of the matters which occurred subsequent to the offer of new terms being made. In particular the fact that the vast majority of staff had accepted the change was significant as were the sound business reasons for the reorganisation.

Quite often the new terms of employment are offered following a reorganisation

In *Catamaran Cruisers Ltd. v. Williams* 1994 the seven complainants were all employed by a cruise company which was taken over when in financial difficulties. The new employers offered new terms and conditions to the staff which were eventually approved by the Union and accepted by the majority of employees. The complainants rejected the new contracts, were dismissed and presented complaints of unfair dismissal. The employers relied on "some other substantial reason" as the reason for dismissal and claimed that it was fair given that it was introduced for a sound business reason. Having compared the old contracts with the new contracts the tribunal held that as the new contracts were much less favourable and the company's financial position was not sufficiently serious to require the imposition of the new terms the dismissals were unfair. The EAT disagreed however and found that there was no principle of law that supported the approach adopted by the tribunal. It was necessary to examine the motives of the employer and *"satisfy itself that they are not sought to be imposed for arbitrary reasons. What has to be carried out is a balancing process"*. The tribunal should *"not look solely at the advantages or disadvantages but should also consider and take account of the benefit to the employers in imposing the changes"*. The question of reasonableness should be determined in the light of the fact that many employees accepted the new terms and the fact that the reorganisation was partly motivated by the need to give more emphasis to safety.

If the reorganisation involves implementing a policy of rationalisation then the fairness of any decision to dismiss must be considered in the light of the policy.

The issue in *Banerjee v. City and East London Area Health Authority* 1979 was whether having decided to replace two part-time consultants in a hospital with a full-time consultant, the decision to dismiss was reasonable as in accordance with the employer's policy of rationalisation. A decision to dismiss in these circumstances could be prima facie fair. The EAT said that *"A question such as that which arose in the present case is very largely a matter for the employer. If an employer can show to the satisfaction of the industrial tribunal that a certain policy has been evolved and that it was considered to be a matter of importance or to have discernible advantages to the organisation, then, subject to there being any effective cross examination, dismissal in accordance with that policy can be said to be for "some other substantial reason."* In 1979 the burden of proving fairness was on the employer, however the EAT still provided instructive guidance on determining the issue of fairness in these circumstances. Certainly it is not enough to simply show that the decision to dismiss was reached in accordance with a particular policy. *"In a case involving dismissal following a policy of rationalisation, this involves other adducing evidence of the relevant minutes of how the decision to rationalise was made, of the pros and cons which were considered and if the importance which was attached to the different features which went into the decision; alternatively, a witness may be called who could show that the reason for the dismissal was that the company considered keeping on the dismissed employee and that the advantages of each course had been weighed".*

In *Scottish Co-operative Wholesale Society v. Taylor* 1993 the EAT held that it was a question of fact based on all the circumstances to decide whether it is reasonable for an employer when implementing a reorganisation to request an employee to move from full-time employment to part-time employment under a shift system.

Also the EAT in *Shevlin v. Coventry Free Church Homes for the Aged* 1993 stressed that the circumstances of the reorganisation must be considered from the viewpoint of both the employer and the employee. Insufficient thought had been given to the impact of a change in a shift system on the employee's domestic circumstances so that her complaint of unfair constructive dismissal was upheld by the EAT when she left her job as a result.

One obvious question is whether an employee who has reluctantly accepted a new contract can still maintain a claim of unfair dismissal.

In *Hogg v. Dover College* 1990 it was held that once action amounting to a dismissal is established the fact that the employee has accepted a new contract will not prevent a complaint of unfair dismissal. This complaint can be pursued before an industrial tribunal while the applicant remains in the employment of the same employer. Applying the rationale of *Hogg in Alcan Extrusions v. Yates* 1996 the EAT reached a similar conclusion when an employer unilaterally changed contracts of employment. *"Where an employer unilaterally imposes radically different terms of employment... there is a dismissal ... if on an objective construction of the relevant letters or other conduct on the part of the employer, there is a removal or withdrawal of the old contract".*

A significant recent trend in employment is the practice of employers offering employees financial incentives to sign so called personal contracts and relinquish the right to trade union representation for the purposes of collective bargaining. In *Wilson v. Associated Newspapers Ltd.* 1993 the Court of Appeal held that this could constitute unlawful action short of dismissal against those employees who refuse the offer. Now s.13 of the Trade Union Reform and Employment Rights Act 1993 amends s.148 of TULRA(C)A 1992 so that if an employer offers enhanced payments to employees who accept personal contracts, provided that the aim of the employer was to change the relationship with a class of employee this will not be unlawful in relation to those who do not accept the change. Unlawful action short of dismissal is considered in Chapter 9.

Case Study

Brinkley Business School - "Ernie's the Name"

Brinkley Business School was set up last year by merging a number of departments in the University of Brinkley. The Director of the School is Miriam Perot who, with her two deputies, comprise the senior management team of the School. The senior management team is the final arbiter on staffing issues in the School, subject to formal ratification by the academic board of the University.

A staff deployment problem has emerged in the area of accountancy and finance in the Business School. Ernie Quinn, a Lecturer in accountancy with twenty three years service at the University was asked by his Resource Director to take responsibility for the development of a course on managing finance in small businesses. This duty was to commence in the next academic year and involved a minimum of eight hours class contact.

Over the years Ernie has built up a solid reputation for his opposition to change and has only recently co-operated in the team approach necessary for the operation of vocational courses with their emphasis on student centred learning. *"Ernie's the name and accountancy is my game"* he has said repeatedly in meetings and to classes over the years.

A major problem faced by the resource director is the dramatic diminution of accountancy courses and courses where accountancy forms an element. For a large part of the present academic year Ernie has operated a timetable which was eight hours short of his contractual teaching requirement with no additional responsibilities. True to form Ernie refuses the offer of course development work point blank, despite the attempt by his Head of Department to persuade him to take on this "challenging work". Subsequently Ernie sent a copy of his statement of terms of employment to the Director of the Business School where he is described as a Lecturer in Accountancy.

Case Study

Dalton West plc - New Technology

Dalton West is a large manufacturer of fork lift trucks with depots and retail outlets situated all over Britain. Nine months ago the clerical staff in Personnel were required to attend a six week intensive in-service training course to equip them with the skills necessary to operate a new computerised system of storing staff records installed at head office. On behalf of the clerical staff, the National Union of Clerical Staff have attempted to negotiate a five per cent pay rise to reflect the willingness of the clerical staff to acquire new skills and use the new technology. The management of Dalton West have rejected the claim for a wage rise out of hand, and argued forcefully that all staff they employ are required to adapt to new working methods in the interests of efficiency. The management also announces that when the new system is operating there will be a twenty per cent reduction in their clerical staff requirements in Personnel. In response, and after consulting their members, the NUCS inform the management of Dalton West that they are in dispute and instruct their members in personnel to boycott the new technology.

For the last three months the gross wages of those staff boycotting the new system have been reduced by one third. Furthermore last week the management wrote to the staff in dispute stating that *"if they continued to boycott the new system their work would be regarded as purely voluntary and no wages would be paid. Failure to report for work will be regarded as implied resignation."* The response of the union is to ballot all their members employed at the Birmingham headquarters to take strike or other industrial action.

The majority of clerical staff at the Birmingham headquarters are members of the National Union of Clerical Staff (NUCS), an independent trade union recognised by Dalton West plc for collective bargaining purposes.

Chapter 8
Health and Safety at Work

Any treatment of the law relating to the workplace should involve an examination of health and safety law. Here the topic is given detailed consideration in an attempt to minimise its complexity and reflect the high priority that should be given to the aim of securing a safe working environment. In addition while health and safety law is embodied within the UK legislation and common law it is an area of business law that has been subjected to dramatic change due to our membership of the European Community. Legal duties in relation to health and safety are imposed with the aim of encouraging a safe working environment and when you consider that in 1999 86 workers were killed on construction sites alone in the UK, enforcement of the law should be a priority.

In the United Kingdom legal intervention in the field of health and safety has a long history and the earliest examples of employment legislation, the nineteenth century Factories Acts, were designed to ensure that a slender cushion of legislative protection was provided for those categories of workers at particular risk. The criminal codes in relation to health and safety law were contained in numerous statutes and statutory instruments e.g. the Factories Act 1961, the Office Shops and Railway Premises Act 1963. Eventually in 1972 the Robens Committee on Safety and Health at work criticised this fragmented state of the law. As a result of the Robens Committee recommendations the Health and Safety at Work Act 1974 was passed.

The aims of the Act were to:

- lay down general duties applicable across the industrial spectrum;

- provide a unified system of enforcement under the control of the Health and Safety Executive and local authorities;

- create the Health and Safety Commission to assist in the process of changing attitudes and producing detailed regulations applicable to each industrial sector backed up by codes of practice designed to give guidance as to how general duties and specific regulations could be satisfied.

By imposing legal duties on employers, employees, contractors, manufacturers and others backed up by criminal sanctions, the 1974 Act is designed to achieve minimum standards of conduct and so minimising the risk of injury and enhancing the welfare of those at the workplace. In addition to criminal sanctions however the possibility of civil redress must also be considered so that those injured at the workplace have a further avenue of redress to secure compensation by relying on common law principles.

European Community Law

As previously stated UK businesses also operate in a European legal framework and health and safety issues are an established part of European Community social policy. Since the adoption of the Single European Act 1986 the regulation of Health and Safety at work in the UK as been refined by European Community law initiatives. In 1990 the Chairman of the Health and Safety Commission said that *"the European Community has now to be regarded as the principal engine of health and safety law affecting the UK not just in worker safety but also major hazards and most environmental hazards"*. Article 22 of the Single European Act 1986 added a new Article 118A to the Treaty of Rome and so introduced a new concept *"the working environment"*. Following the Amsterdam Treaty this article is now contained within article 137

> Article 137 provides that *"Member States shall pay particular attention to encouraging improvements especially in the working environment, as regards the health and safety of workers and shall set as their objective the harmonisation of conditions in this area, while maintaining the improvements made"*.

The significance of Article 137 is that it incorporates the qualified majority procedure rather than unanimity for the adoption of health and safety provisions by the Council of Ministers. (See Chapter 2) Paragraph 2 states that *"In order to help achieve the objective laid down in the first paragraph, the Council acting by a qualified majority on a proposal from the Commission, in co-operation with the European Parliament and after consulting the Economic and Social Committee, shall adopt, by means of directives, minimum requirements for gradual implementation, having regard to the condition and technical rule obtaining in each of the Member States"*.

This means that despite the objection of individual member states the majority view as to setting health and safety standards throughout the European Community will prevail. Furthermore the European Parliament has suggested that the expression *"working environment"* in Article 137 should be given a wide definition so that it could embrace matters such as the arrangement of a workplace as well as physical and psychological conditions at work. The working environment provisions were also acknowledged by the acceptance of the Charter of Fundamental Rights of Workers in December 1989 as an integral part of the development of the internal market.

There is no doubt that recently there has been a dramatic acceleration in the pace of the community legislation on health and safety compared with the minimal achievement of the previous two decades. Between 1970 and 1986 only six Directives aimed specifically at promoting health and safety at work were proposed by the Commission and adopted by the Council.

Despite the worthy aims of the Commission's Action Plans of 1978 and 1984 to promote a programme of health and safety measures, only moderate progress was made. Following the Single European Act, however, there is now a new emphasis in relation to health and safety. In 1987 a third action programme for health and safety was published by the European Commission and subsequently approved by resolution of the Council of Ministers. The programme contemplates a legislative package and a large number of Directives are proposed on a number of topics such as: the organisation of safety; selection and use of plant and machinery; selection and use of personal protective equipment; revision of the safety signs directives; medical assistance on ships; protection of agricultural workers using pesticides; safety in construction; carcinogenic agents; pesticides; amendments to the asbestos directive; and amendments to the lead directive. In December 1988 further Directives were recommended by the Commission to deal with: temporary and mobile work sites; health and safety for fishing vessels; agriculture; modes of transport; extractive industries; and nuclear plants.

Other health and safety Directives promised in the Commission's Action Programme relating to the implementation of the Community Charter of Fundamental Social Rights of Workers are:

- the establishment of a safety, hygiene and health agency;

- information for workers exposed to dangerous agents;

- the protection of workers exposed to physical agents;

- the protection of pregnant women at work; and

- the protection of young people.

The third action programme resulted in the production of a Framework Directive for the Introduction of Measures to Encourage Improvement in Safety and Health of Workers, in March 1989 which was approved by the Council for implementation by member states by January 1 1993. A number of daughter Directives were also proposed to:

- require employers to evaluate health and safety risks;

- introduce preventive measures and develop a preventive policy;

- designate competent personnel or use outside agencies;

- make arrangements for first aid, fire precautions and emergency procedures;

- maintain records and report accidents and diseases;

- provide information to workers;

- consult workers or their representatives on health and safety measures;

- provide health and safety training for workers;

- allow workers' representatives time off with pay; and

- allow them to receive appropriate training.

Health and Safety Regulations

In order to implement numerous directives a number of regulations have been produced clarifying new law and repealing out of date law. In addition, practical guidance in the form of codes of practice have also been produced to ensure compliance with the regulations which have been in force from the beginning of 1993.

The new regulations apply to virtually all work activities and place duties on employers in relation to their employees and in some circumstances to the public and self employed contractors in relation to themselves and others who may be affected by their acts or omissions. The regulations are very comprehensive however it should be stressed that the main focus is initially to promote awareness and enforcement is not likely unless:

- *the risks to health and safety are immediate and evident, or*

- *employers appear deliberately unwilling to recognise their responsibilities to ensure the long term health, safety and welfare of employees and others affected by their activities.*

The Health and Safety (Consultation with Employees) Regulations 1996 require employers to consult with employees who are not covered by safety representatives appointed by recognised unions under them. They are a top up to the 1977 regulations aimed to secure compliance with the Health and Safety Framework Directive which states that *"Employers shall consult workers and/or their representatives and allow them to take part in discussions on all matters relating to health and safety at work"*. There is no doubt that the Health and Safety Commission concluded that those new regulations were necessary following two decisions of the European Court of Justice on the acquired rights directive and collective redundancies directive where the obligation to consult other than where there are recognised trade unions was confirmed.

The Management of Health and Safety at Work Regulations 1992 are aimed at improving health and safety management and apply to almost all work activities in Great Britain and offshore. Under them employers are required to adopt a well organised and systematic approach to comply with their statutory duties in relation to health and safety. In pursuing this objective employers are required to:

- carry out a risk assessment of health and safety so that preventive and protective measures can be identified. While there is an existing obligation in the Health and Safety at Work Act for employers of five or more employees to prepare a written health and safety policy there is now an additional obligation on them to record the findings of the risk assessment.

- make arrangements for putting into practice the health and safety measures that follow from the risk assessment. These arrangements will include planning, organisation, control, monitoring and review and must be recorded by employers with five or more employees.

- appoint competent people to help devise and implement the appropriate measures and ensure that employees including temporary workers are given appropriate health and safety training and understandable information.

- provide appropriate health surveillance for employees and set up emergency procedures where the risk assessment shows it to be necessary.

- consult employees safety representatives, provide facilities for them and co-operate with other employers sharing the same working environment.

Risk assessments should identify hazards and then evaluate risks which should be remedied as soon as possible. The assessment should be carried out by health and safety personnel or suitably qualified line managers. It should be comprehensive covering organisational, job, workplace and individual factors and where sible include the participation of individual employees and safety representatives.

Following amendments to the 1992 regulations resulting from the Pregnant Workers Directive employers are required to address the health risks of pregnant mothers. This involves carrying out a risk assessment, considering preventative measures, attempting to avoid the risk of altering working conditions and suspending the woman on full pay if no suitable alternative work is available.

> In *Day v. T Pickles Farms Ltd.* 1999 the EAT held that the obligations in the regulations are triggered by employing a woman of childbearing age rather than waiting for an employee to become pregnant. Interestingly the EAT also held that failure to carry out a risk assessment could constitute a "detriment" for the purposes of the Sex Discrimination Act and provide a right to damages for the injury caused by the employer's failure.

In relation to employees the regulations require them to follow health and safety instructions and report dangers. Finally as far as the management of health and safety is concerned it should be recognised that there is an overlap between the regulations and some existing requirements contained in duties and regulations. A specific regulation will replace a general duty but there is no requirement to for instance carry out two risk assessments for the purposes of different regulations.

The Provision and Use of Work Equipment Regulations 1992, were replaced by the Provision and Use of Work Equipment Regulations 1998. Under the 1998 regulations general duties are placed upon employers in relation to equipment used at work and minimum requirements are identified to apply to all industries.

The expression *"work equipment"* is given a very wide definition and covers machinery of all kinds ranging from a hand tool to a complete plant. The *'use'* of such equipment includes all activities ranging from installing and repairing to transporting and dismantling.

It should be stressed that employers who already use 'good practice' in the use of work equipment will find themselves in compliance with the new regulations.

The general duties will require an employer to:

- assess working conditions in particular risks and hazards when selecting work equipment.

- ensure that equipment is suitable for its use and that it conforms with EC product safety directives.

- give staff adequate information, instruction and training and maintaining equipment in efficient working order and a good state of repair.

- ensure that work equipment is maintained in an efficient state, in efficient working order and in good repair.

The above duty was interpreted by the Court of Appeal in *Stark v. the Post Office* 2000. The equipment in question was a postman's bicycle which had suffered a wheel lock when part of the brake had broken and became lodged in the front wheel. The court rejected the postman's claim for damages both under the common law and the regulations on the grounds that the brake defect would not have been disclosed on a routine inspection or even a rigorous examination of the bike. The Court of Appeal took a different view construing the regulation as imposing an absolute duty on the employer. Establishing that the mechanism failed to work efficiently and that failure caused the accident is sufficient to impose liability. The court emphasised that absolute liability in these circumstances was the position under previous legislation and the relevant Directive makes it clear that *"the Directive does not justify any reduction in levels of protection already achieved in member states"*.

In addition to the general duties the regulations also contain specific requirements in relation to equipment which will replace existing regulations. They include:

- guarding of the dangerous parts of machines.

- protection against specific hazards such as articles or substances, fire risks and explosion.

- ensuring adequate lighting, maintenance, warnings, stability, control systems and control devices.

The Manual Handling Operations Regulations 1992 are aimed at preventing injuries which occur at the workplace due to the mishandling of loads by incorrect lifting, lowering, pushing, pulling, carrying or simply moving them about. Such operations should have been identified in the risk assessment. The regulations require an employer to ensure that:

- there is a genuine need to move a load and that manual handling is necessary rather than mechanical means

- the weight size and shape of the load is assessed along with the working environment and the handler's capabilities

- in so far as is reasonably practicable the risk of injury is reduced by for example reducing the load, employing mechanical means or training the handler.

The aim of the Workplace (Health Safety and Welfare) Regulations 1992 is to replace numerous parts of existing legislation including the Factories Act 1961 and the Office Shops and Railway Premises Act 1963. They cover many aspects of health safety and welfare at the workplace in particular the working environment which includes temperature, ventilation, lighting, room size, work stations and seating. Facilities at the workplace are covered which includes toilets, washing, eating and changing facilities, drinking water, clothing storage, rest areas and facilities along with the need for cleanliness and effective removal of waste. Specific aspects of safety are included in particular relating to safe passage of pedestrians and vehicles, windows and skylights, doors, gates and escalators and floors.

Regulation 24 of the Workplace Regulations requires that where a person has to wear specialist clothing for the purposes of work then suitable and sufficient changing facilities should be provided. The High Court recently decided that specialist clothing should not be limited to distinct uniforms but should be interpreted to include " *any clothing which would not ordinarily be worn other than for work even if it is worn coming to and from work. As a consequence it did include a postal workers uniform and allowing women to change in the toilets did not satisfy the requirements of the regulations.* "

By the Personal Protective Equipment at Work Regulations 1992 some old law relating to PEP is replaced but more recent legal rules, in particular the Control of Substances Hazardous to Health or Noise at Work Regulations, remain in force. Personal protective equipment includes protective clothing, eye foot and head protection, harnesses, life jackets and high visibility clothing. Where risks are not adequately controlled by other means there is a duty to provide PPE free of charge for employees exposed to risks. The PPE provided must provide effective protection as appropriate to the risks and working conditions, take account of the worker's needs and fit properly. Further regulations are necessary to comply with a separate EC directive on the design certification and testing of PPE. The present regulations require an assessment of risks to determine the suitability of PPE; the provision of storage facilities; adequate training information and instruction; appropriate methods of cleansing maintenance and replacement and effective supervision to ensure its proper use.

The Heath and Safety (Display Screen Equipment) Regulations 1992 apply where an individual habitually uses display screen equipment as a significant part of normal work. Duties are imposed on employers if equipment is used for the display of text, numbers and graphics but some systems are excluded including transport systems for public use, cash registers, window typewriters and portable systems not in prolonged use. The duties require employers to:

- assess display screen work stations and reduce risks revealed.

- ensure that minimum requirements are satisfied in relation to the display screen, keyboard, desk and chair, working environments and task design and software

- plan the work so that there are changes of activity and appropriate breaks and

- provide information and training for display screen users, eye testing and special spectacles if needed.

There is no doubt that under these regulations in particular, employers will have to incur considerable expense to ensure that equipment meets the basic minimum requirements. Existing work stations must be brought up to standard by the end of 1996 and the costs of eye testing spectacles and insurance must all be borne by the employer.

Enforcement of Health and Safety Law

Enforcement of the safety legislation is in the hands of the Health and Safety Executive and local authorities which have a number of powers at their disposal. The main power is to appoint inspectors who have authority to enter premises, take samples and require information to be given. The breach of a general duty or a specific regulation under the Health and Safety legislation is a criminal offence. This can lead to a prosecution in the criminal courts. Less serious offences are dealt with summarily in the Magistrates Court and those of a more serious nature are tried on indictment in the Crown Court. Conviction in summary proceedings carries a fine of up to £5000, or for an indictable offence, an unlimited fine and/or up to two years imprisonment. The fundamental aim of those enforcing the law is to encourage a positive attitude to health and safety at the workplace rather than to take numerous employers through the criminal courts. There is no doubt however that some employers resent the economic cost of health and safety and it may only be the threat of criminal prosecution, that will cause the more recalcitrant employers to respond. Unfortunately enforcement remains inadequate due to under resourcing of the Inspectorate.

A contemporary example of a health and safety prosecution and the imposition of a fine is provided by *R v. Rollco Screw and Rivet Co. Ltd*. 1999. The case concerned the inadequate precautions taken when carrying out shipping of asbestos. Factory staff and public were put in danger when work was carried out without proper precautions. The prosecution was brought against the company and its two directors who had contracted out the work to a firm and who had in turn sub contracted the work. A severe fine was imposed on the company and its directors. On appeal it was argued that the sum the company was ordered to pay was grossly excessive amounting to over seventy thousand pounds payable over six years. The period of repayment was excessive and was reduced by a year and sum payable for the costs element was reduced by £10,000. In assessing fines in health and safety law the Court of Appeal held that two questions should be posed *"first, what financial penalty does the offence merit? Second, what financial penalty can a dependent (whether corporate or personal) reasonably be ordered to meet? That second question invariably raises the question of the time period over which any sum is payable."*

One of the major innovations of the Health and Safety at Work Act was the introduction of constructive sanctions. A Health and Safety Inspector who believes that an employer is contravening one of the statutory provisions may serve on that person an improvement notice requiring that the contravention be remedied within a specific period of not less than twenty one days. The notice will specify the provision which is contravened and state how it is being broken. In cases where the contravention involves an immediate risk of serious injury, the inspector may serve a prohibition notice which will direct that the particular activity is terminated until the contravention is rectified. Such a notice may take immediate effect or be deferred for a specified time. Failure to comply with a prohibition notice, for example by using a machine which has been identified as a serious source of danger, is an offence triable on indictment in the Crown Court.

While liability is generally associated with fault the courts have recently confirmed that even where there was little evidence of personal blame, an occupier of factory premises may still be held liable under the Factories Act 1961 if he fails to make his premises as safe as is reasonably practicable for all persons who may work there, even if they are not employees.

In *Dexter v. Tenby Electrical Accessories Ltd.* 1991 contractors were employed by the defendants to install fresh air fans at their factory premises and for this purpose an employee of the contractor was required to work for a period on the factory roof. Despite the fact that the defendants were unaware that the employee was working on the roof they were nevertheless liable as occupiers of the factory when he suffered injuries after falling through it. The Health and Safety Executive charged the defendant with a contravention of s29(1) of the Factories Act 1961 which provides "there shall, so far as is reasonably practicable, be provided and maintained safe means of access to every place which any person has at anytime to work, and every such place shall, so far as is reasonably practicable, be made and kept safe for any person working there". While the Magistrates accepted the argument that the defendants had no control over the employee's place of work and so there was no case to answer, this was rejected in an appeal by the prosecution to the Queen's Bench Divisional Court. The appeal court held that lack of knowledge was no defence and if a person is ordered by his employer, a contractor, to work on a factory roof, the occupier of the factory is liable under the Act if the roof is in an unsafe condition.

General Duties

Most of the general duties contained in the 1974 Act impose on a number of different categories of person, a standard of care based on the idea of reasonable practicability. The most important general duty is that contained in s.2(1). Section 2(2) identifies matters to which the duty extends:

Under s.2(1) It shall be the duty of every employer to ensure, so far as is reasonably practicable, the health, safety and welfare at work of all his employees.

> (2) *Without prejudice to the generality of an employee's duty under the preceding subsection, the matters to which that duty extends includes in particular-*
>
> (a) *the provision and maintenance of plant and systems of work that are, so far as is reasonably practicable, safe and without risks to health;*
>
> (b) *arrangements for ensuring, so far as is reasonably practicable, safety and absence of risks to health in connection with the use, handling, storage and transport of articles and substances;*
>
> (c) *the provision of such information, instruction, training and supervision as is necessary to ensure, so far as is reasonably practicable, the health and safety at work of his employees;*
>
> (d) *so far as is reasonably practicable as regards any place of work under the employer's control, the maintenance of it in a condition that is safe and without risks to health and the provision and maintenance of means of access to and egress from it that are safe and without such risks;*
>
> (e) *the provision and maintenance of a working environment for his employees that is, so far as is reasonably practicable, safe, without risks to health, and adequate as regards facilities and arrangements for their welfare at work.*

The scope of the general duty, contained in s.2, qualified by the words *"reasonably practicable"* is difficult to determine and little guidance has been provided by the courts. However the meaning of this phrase is obviously crucial in determining the scope of an employer's duty. It would be wrong to assume that it imposes a standard of care comparable with the duty to take reasonable care at common law. The statutory duty requires the employer to take action to ensure health and safety unless, on the facts, it is impracticable in the circumstances. This has been taken to mean that in determining the scope of general duties cost-benefit considerations must be taken account of.

In *Associated Dairies v. Hartley* 1979 the employer supplied his workers with safety shoes which they could pay for at £1 per week. An employee who had not purchased the shoes suffered a fractured toe when the wheel of a roller truck ran over it. There was an obvious risk to workers from roller trucks in the employer's warehouse. Accordingly an improvement notice was served on the employer requiring him to provide his employers with safety shoes free of charge (estimated cost £20,000 in the first year and £10,000 per annum thereafter). The Court of Appeal held that while such a requirement was practicable in all the circumstances of the case, it was not reasonably so, bearing in mind the cost in relation to the risk of injury. The improvement notice was therefore cancelled, the court confirming that in relation to the general duty, practicability alone is not the test, for it is qualified by the term "reasonable".

More recently there is evidence that the courts have adopted a more positive approach to the interpretation of the general duties under s.2(1) and s.2(2).

In *Bolton Metropolitan Borough Council v. Malrod Insulation Ltd.* 1993 a prosecution was brought against the defendant contractors under the general duty in s.2(1) and for failing to provide and maintain safe plant under s.2(2)(a). Following an inspection, an electrically driven decontamination unit, used by the contractors, was found to have defects which could cause electric shocks to those who used it. Following a conviction the defendants appealed on the grounds that the duties owed under s.2 only applied when the employee is at work and at the time of the alleged offences work had yet to begin. The Crown Court, upheld the appeal agreeing with the defendant's interpretation of the section. On further appeal the Divisional Court rejected this interpretation and held that the use of the *"at work"* in s.2(1) could not on any common sense basis mean that the duty to provide safe plant only arises when men are actually at work. This would mean that the health and safety inspectorate would be powerless to act if they discovered unsafe machines on an inspection at the end of the working day. The duty is to *"provide plant"* which is safe, subject to the question of reasonable practicability.

The issue of *'practicability'* under s.2 and its scope in relation to an employer with a large workforce working with contractors was raised *in R. v. Swan Hunter Shipbuilders Ltd., and Telemeter Installation Ltd.* 1981. Here eight men had been tragically killed by a fire which broke out on a ship under construction on the River Tyne. The fire had been fuelled by an oxygen enriched atmosphere caused by the failure of an employee of a sub-contractor (Telemeter) to turn off the oxygen supply over night. Both the employer and the sub-contractor were convicted of offences under the Act in the Crown Court and subsequently appealed to the Court of Appeal. The employer argued that the duty to provide a safe system of work to persons other than their own employees imposed an intolerable burden where there was a large workforce with many different direct employers. The Court however having examined the wording of s.2(1) and s.2(2), decided that providing employees with a safe system of work may involve a duty to an employer to provide instruction and information to persons other than their own employees about potential dangers. Such instructions need not be given if the employer can show on the balance of probabilities that it was not reasonably practicable in the circumstances. Here the employer was aware of the dangers and by sub-contracting the work, they were under a duty to 'inform and instruct'. In the words of Dunn L J *"If the provision of a safe system of work for the benefit of his own employees involves information and instruction as to potential dangers being given to persons other than the employer's own employees, then the employer is under a duty to provide such information and instruction. His protection is contained in the words 'so far as is reasonably practicable' which appear in all the relevant provisions. The onus is on the defendants to prove on the balance of probabilities that it was not reasonably practicable in the particular circumstances of the case".*

The fact that a working practice adopted by employers is universal within the industry is not conclusive evidence that the general duty under s.2(1) has been discharged. The High Court in *Martin v. Boulton and Paul (Steel Construction) Ltd.* 1982 held that a universal practice whilst of great weight, is not conclusive evidence that it was not reasonably practicable to use some other and safer method. *In R. v. Associated Octel Co. Ltd.* 1997 (considered later in the chapter) the Court of Appeal gave further guidances as to reasonable practicability stressing the subjective nature of the concept *"what is reasonably practicable for a large organisation employing safety officers or engineers contracting for the services of a small contractor on routine operations may differ markedly from what is reasonably practicable for a small shopkeeper employing a local builder on activities on which he has no expertise"*

Safety Representatives

A further requirement of s.2 for employers other than those with less than five employees is the obligation to prepare and revise a written statement of their general policy on health and safety and bring this statement to the notice of their employees. The statement should be more than a bland statement of responsibilities but rather a genuine attempt to identify specific health and safety problems of the employer in question and the arrangements that have been made to deal with them. Matters to be included would cover inspection procedures, emergency arrangements, safety precautions, consultative arrangements and training. Under the Safety Representatives and Safety Committee Regulations 1977 it is only recognised trade unions who have the exclusive right to appoint safety representatives and request the creation of safety committees. The functions of safety representatives are laid down in the 1977 regulations and include:

(a) *to investigate potential hazards and dangerous occurrences at the workplace;*

(b) *to investigate complaints by any employee he represents relating to that employee's health, safety or welfare at work;*

(c) *to make representations to the employer on general matters affecting the health, safety or welfare at work of the employees at the workplace;*

(d) *to carry out inspections;*

(e) *to represent the employees he was appointed to represent in consultations at the workplace with inspectors of the Health and Safety Executive and of any other enforcing authority;*

(f) *to receive information from inspectors in accordance with the 1974 Act; and*

(g) *to attend meetings of safety committees where he attends in his capacity as a safety representative in connection with any of the above functions.*

If safety representatives are appointed under s.2 then it is the duty of an employer to consult with such representatives in order to promote health and safety at the workplace. In many cases this will involve consultations with safety committees which have the function of reviewing measures taken to ensure health and safety at work. Safety representatives have a number of powers, including the right to inspect the workplace and require the establishment of a safety committee. The Trade Union Reform and Employment Rights Act 1993 inserted a new right on safety representatives which is included in the Employment Rights Act 1996. Under s.44

safety representatives have the right not so suffer a detriment for carrying out their health and safety functions (see later in the chapter).

By regulation, a safety representative is entitled to paid time off work to undergo such training as is reasonable in the circumstances. It is worth noting that the general duties owed under s.2 apply to employees only and this would not include those training under a Youth Training Scheme as they are not treated as persons working under a contract of service. Following the Health and Safety (Youth Training Scheme) Regulations 1983 however, trainees on YTS are included under the umbrella of the Act.

Duty to Non-Employees

Both employers and those who are self employed are required, in the words of s.3(1), to *"conduct their undertakings in such a way, in so far as is reasonably practicable, to protect persons other than their own employees from risks to their health and safety."* This would require an employer to give anyone who may be affected, information relating to health and safety risks arising from the way in which the business is run.

> In *Carmichael v. Rosehall Engineering Works Ltd.* 1983 an employer was found to be in breach of his duty under s.3(1) when he failed to provide two youths on a work experience programme with suitable clothing for carrying out a cleaning operation using flammable liquid. The failure to give proper instruction and information, as to the possible risks to their health and safety, was a factor which led to the death of one of the boys when his paraffin soaked overalls burst into flames.

Those to whom an employer owes a duty under s.3(1) include contractors and employees of independent contractors.

> In *R v. Associated Octel Co. Ltd.* 1997 the defendant employer was convicted of an offence under s.3(1) when an employee of a contractor engaged to carry out maintenance and repair work suffered severe injury when working at the defendant's chemical plant. On appeal the employer argued that under s.3(1) an employer is not liable for the acts of independent contractors over whom he has no control. The Court of Appeal held that the employer had been correctly convicted. *"The cleaning, repair and maintenance necessary for carrying on the employer's business or enterprise is part of the employee's conduct of its undertaking within the meaning of s.3(1) so as to impose a duty of care with regard to persons not in its employment, whether it is done by the employer's own employees or by independent contractors. The ingredients of an offence under s.3(1) are that the accused is (i) an employer (ii) who so*

conducts his undertaking (iii) as to expose to risk of health and safety (iv) a person not employed by him (v) who may be affected by such conduct of the accused's undertaking …. if there is actual injury as a result of the conduct of that operation, there is prima facie liability subject to the defence of reasonable practicability". A further appeal to the House of Lords was also dismissed, their Lordships holding that the appellants had rightly been convicted of the s.3(1) offence. In relation to determining whether the work involved came within the definition under s.3(1) Lord Hoffman said *"The employer is under a duty s.3(1) to exercise control over an activity if it forms part of the conduct of his undertaking. The existence of such a duty cannot therefore be the test for deciding whether the activity is part of the undertaking or not. Likewise, the question of whether an employer may leave an independent contractor to do the work as he thinks fit depends upon whether having the work done forms part of the employer's conduct of his undertaking. If it does, he owes a duty under s.3(1) to ensure that it is done without risk - subject, of course to reasonable practicability, which may limit the extent to which the employer can supervise the activities of a specialist independent contractor. Although the case was very much on the borderline, I think that there was evidence upon which the justices were entitled to find the particular circumstances of the case that having the asbestos sheets removed was part of the employer's undertaking. The facts were a matter for them and their decision should not have been disturbed."*

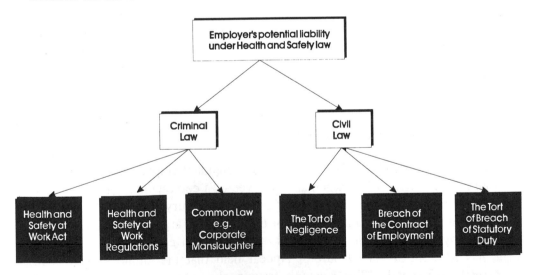

Employer's potential liability under Health and Safety Law

In determining reasonable practicability under s.3(1) it is necessary to consider the extent of control over the contractor, the requirement of instruction as to work methods and safety measures, the degree of risk and the competence and experience of the workmen.

In *R v. Board of Trustees of the Science Museum* 1993 the museum was convicted of an offence under s.3(1) for operating an air conditioning unit in such a way as to produce a risk of legionnaires disease. On appeal the museum maintained that it had not been proved that they had exposed the public to any actual risk of the disease for the purposes of s.3(1) or created any actual condition of danger through escape of bacteria. The Court of Appeal rejected this interpretation of 'risk' under s.3(1) deciding that the word referred to the possibility of bacterial infection rather than actual danger. The court took the view that the legislation exists to put pressure on employers to prevent conditions of risk so that it was enough to show that there was a risk of the escape of bacteria.

Further guidance as to the interpretation of s.3 was provided by the Court of Appeal in *R. v. Mara 1987.* Here the defendant, Mr. Mara, a director of a cleaning company called CMS Ltd., was convicted of an offence in that he had permitted a breach of his company's duty under s.3. The company had failed to conduct its undertaking in such a way as to ensure that persons not in its employment were exposed to health and safety risks. The facts were that the cleaning company had contracted to clean premises owned by International Stores plc on weekdays. This involved using electrical cleaning machines. As the loading bay could not be cleaned because it was in constant use, it was agreed that employees of International Stores should do the work using CMS equipment. One Saturday morning whilst using a CMS cleaning machine, a Store's employee was electrocuted due to the defective condition of the machine's cable. Mr. Mara was convicted and fined for an offence under s.3. On appeal however it was submitted that as the incident occurred on a Saturday morning, when the cleaning company did not work, it was not *'conducting its undertaking'* at all, and so could not be in breach of its duty. The Court of Appeal rejected the submission however, holding that s.3 could not be limited to situations where a company's undertaking is in the process of actively being carried on. The way in which CMS Ltd. conducted its undertaking was to clean during weekdays and leave their equipment for use by their client's employees, at weekends. By failing to ensure that its equipment was safely wired the company was in breach of its s.3 duty to its client's employees. Consequently the director had rightly been convicted of an offence.

This case provides an example of a rare prosecution brought against an individual director of a company rather than the company itself. Under the Act proceedings may be taken against a director of a company which, with his consent or due to his negligence committed an offence. In a prosecution brought against Mr Chapman in

1992 whose company had contravened a prohibition notice, the Crown Court used its powers under the Company Directors Disqualification Act 1986 to ban him from being a company director for two years in addition to a £5,000 fine and a £5,000 fine on the company.

Attorney General's Reference No 2 of 1999, 2000 arose following the prosecution brought as a result of the Southall rail crash in 1997. The defendant company admitted liability under s.3(1) and was fined £1.5 million for what the judge described as *"a serious fault of senior management". Further indictments however for corporate manslaughter failed the judges ruling that to secure a conviction for manslaughter by gross negligence it was necessary to establish a guilty mind and where a corporate is the defendant it may only be convicted via the guilty mind of a human being with whom it may be identified".* This ruling was the subject of an appeal by the Attorney General. The Court of Appeal held that a defendant can be convicted of manslaughter by gross negligence in the absence of evidence as to that defendants state of mind provided his conduct can be judged criminal perhaps through recklessness. However the court further ruled that a corporation cannot be convicted of manslaughter unless an employee embodying the company can be identified as guilty of manslaughter. *"Unless an identified individual's conduct, characterisable as grossly criminal negligence, can be attributed to the company, the company is not, in the present state of the common law, liable for manslaughter."* The High Court in *R. v. Director of Public Prosecution and Others* 2000 stated that *"The test of negligent manslaughter is an objective one, as was made clear in the judgment of the Court of Appeal in Attorney General's Reference No. 2 of 1999. If the accused is subjectively reckless, then that may be taken into account by the jury as a strong factor demonstrating that his negligence was criminal. But negligence will still be criminal in the absence of any recklessness if, on an objective basis, the defendant demonstrated a failure to advert to a serious risk going beyond mere inadvertence in respect of an obvious and important matter which the defendant's duty demanded he should address."*

Duty for Premises and Machinery

By virtue of s.4 a general duty is imposed on those who control work premises to ensure *so far as is reasonably practicable the safety of the premises, any means of access and exit from the place of work, and of any plant or substance provided for use on the premises.*

The duty extends to persons in control of non-domestic premises which are made available as a place of work and is owed to those who are not their employees.

Under s.4(2) "It shall be the duty of each person who has control of non-domestic premises or of the means of access thereto or therefrom or any plant or equipment in such premises, to take such measures as is reasonable for a person in his position to take to ensure, so far as is reasonably practicable, that the premises, all means of access available for use by persons using the premises and any plant or equipment in such premises is safe and without risk to health."

In *H M Inspector of Factories v. Austin Rover Group Ltd.* 1989 the defendants were prosecuted for a breach of s.4(2) when the employee of a contractor working on the defendants' premises was killed following a sudden flash fire where he was working. A combination of breaches of safety instructions had contributed to the cause of the fire and at the original trial the defendants were convicted of a s.4(2) offence for failing to take precautions which would have constituted "reasonable measures" and been "reasonably practicable" for a person in the position of Austin Rover. On appeal and then further appeal to the House of Lords however, it was held that in determining the reasonableness of the measures to be taken under s.4(2) account must be taken of the extent of control and knowledge of the occupier in relation to the actual use to which the premises are put. *"If the premises are not a reasonably foreseeable cause of danger, to anyone acting in a way which a person reasonably may be expected to act, in circumstances which reasonably may be expected to occur during the carrying out of the work, or the use of the plant or substance for the purpose of which the premises were made available, it would not be reasonable to require an individual to take further measures against unknown and unexpected risks."*

A successful prosecution under s.4(2) requires the proof of:

- unsafe premises and a risk to health;

- the identity of the individual having control of the premises; and

- the fact that the person in control ought reasonably to have taken measures to ensure safety.

On proof of these three matters the onus then shifts to the accused to show that it was not reasonably practicable to take such measures. As in the present case, the defendant could not have reasonably foreseen the unknown and unexpected events which made the premises unsafe, they would not be held to be in breach of s.4(2). Lord Jauncey made the important point that the *"safety of premises was not an abstract concept. It must be related to the purpose for which the premises were being used at any one time. Some premises might be unsafe for any normal use, for instance because of large unguarded holes in the floor or unstable walls. Other premises might be completely safe for the purposes for which they were designed but completely unsafe for other purposes, for example, an upper floor warehouse designed to a loading capacity of x lbs might become unsafe if loaded to a capacity of 2xlbs. If A made the warehouse available to B who used it within the designed loading capacity, it could not be said that the warehouse was unsafe and a risk to health under s.4(2) because B at some future date exceeds that capacity contrary to A's instructions".*

A further general duty imposed on those who control work premises is to *use the best practicable means to prevent the emission of offensive substances and to render harmless and inoffensive those substances emitted.*

Those who design, manufacture, import or supply any article for use at work are required under s.6 in so far as is reasonably practicable to ensure the article's safety, to carry out necessary testing and examining and provide sufficient information about the use of the article at work to render it safe and without risks to health.

Finally there is a general duty on every employee while at work under s.7 to take reasonable care for the health and safety of himself and of other persons who may be affected by his acts or omissions at work and to cooperate with employers in the discharge of their health and safety duties. Those employees who act in disregard of health and safety should be counselled but in the end dismissed if they are a danger to themselves or others. Wilful breaches of a safety rule, for instance a no smoking policy was held to be a justifiable reason for dismissal in *Roger v. Wicks and Wilson* 1988.

Certainly there is no room to be complacent about compliance with health and safety law for of the 5000 or so deaths at the workplace over the last ten years in the UK, the Health and Safety Executive estimated that over 70% are due to the failure of companies to provide workers with adequate safety equipment, training, supervision and instruction as they are bound to do under the legislation. Lack of enforcement, particularly against individual directors or managers is a particular cause for concern and the small number of prosecutions that are brought against companies only result in a limited fine in the Magistrates Court.

Civil Redress

A further major objective of the law relating to health and safety at the workplace is to provide a means by which those who have suffered injury may recover compensation. Since the mid 1960s, state benefit has been available for employees who suffer injury from accidents arising out of and in the course of employment or contract prescribed industrial diseases. If injury is caused through fault however, whether of the employer or a fellow worker, an injured person can bring a claim for damages through the courts. If it can be shown that injury has occurred as a result of a failure to comply with a regulation under the Health and Safety at Work Act 1974 or some other statutory obligation, for instance under the Factories Act 1961, then a claim could be brought for damages under a civil action for breach of statutory duty. This action has the status of a separate tort and can provide a means of redress for persons who suffer harm as a result of a breach of a duty imposed by statute.

The Tort of Breach of Statutory Duty

To succeed in an action based upon breach of statutory duty it is necessary to prove:

- that the statute in question imposes a statutory duty on the defendant which is owed to the plaintiff;

- that the defendant is in breach of the statutory duty; and

- that the plaintiff suffered injury as a result and the harm caused was of a kind contemplated by the statute.

In cases where the duty imposed by statute is a strict one, then the burden on the plaintiff is to prove that it has been broken without the need to show any fault on the part of the defendant. In applying s.14(1) of the Factories Act 1961 therefore, *"Every dangerous part of any machinery ... shall be securely fenced unless it is in such a position or of such construction as to be as safe to every person employed or working on the premises as it would be if securely fenced"* , it is necessary to show:

- that the Factories Act applies to the premises in question and that the s.14(1) duty is imposed on the employer and is owed to the employee;

- that the machine in question is a source of danger and that it was not securely fenced;

- that the employee suffered injury as a result of the failure to securely fence and the harm was a type contemplated by the section.

In *Wearing v. Pirelli Ltd.* 1977 the plaintiff suffered a broken wrist when his hand came into contact with a rubber coating around a revolving metal drum which had not been securely fenced. The House of Lords held that the employers were liable for breach of their statutory duty under s.14(1) to fence securely dangerous parts of machinery despite the fact that the employee's hand had come in contact with the rubber coating only, rather than the machinery itself.

The Factories Act 1961 s.29(1) provides that there shall so far as is reasonably practicable, be provided and maintained safe means of access to every place at which any person has at any time to work and every such place shall, so far as is reasonably practicable, be made and kept safe for any person working there.

In *Larner v. British Steel plc* 1993 the Court of Appeal confirmed that in relation to s.29(1) the burden of proof lies with the employer to show what was or was not reasonably practicable. Also the argument by the employer that *'safe'* means safe from reasonably foreseeable danger was also rejected. The word *'safe'* the court said is to be applied as a question of fact and indicates a higher duty of care than that imposed under the common law.

The notion that "reasonable foreseeability" should be imported into s.29(1) was rejected more recently by the Court of Session.

In *Mains v. Uniroyal Englebert Tyres Ltd.* 1995 the plaintiff suffered a hand injury when he was adjusting a tyre building machine but his claims in negligence and for breach of s.29(1) were rejected on the grounds that the accident was not reasonably foreseeable. On appeal the Court of Session took a different view of s.29(1) and held that *"it is not necessary for an employee seeking a remedy under s.29(1) to show that the unsafe state of the place of work causing the accident should have been reasonably foreseeable by the employers. The section imposes a duty on employers to prevent any risk of injury arising from the state or condition of the workplace. There is nothing in the section to suggest that the obligation is only to prevent any risk arising if that risk is of a reasonably foreseeable nature."*

There are of course new health and safety regulations (see earlier in the chapter) which are replacing the factory legislation. Section s.29 is now superseded by the Workplace (Health, Safety and Welfare) Regulations 1992 and now new issues of interpretation such as the burden of proof will arise.

Common Law Negligence

An alternative course of action for an employee who has suffered harm due to the fault of his employer or a fellow employee is to base a claim on common law negligence. Under the common law, an employer owes a legal duty of care to ensure the health and safety of his employees and this duty takes effect on an implied term of the contract of employment. An employer is required to take reasonable care with regard to the safety of his employees by providing a safe system of work. The provision of a safe system of work involves an obligation to provide safe fellow employees, safe plant and equipment, safe working premises and safe working methods. If an employer is in breach of his common law duty to take reasonable care, and damage in the form of injury is caused as a result, he will be liable.

It should be stressed that in civil proceedings it is often the case that a claim is based upon both the breach of a common law duty and for breach of statutory duty if relevant.

In *Smith v. Vange Scaffolding & Engineering Company Ltd. and Another* 1970 the plaintiff scaffolder suffered injury when he fell over a welding cable when walking back from his place of work. The High Court held that the employee's immediate employers were liable for breach of their common law duty of care because they were aware of the dangerous state of the site where their employees worked. In addition the employers were in breach of their statutory duty imposed, by regulation 6 of the Construction (working places) Regulations 1966, to provide a suitable and sufficient access to an egress from the plaintiff's place of work.

Certainly there is no intention that statutory regulation is designed to supersede the common law so that even if an employer has complied with a regulation, for instance to supply his workers with safety equipment, an employee is still entitled to pursue a claim under the common law if he is injured due to a failure to wear it.

In *Bux v. Slough Metals* 1973 the plaintiff lost the sight of one eye as a result of a splash from molten metal when he was pouring it into a die. While safety goggles had been supplied, the plaintiff refused to wear them because they misted up, and no attempt was made to persuade him otherwise. The Court of Appeal held that while the employer had provided suitable goggles for the purpose of safety regulations, they were nevertheless negligent under the common law. The evidence suggested that the plaintiff would have followed clear instructions to wear the goggles, and that the question whether or not an employer's common law duty of care extended to instructing, persuading or insisting on the use of protective equipment depended on the facts. By failing to make use of the goggles the plaintiff was guilty of contributory fault and damages were reduced by forty percent.

As far as safety equipment is concerned, the contemporary view seems to be that the common law duty to make it available and ensure that employees are aware of it does not necessarily carry with it any further obligation to inspect it or insist that it is worn. Obviously there is some obligation on the employee to take some responsibility for his own safety by ensuring that safety equipment is renewed when necessary.

In *Smith v. Scott Bowyers Ltd.* 1986 the plaintiff, who was just twenty years of age, and employed by the company for nineteen months, suffered injury when he slipped on the greasy factory floor. To help minimise the risk the employer provided the workers with wellington boots with diamond ridge soles and they were renewed on request. Having already replaced one pair of boots the accident was due to the plaintiff's failure to renew the replacement pair which had also worn out and were a danger. In an action for damages for breach of the employer's duty of care, the High Court found that the failure of the employers to emphasise the danger and carry out checks of the safety equipment made them in breach of the legal duty of care they owed to the plaintiff. Damages were to be reduced by one third however, due to the plaintiff's contributory fault. On appeal however, the Court of Appeal reversed the decision and held that there was no breach of the employer's duty to take reasonable care. The failure of the employee to renew the boots was due to his own lack of care and could not be taken as the fault of the employer. *"The employer's duty to provide employees with properly designed Wellington boots would not be filled out with any further obligation to instruct them to wear them or to inspect the condition of the soles from time to time."*

In *Pape v. Cumbria County Council* 1991 the plaintiff had been employed as a cleaner by the council for many years and her job involved the use of chemical cleaning materials and detergents. While rubber gloves were supplied they were rarely used the employer failing to point out the dangers of frequent contact of the skin with cleaners or encouraging the use of gloves. In 1982 the plaintiff was diagnosed as suffering from dermatitis and told by a consultant to protect her skin at work. This she did but her medical condition deteriorated so that all her skin became infected and in 1989 she gave up her job as a result. Mrs Pape claimed damages against her employer for negligence in that her dermatitis resulted from exposure to chemicals in the course of her employment and the employer was in breach of a clear duty to warn of the dangers and persuade staff to take preventative measures. The High Court awarded her £58,000 in damages stating that *"there is a duty on an employer to warn cleaners of the dangers of handling chemical cleaning materials with unprotected hands and to instruct them as to the need to wear gloves all the time. The argument on behalf of the defendant that an employer's duty to his office cleaners is fully discharged when he provides them with gloves could not be accepted."* The risk of dermatitis was not an obvious risk to the cleaners but should be appreciated by a reasonable employer.

The common law duty encompasses an obligation to provide safe plant and appliances. If an employer was aware that machinery or tools are not reasonably safe, and an employee is injured as a result, the employer will be in breach of his duty under the common law.

In *Bradford v. Robinson Rentals* 1967 the employer provided an unheated van for the employee, a 57 year old, to make a 400 mile journey during the winter, which would involve him in at least 20 hours driving. The court held that the employer was liable for the employee's frost bite, which was the type of injury that was reasonably foreseeable from prolonged exposure to severe cold and fatigue. The court also confirmed that even if the plaintiff had been abnormally susceptible to frost bite he would still be entitled to succeed under the rule that the defendant must take his victim as he finds him.

In the past an employer could satisfy his duty to provide safe equipment by showing that he purchased the equipment from a reputable supplier and that he had no knowledge of any defect. Now however, following the Employers Liability (Defective Equipment) Act 1969, injury occurring to an employee under those circumstances may be attributed to the deemed negligence of the employer. If damages are awarded against the employer then it is up to him to seek a remedy from the supplier of the defective equipment.

In *Knowles v. Liverpool City Council* 1993 a council *"flagger"* was injured when a flagstone he was handling broke because it had not been properly cured by the supplier. He relied on the Employer's Liability (Defective Equipment) Act 1969 to impose liability on his employer who is deemed to be negligent if injury occurs as a result of equipment provided from a supplier. The main issue before the court was whether equipment defined as plant and machinery vehicles, aircraft and clothing, would cover a flagstone which seems to fall in the category of work materials. The Court of Appeal and subsequently the House of Lords agreed with the county court and held that the term equipment should be interpreted broadly to include *the "materials which an employee is given by his employer to use to do his job. Such a broad approach reflects the general purpose of the legislation and is consistent with the ordinary meaning of the word in the context of an employee carrying out his job"*. As a consequence the employer was liable under the 1969 Act for the injuries sustained by the plaintiff by the defective equipment used in the course of employment.

The obligation to provide a safe system of work also encompasses a requirement to provide safe fellow employees. If there are untrained or unskilled people employed at the workplace then a higher standard of care is owed by the employer to ensure their safety and the safety of those who work with them.

In *Hawkins v. Ross Castings Ltd.* 1970 the plaintiff was injured following a spillage of molten metal, due partly to the employer's failure to comply with safety regulations in relation to the maintenance of a safe pouring systems. An additional contributing factor was the fact that the plaintiff was working closely with a seventeen year old untrained Indian who spoke little English and yet was required to carry and pour molten metal with the plaintiff. This factor contributed to the employer's liability.

The conduct of fellow employees of contributing to an unhealthy working environment by smoking could be the responsibility of the employer in relation to an employee who suffers damage to health through passive smoking. The judgment in *Dryden v. Greater Glasgow Health Board* 1997 makes it clear that an employee who smokes cannot insist on an implied term entitling him to smoke or have access to smoking facilities. If a no smoking policy is introduced for a legitimate purpose, the health and welfare of the staff, the fact that it makes life difficult for non smokers is of no consequence. The later case of *Walton and Morse v. Dorrington* 1997 establishes a clear duty on employers in relation to the health of non smokers to ensure that they do not suffer the effects of passive smoking.(see Chapter 10).

The duty to provide safe fellow employees exists irrespective of any issue of the employer's vicarious liability for the actions of his employees. Vicarious liability is considered later in the chapter. If an employee is injured through the negligence of some third party then the court must decide in the circumstances whether this constitutes a breach of the employer's duty of care ar J so imposing liability.

> In *Reid v. Rush & Tompkins Group* 1989 the plaintiff driver claimed that his employer was in breach of their duty of care in failing to insure him or advising him to obtain insurance cover when driving abroad. The plaintiff had suffered severe injuries as a result of an accident which occurred in Ethiopia resulting from the negligence of another driver. Both the High Court and the Court of Appeal were reluctant to impose liability on the employer for the loss sustained by the employee. *"It was impossible to imply into the plaintiff's contract of service any term a breach of which would entitle him to recover damages from the defendants for the loss he sustained. There was no basis on the facts as pleaded for holding that the defendants gave an implied undertaking to insure his plaintiff against the risk of uncompensated injury caused to him, while acting in the course of his employment in Ethiopia, by third party drivers."*

The employer's common law duty also imposes an obligation to provide safe working methods and safe working premises. To determine whether an employer is providing safe working methods, it is necessary to consider a number of factors including:

- the layout of the work place;

- training and supervision;

- warnings; and

- whether protective equipment is provided.

It should be stressed that the common law duty on an employer is to take reasonable care, and if he gives proper instructions which the employee fails to observe then the employer will not be liable if the employee is then injured.

In *Charlton v. Forrest Printing Ink Company Ltd.* 1980 the employer gave proper instructions to an employee who was given the job of collecting the firm's wages. The instructions required the employee to vary his collecting arrangements to prevent robbery. The employee failed to do this and suffered severe injury when he was robbed. The Court of Appeal held that the employer was not liable as he had taken reasonable steps to cut down the risk. The normal industrial practice of firms of that size in that area was to make their own payroll collection rather than employ a security firm. The employers *"did what was reasonable in the circumstances to eliminate the risk and no more could have been expected of them. They could not be held liable for the injuries incurred by the employee"*.

It should be stressed that the common law duty is not one of strict liability but rather a duty to take reasonable care in the circumstances.

In *Latimer v. AEC* 1953 after a factory was flooded, the employer asked his workforce to return, warning them of the dangerous state of the factory floor. Sawdust had been used to cover most of the damp areas but not enough was available, and the plaintiff slipped, and was injured. To determine whether the employer had broken the common law duty of care he owed his employees the court weighed the cost of avoiding the injury against the risk of injury and held that the employer had acted reasonably in the circumstances.

In *Dixon v. London Fire and Civil Defence* 1993 the fire authority was held not to be in breach of its common law duty of care to an officer who slipped and fell as a result of a wet floor. The fact that water had leaked on to the floor of the fire station from an appliance did not constitute negligence for such an occurrence was endemic in the fire service and appeared to be insoluble.

If the plaintiff is a trained professional it may be reasonable to allow the employer to rely on the plaintiff's expertise without the need for warnings or instruction.

In *Woolgar v. West Surrey and Hampshire Health Authority* 1993 the Court of Appeal held that the defendant was not in breach of duty when it failed to warn a nurse against the use of a method of lifting a patient which caused the nurse back injury. The nurse should have realised the likely consequences of her action and used her own reasonable skill and judgement.

The courts have recognised that to require an employee to work long hours, which is related to health problems, could put an employer in breach of his common law duty.

In *Johnstone v. Bloomsbury Health Authority* 1991 the plaintiff, a senior house officer, was required to work forty hours by his contract with an additional average of forty eight hours per week on call. He alleged that some weeks he had been required to work for one hundred hours with inadequate sleep and as a consequence he suffered from stress, depression, diminished appetite, exhaustion and suicidal feelings. It was claimed that the employers were in breach of the legal duty to take reasonable care for the safety and well being of their employee by requiring him to work intolerable hours with deprivation of sleep. The majority of the Court of Appeal held that an employer's express contractual rights had to be exercised in the light of their duty to take care of the employee's safety and if the employer knew that they were exposing an employee to the risk of injury to health by requiring him to work such long hours, then they should not require him to work more hours than he safely could have done.

Although only a majority decision, the Court of Appeal by this judgment is recognising that the implied objective of health and safety in an employment contract may override a clear express contractual right in relation to the hours of work.

There is an increased recognition that individual employees may suffer stress as a direct result of their work. If an employer has reason to believe that this is the case and takes no steps to alleviate the problem there is now authority to suggest he could be in breach of duty.

In *Walker v. Northumberland CC* 1995 the High Court held that a local authority was in breach of duty if care to a senior social worker who was required to cope with an increased workload despite the fact the employer was aware of his susceptibility to mental breakdown. Mr Justice Coleman said that *"An employer owes a duty to his employees not to cause them psychiatric damage by the volume or character of the work which they are required to perform. Although the law on the extent of the duty on an employer to provide an employee with a safe system of work and to take reasonable steps to protect him from risks which are reasonably foreseeable has developed almost exclusively in cases involving physical injury to the employee, there is no logical reason why risk of injury to an employee's mental health should be excluded from the scope of the employer's duty. The standard of care required for performance of that duty must be measured against the yardstick of reasonable conduct on the part of a person in the employer's position. What is reasonable depends on the nature of the relationship, the magnitude of the risk of injury which was reasonably foreseeable, the seriousness of the consequences for the person to whom the duty is owed of the risk eventuating, and the cost and practicability of preventing the risk. The practicability of remedial measures must take into account the resources and facilities at the disposal of the person or body who owes the duty of care, and purpose of the activity which has given rise to the risk of injury".*

It should be noted that a material fact in deciding liability in the Walker case was that the plaintiff complained of his employers breach of duty in relation to a second nervous breakdown which was reasonably forseeable.Previously Mr Walker had suffered a breakdown due to the stress caused by his heavy workload which was not reasonably foreseeable and for which there would have been no breach of duty. By allowing Mr Walker to be exposed to the same workload as before however the employer should have appreciated that he was as a result of the first breakdown more vulnerable to psychiatric damage.

Employers should be aware of the case of stress and can obtain that stress by carrying out a full assessment of

- factors that could lead to stress including the stress levels of particular job functions

- training requirements for staff, particularly those changing job functions

- individual needs and the requirement to record individual progress

- potential signs of deterioration due to work loads.

In *Lancaster v. Birmingham City Council* 1999 the employee had been moved from a technical environment to a customer contact role in the housing department. Unfortunately no adequate training had been provided to deal with the particular stresses that the job entailed. When she suffered mental illness as a result of the change the court found that the employers had taken no obvious steps to deal with the problem. An award of £67,000 in damages was made against her employer.

In *White v. Chief Constable of South Yorkshire Police* 1999 a claim for damages in the tort of negligence was brought by police officers who suffered post traumatic stress disorder as a result of tendering the dead and injured following the Hillsborough disaster in 1987. They claimed that their employer owed them a duty of care as employees/rescuers to avoid exposing them to increasing risk of physical or psychiatric injury. Claims by police officers who had actually dragged dead and injured spectators from the scene and risked injury themselves had earlier been conceded and settled by their employers. By a majority the Court of Appeal held that a duty of care was owed to those officers at the ground who suffered psychiatric harm as rescuers and the primary victims of their employer's negligence. On further appeal to the House of Lords the decision was reversed by a majority and the door seems to be closed on further expansion of potential liability for psychiatric loss. The police officers could not be classified as primary victims of the defendants negligence for it does not follow that a duty to avoid causing physical harm extends to psychiatric injury except in stress related cases such as *Walker v. Northumberland County Council 1995*. Here the harm resulted from a traumatic experience as a secondary victim and as the police officers lacked the close ties of love and affection with the victims a duty of care could not extend to them. Also to qualify as rescuers their psychiatric harm must result from a fear of foreseeable physical injury and this was held not to be the case here.

The standard of care owed by an employer will vary with regard to each individual employee. A young apprentice should be provided with effective supervision while this may not be required for an experienced employee.

In *Paris v. Stepney BC* 1951 the plaintiff, a one-eyed motor mechanic, lost the sight of his good eye while working at chipping rust from under a bus. Despite there being no usual practice to provide mechanics with safety goggles, the court decided that they should have been provided to the plaintiff. The defendants were liable as they could foresee serious consequences for the plaintiff if he suffered eye injury. *"The special risk of injury is a relevant consideration in determining the precautions which the employer should take in the fulfilment of the duty of care which he owes to the workman."*

If an employer is in breach of the implied common law duty that he owes to an employee this could lead to a claim for unfair constructive dismissal.

In *Pickford v. Imperial Chemical Industries* 1998 a secretary who suffered *repetitive strain injury* due to her secretarial duties claimed that her employer had been negligent in failing to instruct her about the need for rest breaks and work organisation to alleviate the need for long periods of typing. By a majority decision the Court of Appeal reversed the decision of the High Court and found that the employer was in breach of the duty of care he owed to his employee. A majority of the House of Lords however reversed the Court of Appeal and confirmed the decision of the High Court and dismissed the claim. They felt that Ms Pickford as a general secretary had a number of duties other than typing and would have organised her own rest periods from the word processor. In addition they thought that the medical evidence was insufficient to prove that her condition was caused by repetitive movements while typing.

In *Pagano v. HAS* 1976 the complainant employee was a gas converter who had made a number of complaints about the unfit state of the company vans he was required to use in his job without a constructive response from the employer. When he was issued with a van with faulty brakes he drove it to the Department of the Environment's vehicle testing station and submitted the van for inspection. After the test a prohibition ban was issued on the vehicle and the complainant resigned, concerned for his own safety and his own potential liability under the Road Traffic Acts. His claim of constructive dismissal was upheld in the tribunal (see Chapter 10).

Defences Available to the Employer

In very exceptional cases the plaintiff may be taken to have consented to the risk of injury and the defence of "volenti non fit injuria" (no wrong is done to one who consents) established.

In *Imperial Chemical Industries v. Shatwell* 1965 two employees, both experienced shot firers, in contravention of specific safety instructions, fired a shot causing injury to both of them. The House of Lords held that the employer could rely on volenti as an absolute defence to the action, due to the act of gross disobedience.

It is more likely that the employer will be able to rely on the Law Reform (Contributory Negligence) Act 1945 which provides a partial defence. If the employer can show that the injured employee contributed to his injury by his own fault then damages may be reduced to *"such extent as the court thinks just and equitable having regard to the claimants share in the responsibility for the damage"*.

If the employer can show that the injured employee contributed to his injury by his own fault then damages may be reduced to *"such extent as the court thinks just and equitable having regard to the claimants share in the responsibility for the damage"*.

You will remember that in the case of *Bux v. Slough Metals* 1973 (mentioned earlier in the chapter) the damages awarded were reduced by forty percent to reflect the employees contributory fault.

Unfair Dismissal

As we mentioned earlier, part of the common law duty is that an employer must take reasonable care to ensure that he provides his workers with safe fellow workers. To engage an employee who has a past record of dangerous behaviour could put the employees at risk and constitute a negligent act on the part of the employer for which he could be made directly liable. Certainly if an employer is aware of an employee who by incompetence or practical jokes is creating a dangerous situation at work he should take steps to discipline him and if necessary dismiss him. In such circumstances a qualified employee could potentially present a complaint of unfair dismissal but as we shall see in Chapter 11 the determination of such an issue will depend upon the tribunal's view of the reasonableness of the employer's action.

Under the Trade Union Reform and Employment Rights Act 1993 a new category of automatically unfair dismissal was introduced as it is now found in s.104 of the Employment Rights Act 1996. The new right applies irrespective of an employee's length of service. It covers the situation where an employee is dismissed for acting as a safety representative or bringing health and safety matters to the employers attention. Dismissals under s.104 are covered in Chapter 11 on Unfair Dismissal.

A new right on employees not to suffer a detriment by an employer for carrying out health and safety activities has also been inserted as s.44 of the Employment Rights Act 1996.

Under s.44(1) An employee has the right not to be subjected to any detriment by any act, or any deliberate failure to act, by his employer done on the ground that-

(a) having been designated by the employer to carry out activities in connection with preventing or reducing risks to health and safety at work, he carried out, or proposed to carry out, any such activities,

(b) being a representative of workers on matters of health and safety at work, or a member of a safety committee the employee performed, or proposed to perform, any functions as such a representative or a member of such a committee,

(c) being an employee at a place where-

(i) there was no such representative or safety committee, or

(ii) there was such a representative or safety committee but it was not reasonably practicable for the employee to raise the matter by those means,

he brought to his employer's attention, by reasonable means, circumstances connected with his work which he reasonably believed were harmful or potentially harmful to health or safety,

(d)   *in circumstances of danger which he reasonably believed to be serious and imminent and which he could not reasonably have been expected to avert, he left, or proposed to leave, or (while the danger persisted) refused to return to, his place of work or any dangerous part of his place of work, or*

(e)   *in circumstances of danger which he reasonably believed to be serious and imminent, he took, or proposed to take, appropriate steps to protect himself or other persons from the danger.*

The new right not to suffer a detriment for carrying out health and safety functions applies to safety representatives and individual employees who raise health and safety matters with the employer where there is no safety committee. If a health and safety risk is perceived to be a serious danger the section also purports to confer protection on employees who refuse to work. The right under s.44 is enforceable by means of a complaint to the employment tribunal.

The legal responsibility of an employer extends to where an employee under his control causes harm to a fellow employee or a third party by some wrongful act. This is by virtue of vicarious (substituted) liability, an important feature of an employer's responsibility to which we should devote some attention.

Vicarious Liability

There are some situations where the law is prepared to impose vicarious (substituted) liability on an individual who is not at fault for the commission of the wrongful (tortious) act of another. The best known example of this situation is the common law rule which imposes vicarious liability on employers in respect of torts committed by their employees during the course of their employment. Accordingly, if one employee (Jones) by his negligent act causes harm to a fellow employee (Smith) then in addition to the possibility of (Smith) pursuing a legal action against (Jones) he may have the further option of suing his employer who will have become vicariously liable if the negligent act occurred during the course of Jones's employment. The same principle applies equally where the injuries are caused by an employee to some third party. However, while employers have a choice as to whether they insure against the risk of injury to third parties, under the Employer's Liability (Compulsory Insurance) Act 1969, an employer is required to insure himself in respect of injuries caused by his employees to their colleagues.

The imposition of vicarious liability does not require proof of any fault on the employer's part, or any express or implied authorisation to commit the wrongful act. All that must be proved for the purpose of vicarious liability is:

(1)   *an actionable wrong committed by the worker;*

(2)   *that the worker is an employee;*

(3)   *that the wrongful act occurred during the course of his employment.*

What then is the *theoretical* basis for imposing liability in these circumstances? A number of reasons have emerged, such as he who creates and benefits from a situation should assume the risk of liability arising from it. There is also the idea that if an organisation embarks on an enterprise and as a result harm is caused by one member of the organisation, it should be the responsibility of the organisation to compensate for the harm. It is after all the employer who selects and controls the employees who work for him. The employer has the responsibility of training staff and can of course dismiss those whose work is performed incompetently. The practical reason for vicarious liability is of course that if the employee were solely liable he would have to insure himself, and the cost of this would be indirectly borne by the employer in the form of higher wages. Under the present system insurance costs are borne directly by the employer who, as a principle of sound business practice, will normally carry adequate insurance.

To determine an employer's liability it is first necessary to establish the employment status of the worker who is alleged to have committed the wrongful act. This is because the legal position differs dramatically depending on whether the worker is employed as an employee under a contract of service rather than as a self employed contractor under a contract for services. Usually this issue may be settled without argument but in the small proportion of cases where there is doubt the courts are left with the task of identifying the true contractual status of the worker by applying the law contained in Chapter 3. It is convenient to deal with the legal position of employees and independent contractors separately.

Employees

As a general principle an employer is vicariously liable for the tortious acts of his employees committed during the course of their employment. The *phrase course of employment* has produced numerous interpretations in the courts, but essentially it concerns the question of whether the employee was doing his job at the time of the *tortious act*. It should be emphasised that an employee will have both express and implied authority to perform work for his employer and while he will normally have no authority to commit torts, he may nevertheless be guilty of a tortious act in the performance of his authorised duties.

In *Century Insurance Ltd. v. Northern Ireland Road Transport Board* 1942 a tanker driver while delivering petrol at a garage, lit a cigarette and carelessly threw away the lighted match which caused an explosion and considerable damage. His employer was held to be vicariously liable for his negligence as the employee had acted within the course of his employment. By supervising the unloading, the employee was doing his job, but by smoking he was doing it in a grossly negligent manner.

Even if an employee is carrying out an act outside the basic obligation of his contract of employment, his employer may nevertheless be made vicariously liable if the act is carried out for the benefit of the employer.

In *Kay v. ITW* 1968 the employee injured a colleague when he negligently drove a five ton diesel lorry which was blocking his way. Despite the fact that he was contractually authorised to drive only small vans and trucks, his employer was held to be vicariously liable for his action.

In *Iqbal v. London Transport Executive* 1974 a bus conductor had clearly stepped outside the course of his employment when he drove the bus and injured the plaintiff so that his employer could not be held responsible. In *Ilkiw v. Samuels* 1963 however the employer could be held liable for the driver's negligence when he allowed an unauthorised person to drive.

If an employee is doing something of purely personal benefit at the time of the negligent act then he may be regarded, to quote from the colourful language of the Victorian era as *"off on a frolic of his own"*, and his employer will not be responsible.

In *Hilton v. Thomas Burton (Rhodes) Ltd.* 1961 the plaintiff's husband was a demolition worker who was killed through the negligent driving of one of his colleagues. The defendant employer denied vicarious liability as, at the time of the accident, the van was being driven from a cafe on an unauthorised break. The court held that although the van had been driven with the permission of the employer, at the time of the incident the driver was not doing that which he was employed to do. Accordingly the employer was not liable for the negligent driving.

Guidance in relation to the possibility of vicarious liability being imposed when industrial action causes damage to property was provided by the Judicial Committee of the Privy Council in *General Engineering Services Ltd. v. Kingston and St. Andrews Corporation* 1989. The claim was based upon the notion that the corporation, having a statutory duty to extinguish fires, were vicariously liable for the negligence of the members of their fire brigade who had failed to respond promptly to an emergency call. The reason for the delay was that the fire brigade, in dispute with their employer, were operating a go slow. As a consequence of taking seventeen rather than three minutes to respond to a fire, a building and its contents were burned to the ground. Both the court of first instance and the Jamaica Court of Appeal held that in operating the go slow the brigade were not acting in the course of their employment, so that the employers could not be made vicariously liable. This was confirmed on final appeal to the Judicial Committee of the Privy Council. Here it was held that an act is deemed to have been done in the course of employment if it is either a wrongful act and authorised by the employer, or a wrongful and unauthorised mode of doing some authorised act. If however the employee's unauthorised and unlawful act could be regarded as independent and not connected with the authorised act so as to constitute a mode of doing it, the employer is not responsible. Here by operating a go slow the fire brigade were not carrying on a wrongful or authorised mode of doing an otherwise authorised act. By stopping and starting on their way to a fire this manner of driving had no connection with the authorised activity of driving to the scene of a fire as quickly as possible.

Taking industrial action therefore in furtherance of an industrial dispute, may have the effect of repudiating an essential obligation of the contract of employment, and if so unconnected with the employee's job, take him outside the course of his employment for the purpose of vicarious liability.

The extent to which an express prohibition by the employer will prevent vicarious liability will depend upon the nature of the prohibition. If it merely attempts to instruct the employee how he is to do his job, the employee may still be within the course of his employment for the purposes of vicarious liability.

In *Rose v. Plenty* 1976 a milkman, contrary to an express prohibition, engaged a thirteen year old boy to help him deliver the milk. The boy was subsequently injured by the milkman's negligent driving and sued both the milkman and his employer. The Court of Appeal held that despite the prohibition of the employer, he remained vicariously liable as the milkman had acted within the course of his employment. Scarman L.J. having considered the prohibition stated that *"There was nothing in the prohibition which defined or limited the sphere of his employment, the sphere of his employment remained precisely the same as before the prohibition was brought to his notice. The sphere was as a roundsman to go the rounds delivering milk, collecting empties and obtaining payment. Contrary to instructions the roundsman chose to do what he was employed to do in an improper way. But the sphere of his employment was in no way affected by his express instructions"*.

It seems therefore that only an express prohibition which effectively cuts down the *sphere of employment* will prevent the establishment of vicarious liability. The fact that contemporary courts seem to favour the idea of a very wide sphere of employment in individual cases, severely limits the opportunity of employers to restrict liability by express instruction. It is only by deciding the authorised parameters of an individual's job, and deciding that the act complained of fell outside these parameters that vicarious liability can be successfully denied.

Two recent decisions of the Court of Appeal confront the issue of course of employment and the potential common law liability of an employer for the abuse of children by school masters responsible for their care. In *ST v. North Yorkshire County Council* 1999 the county court had found the local authority employer vicariously liable for an alleged indecent assault by a deputy headmaster on the claimant, a mentally handicapped pupil in his care. Deciding that what occurred could not be described as a mode, authorised or not, of carrying out his work, the headmaster had stepped outside the course of employment when he committed the act so that the employer was not liable. The Court of Appeal also stressed that while this was the common law position different principles governed potential statutory liability.

The second case *L and Others v. Hesley Hall Ltd.* 1999 involved a similar issue of abuse by a housemaster of vulnerable boys in his care in a residential home. While accepting that there could be no vicarious liability for the acts of abuse the argument was advanced that the employer should be liable for the failure of the housemaster to report the fact that children had been traumatised and arrange treatment and protection. This argument was rejected however the court deciding that the failure to take remedial action was also part of a wrongful and unauthorised course of conduct outside the course of employment of the housemaster so the employer could not be made vicariously liable for it.

In *Joseph Rand v. Craig* 1919 carters employed to take rubbish to a tip were subject to an express prohibition against tipping other than on the authorised dump. On the question of liability for unauthorised tipping the court held that as the carters were employed to transport the rubbish to and from defined places, by unauthorised tipping they had stepped outside the course of their employment and so their employer could not be held liable for their conduct. If the act is done on the employer's premises with the employer's interest in mind, the employer may be made liable provided the act has a close connection with the employee's job.

Similarly in *Compton v. McClure* 1975 the employer was held to be vicariously liable for the negligence of an employee who, when late for work, caused an accident when driving negligently on the factory road.

Even the manager in a public house in *Stone v. Taffe* 1974 was held to be within the course of his employment when he negligently failed to ensure that a stairway was properly lighted for a customer, despite the fact that the injury occurred two and a half hours after licensed closing time.

The question as to whether an employee is acting within the course of his employment while required to travel from home to a workplace other than his regular one was addressed by the *House of Lords in Smith v. Stages and Another* 1989. Here an action was brought on behalf of an employee, who as a passenger in the defendant's car, suffered personal injuries as a result of the negligent driving of the defendant, a fellow employee. Despite the fact that the employers neither required nor authorised the journey by car to and from their particular workplace they were joined as second defendants on a claim that they were vicariously liable for the driver's negligence. The House of Lords held that employees who are required to travel to and from non regular workplaces, and in receipt of wages for doing so, remain within the course of their employment, even if they have a choice as to the mode and time of travel. Here the employee chose to travel in his own vehicle with the employer's knowledge and so the employers were vicariously liable for his negligent driving. Employees are in the course of their employment when going about their employer's business, and this will be the case if an employee is 'on duty' on his way to and from the workplace. This would not be so in relation to an employee travelling from home to and from his regular workplace whatever the mode of transport, unless obliged by his contract of service to use the employer's transport.

A number of prima facie propositions were suggested by the House of Lords in relation to the question as to whether an employee is acting in the course of his employment during travelling time. The receipt of wages would indicate that an employee was travelling in his employer's time, and acting in the course of his employment. Equally so would an employee travelling in the employer's time between different workplaces. An employee travelling in his employer's time from his ordinary residence to a workplace, other than his regular workplace, to the scene of an emergency such as a fire accident or mechanical breakdown of plant, would also be acting in the course of his employment. Deviations or interruptions of a journey undertaken in the course of employment unless merely incidental would normally take an employee outside the course of his employment.

While it may be reasonable for an employee to use a degree of force in protection of his employer's property, or to keep order, an employee who commits an assault which has no connection with his work will be solely liable for his conduct.

So in *Warren v. Henleys Ltd.* 1948 the employer was held not to be vicariously liable for a physical attack by a petrol pump attendant on one of his customers. The claim that the attendant was acting within the scope of his employment was rejected, for while the attack developed out of an argument over payment for petrol, it was in reality motivated by an act of private vengeance.

It is important to draw distinction between vicarious liability and the direct or primary liability of an employer.

In *Carmarthenshire County Council v. Lewis* 1955 a child at a local authority nursery school wandered from the school yard onto the highway and caused the death of a lorry driver who had swerved to avoid the child. An action was brought against the council in negligence on the grounds that the child's teacher left her unattended for a short time. In fact at the relevant time the teacher was attending to the needs of another child. The court held that the teacher had in fact fulfilled the common law duty of care required of her by acting as a prudent parent would in the circumstances. Consequently there could be no vicarious liability imposed on her employer. However, the fact that the child could reach the street so easily, indicated that the council were failing in their legal duty to operate a safe system at the school, and so were held to be directly liable for their primary negligence.

Another example of the distinction between the direct and vicarious liability of an employer is provided by the decision in *Nahhas v. Pier House (Cheyne Walk) Management* 1984. Here the tenant of a luxury flat deposited the key with a porter during a stay in hospital. This was the normal system operated by the owners, but unfortunately a porter, one of their employees, used the key to steal jewellery from the plaintiff's flat. In fact the porter had a long criminal record involving eleven prison terms of which his employer, the owners, were unaware. The court held that while the system of depositing keys was not negligent, the failure by the employer to thoroughly check the porter's background constituted a breach of the legal duty of care owed to the tenants which resulted in damage. Consequently the employers were liable for their primary negligence and also responsible vicariously for the criminal act of the porter carried out during the course of his employment.

Certainly to impose liability on an employer for the tortious or criminal acts of an employee under his control, there must be a connection between the act complained of and the circumstances of employment. The fact that employment gives the employee an opportunity to commit the wrongful act is insufficient to impose vicarious liability on the employer.

In *Heasmans v. Clarity Cleaning Company* 1987 the Court of Appeal found it possible to absolve the defendant cleaning company from liability for the acts of one of their cleaners who, while employed on the plaintiff's premises, used the plaintiff's telephone to make international telephone calls to the value of

£1411. The mere fact that the cleaner's employment provided the opportunity to fraudulently use the plaintiff's telephone was not itself sufficient to impose liability on the defendant.

Statutory Torts

An employer can be vicariously liable for the statutory torts of sex, race or disability discrimination committed by employees during the course of employment unless he can show that he took such steps as were reasonably practicable to prevent the employee from committing the act of discrimination. A contentious issue is the extent to which an employee can be regarded as acting within the course of employment when committing an act of racial or sexual harassment.

In *Irving & Irving v. Post Office* 1987 the complaint of race discrimination was based on the conduct of an employee of the post office who when sorting the mail had written a racially insulting comment on a letter addressed to his neighbours who were of Jamaican origin. The issue before the Court of Appeal was whether the employee was acting in the course of his employment so that the Post Office could be made vicariously liable for the discriminatory act. The employee's act of writing on the mail was clearly unauthorised so the question was whether the act was an unauthorised mode of doing an authorised act. Here the misconduct formed no part of the postman's duties and could not be regarded as an unauthorised way of performing his work. *"An employer is not to be held liable merely because the opportunity to commit the wrongful act had been created by the employee's employment, or because the act in question had been committed during the period of that particular employment".*

In *Bracebridge Engineering v. Derby* 1990 the complainant was the victim of serious sexual harassment by her supervisor which constituted unlawful discrimination. The employer was vicariously liable for the misconduct as at the time the act of sexual harassment took place the perpetrators were supposedly engaged in exercising their disciplinary and supervisory functions and were in the course of their employment. Here the court applied a liberal interpretation of course of employment.

In *Jones v. Tower Boot Co Ltd*. 1997 the EAT held that racial taunts of fellow workers were not an unauthorised wrongful act connected with employment so as to make the employer vicariously liable. *"The phrase in the course of employment has a well established meaning in law. The nub of the test is whether the unauthorised wrongful act of the servant is so connected with that which he was employed to do as to be a mode of doing it. That has to be judged by reference to all the circumstances of the case. Applying that test to the facts of the present case, the acts complained of, including the deliberate branding with a hot screwdriver and whipping, could not be described by any stretch of the imagination, as an improper mode of performing authorised tasks."* Adopting a sensible pragmatic approach to this type of case, the Court of Appeal, in giving emphasis to the object of the legislation gave the phrase *"course of employment"* different interpretation from that applied when potential vicarious liability is determined in relation to common law tort. For the purposes of statutory torts, such as race discrimination the court held that course of employment should be given an everyday meaning so that if an employee commits an act of race discrimination at the workplace his employer would be held liable.

This novel approach to the liability of employers for the statutory torts of their employees was further tested in *Chief Constable of the Lincolnshire Police v. Stubbs* 1999. Here the EAT upheld the tribunal's decision that a police officer was acting the course of his employment when he subjected a fellow officer to sexual harassment contrary to the Sex Discrimination Act 1975. The EAT found the employer vicariously liable despite the fact that the conduct complained of occurred at social events outside the police station. The tribunal had decided that such gatherings were extensions of the working day and so within the course of employment for the purposes of liability.

The issue in *Sidhur v. Aerospace Composite Technology Ltd.* 2000 was whether the events on a family day out organised by the employer would be regarded as within the course of employment. The Court of Appeal thought not as the employees were not at their place of work during working hours and the majority of participants were family and friends. The Employment Tribunal had correctly applied the statutory test for vicarious liability and their conclusion that the incident was not in the course of employment was a finding of fact that should not be interfered with.

While there is no doubt that this interpretation of *'course of employment'* represents a dramatic but sensible change of the law of vicarious liability in relation to statutory torts it should be stressed that there is a possible defence to a statutory claim. The employer can avoid responsibility if he can prove that he had taken such steps as were reasonably practicable to prevent the employee from committing the unlawful act.

Loaned Employees

Occasionally the courts have been faced with the issue of vicarious liability for the tortious acts of an employee committed when he has been hired out by his primary employer to another employer.

In *Mersey Docks and Harbour Board v. Coggins & Griffith Ltd.* 1947 a crane and its driver had been hired out by one employer to another. The question before the House of Lords was which employer should be made liable for its negligent operation by the crane driver. Their Lordships held that while the crane driver remained an employee of his primary employer, for the purpose of vicarious liability, responsibility depended upon whether a sufficient degree of control over his acts had passed to the primary employer. *"The workman may remain the employee of his general employer, but at the same time, the result of the arrangements may be that there is vested in the hirer a power of control over the workman's activities sufficient to attach to the hirer responsibility for the workman's acts and defaults and to exempt the general employer from that responsibility"*. In this case control had passed over and consequently it was the hirer of the crane who was made liable.

A further difficulty in relation to the loaned employee is the question as to which employer is responsible if he suffers injuries due to the negligence of a fellow employee. In such cases the employee is usually advised to sue both his general employer and the employer to whom he was loaned.

This was the situation in *Thompson v. T. Lohan (Plant Hire) Ltd. and J.W. Hurdiss Ltd.* 1987 where an action was brought by Mr. Thompson's widow alleging that her husband's death was due to the negligence of a fellow worker. Mr. Thompson, who was employed by the first defendants, (the plant owners) as a JCB driver, was killed as a result of an incident which occurred whilst he and his machine were on hire to the second defendants (the hirers). The High Court held that the claim in negligence had been proved and Mr. Thompson's employer, (the plant owners), were liable for damages. A major point of issue however, was whether the plant owners were entitled to be indemnified against liability by the hirers because of certain clauses in the hire contract to that effect. All hirings by the plant owners were made subject to the terms of the Contractors Plant Association conditions of hire, two of which were relevant in this case. Condition 8 provided that: *"When a driver or operator is supplied by the owner of the plant... such person shall be under the direction and control of the hirer... Such drivers or operators shall for all purposes in connection with their employment in the working of the plant be regarded as the servant or agents of the hirer....who alone shall be responsible for all claims arising in connection with the operation of the plant by the said drivers or operators"*. Condition 13 went on to provide that: *"During the continuance of the hire period, the hirer shall...fully and completely indemnify the owner in respect of all claims by any such person whatsoever, for injury to persons or property caused by or in connection with or arising out of the use of the plant and in respect of all costs and charges herewith whether arising under statute or common law"*. In the light of the above clauses the High Court held that the hirers should indemnify the plant owners against the damages and costs recovered by Mrs. Thompson. On further appeal to the Court of Appeal however it was argued that the indemnity clause was in fact inoperative as it conflicted with s.2(1) of the Unfair Contract Terms Act 1977 which states that *"A person cannot by reference to any contract term or to a notice given to persons generally or to particular persons exclude or restrict his liability for death or personal injury resulting from his negligence"*. The Court of Appeal held that as the intention of this clause was to protect the victims of negligence, there was nothing in s.2(1) to prevent a person at fault making arrangements with others to share or bear the burden of compensating those victims of negligence. The plaintiff was in no way prejudiced by the operation of the contract clauses which operated to require the hirer to indemnify the plant owner against the damages and costs recovered by the plaintiff.

The increasing practice of employees contracting out areas of work to contractors and sub contractors has important implications when determining liability for injuries caused due to negligence at the workplace.

In *Sime v. Sutcliffe Catering Scotland Ltd.* 1990 an employee brought a claim alleging negligence by the above catering company when, carrying out her work as a canteen assistant she slipped on some food dropped by a fellow worker and suffered injury. The case was complicated by the fact that the employee was not directly employed by the catering company but by a paper manufacturer, Tullis Russell and Company. Previously the paper manufacturer had contracted out the management of the canteen to the above company, but following pressure from the trade union, had agreed to retain existing canteen staff, including the employee. It was never established whether the worker who had dropped the food was an employee of the catering company or not. The issue therefore was whether the catering company could be held liable vicariously to a worker for the possible negligent act of a worker who they did not employ. The Scottish Court of Session held that responsibility should be with the employer in control. Although not directly employed by the catering company, whether the employer relationship is *"such as to render the company liable for the negligence depends upon whether the substitute employer has sufficient power of control and supervision purely to be regarded as the effective employer at the critical time"*. As the *"whole day to day management of the catering operation and staff was undertaken by the catering company and the canteen manager had complete control over the way in which all the canteen workers did their job"*…and *"since one of the employed persons caused the accident by being negligent in dropping food stuff onto the floor and failing to clean it up the company had to accept responsibility for that negligence"*. The fault of the injured employee was also recognised and damages were reduced by twenty five percent to reflect her contributory negligence. *"Where a person is working in or near a kitchen where a number of people are working with food or dirty dishes and where it is quite predictable that food might be spilt it is reasonably necessary that a look out be kept for any wet or slippery patches on the floor. "*

Independent Contractors

Generally vicarious liability has been confined to the employer/employee relationship and where contractors are employed, responsibility for their wrongful acts is solely their own. The justification for not extending vicarious liability to employers of contractors, other than in exceptional cases, stems from the fact that the contractor is not subjected to his employer's control in the same way as an employee. One important exception, which in recent times has assumed significance, is the situation where the contractor has been employed to carry out a statutory duty imposed on the employer. This is because of the recent move towards requiring public bodies to put out many of their statutory functions for competitive tender among contractors and so the possibility of imposing liability on employers for the tortious acts of a contractor have increased significantly. The law in this area is not new.

> The case of *Hardaker v. Idle District Council* 1896 remains the leading authority in relation to the delegation of statutory duties. The council acting under a statutory power to construct a sewer, employed a contractor to carry out the work. The contractor negligently pierced a gas main and the plaintiff's property was damaged by the resultant explosion. In an action by the plaintiffs against the contractor and the council employer, the court held that in exercising their statutory power the council owed an overriding duty to the public. This duty was to construct a sewer so as not to damage the gas main and put the public at risk. The council could not discharge this duty by simply employing a contractor to carry out the work, and accordingly they remained responsible to the plaintiff for its breach.

There are then certain legal duties that cannot be delegated, and if the wrongful act of a contractor constitutes a breach of such a duty, owed by an employer to a third party, then the contractor's employer may be made vicariously liable for the default.

> In *Rogers v. Nightriders* 1983 a mini cab firm undertook to provide a hire car to the plaintiff for a journey and did so by engaging a contractor driver. The plaintiff was injured in an accident caused by the negligent maintenance of the mini cab by the contractor. In an action against the mini cab firm the court held that they were not liable as an employer could not be made vicariously

liable for their contractor's default. On appeal however, it was held that as the employer had undertaken to provide a vehicle to carry the plaintiff, and since they ought to have forseen harm to the plaintiff if the vehicle was defective, they owed a duty of care to the plaintiff to ensure that the vehicle was reasonably fit. Such a duty could not be delegated to a contractor and accordingly the employers were liable for breach of the primary duty that they owed to her.

This case is a further example of the distinction that must be drawn between vicarious and direct or primary liability previously considered. By providing a negligent contractor, the employer in *Rogers v. Nightriders* had failed to fulfil a direct duty of care he owed to those he could reasonably foresee being affected.

Case Study

Dalton West plc - The Oil Spillage

Dalton West is a large manufacturer of fork lift trucks with depots and retail outlets situated all over Britain.

David Hall has been employed as a machine fitter by Dalton West plc at their Coventry factory for the past six years. He is a member of the Fitters and General Workers Union. As part of safety equipment supplied to him on the commencement of his employment David was supplied with a pair of work boots with a steel toe cap and a heavy tread. It was explained to David by his supervisor that all safety equipment supplied was renewable on request.

Last Tuesday afternoon a drum of oil thinner was accidentally spilt onto the factory floor near to David's work station. While cleaning up operations were put into effect almost immediately, part of the factory floor was still in a highly dangerous state on the Wednesday morning. Last thing on Tuesday afternoon David had heard the works manager warn, over the firm's tannoy, of the increased risk of injury caused by the spillage and the need for increased vigilance when walking across the factory floor. Despite the warning however when making his way to his machine on Wednesday morning, David slipped on a mixture of oil thinner and grease and landed on the base of his spine. As he was in severe pain David was immediately taken by ambulance to hospital. The initial medical opinion is that while the fall was not of itself serious, it has further exacerbated a back condition from which David already suffered and as a consequence David may be unfit for work for a considerable period. David has an appointment to be examined by a back consultant in three weeks time.

Chapter 9

Statutory Employment Rights at Work and Continuity of Employment

In this chapter it is proposed to examine a number of the many statutory employment rights which apply to employees in the workplace and the rules relating to establishing a continuous period of employment.

The table on the following pages identifies the main statutory employment rights, their source and the means of enforcement. As a number of rights arise only after a period of continuous employment, this has also been included where appropriate. Rights are only exercisable within strict time limits and these are shown, along with the various types of redress available if the right has been infringed.

For each of the following rights under statute there is reference to the person qualified to benefit, the statutory source and the time period and means by which the right is legally enforceable. The Employment Rights Act 1996 is the source of the majority of individual employment rights.

Table of Statutory Rights

Statutory right	Statutory source	Means of Enforcement	Time limits	Redress
To be given a written statement of employment particulars within two months from the start of employment	ERA 1996 s.1	Complaint by an employee to a Tribunal	Within three months of cessation of employment (where appropriate)	A declaration and/or compensation
Not to have unauthorised deductions made from wages or salaries	ERA 1996 s.13	Complaint by an employee to a Tribunal	Within three months of the date of the deduction	A declaration and/or an order for repayment of the deduction
To be given an itemised pay statement in writing containing specified particulars	ERA 1996 s.8	Complaint by an employee to a Tribunal	Within three months of cessation of employment (where appropriate)	A declaration and/or compensation
To notice on the termination of employment for an employee with continuous employment of not less than one month	ERA 1996 s.86	Complaint by an employee to the Court	Within six years of the breach of contract	An award of damages
To a written statement of the reasons for dismissal for employees with one years continuous employment	ERA 1996 s.92	Complaint by an employee to a Tribunal	Within three months of the effective date of termination	An award of two weeks pay
Not to be unfairly dismissed for an employee with one years continuous employment	ERA 1996 s.94	Complaint by an employee to a Tribunal	Within three months of the effective date of termination	An award of compensation, reinstatement or re-engagement
Not to be dismissed for trade union membership and activities	TULR(C)A 1992 s.152	Complaint by an employee to a Tribunal	Within three months of the effective date of termination	An award of compensation, reinstatement or re-engagement

Statutory right	Statutory source	Means of Enforcement	Time limits	Redress
Not to have action short of dismissal taken because of trade union membership or activities	TULR(C)A 1992 s.146	Complaint by an employee to a Tribunal	Within three months of the effective date of termination	An award of compensation
Not to suffer a detriment in Health and Safety cases	ERA 1996 s.44	Complaint by an employee to a Tribunal	Within three months of the act or failure to act	Declaration an award of compensation
Not to be unreasonably excluded or expelled from membership of a trade union where a closed shop is in operation	TULR(C)A 1992 s.174	Complaint by an employee to a Tribunal	Within six months of the act complained of	A declaration and/or compensation
Not to be unjustifiably disciplined by a trade union for refusing to participate in industrial action	TULR(C)A 1992 s.64	Complaint by a trade union member to a Tribunal	Within three months of the allegation that the right has been infringed	A declaration
Not to be called to participate in industrial action without the approval of a secret ballot	TULR(C)A 1992 s.62	Complaint by a trade union member to a Court	After the internal grievance procedure or six months after invoking the procedure and it is not complete	A court order that is 'appropriate'
Not to be refused employment because of membership or non-membership of a trade union	TULR(C)A 1992 s.137	Complaint to a Tribunal	Within three months of the conduct complained of	A declaration or compensation/ recommendation
To prevent a trade union indemnifying an individual in respect of penalties for relevant offences or contempts	TULR(C)A 1992 s.15	Complaint to the court	Within three months of the conduct complained of	A court order that is appropriate

Statutory right	Statutory source	Means of Enforcement	Time limits	Redress
Right to ordinary maternity leave for a period of eighteen weeks from its commencement or childbirth if later	ERA 1996 s.71	Complaint to a Tribunal	Within three months	A declaration or compensation
Right to additional maternity leave for twenty nine weeks after childbirth for employees with one years continuity	ERA 1996 s.79	Complaint to a Tribunal	Within three months	A declaration or compensation
Time off for ante natal care for pregnant employees	ERA 1996 s.55	Complaint to a Tribunal	Within three months of the refusal	A declaration or compensation
To take paid time off to carry out trade union duties for an employee who is an official of a recognised trade union	TULR(C)A 1992 s.168	Complaint to a Tribunal	Within three months of the failure	A declaration or compensation
To take paid time off for trade union activities for an employee who is a member of a recognised independent trade union	TULR(C)A 1992 s.170	Complaint to a Tribunal	Within three months of the failure	A declaration or compensation
To have preferential status in relation to certain payments from an insolvent employer	Insolvency Act 1986	Complaint to a Tribunal	Within three months	A declaration or compensation
To take up to thirteen weeks parental leave during five years from birth for employees with one years continuity	Maternity and Parental Leave Regulations	Complaint to a Tribunal	Within three months of the failure	A declaration or compensation

Statutory right	Statutory source	Means of Enforcement	Time limits	Redress
To a redundancy payment for an employee who has been continuously employed for two years	ERA 1996 s.135	Complaint to a Tribunal	Within six months of relevant date	A declaration or compensation
Not to be discriminated against because of race, gender, marital status, or disability in securing work, at work or in the case of dismissal	Sex Discrimination Act 1975; Race Relations Act 1976; Disability Discrimination Act	Complaint to a Tribunal	Within three months of act of discrimination	A declaration or compensation
To equal pay when engaged on like work or equivalent work	Equal Pay Act 1970 (as amended)Equal Treatment Directive	Complaint to a Tribunal	Within six months of termination of employment	A declaration or compensation

To seek redress for the alleged infringement of a statutory right it is crucial that the prospective complainant presents a complaint within the appropriate time limit. As you will see from the table above the time limits attached to statutory claims before industrial tribunals are nothing like as generous as common law claims for example for breach of contract. Three months beginning with the unlawful act complained of is the usual period within which the complainant must act in relation to pay issues, unfair dismissal, time off work, discrimination and trade union rights. The law relating to time limits, particularly in relation to discrimination and unfair dismissal is dealt with in Chapters 5 and 11. In this chapter we will concentrate on statutory rights in relation to the payment of wages, sickness, working time, disclosure of matters of public concern guarantee payment and trade union membership and activities. The majority of statutory employment rights depend upon the existence of a valid contract of employment involving an employer/employee relationship but we shall see that more contemporary rights such as the minimum wage, maximum working hours and public interest disclosure are conferred on the wider category of 'workers'. If the contract proves to be unenforceable because of illegality then the employee is prevented from relying on statutory rights.

To qualify for a number of the statutory rights, in particular redundancy, unfair dismissal and maternity, you will notice that an employee must establish a minimum period of continuous employment. It is considered appropriate therefore to consider the law relating to continuity of employment including business transfer at this point and then deal with the major statutory rights and obligations that apply in a subsisting employment relationship.

Continuity of Employment

To qualify for the majority of statutory employment rights, an employee, full or part-time, must establish a period of continuous employment. In addition to calculate statutory redundancy pay or the basic award for unfair dismissal it is necessary to refer to the period of continuous employment. To calculate this period it will be necessary to establish the date of the commencement of employment and if relevant the effective date of termination. Issues such as breaks in continuity and the change of an employer may have to be addressed and the increasing practice of employing individuals on a succession of fixed term contracts over a period of time. The relevant rule on continuity are contained in primary and secondary legislation and are often the subject of judicial interpretation.

Continuous Employment

Periods of continuous employment to qualify for the above statutory rights vary from one month to three months and as long as two years to qualify for a redundancy payment or one year to present a complaint of unfair dismissal.

The basic rules to establish the period of continuous employment are contained in ss.210-219 of the Employment Rights Act 1996. Under s.211 an employee's period of continuous employment begins with the day on which the employee starts work. Under s.212(1) any week during the whole or part of which an employee's relations with his employers are governed by a contract of employment counts in computing the employee's period of employment. Continuity is preserved while the contract of employment is in existence so that absence from work due to sickness, injury, pregnancy, or temporary cessation of work will count as periods of continuous employment.

> In *Sweeney v. J & S Henderson Ltd.* 1999 it was alleged that the complainant's continuity of employment was broken when he resigned and tried employment with a different employer but then obtained re-employment all in the same week. The EAT confirmed that s.212 (1) plainly contemplates that continuous employment can include gaps and the reason for the gap is immaterial. Here continuity was preserved because during the relevant week there was at least one day governed by a contract with the relevant employer.

Earlier in Chapter 4 we said that if the contract of employment is illegal then any statutory rights which would otherwise have accrued due to continuous employment are unenforceable. Certainly if an employee is aware of the illegality surrounding his employment contract, by participating further in the contract he may prejudice his rights to pursue statutory rights.

In *Ali Begacem v. Turkish Delight Kebab House* 1987 the applicant was paid between £90 and £120 in cash and received no pay slip. While he was informed by the DSS that no National Insurance contributions had been paid and by the Inland Revenue that no tax had been deducted the applicant merely mentioned the matter to his employer and was satisfied with a cursory response. The EAT upheld the tribunal's decision to dismiss the applicant's unfair dismissal complaint on the grounds that the contract was illegal and the applicant was at fault in not making further enquiries as to his legal position.

Any period that the contract operates illegally will not count towards the period of continuous employment for the purposes of statutory rights.

In *Hyland v. J H Barber (North West) Ltd.* 1985 it was held that a contract of employment became illegal during a four week period when a tax-free lodging allowance was paid. This period could not therefore count toward continuity for the purposes of statutory rights.

Following the important decision of the House of Lords in *R v. Secretary of State for Employment ex parte EOC* 1994 the legal position of a part-time employee in relation to continuity for the purposes of unfair dismissal and redundancy is now the same as a full-time employee. The previous longer qualification period was held to be indirectly discriminatory under EC law and the UK government, committed to amending the legislation, achieved this in the Employment Protection (Part-Time Employees) Regulations 1995.

Even if the employee is away from work without a contract, continuity is not broken if he returns and the absence was under s.212(3) because the employee was:

(a) incapable of work through sickness or injury up to 26 weeks;

(b) absent from work through a temporary cessation of work;

(c) absent from work in circumstances such that, by arrangement or custom, he is regarded as continuing the employment for any purpose.

In *Booth v. United States of America* 1999 the applicants were employed by the United States Army under a series of fixed term contracts with a break of at least two weeks between each contract. The breaks were designed to prevent the applicants securing sufficient continuity of employment for the purposes of redundancy and unfair dismissal. The applicants argued that the breaks fell within s.212(3)(c) of the 1996 Act which provides that absence from work by arrangement or action is regarded as continuing of employment. This argument was rejected by the EAT who felt the employee's clearly did not want the employment relationship to continue and there was no evidence to suggest that there was a custom or arrangement that it should continue, merely an expectation that the applicants would be re-employed. *"If by so arranging their affairs, employers lawfully are able to employ people in such a manner that the employees cannot complain of unfair dismissal or seek a redundancy payment, that is a matter for them. It is for the legislators, not the courts, to close any loopholes that might be perceived to exist."*

Unfortunately here the EAT failed to consider the substance of these employment practices and declare them to be devices or shams. The arrangements here were designed to prevent employees acquiring statutory rights and the tribunal effectively supported the employees prerogative to achieve that aim.

Temporary Cessation of Work

It has been argued that the expression *"temporary cessation of work"* should apply to preserve continuity of employment where there has been a succession of fixed term contracts.

In *Ford v. Warwickshire County Council* 1983 a *'part-time temporary'* teacher in a further education college claimed that as she had been employed from September 1971 to July 1979 on a succession of fixed term temporary contracts which terminated each July and then recommenced in the September, the periods of summer vacation when she was not employed should count as temporary cessation of work. It was necessary to establish the period of continuous employment to maintain a claim for unfair dismissal and a redundancy payment. While the industrial tribunal, the EAT and the Court of Appeal all found that the continuity was broken each summer and the teacher was not absent from work but simply unemployed, the House of Lords on final appeal took a different view. The Lords held that the applicant's absence from work during the summer vacation could properly be described as *"on account of a temporary cessation of work"*, particularly when there was a regular pattern of employment and continuity was not broken.

In deciding whether a cessation of work is temporary or not, it is necessary to take account of all the relevant circumstances, in particular the length of period of absence in the context of the period of employment as a whole. *In Flack v. Kodak Ltd.* 1986 the Court of Appeal held that a long gap in the course of employment over a number of years may be considered temporary in the circumstances of the case.

Certainly to determine whether there has been a temporary cessation of work, the whole history of the employee's intermittent employment must be considered bearing in mind the nature of the industry in which he was employed. A failure by the tribunal in *Olla v. Sutcliffe Catering (UK) Ltd.* 1995 to take account of an employee's history of employment was held by the EAT to be fatal in deciding whether a three month break constituted a temporary cessation of work.

> In *Tipper v. Roofdec Ltd.* 1989 the EAT held that continuity of employment is not broken even if there is a change of work, and that the precise reason for the change of work is irrelevant. Here a lorry driver who could no longer drive because of a twelve month driving ban was offered and accepted labouring work by his employer. Terminating the job as a driver on the Friday and then being re-employed as a full-time labourer on the Monday meant that there was continuity of employment. Accordingly the driver had sufficient service to be able to claim a redundancy payment when he was dismissed when the labouring job came to an end.

Continuity may also be preserved if the absence is due to an established arrangement or custom. The arrangement could cover leave of absence, secondment or even being placed on a reserve list of employees. In some industries employers rely heavily on a pool of casual or temporary employees who may be called upon subject to production or seasonal demands. Many temporary workers have a long period of service with their employers but with numerous breaks in employment. Such breaks in employment could constitute temporary cessation of work or absences due to custom and practice which under s.212(3) would not break continuity of employment for the purposes of statutory rights. In *Hygena Ltd. v. Cook and Others* 1996 a furniture manufacturer maintained a pool of temporary employees to fill full-time absences. When choosing workers from the pool a custom developed that priority should be given to the longest serving pool members. The EAT held that the purpose of the pool was to provide the employer with access to skilled and experienced workers when required and the fact that priority was given to long serving members was consistent with regarding them as continuously employed for the purpose of statutory rights, despite breaks in employment.

Under s.216 periods of industrial action which involve no work due to strikes or lock outs will not count towards the period of continuity but will not break it.

Under the Employment Protection (Continuity of Employment) Regulations 1993 a dismissed employee's continuity of employment is preserved under the relevant legislation if she is reinstated or re-engaged by the employer or an associate following ACAS conciliation, a compromise agreement, or the order of a tribunal.

Change in the Employer

It is generally only continuous employment with the same employer that is calculated to determine an employee's length of continuity of employment for the purpose of statutory rights. If an employee changes his job then previous periods of employment with the old employer are ignored for the purposes of calculating continuity with the new employer. Under the common law this is also the position when the employer changes because the business is sold. The effect of the change is to discharge the contracts of employment with the old employer and start afresh with new contracts of employment with the new employer. There are however a number of exceptions to this rule, in particular contained in:

(a)   section 218 of the Employment Rights Act 1996; and

(b)   the Transfer of Undertakings (Protection of Employment) Regulations 1981.

It should be stressed from the outset that these are complex provisions with a considerable degree of overlap, so that a business transfer could be covered by both s.218 of the 1996 Act and the 1981 TUPE regulations. Also both s.218 and the 1981 regulations only apply to the take-over of a business as a going concern rather than a sale of the business assets which could include the employees. Continuity will be broken in such circumstances and the employees affected will negotiate new contracts with the transferee employer. They will also have the right to proceed against their old employer in relation to the termination of their original contracts for wrongful dismissal, unfair dismissal or redundancy payments where appropriate. It should also be stressed that the majority of business take-overs in England and Wales are effected by acquiring the shares of a limited company in which case the contracts of employment of the company employees will remain unaffected by the business transfer.

Under s.218(2), if a trade or business or an undertaking is transferred from one person to another, the period of employment in the trade or business or undertaking shall count as a period of employment with the transferee and the transfer shall not break continuity. Furthermore under s.218(4) continuity will not be broken if the employer dies and the employee is kept on by the Personal Representatives or trustees of the estate.

The EAT in *Williams v. Evans* 1992 decided that the sale of a member's club to to an individual proprietor was a business transfer for the purposes of the Act. It was not simply a sale of business assets but the transfer of a going concern and *"the reality of the situation is that the club is carrying on"*. As a consequence the continuity of employment of the club's sole employee was not broken by the transfer and she was qualified to present a complaint of unfair dismissal.

For a s.218(2) transfer, continuity is preserved only if the new business carried on is the same as the old business.

> In *Macer v. Abafast Ltd.* 1990 the EAT in considering the section decided that *"provided that there has been a valid transfer of a business from A to B then the continuous period of service with A may be added to the continuous period of service of an employee with B so as to establish a qualifying period of employment"*. The EAT stated there are four essentials to the section:
>
> * the transfer of the business;
>
> * employment by the owner before the transfer and after the transfer;
>
> * a period of service with the old owner and new owner which is continuous;
>
> * the combined periods of service satisfying the statutory qualification period.

This interpretation of s.218(2) suggests that the fact that the employee is not employed in the business *'at the time of the transfer'* does not necessarily break continuity. A gap in employment by the old employer and the new employer which is related to 'the transfer' is permissible, but if it is too long it may not be viewed as related to the 'machinery of the transfer' and so break continuity. In interpreting these provisions, the court *"should lean in favour of that interpretation which best gives effect to the preservation of continuity of service and hence the preservation of the rights of the employee and so obviate and discourage a tactical manoeuvre which seeks to avoid the clear intention of Parliament"*.

> In *A & G Tuck Ltd. v. Bartlott and A & G Tuck (Slough) Ltd.* 1994 the issue was whether the complainant's employment and consequently continuity had been preserved and transferred when he remained in the employment of the transferor at the time of the transfer and joined the transferee two weeks later. The EAT held that the tribunal was correct to conclude that nevertheless the section *"applied to circumstances in which the complainant entered the transferee's employment in connection with the transfer and after a gap which was related to the machinery of the transfer"*.

> In *Justfern Ltd. v. Dingerthorpe and others* 1994 the complainant a college lecturer made a claim for unemployment benefit when his college employer closed down. One week later the college was purchased and reopened with the complainant accepting re-employment. Despite the gap in employment of

more than a week and the claim for benefit, the EAT held that the employee was still employed in the business at the time of the transfer. *"A liberal construction of the words at the time of the transfer accords with the evident policy of the legislature to preserve continuity of employment"*. The section operated, moreover to preserve continuity of employment even though the termination of employment by the original employer was for commercial reasons of insolvency rather than as a step in the transfer of the business. The motivation for the termination of the employment by the transferor employer is not in direct significance. The question is whether there was a transfer of a business in relation to which an employee's employment can also be regarded as transferred. It is a necessary implication of that the business and the employment of the relevant employee should survive sufficiently as to be susceptible to transfer. If the old employer closes down the business so completely that the new employer was effectively starting a new business, that necessary implication would not be satisfied.

Section 218(5) deals with a change in business partners, personal representatives or trustees who employ any person and provides that the employee's period of employment at the time of the change shall count as a period of employment after the change and continuity is not broken.

Employers are treated as associated if one is a company of which the other (directly or indirectly) has control or if both companies are under the control (directly or indirectly) of a third person. Under section 218(6), if an employee is transferred from one employer to an *"associated employer"* then continuity of employment is preserved. Under section 231 Employment Rights Act 1996 any two employers are to be treated as associated if one is a company of which the other (directly or indirectly) has control, or if both are companies of which a third person (directly or indirectly) has control. Continuous employment for associated employers may be aggregated in computing an employee's total period of service for the purpose of statutory rights.

> In *Hancill v. Marcon Engineering Ltd*. 1990. The employee in question had worked abroad for an American firm and then returned to the United Kingdom to work for a British Company which eventually dismissed him. Both undertakings were wholly-owned subsidiaries of a Dutch Company. In order to show the requisite period of continuous employment to qualify to bring a complaint of unfair dismissal the employee sought to include his period of employment with the American firm in the computation. The industrial tribunal however rejected the claim that the American firm was an *"associated company"*, as it was not a *"Limited Company"* as required by the section. This strict interpretation of the term *"company"* was not followed in the EAT which concluded that *"it is difficult to see quite how 'Inc' differs in its constituent parts from a company incorporated under the Companies Act. It*

seems to us that it would be entirely appropriate in the application of this branch of the law to contracts of employment that if the overseas subsidiary is a company which in its essentials is to be likened to a company limited under the Companies Act, then it would be right, fair and indeed in accordance with the principles of presumption of continuity under the Act that the company should be recognised as a company for the purpose of the definition section of associated employer". Concerned that without such an interpretation there would be obvious possibilities of transferring employees to overseas subsidiaries and so preventing them from acquiring statutory employment rights dependent on continuous employment, the President of the EAT said that *"our task is to look to the true intent of the legislation and so to interpret the provisions of the Act and so far as we can properly do so as to give effect to that intention. It seems to us here that a coach and four could easily be driven round a few comers and then straight through the provision of this legislation if the word 'company' were only to include a UK Ltd. Company when the overseas vehicle is to all intent and purposes identical".*

The TUPE Regulations

Further rights relating to the preservation of continuity are contained in the Transfer of Undertakings (Protection of Employment) Regulations 1981. These regulations were passed to give further protection to workers in a business transfer and as so, give effect to EC Council Directive 77/187 (the Acquired Rights Directive). The aim of the regulations is to ensure that on the transfer of an undertaking, the contractual rights of the employees, including continuity, are preserved.

An employee is defined in regulation 2(1) as *"any individual who works for another person whether under a contract of service or apprenticeship or otherwise but does not include anyone who provides services under a contract for services".*

In *Cowell v. Quilter Goodison Company Ltd. and QG Management Services Ltd.* 1989 the Court of Appeal held that an equity partner for a firm which had transferred its business could not count his prior service as a partner for the purposes of showing two years' service as an employee to qualify for a claim of unfair dismissal. An equity partner does not work for another person under a contract of service and nor does he have an employment relationship with any or all of the partners. His relationship is governed by the definition of a partnership under the Partnership Act under which partners are required to provide services under a contract for services for the benefit of the partnership.

Originally the TUPE regulations only applied to business transfers which were of a *"commercial venture"*. Following the decision of the European Court of Justice in

Dr Sophie Redmond-Stitching v. Bartol 1992 it became necessary to bring the TUPE regulations in line with the Acquired Rights Directive and the regulations were amended by the Trade Union Reform and Employment Rights Act 1993. Following the TURERA amendments the regulations will apply to all relevant transfers rather than just where the undertaking is a commercial venture. The defective implementation of the Acquired Rights Directive in TUPE so that *"non-profit making undertakings"* were excluded was confirmed by a ruling of the European Court of Justice in *The Commission of the European Communities v. UK* in June 1994. As a result all those employees whose jobs were lost or accepted inferior terms and conditions of employment resulting from the contracting out of public services prior to the TURERA amendments have potential claims. The argument is that had the law been properly implemented their position would have been safeguarded. Such claims however should have been lodged within three months of the TUPE amendments coming into force, subject to the Tribunal's discretion. Alternatively there is a potential action against the Government under the Francovitch principle for failing to properly translate the Directive into national law.

In *Kenny and others v. South Manchester College* 1993 the High Court ruled that the contracting out by the Home Office of the education service at a young offenders institution is a transfer covered by the TUPE regulations. The further education college which won the contract was therefore bound by the terms and conditions in the contracts of the existing staff who were previously employed by the local authority.

Both the European Court of Justice in *Rask and another v. ISS Kantineservice A/S* 1993 and the Court of Appeal in *Dines and others v. Initial Health Care Services and Pall Mall Services Group Ltd.* 1993 make it clear that a business which comprises of only the provision of labour is capable of being an economic entity within the meaning of the TUPE regulations and the Business Transfer Directive.

In *Rask and Christensen v. ISS Kantineservice A/S* 1992 the European Court of Justice ruled that the Business Transfer Directive may cover the contracting out of a canteen service even though the service is incidental to the transferors main business and the transferee receives only a fixed fee for running the service. If a transfer which falls within scope of the Directive has occurred, the transferors rights and obligations in relation to the affected employees are transferred to the transferee. The transferee cannot therefore alter the date on which the employee's wages are paid or the constituent parts of their wages unless the transferor would have had the same rights in a non transfer situation.

In *Workman and Birckley v. Servisystem Ltd.* 1994 the EAT held that when cleaning services at a local authority college are transferred from the council to a private contractor and then to another contractor, this was the transfer of an *"economic entity"* to which the TUPE regulations applied. As a consequence two cleaners who moved on two occasions to the contractors retained their continuity of employment for the purposes of their complaints of unfair dismissal.

Following amendments to TUPE regulations by TURERA 1993 all transfers which occur after August 30th 1993 are covered by the regulations even if they do not involve a transfer of property or relate to a non-commercial venture. This means that almost all public sector contracting out scenarios are now covered by the regulations.

Equally there is not a transfer of an undertaking merely because assets are disposed of. The relevant question is whether the business was transferred as a going concern indicated by the fact the new employer continues the same activities. An important question is whether on the transfer the business retains its identity. All the circumstances surrounding the transfer must be considered including the type of business, the proportion of employees transferred, the impact on customers/clients, and the extent to which tangible and intangible business assets are transferred. In a significant case the judgment the European Court of Justice *in Suzen v. Zehnacher Aebaudereinigung GmbH Krankenhausservice and Another* 1997 held that the Business Transfer Directive *"does not apply to a situation in which a person who had entrusted the cleaning of premises to a first undertaking, terminates the contract and for the performance of similar work enters into a contract with the second undertaking, if there is no concomitant transfer from one undertaking to the other of significant tangible or intangible business assets or taking over by the new employer of a major part of the workforce, in terms of their numbers and skills, assignment by the predecessor to the performance of the contract".*

Under regulation 5(1) the transfer of an undertaking *"shall not operate so as to terminate the contract of employment of any person employed by the transferor... but any such contract ... shall have effect after the transfer as if original made between the person so employed and the transferee".* This means that the contract of employment still subsists after the transfer and consequently continuity of employment is preserved. This process under the regulations of preserving rights by deeming that a contract is *"as if originally made between the person so employed and the transferee"* is an attractive one, so that if a business transfer is covered by both the regulations and paragraph 17, then the regulations would normally be applied.

A further reason for applying the regulations is that they are wider than paragraph 17 in conferring additional rights on employees. Under regulation 5(2) *"all the transferor's rights, powers, duties and liabilities under or in connection with ... the contract shall be transferred to the transferee; and anything done before the transfer is completed by or in relation to the transferor in respect of that contract ... shall be deemed to have been done by or in relation to the transferee"*. This means that an employee can pursue his rights against the transferee business even where breaches of contract occur prior to the transfer. Also an employee's contractual rights on redundancy will transfer to the new employers. If an employee objects to the transfer he will not be transferred and his contract will terminate. By showing that the transfer would have a detrimental affect on his contract however such an employee could claim constructive dismissal by reason of the transfer under regulation 5(5).

Potential liability for failure to consult with employee representatives prior to a TUPE transfer will pass by virtue of Reg 5 from the transferor to the transferee. So held the EAT in *Kerry Foods Ltd. v. Kreber* 2000 ruling that the duty to consult is a right which arises from individual worker's contracts and is therefore covered by Reg 5. The maximum compensation for failing to consult is now increased from 4 weeks pay to 13 weeks pay so that there could be a substantial liability on the transferee.

The EAT in two cases in 1997, *BET Catering Services Ltd. v. Ball and Others and Wheat and Others v. Cartledge Ltd.* held that under regulation 5, on a TUPE transfer from the public sector to the private sector, a collective agreement under which pay rates were varied transferred to a private contractor without modification or amendment. This meant that a private employer who was not a party to the collective agreement was bound to pay collectively bargained rates of pay to the transferred employees as their terms and conditions remained the same after the transfer.

In *Bernadone v. Pall Mall Services* 2000 the Court of Appeal held that tortious liability transfers under TUPE. Therefore a transferee is liable for any negligence or breach of statutory duty by the transferors in connection with a claimants accident at work prior to the transfer of the undertaking. The obligations of a transferor to compensate an employee as a consequence of negligence by the employer arises *"in connection with"* the employee's contract of employment within the meaning of the TUPE since the duty of care arose by virtue of the contract of employment. Of great practical significance was the further ruling that the right to be indemnified under the employers liability insurance policy was also transferred along with the undertaking. Reg 5(2). TUPE confers on the transferee the right of an indemnity under the insurance policy between the transferor and their insurers in respect of the employee's claim. The position is therefore satisfactory for the transferee as the transferor is obliged by statute to have the relevant employer's liability insurance cover.

A question of considerable practical importance on a business transfer is whether TUPE would preserve the employee's right to share in profits earned by the former employer. Also is there any obligation on the transferee to create a comparable profit sharing scheme.

In *Unicorn Consultancy Services Ltd. v. Westbrook* 2000 the EAT upheld a finding that the employees were entitled to profit related pay earned by the date of the transfer and the transferee was liable for this under TUPE. While the employee's acquired right should be an obligation on the transferee there was no obligation under TUPE for the transferee to replicate the former employers scheme.

If as a result of the transfer, an employee is dismissed, then the right to pursue a claim for unfair dismissal is provided for in regulation 8(1). *"Where either before or after a relevant transfer, any employee of the transferor or transferee is dismissed, that employee shall be treated ... as unfairly dismissed if the transfer or a reason connected with it is the reason or principal reason for his dismissal."* The regulations provide therefore, that a dismissal in connection with a business transfer is to be regarded as automatically unfair unless the employer can establish a regulation 8(2) defence. Rights relating to unfair dismissal on a business transfer are considered in Chapter 11. Similarly an employer's liability on a business transfer to make a redundancy payment to an employee dismissed by reason of redundancy is examined in Chapter 12.

The Payment of Wages

We considered the payment of wages and salaries in Chapters 4 and 7 as the employer's fundamental obligation under a contract of employment. Here it is proposed to examine statutory rights in relation to the payment of wages in particular protection in relation to unlawful deductions and the right to a national minimum wage. Over 20% of claims before employment tribunals are concerned with unlawful deductions from wages.

Earlier when we explored the formation of a contract of employment in Chapter 4, it was stated that while there is no legal requirement that an employment contract be in writing, under s.1 of the Employment Rights Act 1996, an employee is entitled to be supplied with a written statement of the main terms and conditions of employment. Section 8 of the 1996 Act further provides that every employee has the right to be given a written itemised pay statement at the time or before wages or salary are paid. Following the Employment Protection (Part-time Employees) Regulation 1995, part-time employees are also entitled to a written itemised pay statement. Certain particulars must be included on the statement:

- the gross amount of the wages or salary;

- the amount of any variable and fixed deduction and the purpose for which they are made;

- the net amount of the wages or salary; and

- where different parts of the net amount are paid in different ways, the amount and method of each part-payment.

In relation to fixed deductions a further option is for the employer to provide his employees with a standing statement of fixed deductions. If this statement is kept up to date on an annual basis then the employee need only include the aggregate amount of fixed deductions in the pay statement. If an employer fails to comply with a s.8 obligation to provide a complete and accurate itemised pay statement, the remedy for an employee is to make an application under s.11 to the employment tribunal within three months for a declaration to that effect.

In *Coates v. John Wood & Company* 1986 the tribunal took the view that as the employee in question had never been denied the right to an itemised statement, and details of deductions had been shown to her whenever requested, then s.8 had not been infringed. On appeal however, the EAT disagreed and made a declaration to the effect that there had been non compliance with the statutory right. The EAT stated that *"s.8 establishes an inherent right which creates an inherent obligation on an employer to provide the employee with an itemised pay statement at or before the time at which any payment of wages or salary is made and that right exists whether or not the employee exercises any claim under it"*.

Statutory intervention in the payment of wages has a long history and under the Truck Act 1831 employers were required to pay the wages of manual workers in current coin of the realm and obtain their written consent to any deductions. This was designed to prevent abuse by employers who were forcing workers to accept wages in the form of tokens or in kind. The Truck Acts 1831-40 were finally replaced by the Wages Act 1986 which in turn has now been incorporated into the Employment Rights Act 1996. Sections 13-27 regulate the mode and method of the payment of wages.

As a result of the wages legislation workers no longer have the right to be paid in cash and must agree to other forms of payment such as direct debit etc.

Unlawful Deductions

The provisions of the Act are designed to extend beyond those working under a contract of service and would cover apprentices and even contractors provided they were performing personal services. This is a good example of a major part of the ERA that applies to workers.

One of the main aims of the Wages Act, now incorporated into the ERA is to introduce restrictions on the right of employers to make deductions from the wages of employees and to receive payments from employees.

Under section 13(1) An employer shall not make any deduction from any wages of any worker employed by him unless:

(a) the deduction is required or authorised to be made by virtue of any statutory provision or a relevant provision of the worker's contract; or

(b) the worker has previously signified in writing his agreement or consent to the making of the deduction.

An employer should not receive any payment from any worker employed by him unless the payment satisfies one of the conditions set out in paragraphs (a) and (b) of section 13(1).

In *Fairfield Ltd. v. Skinner* 1993 the EAT considered an employer's argument that the Act only permits a tribunal to interpret contractual terms to determine whether a deduction is authorised and not investigate the facts of the case to see whether the deduction is justified. The EAT ruled that is is perfectly proper for a tribunal to decide that while a deduction is contractually authorised on the evidence before it the deductions were not justified.

The expression wages is given a wide definition under the Act and includes under s.27(1) any fee, bonus, commission, holiday pay or other emolument referable to his or her employment whether payable under his or her contract or otherwise. Wages would also include non contractual bonuses, payment in pursuance of reinstatement or re-engagement orders (see Chapter 11) and numerous statutory payments in lieu of wages such as guarantee payments, time off payments, sick pay and maternity pay. Section 27(2) excludes a number of payments including those made by way of an advance for a loan or wages, expenses, pension allowance and redundancy.

In *Kent Management Services Ltd. v. Butterfield* 1992 the EAT agreed with the tribunal's view that a commission and bonus scheme, which was expressly described as *"discretionary"*, *"ex gratia"* and *"non contractual"* constituted wages under the Act. Despite the fact that the Act stated that non contractual bonuses were considered to be wages once they had been paid the EAT nevertheless held that a non contractual commission, once calculated but not paid was still wages under the Act. The commission was a sum payable *"in connection"* with the worker's employment since it was within the reasonable contemplation of both parties that in ordinary circumstances it would be paid.

In *Robertson v. Blackstone Franks Investment Management Ltd.* 1998 the Court of Appeal held that commission that became payable after termination of a contract were wages under the Act.

In *Edinburgh Council v. Brown* 1999 the EAT held that a regrading policy between the employer and a Trade Union in a collective agreement had become incorporated into individual contracts of employment. Accordingly the failure to implement the policy in relation to the claimant so that his new wage following a regrading was backdated to the date of approval constituted an unauthorised deduction from his wages in contravention of s.13.

Following a number of conflicting decisions it now seems that payments made in lieu of notice following a summary dismissal are not "wages" under the Act.

In *Delany v. R J Staples* 1990 the Court of Appeal upheld both the EAT and the tribunal in deciding that a claim for payment in lieu of notice was in effect a claim for damages for wrongful dismissal and so did not come under the Wages Act. The House of Lords attempted to clarify the position by identifying the various payments that could be made on contractual termination most of which fell outside the Act. There is no payment of wages if:

- The contract of employment expressly provide for summary termination with payment in lieu of notice.

- There is a mutual agreement on summary termination for a payment in lieu.

- There is a summary dismissal and payment in lieu is tendered in respect of proper notice.

Their lordships did decide however that the Act does apply if the employer gives proper notice but tells the employee that he need not work and gives wages attributable to the notice period in a lump sum (garden leave). Here there is no breach of contract by the employer and the employment continues until the notice expires, the lump sum being an advance of wages.

It is now possible of course to use the employment tribunals contractual jurisdiction to pursue a claim for wrongful dismissal and claims for payment in lieu as well as retaining the right to sue in the ordinary courts.

A deduction for the purposes of the Act covers any shortfall in payment of the amount properly payable leaving aside errors of computation. This includes any deductions which an employer alleges that he is entitled to make, but also disputes about whether wages are due or the amount payable.

The Act excludes a number of deductions or payments from its provision and under s.14(1) section 13 does not apply:

to a deduction from a worker's wages made by his employer, where the purpose of the deduction or payment is the reimbursement of the employer in respect of:

    (a) any overpayment of wages, or

    (b) any overpayment in respect of expenses incurred by the worker in carrying out his employment,

made (for any reason) by the employer to the worker;

 in addition s.13 does not apply

- *to deductions in consequence of disciplinary proceedings;*

- *any deduction from a worker's wages in pursuance of any requirement imposed on the employer by any statutory provision;*

- *deduction form a worker's wages made by his employer to a third party where the worker has given prior written or contractual consent:*

- *a deduction from a worker's wages made by his employer, or any where the worker has taken part in a strike or other industrial action;*

- *a deduction from a worker's wages made by his employer with his prior agreement or consent signified in writing, to satisfy an order of a court or tribunal.*

In *Home Office v. Ayres* 1992 The EAT suggested that the s.14(1) exception had to be read as if the word lawful was inserted in the provision so that if it is claimed by an employer an employee is entitled to raise a number of defences. The employee could argue that there was *"no overpayment, incorrect amount of deduction; the purpose of the deduction was not to reimburse; or some defence under the general law to the claim to deduct"*.

It now seems however that this is not the approach to be adopted when s.14 is raised. The determination of the question in any given case as to whether a deduction falls within s.14 and is lawful does not fall within a tribunal's statutory jurisdiction, rather it is a common law contractual matter subject to proceedings in the ordinary courts.

In *Sip (Industrial Products) Ltd. v. Swinn* 1994 the complainant was dismissed for dishonesty relating to a fraudulent claim for expenses. The employer then deducted a sum of money due to him in respect of wages and holiday pay against the money he had dishonestly obtained. A complaint was presented that this deduction was in breach of the Wages Act to which the employer argued that the deduction constituted a reimbursement. The tribunal held that the deduction was not a reimbursement therefore was not a lawful deduction. On appeal the EAT said that it was not part of the tribunal's jurisdiction to decide the lawfulness of the deduction. *"An industrial tribunal has no jurisdiction to enquire into or determine the issue of the lawfulness of a deduction of a kind falling within one of the categories of the section". The section disapplies the provision off the Act where there is any deduction lawful or unlawful falling within one of the specified categories. Where a deduction is made in these circumstances the appropriate procedure is to institute proceedings in the civil courts for alleged breach of contract and recovery of the sum deducted."*

If a deduction is made the tribunal must ask whether the sum was properly payable or not.

In *Grey May (CF&C) v. Dring* 1990 the employer refused to pay accrued holiday pay on dismissal relying on an express term in the employee's contract that it was not payable if the dismissal was for gross misconduct. The pay was held to be properly payable as the EAT did not believe that the facts constituted gross misconduct.

The Court of Appeal's decision in *Delany v. Staples* 1990 (previously mentioned) confirms that if wages are properly payable and not paid, then non payment is to be regarded as a deduction and the industrial tribunal has jurisdiction to determine the issue *"a dispute on whatever ground, as to the amount of wages properly payable cannot have the effect of taking the case outside the Act. It is for the industrial tribunal to determine that dispute, as a necessary preliminary to discovery whether there has been an unauthorised deduction. Having determined any dispute about the amount of wages properly payable, the industrial tribunal will then move on to consider and determine whether, and to what extent, the shortfall in payment of that amount was authorised by the Statute or was otherwise outside the statutory provision".*

There is a deduction of wages under the Act if an employer unilaterally revises or reduces any element of a worker's wage whether temporarily or permanently.

In *Bruce and Others v. Wiggins Teape (Stationery) Ltd.* 1994 the employer unilaterally withdrew enhanced contractually agreed overtime rates and the employees continued to work overtime in protest. The EAT said that the issues in this type of case were identifying the wages, deciding whether a deduction had been made and determining whether the deduction was unlawful. The EAT confirmed that *"no valid distinction is to be drawn for the purposes of the Wages Act between a deduction from wages on the one hand, and a reduction of wages on the other. Overtime payments are wages so the question is whether for whatever reason, apart from an error of computation, the worker is paid less than the amount of wages properly payable to him. In the present case, the amount of wages properly payable to the employees included the enhanced overtime rate"*. There had been no express or implied acceptance of the reduced overtime rates and as the employer had no contractual right to reduce wages the Act was applicable. In *Rigby v. Ferodo* 1987 the court confirmed that a worker could continue to work under protest without impliedly accepting a reduction in wages. Here the deductions were unauthorised and unlawful.

In *Chiltern Houses Ltd. v. Chambers* 1990 the EAT held that it was unlawful under the Wages Act to deduct wages from am employee in order to satisfy a prospective action by the employer for breach of contract against the employee.

In *Yemm v. British Steel* 1994 four shift workers made a complaint under the Wages Act claiming they had not been paid the correct shift allowance for a three month period and this constituted an unlawful deduction. The employers maintained that the correct shift allowance had been paid reflecting a change in shift patterns. The tribunal held that the under payment was due to an error of computation and not therefore deemed to be a deduction from wages. Under the Act it is defined as an *"error of any description on the part of the employer affecting the computation by him of the gross amount of the wages that are properly payable by him to the worker on that occasion"*. The EAT disagreed with the tribunal and found that here there was no error of computation *"An employer who makes a conscious decision not to make a payment because he believes that the contract entitles him to take that course is not making an error of computation ... he may be mistaken about the terms and the effect of the contract but such an error cannot be characterised as an error of computation. If it could then in every case involving a contractual dispute about entitlement to pay it would be open to the employer to take the point and say that the Wages Act had no application to the facts of such a dispute"*.

The decision of the EAT in *Morgan v. West Glamorgan County Council* 1995 provides further guidance in relation to the meaning of the expression 'error of computation' under the Act. The EAT stated that: *"A deduction from wages made in consequence of a deliberate decision, even if that decision is legally erroneous, is not a deduction which is attributable to an "error of computation" within the meaning of the Act. Although the Act refers to an "an error of any description", it does not include an error of law. It must be (a) an "error" on the part of the employer and (b) an error which affects the computation of gross wages. An "error" is a mistake, something incorrectly done through ignorance or inadvertence. "Computation" of wages is a matter of reckoning the amount, of ascertaining the total amount due by a process of counting and calculation. In the present case the reduction in the employee's wages was attributable to a deliberate decision to demote him and reduce his salary. Although that decision was itself the result of an erroneous or mistaken view of the legal and factual position, the reduction in salary and the consequent deduction from the wages paid to the employee were attributable to that decision and not to any error of computation. The short fall was a "deduction" from wages within the meaning of the Act. If there was no right to demote him the employee remained in his original position and the amount of wages which were properly payable by the employers remained the same. Since the employers paid him less than he had previously been paid the amount of the deficiency fell to be treated as a deduction."*

Lawful deductions are those which are:

- authorised by statute; or

- covered by a contractual term; or

- previously consented to in writing.

Statutry authorisation would cover deductions for income tax, national insurance and attachment of earnings orders. Contractual authorisation means a written contractual term transferred to the worker prior to the deduction. The term must authorise the deduction so that a tribunal could be called on to determine whether it is justified. Certainly an employer cannot rely on a term of the contract which is a contractual variation which took effect before the conduct which led to the deduction.

If management and union negotiations produce oral agreements as to proposed variations of individual contracts of employment, the variations will be effective from the date of the oral agreement rather than the date that a collective agreement is reduced to writing and signed by the parties.

In *York City and District Travel Ltd. v. Smith* 1990 a deduction had been made from the wage of a traffic office clerk in respect of missing money. On an allegation that such a deduction was unlawful under the Wages Act 1986, the employer argued that it was lawful as it was made in accordance with a relevant provision of the worker's contract. The provision relied upon was included in the 'Booking Office Clerical Responsibilities', the subject matter of management/union negotiations in 1988 and not part of the complainant's original contract. By such agreement, the employer argued, the complainant's contract had been varied to include the clause. Also the Wages Act provides that *"In this section 'relevant provision ' in relation to a worker's contract, means any provision of the contract comprised and if express whether oral or in writing) whose existence and effect on any such occasions."* The fact that the deduction was made after the contractual variation had been agreed between management and the union but before the agreement had been formally ratified and signed, convinced the tribunal that it was not sanctioned by a relevant provision in the employee's contract and consequently unlawful. The EAT disagreed and held that the contract of employment had been varied by the relevant clause which authorised the deduction. *"Although a variation to an employee's contract entitling the employer to make a deduction from wages must have been agreed before the conduct or events on account of which the deduction was made and must have been notified to the employee in writing prior to the date of deduction, the Act permits the agreement to vary the contract to be oral. There is nothing to indicate that there is a general practice or rule of good industrial relations that agreements varying the terms of contracts of employment should always be or almost always are, reduced into writing and unless there is evidence before an industrial tribunal to justify the inference that such an agreement must be in writing, it is an error to approach consideration of a case of this kind with that fixed notion."*

A third way a legitimate deduction can be made is to rely on the previous consent in writing of the worker that the deduction could be made. Once again the consent must be given before the conduct which gives rise to the deduction occurs.

In *Discount Tobacco and Confectionery v. Williamson* 1993 on the consent authorising the deduction was given after the considerable stock shortages had been discovered so the EAT held that the authorisation did not make the deductions lawful.

In *Pename Ltd. v. Paterson* 1989 a deduction of one week's pay from a worker who had left without giving notice was held to contravene the Act. This was despite the fact that the employee had orally agreed to such a deduction in these circumstances and had that confirmed in a letter. Such deductions are unlawful unless the employer positively signifies his consent in writing.

While the Act indicates that the sole remedy for breach is by way of complaint that does not exclude the right to pursue contractual remedies in the ordinary courts or now before the tribunal. The usual three months time limit applies and for a series of deductions the time begins to run with the last deduction. If a claim is successful the tribunal must make a declaration to the effect and order repayment of the amount deducted.

Minimum Wage

One of the commitments of the labour government was to extend the floor of workers rights and introduce minimum wage legislation in line with other EU States. This it has done by virtue of the National Minimum Wage Act 1998. As with wage deduction rights the minimum wage legislation applies under s.1 not just to employees but to workers generally so that an employer will not avoid its impact by simply designating staff as contractors/casuals.

The Act adopts a wide definition of worker as *an individual who has entered into, works under or who has worked under a contract of employment or any other contract where the individual undertakes to do or perform work or services for another party whose status is not by virtue of the contract that of a client or customer of any profession or business undertaking carried on by the individual.*

The aim of the definition is to exclude all but the genuinely self employed from its ambit. In Chapter 3 we considered the recent case of *Edmunds v. Lawson* 2000 where a pupil barrister claimed that she should be classified as a worker and so entitled to the national minimum wage. While the High Court accepted that her apprenticeship contract brought her within the statute the Court of Appeal disagreed and held that the pupillage contract that she had entered into did not make her a worker for the purposes of securing a minimum wage.

The 1998 Act contains the basic framework of the statutory scheme supported by the National Minimum Wage Regulations 1999 which detail the applicable rate and the method of calculation. (£3.70 per hour from October 2000). One of the most controversial aspects of the minimum wage regulations is to reduce the standard minimum rate of pay for those aged between 18-21 (now £3.20 an hour). Also there is no requirement stipulating an annual uprating or even a review. Inevitably there is a requirement on the employer to maintain appropriate records which are subject to inspection and it is a criminal offence to fail to do this or indeed pay the minimum wage.

Under s.17 of the Act the right to a minimum wage takes effect as a contractual term so that an individual worker could potentially commence proceedings for its breach. Later in the chapter we will consider *Barber v. Mining (UK) Ltd.* 1999 where the

High Court held that the maximum 48 hour working week contained in the Working Time Regulations take effect as a statutory implied term in all contracts of employment.

Sickness

While there is no legal requirement to continue to pay wages to an employee who is absent from work due to illness, it is often the case that an express term of the contract of employment will make provision. The contract could provide that full wages are payable to the employee during a specified period of sickness and then a proportion of the pay in cases of long absence, depending on length of service. In the absence of an express term, the courts are reluctant to imply a right to sick pay.

> In *Mears v. Safecar Security* 1983 the plaintiff who had been employed as a security guard for fourteen months, had been absent from work for half that period and received no sickness benefit. On a complaint brought to require the provision of a statutory statement of the main terms and conditions of employment including reference to the right to sick pay, the Court of Appeal held that a term requiring the payment of sick pay should only be implied into a contract of employment after considering all the facts and circumstances. Here no such term would be implied into the contract.

Under the Social Security Contributions and Benefits Act 1992 an employee is entitled to be paid statutory sick pay (SSP) by the employer during periods of absence from work due to illness. Employers are obliged to administer the scheme in relation to qualified employees and there is no provision for contracting out. Also, significantly, the Statutory Sick Pay Act 1994 now abolishes the employers right to reimbursement of 80% of sums paid out by way of SSP and this Act is in force from 6th April 1994. There is relief however for small employers to which the reimbursement rules still apply. A small employer is defined as one whose national contributions for the qualifying tax year 1993/94 did not exceed 20,000. Such employers get 100% reimbursement of SSP payments made from their NIC payments but only in respect of sick absences of four weeks or more.

The maximum entitlement under the scheme is to twenty eight weeks SSP in any three year period. To qualify for a payment the claimant must be an employee, which would include an office holder or even someone in part-time employment, and both man and women are eligible up to the age of 65. The claimant must satisfy three conditions:

(1) *There must be a period of incapacity for work (PIW) and that is a period of four or more consecutive days of incapacity which may include Sundays and holidays.*

(2)   *The period of incapacity must fall within a period of entitlement (PE). A PE commences with the PIW and ends on the occurrence of the first of the following:*

- *the day the employee returns to work;*

- *after twenty eight weeks during a three year period;*

- *the termination of the contract of employment;*

- *when a pregnant employee reaches the beginning of the eleventh week before the expected week of confinement; or*

- *the day the employee leaves the European Community or is detained in custody.*

(3)   *Statutory Sick Pay is only payable in respect of qualifying days in any PIW. They are normally agreed with the employer and include all days which are normal working days.*

The first three qualifying days are waiting days for which no SSP is payable. From the fourth qualifying day SSP becomes payable the weekly rate for which is calculated according to the claimant earnings.

The rate of payment in force from 6th April 1997 is under the Social Security Benefits Up-rating Order 1997 £55.70 per week.

If there is any conflict as to entitlement, the matter can be referred to an insurance officer (civil servant) who will give a written decision, with possible appeal to a local Appeal Tribunal, and from there to a Social Security Commissioner. Later when we consider the termination of employment and unfair dismissal, we shall see that long term sickness could amount to a fair reason for dismissal or result in a contract of employment being brought to an end by the operation of the doctrine of frustration.

Guarantee Payments

One of the least known statutory rights contained in the Employment Rights Act 1996 is to a guarantee payment in respect of any day during which an employee is laid off due to a reduction in requirements for work of the kind that he is normally employed to do. Such payments are of limited importance in the present day however, due to the fact that the majority of employees are contractually entitled to a payment for periods of not working, often the full wage, and that a contractual payment will normally exceed the usual maximum guarantee payment of £11.85 per day. Continuous employment for at least one month is necessary for the right to arise and the lay-off must be for the whole of the normal working hours the employee is normally required to work. The employee must be available for work and have complied with any reasonable requirement imposed by the employer and not have unreasonably refused an offer of suitable alternative employment'. Also the lay-off must not be due to a strike, lockout or after industrial action. Under the Act there is a maximum entitlement of five guarantee payments in any three month period and twenty days over a year. Enforcement of the right is by way of a complaint to the tribunal within three months of the day in question and if the complaint is made out, the tribunal could order the employer to make a payment of the amount due.

Working Time

The saga of the Working Time Directive was dealt with in Chapter 1 where we used it as an example of the previous government challenging its legal validity. The present government sought to implement the Directive in the Working Time Regulations 1998. As with the minimum wage the regulations apply not just to employees but to workers, but who that includes is not always straightforward. In *Willoughby v. County Home Care Ltd.* 1999 a freelance care assistant was able to establish that she was a worker for the purposes of the regulations and able to claim accrued holiday entitlement.

Workers in transport, sea fishing, off-shore oil and gas work and junior doctors in training are presently excluded but this may change. Under the regulations there is a maximum working week of 48 hours and a standard reference period for average hours of work of 17 weeks. It is possible for a worker to agree to work in excess of this limit in a written agreement subject to a right to terminate the agreement on notice. Strict records must be kept of all such agreements and how they operate. There is a minimum rest break of 20 minutes after 6 hours work which may be taken by workers.

For the first time annual leave is included in legislation so that all workers are entitled to three weeks paid leave rising to four weeks from 23 November 1999. There is a qualifying period of 13 weeks before a worker is entitled to accrue annual leave entitlements. Presently there is a challenge to the legality of the 13 weeks qualifying period which was referred to the European Court for a preliminary ruling in April 1999.

Suspension from Work on Medical Grounds

This right arises also after one month's continuous employment and provides that an employee is entitled to be paid for up to twenty six weeks during which the employee is suspended from work on medical grounds. The suspension must be in consequence of a requirement imposed under statute or a code of practice issued under the Health and Safety at Work Act 1974. Basically then, if an employee is suspended due to a relevant health hazard, he is entitled to be paid provided he is available for work, has complied with any reasonable requirements imposed by the employer and has not unreasonably refused an offer of suitable alternative employment. Once again the right is enforced by means of a complaint to an industrial tribunal within three months of any day to which it is claimed. The tribunal can order the employer to make a payment of any remuneration due if it finds the complaint made out.

Rights in Relation to Trade Union Membership and Activities

A number of rights are conferred on employees by the Trade Union and Labour Relations (Consolidation) Act 1992 in relation to the membership of independent trade unions and taking part in their activities.

- The right not to refused employment on grounds relating to trade union membership under s.137 TULR(C)A 1992 is explored in Chapter 5.

- The right not to be dismissed on grounds relating to trade union membership or activities under s.152 TULR(C)A 1992 is considered in Chapter 11 and referred to in Chapter 3.

Here it is proposed to examine the right not to have action short of dismissal taken against an employee on grounds related to union membership or activities.

Action Short of Dismissal

Under TULR(C)A 1992 s.146(1) An employee has the right not to have action (short of dismissal) taken against an individual by his employer for the purpose of:

(a)   preventing or deterring him from being or seeking to become a member of an independent trade union or penalising him for doing so; or

(b)   preventing or deterring him from taking part in the activities of an independent trade union at any appropriate time, or penalising him from doing so; or

(c)   compelling him to be or become a member of a trade union.

The section requires the proof of an intention by the defendant to deter the complainant from trade union membership or activities. The words *"for the purpose of"* suggest that the employer has an object which he desires to be achieved.

In *Gallacher v. Department of Transport* 1994 the Court of Appeal held that there had been no breach of the section when the employer indicated that to gain promotion to a senior post it was necessary for the applicant to demonstrate management skills and this would involve a return to a line job. The fact that the effect of such a requirement would prevent the applicant continuing his full time union duties did not put the employer in breach of the section. *"The word 'for the purpose of' in the section connote an object which the employer desires or seeks to achieve. The purpose of an action must not be confused with its effect."*

There is no requirement for an employee to qualify by means of a period of continuous employment to take action under s.146. An individual who believes that the section has been contravened may present a complaint to a tribunal within three months of the act complained of and if the complaint is well-founded the tribunal will make a declaration to that effect and may award compensation. The type of action envisaged by s.146 would include demotion, suspension or withholding financial benefits from an employee because of his trade union activities. In the few reported cases, the courts have accepted less serious conduct by the employer as infringing s.146.

In *Brassington v. Cauldon Wholesale* 1977 three members of the TGWU presented a complaint that the conduct of their company chairman constituted action short of dismissal because of trade union membership. During a recognition enquiry, the chairman, had threatened the trade union representatives to the effect that he would rather close the factory than recognise the union. The EAT upheld the complaint that such a threat was action short of dismissal for the purpose of deterring employees from becoming or remaining members of an independent trade union.

In *Carlson v. The Post Office* 1981 the EAT held that 'penalising' for the purposes of the section cannot be limited to the imposition of a positive punishment or to a financial penalty. Here the refusal of a parking permit because of trade union membership subjected the individual to a disadvantage and that was sufficient to amount to penalising' him for the purposes of the section.

In *Carter v. Wiltshire County Council Ltd.* 1979 the employer threatened disciplinary action against members of an independent trade union for holding a trade union meeting on the employer's premises after working hours but without his permission. Here it was held that as the request to hold the meeting involved minimal expense or harm for the employer and the employees were entitled to be on the employer's premises, the threat of disciplinary action constituted unlawful action short of dismissal.

Similarly in *British Airways v. Clark* 1982 trade union representatives were disciplined for attending a trade union meeting without permission. The EAT held that this amounted to action short of dismissal. Furthermore, the three month's time limit in presenting the complaint was held to run from the date of the final appeal against the decision to discipline the men rather than the date of the original hearing.

A major source of conflict in relation to the section was whether the right is restricted to preventing action targeted against an employee or an individual or whether it extends to protect an employee who is discriminated against on the basis of his membership of a trade union or of a particular trade union.

The matter was considered by the Court of Appeal in *Ridgeway and Fairbrother v. National Coal Board* 1987. Here employees complained that as members of the National Union of Mineworkers they had directly suffered when they did not receive a pay increase that had been restricted to members of the Union of Democratic Mineworkers. The Court reversing the decision of the EAT held that the NUM employees had been discriminated against directly because of their membership of a particular trade union for they did not receive the pay increase which was a direct loss to them as individuals. Accordingly their right not to have action taken against them as individuals for the purpose of preventing or deterring them from being a member of an independent trade union (the NUM) had been infringed.

In *Farnsworth Ltd. v. McCoid* 1999 the employer exercised the right in a collective agreement to derecognise the claimant as a shop steward because of his conduct. The claimant's allegation of a breach of s.146 was upheld by the Court of Appeal which found that the derecognition was action taken against him as an individual with the meaning of s.146(1).

Under s.148 when an employee complains to an industrial tribunal about an alleged breach of s.146 it is for the employer to show the purpose for which the action was taken against the employee.

In *Palmer v. Associated British Ports* 1993 and *Wilson v. Associated Newspapers Ltd.* 1993 the Court of Appeal held that the employers had infringed s.146 in relation to certain trade union members who had refused to accept personal contracts and give up their rights to union representation in collective bargaining. By withholding pay rises from such members the employer was penalising them for trade union membership and this constituted unlawful action short of dismissal.

In an immediate response to the judgment the Government proposed an amendment to the Trade Union Reform and Employment Rights Bill which would have the effect of overturning the above judgments and limiting action short of dismissal to cases of individual victimisation rather than organisational changes. A new s.148(3) was inserted into TULR(C)A 1992 by s.13 of the Trade Union Reform and Employment Rights Act 1993.

Under s.148(3) In determining what was the purpose for which action was taken by the employer against the complainant in a case where–

(a) there is evidence that the employer's purpose was to further a change in his relationship with all or any class of his employees, and

(b) there is also evidence that his purpose was one falling within s.146.

the tribunal shall regard the purpose mentioned in paragraph (a) (and not the purpose mentioned in paragraph (b)) as the purpose for which the employer took the action, unless it considers that the action was such as no reasonable employer would take having regard to the purpose mentioned in paragraph (a).

The effect of the new s.148(3) is that even if an act may at first seem to amount to a breach of s.146 it is nevertheless open to the employer to show that it had another purpose, for instance to effect a change under s.148(3)(a) and that is the purpose which must prevail.

The amendment therefore severely limits the scope of s.146 as protection for trade union members if an employer is determined to derecognise a union, establish single union bargaining or introduce personal contracts (see Chapter 7).

Time off for Trade Union Officials to carry out Trade Union Duties

The right to paid time off for trade union officials was considerably narrowed by the Employment Act 1989 and is now contained in s.168 of TULR(C)A 1992.

Under s.168(1) An employer shall permit an employee of his who is an official of an independent trade union recognised by the employer to take time off during his working hours for the purpose of carrying out any duties of his, as such an official, concerned with

(a)   *negotiations with the employer related to or connected with matters falling within section 178(2) (collective bargaining) in relation to which the trade union is recognised by the employer, or*

(b)   *the performance on behalf of employees of the employer of functions related to or connected with matters falling within that provision which the employer has agreed may be so performed by the trade union.*

(2)   *He shall also permit such an employee to take time off during his working hours for the purpose of undergoing training in aspects of industrial relations*

(3)   *The amount of time off which an employee is to be permitted to take under this section and the purposes for which, the occasions on which and any conditions subject to which time off may be so taken are those that are reasonable in all the circumstances having regard to any relevant provisions of a Code of Practice issued by ACAS.*

The Code of Practice referred to by the section is ACAS Code of Practice 3: Time Off for Trade Union Duties and Activities (1991).

Originally the Employment Protection (Consolidation) Act 1978 provided that if an employer recognised an independent trade union for the purpose of collective bargaining then he was obliged to permit an employee of his who is an official of that union to have *'reasonable'* time off work with pay during working hours to enable him:

(a)   *to carry out those duties as an official concerned with industrial relations between employer and employees; or*

(b)   *to undergo training in aspects of industrial relations.*

A trade union official would include anyone appointed to be a representative of members of an independent trade union, for instance, a steward, safety representative or branch secretary. It seemed that the *words "concerned with industrial relations between employer and employees"* were not to be interpreted too strictly.

In *Beal v. Beecham Group Ltd.* 1982 the issue was whether attendance by seven union officials of the ASTMS at a National Advisory Committee for the Beecham group, with the object of planning a co-ordinated strategy to ensure minimum allowances and health and safety standards for all employees of the various groups was a duty *"concerned with industrial relations"*. It was held that to restrict the duty to when officials are actually engaged in transacting industrial relations business is too narrow an interpretation. Here the meeting in question was designed to make concrete policy decisions as to how industrial relations should be negotiated in the future and attendance was a duty for which time off should be allowed.

In *Young v. Carr Fasteners* 1979 when the employer set up a pension scheme for the staff, a steward of the recognised trade union went on a course to the trade union college entitled *"Pensions and Participation"*. In deciding whether she was entitled to paid time off, the EAT held that the question to be asked was whether what the trade union official was seeking to do was to undergo training in some aspect of industrial relations relevant to the carrying out of her duties. Advising and negotiating on pension rights was as much industrial relations as advising on wages and she was entitled to paid time off.

This broad view of industrial relations training and duties taken by industrial tribunals led the government to intervene and considerably narrow the scope of the right in the Employment Act 1989, now included as s.168 TULR(C)A 1992. In s.168(1) above reference is made to s.178(2) which relates to collective bargaining matters for which the trade union is recognised.

As a result of the amendments it seems that there is no right to paid time off for matters in respect of which the union is not recognised by the employer unless the employer has specifically agreed that the union may act on behalf of the employees. The right to time off depends on whether the trade union is recognised and the extent of recognition is crucial in determining the purposes for which time off can be claimed. Nevertheless there is still a view that s.168 should be broadly interpreted.

In *STC Submarine Systems v. Piper* 1993 the complainant branch secretary of the TGWU asked for paid time off to attend a training course on sex discrimination in pension plans. This request was refused and he claimed that this was in breach of statutory rights to paid time off. The TGWU is independent and recognised for collective bargaining purposes by the employer. Also one of the complainants roles was to advise company employees on pensions and he was also on the consultative committee of the company's group pension scheme. The issue was whether the training course was relevant to his function as branch secretary concerned with negotiations about terms and conditions of employment. To assist in its deliberation the industrial tribunal referred to the 1991 Code of Practice relating to time off which states that time off could be considered for training particularly where an official has special responsibilities. The EAT agreed with the tribunal that time off should have been given emphasising that the phrase special responsibilities was useful and tended to show that they may well be functions which were part and parcel of the efficient carrying out of an official's position and were incidental to the office, even though they did not fall within a strict interpretation of the word *'duties'*. The argument that the pension scheme was not negotiable was also rejected by the EAT who decided that information the branch secretary gave to shop stewards about pensions was nevertheless relevant to their negotiations.

In *Ryford Ltd. v. Drinkwater* 1996 the EAT considered the operation of s.168 in relation to the right of a trade union official to take time off for the purpose of trade union duties. To establish a breach of s.168 the EAT prescribed that the official had to establish on the balance of probabilities, that a request for time off was made, that it came to the notice of the employer's appropriate representative, and that they either refused it, ignored it or failed to respond to it. Obviously the employer must be aware of the request before he can "fail" to "permit" time off.

Trade union officials are entitled to be paid for time off approved under s.168

> *Under s.169(1) An employer who permits an employee to take time off under section 168 shall pay him for the time taken off pursuant to the permission.*

> *(2)   here the employee's remuneration for the work he would ordinarily have been doing during that time does not vary with the amount of work done, he shall be paid as if he had worked at that work for the whole of that time.*

> *(3)   here the employee's remuneration for the work he would ordinarily have been doing during that time varies with the amount of work done, he shall be paid an amount calculated by reference to the average hourly earnings for that work.*

Time off for Trade Union Members to take part in Trade Union Activities

A member of a recognised independent trade union has under s.170(1) the right to be given reasonable time off during working hours to take part in a trade union activity.

> *Under s.170(1) An employer shall permit an employee of his who is a member of an independent trade union recognised by the employer in respect of that description of employee to take time off during his working hours for the purpose of taking part in–*

> > *(a)   any activities of the union, and*

(b) any activities in relation to which the employee is acting as a representative of the union.

(2) The right conferred by subsection (1) does not extent to activities which themselves consist of industrial action, whether or not in contemplation or furtherance of a trade dispute.

(3) The amount of time off which an employee is to be permitted to take under this section and the purposes for which, the occasions on which and any conditions subject to which time off may be so taken are those that are reasonable in all the circumstances having regard to any relevant provisions of a Code of Practice issued by ACAS.

(4) An employee may present a complaint to an industrial tribunal that his employer has failed to permit him to take time off as required by this section.

Again the relevant Code of Practice is ACAS Code of Practice 3: Time off for Trade Union Duties and Activities (1991).

Following the Employment Protection (Part-Time Employees) Regulations 1995 this right applies to all employees whether or full-time or part-time.

Specifically excluded from the expression *'trade union activity'* is industrial action whether or not in contemplation or furtherance of a trade dispute.

In *Luce v. Bexley LBC* 1990 the EAT held that for the purposes of this section the lobbying of Parliament in connection with proposed legislation which affected the teaching profession was not a 'trade union activity' which enables a member of the National Union of Teachers to take time off work. While the lobbying of Parliament could amount to a *'trade union activity'* in appropriate circumstances, if it merely has the object of conveying political and ideological objections to proposed legislation, that could not be regarded so. For the purpose of the section the role of the industrial tribunal was: *"first to decide whether on the facts the request fell within the section, and then it had to apply the provisions of reasonableness."*

Public Duties

An employee, whether full-time or part-time, is entitled by virtue of s.50 of the Employment Rights Act 1996 to take time off during working hours to undertake certain public duties such as in the capacity of a Justice of the Peace or a local councillor. Once again the amount of time off must be reasonable bearing in mind the amount of time off needed to perform the public duty and the effect of the absence on the employer's business.

> In *Borders Regional Council v. Maule* 1993 the EAT provided some guidance as to how the section should be interpreted so that *"time off"* is reasonable in the circumstances. The EAT thought that the onus lay with the employee to plan absences and through discussion with the employer scale down the level of commitment to produce a pattern which is reasonable in the circumstances. *"In determining whether an employer was in breach of the section in refusing to permit an employee to take time off for public duties the statute requires the tribunal to consider the whole circumstances including the number and frequency of similar absences which have been permitted by the employer".*

Time off to Look for Work or Arrange for Training

Later in the text the concept of redundancy is explored. If an employee is dismissed by reason of redundancy rather than being warned of impending redundancy, he is entitled, before his notice period expires, to be allowed to have a reasonable amount of paid time off during working hours to search for new employment or make arrangements for training for future employment. If such time off is unreasonably refused, the employee may within three months present a complaint to an industrial tribunal who may declare that fact if they feel the claim is well founded, and award compensation. To qualify for this right the employee must have been employed for a continuous period of two years at the time the notice period expires.

Time Off for Dependents

A new right to time off for dependents was introduced as a result of the Parental Leave Directive and was in force on 15 December 1999. The aim of the directive was to give workers time off for urgent family reasons in cases of sickness or accident making the presence of the worker indispensable. This right along with maternity and parental leave (see Chapter 6) is an example of the government's commitment to family friendly policies in the working environment.

Schedule 4 of the Employment Relations Act 1999 adds a new s.57A to the Employment Rights Act 1996 containing the provision.

The right is to a reasonable amount of time off during working hours to take action in the following circumstances:

- to provide assistance when a dependent falls ill, gives birth, is injured or assaulted;

- to make arrangements for the provision of care for a dependent who is ill or injured;

- upon the death of a dependent;

- due to the unexpected disruption or termination of the arrangements for the care of a dependent;

- to deal with an incident involving a child during the time when an educational establishment has the care of that child.

Significantly the rights to time off in the above circumstances does not carry with it any right to be paid during the period of time off. Also the period is that which is reasonable and so left to the interpretation of a tribunal in a case where enforcement is necessary. A complaint may be made s.57B within three months of an unreasonable refusal and compensation which is just and equitable may be awarded for an infringement of the right.

Disclosure of Public Interest Matters

The Public Interest Disclosure Act 1998 was brought into force on July 2 1999 its provisions being incorporated into the Employment Rights Act 1996. Its aim is to provide protection for workers who wish to speak out about matters of public concern. Notice that the Act confers protection on a 'worker' which would include a full-time or part-time employee and a contractor providing personal services as well as agency workers. Fear of unjustifiable disciplinary action or victimisation has in the past deterred workers from making known matters of public concern and the aim of this legislation is to provide them with some degree of protection. Health and safety issues should always be raised and addressed without fear of intimidation, particularly where staff are temporary or on short term contracts. There is evidence that disasters such as Piper Alpha, The Herald of Free Enterprise and Clapham Junction would have been prevented if a different culture of raising genuine concerns about health and safety had been in place. More recent concerns about the standard of some of the work carried out in the health service also points to the need to encourage whistle-blowing for the protection of the public.

Under the Act protection is offered to a whistle-blower provided that the disclosure is proportionate and made in good faith on a matter of public concern. Two key considerations are:

- the subject matter of the disclosure;

- to whom the disclosure is made.

Only a disclosure which is the reasonable belief of the worker and relates to one of six specified categories may qualify for protection, called "qualifying disclosures". The categories are contained in s.43B

- actual or apparant breaches of the criminal law

- a failure to comply with a legal obligation

- a miscarriage of justice

- endangering of an individuals health and safety

- damage to the environment

- concealment of any of the above.

The Act differentiates between disclosure to an employer or other responsible person and disclosure to outsiders. In relation to employers a worker who makes a qualifying disclosure is protected under s.43C provided he acted in good faith and reasonably believes that the information tends to show the malpractice or misconduct. There are numerous regulatory bodies who may have an interest in hearing certain disclosures (eg the Health and Safety Executive, the Financial Services Authority). A worker who makes a qualifying disclosure to such a body will be protected if he acts in good faith and reasonably believes that the malpractice falls within the matters for which the body is responsible and reasonably believes that the information disclosed and allegations in it is substantially true.

If disclosure is made externally on a wider scale then under s.43G there are significant additional requirements before protection is offered in such cases. The subject of the disclosure must be exceptionally serious or the workers must show that they reasonably believe that they will be victimised for making the disclosure internally or that there will be a cover up. In addition the disclosure must be reasonable in the circumstances. Certainly there will be no protection if disclosure is made for personal gain or for example to the press rather than to the police who could address the issue. A worker has the right under s.47B not to be victimised for making a protected disclosure. In cases involving dismissal an employee has the right to claim unfair dismissal with no qualifying period and no upper limit on potential compensation. If it is established that the applicant has been dismissed as a result of making a protected disclosure then under s.103A the dismissal will be automatically unfair (see Chapter 11).

Case Study

Dalton West plc - Trade Union Duties and Activities

Dalton West is a large manufacturer of fork lift trucks with depots and retail outlets situated all over Britain.

Jim White is the branch secretary of the Fitters and General Workers Union at the Coventry factory. Supported by fifteen shop stewards Jim is responsible for about twelve hundred members at Coventry. Inevitably he finds that a large part of his working day is devoted to union business and in the interests of "good industrial relations" this is done with the approval of the management. With such a large membership there are always employment problems to deal with and they usually have legal implications. At present Jim is faced with three issues involving statutory rights.

1. *The first problem involves the payment of wages. The company decided last month to withdraw enhanced overtime rates for production workers in the factory and since then overtime has been worked but under protest. Also a festering issue relates to lasts years Christmas bonus which was calculated for all factory staff but then withdrawn for maintenance workers who failed to achieve their productivity targets.*

2. *Bill Pearson a foreman in production has been encouraged by the management to apply for the post of supervisory chargehand carrying additional responsibilities. He complains to Jim that the production manager indicated to him that to secure the post he should consider whether as a prospective supervisor he should retain his union membership.*

3. *Jim applied three months ago for paid time off work to attend a union training course on discrimination in pension plans. Advising the stewards and the shop floor on pension matters is one of the functions of the branch secretary. Jim's request has been refused by management on the grounds that the course has nothing to do with industrial relations.*

Chapter 10
The Termination of Employment

Legal conflict between employer and employee arises most usually when the employment relationship comes to an end. Important statutory rights, such as unfair dismissal and redundancy, and common law rights, such as a wrongful dismissal all depend upon showing that the employment relationship was terminated by means of a dismissal. For this purpose therefore, it is necessary to explore the various modes of termination of the employment relationship and identify when a dismissal, whether express or implied has occurred.

Dismissal and Notice

If an employer or an employee wishes to terminate a contract of employment they are required to comply with the employee's contractual requirements in relation to notice. Generally the length of the notice period will depend upon the nature of the employment and may increase in relation to the number of years' service. In addition, the Contracts of Employment Act 1963 introduced statutory minimum periods of notice that apply where the contract is silent or provides for less favourable periods. The statutory statement of the main terms and conditions of employment supplied under s.1 of the Employment Rights Act 1996 will stipulate the minimum notice period to which the employee is entitled.

Under s.86 The notice required to be given by an employer to terminate the contract of employment of a person who has been continuously employed for [one month] or more

(a) *shall be not less than one week's notice if his period of continuous employment is less than two years;*

(b) *shall be not less than one week's notice for each year of continuous employment if his period of continuous employment is two years or more but less than twelve years; and*

(c) *shall be not less than twelve weeks' notice if his period of continuous employment is twelve years or more.*

(2) *The notice required to be given by an employee who has been continuously employed for [one month] or more to terminate his contract of employment shall be not less than one week.*

If the contractual notice period is less than the statutory minimum period then the statutory minimum period will apply. This minimum period is often triggered in the case of employees who have been employed for twelve years or more and are entitled to 12 weeks notice under s.86. Following the Employment Protection (Part-Time Employees) Regulations 1995, the right to a statutory minimum period of notice extends to part-time employees regardless of their hours of work.

One further complication is that if the contract is silent as to the notice period, there is an implied term under the common law that the notice given will be reasonable and such a notice period may, in exceptional cases, exceed the statutory minimum. Certainly the seniority of the employee, the nature of his job, and the length of service could dictate that a relatively long period of notice is required. In *Hill v. Parsons & Company Ltd.* 1972 a senior engineer was held to be entitled to notice of six months under the common law, well in excess of the statutory rights.

There is nothing to prevent an employee from waiving his right to notice or, in fact, accepting a lump sum payment in lieu of the notice period to which he is entitled. Failure by the employer to comply with notice requirements would entitle the employee to bring an action for damages in the ordinary courts or now in the employment tribunal based on breach of contract. Such a claim is known as 'wrongful dismissal' referring to the wrongful manner in which the contract of employment has been terminated.

Wrongful Dismissal

Summary dismissal occurs when the contract of employment is terminated instantly without notice and it is prima facie wrongful. Such a dismissal is justifiable under the common law, however, if it can be shown that the employee is in repudiatory breach of the contract of employment because of his *gross misconduct*. By summarily dismissing, the employer is accepting the repudiatory breach of the employee and treating the contract as discharged. Whether the alleged misconduct may be classified as gross is a question of fact and degree, but it would normally include conduct such as disobedience, neglect, dishonesty, or misbehaviour. Certainly early cases must now be viewed with caution. The summary dismissal of a housemaid in *Turner v. Mason* 1854 because she went to visit her sick mother in contravention of her employer's instructions was held not to be wrongful but would be unlikely to constitute gross misconduct in the present day. Until recently an action for wrongful dismissal was a common law claim for breach of contract and could only be dealt with in the ordinary courts. Now employment tribunals also have jurisdiction to hear an action for wrongful dismissal.

A fundamental question that is often asked is whether the employment relationship can survive the nature of the misconduct.

In *Pepper v. Webb* 1969 the action of the head gardener in wilfully disobeying a reasonable order was sufficient to amount to gross misconduct and provide grounds for summary dismissal, despite the contract of employment providing for three months' notice. It should be stressed, however, that the reaction of the gardener in this case represented the culmination of a long period of insolence, and the isolated use of choice obscenities by an employee to an employer may not amount to gross misconduct if there is provocation.

Also, in *Laws v. London Chronicle* 1959 an employee who disobeyed an express order of her managing director was nevertheless held to be wrongfully dismissed in the circumstances. The employee had acted out of loyalty to her immediate superior when she walked out of an editorial conference despite the express instruction of her managing director to remain.

The action of a betting shop manager in *Sinclair v. Neighbour* 1967 in borrowing £15 from the till and leaving a IOU, contrary to express instructions, was regarded as sufficient grounds to justify summary dismissal.

In *Denco Ltd. v. Joinson* 1991 the EAT felt that if an employee uses an unauthorised password in order to enter a computer known to contain information to which he is not entitled that of itself is gross misconduct which could attract summary dismissal. In such cases the EAT thought it desirable that the management should stress that such dishonesty will carry with it severe penalties.

In determining whether an employer is entitled to dismiss summarily for gross misconduct it is usually necessary to interpret the employee's contract of employment. In *Dietman v. London Borough of Brent* 1988 following a critical report on the performance of a senior social worker in relation to the death of child her employer instantly dismissed her without notice, payment in lieu of notice, or an opportunity to defend herself in a disciplinary hearing. This was despite the fact that the councils contractual disciplinary procedure was that in the case of more serious offences the employee should be invited to a formal disciplinary meeting and be represented. Her contract also provided that "any breach of disciplinary rules will render you liable to disciplinary action which will normally include immediate suspension followed by dismissal, or instant dismissal for offences of gross misconduct". Gross misconduct was defined as misconduct of such a nature that the authority is justified in no longer tolerating the continued presence at the place of work of the employee who commits an offence of gross misconduct. On a claim for wrongful dismissal the High Court held that on a proper construction of these terms the employer was not entitled to dismiss the employee without giving her the right to a disciplinary hearing.

On appeal the council argued that the employee's gross negligence constituted gross misconduct under the contract and instant dismissal without suspension or a disciplinary hearing was permissible. This argument was rejected by the Court of Appeal who felt that in relation to gross misconduct the agreed procedure was suspension pending the outcome of a disciplinary hearing and this construction was in accordance with the ACAS code of practice. Furthermore the Court of Appeal agreed that gross negligence did not constitute gross misconduct as defined in the contract. Gross negligence lacks the element of intention and is conduct which is neither dishonest or disruptive but rather a serious failure to perform professional duties to the required standard.

The courts have recognised that a summary dismissal could occur despite the fact that an employee is already under notice of dismissal. In *Stapp v. Shaftesbury Society* 1982 there was held to be a summary dismissal when an employee, already serving a notice of dismissal, was sent a letter by the employer asking him to *"relinquish your duties with effect from today"*.

The remedy for a successful claim of wrongful dismissal is an action for damages amounting to the loss of wages payable during the notice period.

> In *Addis v. Gramophone Company Ltd*. 1909 the House of Lords ruled that when a servant is wrongfully dismissed from his employment, the damages for the dismissal cannot include compensation for the manner of the dismissal, for his injured feelings, or for the loss he may sustain from the fact that the dismissal in itself makes it more difficult for him to obtain fresh employment.

It seems therefore that if an employer pays the employee an appropriate lump sum on summary dismissal, which represents a full payment of pay in lieu of notice, there would be little point in bringing a claim for breach of contract as no further damages would be payable. In *G Cox v. Philips Industries* 1975 there was some retreat from this somewhat harsh position. Here the plaintiff was dismissed and given five months' salary in lieu of notice, the appropriate compensation under his contract of employment. He nevertheless sued for further damages for breach of contract. Prior to his dismissal the plaintiff had been demoted to a position of less responsibility and relegated to duties which were vague and inadequately expressed and this constituted a breach of his contract of employment. The High Court held that *"it was in the contemplation of the parties that such a breach of contract would expose the plaintiff to the degree of vexation which he did in fact suffer (depression, anxiety, frustration and sickness). Although it was argued by the defendants that damages for such a breach should only be awarded in funeral, wedding and holiday cases, there was no reason in principle why they should not apply to a case like the present one. Thus the plaintiff would be awarded £500".*

In *Bliss v. South East Thames Regional Health Authority* 1985 the Court of Appeal re-emphasised the ruling of the House of Lords in *Addis v. Gramophone Company Ltd.* 1909 and reversed the decision of the High Court in the case before it to award damages to a consultant orthopaedic surgeon who had suffered frustration, vexation, and distress from the repudiatory breach of contract by his employer. *"The general rule laid down by the House of Lords in Addis v. Gramophone Company Ltd. is that where damages fall to be assessed for breach of contract rather than tort, it is not permissible to award general damages for frustration, mental distress, injured feelings or annoyance caused by the breach. Unless and until the House of Lords has reconsidered its decision in Addis, the view taken in Cox that damages for distress, vexation and frustration could be recovered for breach of a contract of employment if it could be said to have been in the contemplation of the parties that the breach would cause distress was wrong".*

You will remember that in the important House of Lords decision in *Malik v. BCCI* 1997 the court confirmed that damages could be awarded for breach of trust and confidence caused by the stigma attached to working for an employer who had been guilty of serious misconduct. (See Chapter 4).

In *Johnson v. Unisys Ltd.* 1999 the applicant having succeeded in an unfair dismissal claim made a further claim for substantial damages for wrongful dismissal alleging that because of the manner of dismissal he had suffered a mental breakdown and was unable to work. The Court of Appeal felt that the claimant was not entitled to damages in these circumstances. The court reaffirmed that where there is an express dismissal Addis remains authority for the principle that damages for wrongful dismissal cannot include compensation for the manner of the dismissal, for the employee's injured feelings or for the loss he may sustain from the fact that the dismissal itself makes it too difficult to obtain new employment. The court stressed that the House of Lords decision in *Malik v. BCCI 1997* did not overrule Addis and dealt with the breach of the implied term of trust and confidence rather than the manner of dismissal.

A contract of employment could make provision for a minimum period of notice on termination, and also provide that the employer *"may make a payment in lieu of notice".*

In *Cerbus Software Ltd. v. Rowley* 1999 the complainant employee was dismissed in breach of such a term and claimed damages for wrongful dismissal. His award of six months wages in lieu of notice was challenged by the employer who contended that the complainant was under a duty to mitigate his loss and as he had obtained more lucrative employment during the notice period account should be taken of it in determining his loss. The EAT upheld the tribunal's decision deciding that *"monies in lieu are claimable either as monies due under the contract or as damages for breach of contract putting the employee in the position he would have been had the breach not be committed. In neither event was the employer entitled to receive the benefit of the employee's mitigation of his damage"*.

The contact could also make provision for its summary termination on the occurance of a particular event. In *T & K House Improvement Ltd. v. Shilton* 2000 a double glazing sales director had a term in his contract which provided that if he failed to make sales targets *"you may be dismissed with immediate effect"*. The employer sought to trigger the clause with no notice or wages in lieu and the employee claimed breach of contract. The Court of Appeal held that the claimant was entitled to three months pay in lieu of notice when he was dismissed in such circumstances. The power to dismiss with immediate effect did not override the employee's contractual right to notice. It did have the effect of terminating the employee's right to work but did not destroy all other contractual rights.

There is an increasing practice for senior post holders in organisations to negotiate long periods of notice to terminate their contracts of employment. Inevitably a substantial sum would become payable if an employer wishes to terminate such a contract without giving the notice to which the employee is entitled under the contract.

In *Clark v. BET Plc* 1997 following a takeover the chief executive of BET was dismissed without the three years notice to which he was entitled under his contract. Liability for wrongful dismissal was not denied by the employer but the parties litigated in the High Court over the level of damages. The plaintiff's contract of employment provided that his considerable salary should be reviewed annually and increased at the boards discretion. In addition the contract stated that "The executive will participate in a bonus arrangement providing a maximum of 60% basic salary in any year". For the previous five years the plaintiff was given a 10% salary increase and the maximum bonus. The High Court held that the damages for wrongful dismissal should reflect a 10% salary increase over the three year notice period, for the plaintiff had a contractual right to an annual upward adjustment in salary. A 50% bonus of salary for each of the three years was also payable as a realistic assumption of the plaintiff's position had he stayed with the company, The figure of 2.85 million paid in damages demonstrates the need for careful drafting in the contracts of high earners.

It is obvious in some cases that the employer has dismissed without notice to prevent the employee acquiring sufficient continuous employment for the purposes of qualifying for an unfair dismissal complaint. In *Stapp v. Shaftesbury Society* 1982 the court held that if there is no adequate reason which would justify summary dismissal, and if by the summary dismissal the employee as a consequence is deprived of his right to bring a claim for unfair dismissal by shortening the relevant period of continuous employment, the employee could have a remedy at common law for unfair dismissal. The measure of damages payable *"might include the loss of the right to complain of unfair dismissal which the employee would have had, had he not been summarily dismissed"*.

Raspin v. United News Shops 1999 is the first case where the EAT has confirmed that an award of damages can be made against an employer to reflect the fact that a wrongful dismissal prevented an employee from acquiring the necessary service to qualify to make a complaint of unfair dismissal. The damages should equate with the loss which could be the opportunity to succeed in an unfair dismissal claim against the employer.

Of course since 1971 an aggrieved employee who is qualified has the further option of complaining to a tribunal that the dismissal is without good reason and unfair. (See Chapter 11).

In relation to breaches of discipline it is often the practice that express agreement will be reached between the employer and a trade union to identify types of conduct and classify it as *'gross misconduct'* which will warrant instant dismissal. This was the position in *W Brooks & Son v. Skinner* 1984 where the employer had agreed with the trade union that anyone who became drunk at the firm's Christmas party, so that he was absent from the next shift, would be instantly dismissed. In accordance with the agreement the complainant was instantly dismissed and brought a claim of unfair dismissal. Agreeing with the tribunal the EAT held that failure to communicate to the employees the consequences of absence from work after the party, made the decision to dismiss summarily an unfair one. *"Whether or not an employer is justified in treating a particular matter of conduct as sufficient to justify dismissal must include in the particular case, that the employee knew that his conduct would merit summary dismissal. Though there is much conduct which any employee will know will result in instant dismissal, there are also instances of conduct, particularly those which have been dealt with in other ways at other times by the employer, which the employee may well consider will not merit summary dismissal."*

In the above case, therefore, it is the manner of dismissal which leads the tribunal to conclude that the employer has acted unreasonably for the purposes of unfair dismissal. Non-compliance with disciplinary procedures in relation to dismissal is considered in Chapter 11 where the law of unfair dismissal is explored.

It has been argued that in the case of a dismissal in breach of contract, where the employer ignores disciplinary and appeals procedures the employee in question should be able to rely on the implied contractual rights not to be unfairly dismissed. Damages equivalent to the compensatory award for unfair dismissal were awarded in such circumstances by the tribunal in *Fosca Services (UK) Ltd. v. Birkett* 1996. The tribunal held that while the employee could not claim unfair dismissal because he did not have sufficient service *"the effect of the terms of the contract of employment in this case is to give Mr Birkett the right not to be unfairly dismissed as a right under his contract"*. On appeal the EAT strongly reversed the decision and made it clear *"It was not open to the chairman to imply a term of the contract that the respondent would enjoy the equivalent of the statutory right not to be unfairly dismissed. None of the recognised tests for implying such a term are made out. The fallacy, in our judgment, in the chairman's reasoning is to disregard the normal common law rules as to loss in cases of wrongful dismissal. That loss is limited to the sums payable to the employee had the employment been lawfully terminated under the contract. Once a dismissal has taken place, as was accepted and found in this case, it is irrelevant to consider what might have happened had a contractual disciplinary procedure been followed. An employer is entitled to dismiss on contractual notice at common law for whatever reason"*.

It may be that there are grounds for alleging that the summary dismissal of the employee is both wrongful and unfair. In such a case it would technically be possible to pursue a common law claim for wrongful dismissal based upon breach of contract and claim under statute for unfair dismissal in the industrial tribunal. The Court of Appeal in *O'Laoire v. Jackel International Ltd.* 1991 confirmed that the High Court was wrong to deduct an award of the maximum compensation for unfair dismissal (then £8,000) from the damages recoverable by the plaintiff in an action for wrongful dismissal for loss of earnings during the notice period. *"Unless the defendants can prove a double recovery for the same loss, there is no basis for setting off an unfair dismissal compensatory award against common law damages for wrongful dismissal. For the rule against double recovery to be involved, it must be shown that the plaintiff would be obtaining compensation under two heads for the same loss"*.

A number of cases in the 1980s culminating in *Robb v. London Borough of Hammersmith and Fulham* 1991 suggest that in cases involving a dismissal in breach of contract an interlocutory (temporary) injunction to restrain the dismissal and preserve the contract of employment so compelling the employer to go through the contractual disciplinary procedure may be the most effective remedy. Here an injunction was granted by the High Court against the employer to restrain the dismissal and treat the plaintiff as suspended on full pay until the contractual disciplinary procedure had been complied with. The employer was clearly in breach of contract and while there was no longer trust and confidence between employer and employee the injunction was workable.

Modes of termination of a Contract of Employment

Normal contractual principles would suggest that *an "unaccepted breach of contract is a thing writ in water"* and if the letter of dismissal is a repudiatory breach of contract it is not effective until the breach is accepted by the employee. As far as the Employment Rights Act 1996 is concerned however, such a letter can unilaterally terminate a contract of employment.

In *Marsh v. National Autistic Society* 1993 the High Court confirmed that a contract of employment repudiated by the employer can no longer subsist in practice as the employee has been excluded from the employment. The contract does not continue on until either the repudiatory breach has been accepted by the employee or the contract has been terminated lawfully by proper notice. The employee in this case had no right to payment of salary up until the time the contract was lawfully terminated.

In cases where a fixed term contract is prematurely brought to an end by the employer's repudiatory breach, a claim for damages for breach of contract may be the more appropriate avenue for redress, for the sum due under the unexpired term of the contract may be well in excess of the possible compensation available for unfair dismissal. Such claims are more prevalent with the increased use of fixed term contracts which are usually terminated by mutual consent. Wrongful dismissal is dismissal in breach of contract and while it is usually alleged in relation to the notice period, in *Jones v. British Telecom* 1987 the allegation was that the dismissal itself was a breach of contract. The plaintiff unsuccessfully argued that the employer had a contractual duty to employ him beyond the age of 60 provided he fulfilled certain retention criteria.

Statutory Dismissal

For the purposes of unfair dismissal the meaning of 'dismissal' is defined in s.95 of the Employment Rights Act 1996.

Section 95(1) provides that: *an employee shall be treated as dismissed by his employer if, but only if;*

(a) *the contract under which he is employed is terminated by the employer, whether it is so terminated by notice or without notice, or*

(b) *where under the contract he is employed for a fixed term, that term expires without being renewed under the same contract, or*

(c) *the employer terminates the contract, with or without notice, in circumstances such that he is entitled to terminate it without notice by reason of the employer's contract.*

The section envisages a dismissal arising expressly, by the employer terminating the contract under s.95(1)(a), impliedly where a termination occurs on the expiration of a fixed term contract of employment under s.95(1)(b) and constructively when the employee terminates the contract in response to the employer's conduct under s.95(1)(c).

Express Dismissal

Under s.95(1)(a) an express dismissal occurs where the employer terminates the contract of employment with or without notice.

We have already said that an employer is normally required to give the employee notice in accordance with the terms of the contract or least the statutory or common law minimum period. For a dismissal with notice, therefore, there is normally no room for any misunderstanding in relation to the employer's intentions. In cases of alleged summary dismissal, however, where there is no notice, there have been claims by the employer that it was not his intention to dismiss but rather merely to discipline. While the words, "you're dismissed, fired, sacked", etc. leave little doubt as to the employer's intentions, if he uses more ambiguous language, perhaps to register his discontent with the employee, the argument that there has been no express dismissal could have some merit.

In *Tanner v. D T Kean* 1978 the complainant had been told that he could not use the company van outside working hours. When the employer discovered that he was doing so, after abusing the employee, he said to him, "that's it, you're finished with me". The EAT held that in deciding whether the words or actions of the employer amounted to a dismissal, all the circumstances should be considered. *"A relevant and perhaps the most important question is how would a reasonable employee in all the circumstances have understood what the employer intended by what he said and did?"* Here the words spoken in the heat of the moment indicated a reprimand rather than a dismissal.

In *Rees v. Apollo Watch Repairs Plc* 1996 the employer wrote to an employee who was taking maternity leave stating that *"I am no longer able to guarantee that you are able to return ..... I am unable to keep the job for you"*. This letter was held to be an express dismissal.

The custom and practice of the trade are also considerations to bear in mind to determine the interpretation to be placed on the language used.

In *Futty v. Brekkes Ltd.* 1974 the tribunal was called on to place an interpretation on the quaint language used on the Hull dock. During an altercation with his foreman the complainant fish filleter was told, "If you do not like the job, fuck off". The complainant took this as a dismissal, left, and found a job elsewhere. For the purposes of an unfair dismissal claim the employer argued in his defence that there had been no dismissal. Here the words were to be considered in the context of the fish trade, and in these circumstances were taken to mean that if you do not like the work you are doing, clock off and come back tomorrow. The custom of the fish trade was that, for a dismissal, the language used was clear and formal. The tribunal agreed with the employer's view and held that the complainant had terminated his own employment by deciding on this occasion that he would leave and subsequently find himself alternative employment.

If the conduct of the employer demonstrates a firm and settled intention to treat the contract of employment as at an end, then this would constitute an express dismissal for the purpose of s.95(1)(c).

In *Boyo v. London Borough of Lambeth* 1995 following an allegation of fraud made against an accountant, his employer the local authority, wrote to him stating that his action had effectively frustrated his contract of employment and as a consequence his salary was to cease at the end of the month. The Court of Appeal held that despite the assertion of frustration, a firm and settled intention to stop paying salary and treat the contract as at an end constituted a dismissal. The meaning and effect of the letter did not depend upon the accuracy of the legal reasoning upon which it was based.

It should be noted, of course, that a failure to treat employees with respect could indicate a breakdown in trust and confidence so as to entitle an employee to walk out and regard himself as constructively dismissed.

An important development in the law relating to express dismissal is the notion that if an employer unilaterally imposes a fundamental change in employment terms that could constitute an express dismissal from a previous contract of employment. This possibility was first recognised in *Hogg v. Dover College* 1990 where a Head of Department was informed that he would in future be employed as a part-time teacher on half his previous salary. The EAT concluded that *"both as a matter of law and common sense, he was being told that his former contract was from that moment gone. There was no question of any continued performance of it. It is suggested, on behalf of the employers, that there was a variation, but again, it seems to us quite elementary that you cannot hold a pistol to somebody's head and say henceforth you are to be employed on wholly different terms which are in fact less than 50% of your previous contract".*

Applying the rationale of Hogg in *Alcan Extrusions v. Yates* 1996 the EAT reached a similar conclusion. Here staff had objected to a fundamental change in shift patterns which affected overtime and holidays. When the change was imposed unilaterally a number of staff responded by claiming that it constituted a fundamental breach of contract tantamount to dismissal. Continuing to work under protest they lodged unfair dismissal clauses and the EAT supported the tribunal's decision that the staff had indeed been expressly dismissed from their previous contracts. The EAT concluded *"that the applicants former contract of employment providing for employment in jobs with a steady and predictable pattern of shift employment were removed from them and replaced by an altogether more demanding and previously uncontemplated regime of rolling shift pattern work which the applicants were certainly not obliged to undertake by their contracts of employment.... Where an employer unilaterally imposes radically different terms of employment, applying the principle in Hogg v. Dover College, there is a dismissal under s.55(2)(a) (now s.95(1)(a)) if, on an objective construction of the relevant letters or other conduct on the part of the employer, there is a removal or withdrawal of the old contract."*

The significance of classifying a change of contract as an express dismissal rather than a fundamental breach for the purposes of constructive dismissal (considered later in the chapter), is that an employee may lodge a claim for unfair dismissal and yet retain his status in an employment relationship, albeit under the new contract.

There is a line of cases from the early 1970s which seemed to suggest that an employee's act of serious misconduct could be regarded as amounting to a self dismissal constituting constructive resignation. In *Rasool v. Hepworth Pipe Company Ltd.* 1980 the Court of Appeal disapproved of that approach and suggested that is the acceptance by the employer of the employee's repudiatory breach which constitutes the dismissal in such circumstances.

The date of dismissal may be significant, particularly in relation to time limits. A dismissal does not take effect until the employee is told or has been given a reasonable opportunity of reading the notice of dismissal.

Implied Dismissal

Previously we said that if a fixed term contract is terminated by either party prematurely without good reason or authorisation under the contract then an action may lie for damages for breach of contract. If the contract runs its course however under s.95(1)(b) there is an implied dismissal of the employee when the term expires. Potentially therefore if the fixed term contract is not renewed the employee is entitled to present a complaint of unfair dismissal. The ERA 1996 provided that an employer under a fixed term contract could expressly exclude unfair dismissal and redundancy rights. Under s.197(1) the right to claim unfair dismissal did not apply to a fixed term of one year or more which has expired, if the parties had previously agreed in writing to exclude unfair dismissal rights. This section has now been repealed by the Employment Relations Act 1999 which has removed the right to contract out of unfair dismissal in fixed term contracts. Of course in the majority of fixed term arrangements the reason for non renewal of the contract may be redundancy which is potentially a fair reason for dismissal. Also the right to exclude redundancy payments from fixed term contracts has been unaffected by the 1999 Act so that under s.197(3) of the ERA 1996 most employers would ensure that a fixed term contract of employment contains such an exclusion.

It is usual under s.197(3) to exclude the right to a redundancy payment if the term of the contract is two years or more.

> In *Mulrine v. University of Ulster* 1993 the Northern Ireland Court of Appeal held that if the parties to a two year fixed term contract of employment agree to waiver statutory rights to claim unfair dismissal and/or redundancy on the contracts' termination then this waiver will apply if the parties agree and the contract is extended for a further term of four months. As its only possible to waive statutory rights in a fixed term contract of one year or more under, here it was argued that if the four months extension constitutes a new contract, the waiver should not apply. The Court of Appeal held however that the second shorter term was clearly an extension of the first and as the fixed term was now two years and four months, statutory rights were validly excluded by the waiver.

An increasingly popular employment practice in the UK is to employ individuals on a series of short fixed term contracts. We saw in Chapter 8 that in such circumstances if there is no breach in continuity then an employee, full-time or part-time, with a series of contracts extending over two years can qualify for unfair dismissal and redundancy rights. On the termination of each fixed term contract there is potentially a dismissal under s.95(1)(b) for the purposes of unfair dismissal and redundancy. An excellent example is provided in the field of further and higher education where college employers rely heavily on a pool of part-time lecturing staff normally employed for a fixed term over an academic term or semester.

> In *Pfaffinger v. City of Liverpool Community College* 1996 the complainant had been employed as a part-time lecturer at Liverpool Community College under a number of fixed term contracts for each term for a period of thirteen years. When the employer negotiated a reduced hourly rate of pay for part-time staff the complainant refused the offer of a new contract and claimed unfair dismissal and a redundancy payment. The EAT rejected the tribunal's analysis of the legal position and applying s.95(1)(b) held that an employee employed on a succession of fixed term contracts is dismissed for redundancy on the expiration of each contract. Consequently a college lecturer who has three contracts over an academic year could be dismissed three times for redundancy. The redundancy position in relation to the complainant's last contract arose because *"the Liverpool College's need for part-time lecturers to carry out the function of part-time lecturing ceased or diminished from the beginning of the vacation to the start of the new term. This is a redundancy situation and the complainant is entitled to redundancy payment."*

Constructive Dismissal

In a large number of cases it may seem superficially that the contract of employment has been terminated by the employee's conduct in `walking out' and treating the contract as at an end. Where however, the reason for leaving was due to the conduct of the employer or those under his control, it may be that the employee could show that the employer is responsible for the contractual termination. In such circumstances an employee could argue that he has been impliedly dismissed under s.95(1)(c). Such a dismissal is commonly referred to as a constructive dismissal and if established will usually provide the applicant with sufficient evidence to secure a remedy for unfair dismissal.

> In *Edwards v. Surrey Police* 1999 Mr Justice Morison, President of the EAT, examined the circumstances of a constructive dismissal scenario and concluded that there must be a clear indication by the employee's words or conduct that the employment relationship has terminated. He felt that *"an employee alleging constructive dismissal, must communicate to the employer the fact that they are terminating their employment. It is not an infrequent occurrence that employees find their working life intolerable, walk out in a huff, but do not intend to bring their employment relationship to an end. Unless there has been a proper communication by the employee of the fact that they are regarding themselves as no longer employed, whether by words or conduct their employment relationship has not terminated".*

Originally the test for determining whether a constructive dismissal had taken place was to judge the reasonableness of the employer's conduct according to the language of s.95(1)(c). Since *Western Excavating (ECC) Ltd. v. Sharp* 1978 however, the Courts have rejected that approach as being too vague and now the so called 'conduct test' is to be applied based upon strict contractual principles. The aim of the conduct test is to bring some degree of certainty to the law by requiring the employee to justify his leaving as a response to the employer's repudiatory conduct. Ld Denning MR stated that *"If the employer is guilty of conduct which is a significant breach going to the root of the contract of employment, or which shows that the employer no longer intends to be bound by one or more of the essential terms of the contract then the employee is entitled to treat himself as discharged from any further performance."*

A breach by the employer of the express terms of the contract of employment covering such matters as wages, job location, contractual duties and job description, normally comes about when the employer unilaterally attempts to impose a change on the employee without his consent. In *Hill Ltd. v. Mooney* 1981 the EAT held that an attempt by an employer to unilaterally alter his obligation to pay the agreed remuneration was a breach which went to the root of the contract and consequently constituted a repudiation of it. The complainant was entitled therefore to regard himself as constructively dismissed when he resigned following the employer's decision to unilaterally change the basis upon which sales commission was payable to him. *"Although a mere alteration in the contractual provisions does not necessarily amount to a fundamental breach constituting repudiation, if an employer seeks to alter that contractual obligation in a fundamental way such attempt is a breach going to the very root of the contract and is necessarily a repudiation. The obligation on the employer is to pay the contractual wages, and he is not entitled to alter the formula whereby those wages are calculated."*

In *Reid v. Camphill Engravers* 1990 the breach complained of was the failure of the employer to pay the statutory minimum rate of remuneration set out in the Wages Council Order. Such a breach was of a sufficiently serious nature to be repudiatory and justify a constructive dismissal when the employee resigned as a result. The issue in the case however was whether the breach, having continued for three years, had been affirmed by the employee. The EAT held that in the case of a continuing breach the employee is still entitled to refer to the initial breach to show constructive dismissal. *"In any event where an employer has a statutory obligation to make the appropriate weekly payments, it is not open to an employee to agree and affirm the contract for a lower sum in wages than decreed by Parliament. In the present case therefore affirmation by the complainant could not apply."*

In a constructive dismissal scenario it has been suggested that the employee must leave in circumstances that make it clear that he is leaving because of the employer's breach of contract and not for some other reason. In *Holland v. Glendale Industries* 1997 the EAT said that the statutory definition of constructive dismissal should be considered in the light of ordinary contractual principles. Where one party by his conduct repudiates the contract and the other party wishes to rely on the repudiation the latter must make it clear that he is accepting the repudiation and that is the reason for the termination of employment. This requirement as a matter of law has been overruled by the Court of Appeal in *Weathersfield Ltd. t/a Van and Truck Rental v. Sargent* 1999. This case was considered in Chapter 6 as it involved an employee who left her employment because of a racially discriminatory instruction from her employer. The court clearly stated that in a claim of constructive dismissal there is no requirement as a matter of law that an employee must state his reason for leaving. *The holding of the EAT in Holland v. Glendale Industries that constructive dismissal cannot be established unless it is made clear to the employer that the employee is leaving because of the employer's repudiatory conduct was incorrect as a principle of law.*

By demoting an employee and failing to provide him with suitable office accommodation an employer could be held to be in fundamental breach of the contract of employment. Such an employee could accept the repudiatory breach and regard himself as constructively dismissed.

This was the case in *Wadham Stringer Commercials (London) Ltd. & Wadham Stringer Vehicles Ltd. v. Brown* 1983 where a fleet sales director was effectively demoted to no more than a retail salesman. At the same time he was moved from reasonable accommodation to an office 8ft x 6ft with no ventilation, next to the gentleman's lavatory. As a consequence the employee eventually resigned and claimed a constructive dismissal which was unfair. The EAT agreed that there had been a fundamental breach of contract, accepted by the employee, and following *Western Excavating (ECC) Ltd. v. Sharp*, a constructive dismissal. The employer's argument that their actions were the result of economic necessity were relevant, but only in deciding the reasonableness of their conduct for the purposes of the test of fairness or for the purpose of assessing the level of compensation in an unfair dismissal claim.

In *Brown v. Merchant Ferries Ltd.* 1998 the Northern Ireland Court of Appeal considered the circumstances of an employee who had resigned from his position as manager because of his employer's conduct. He claimed that his position had been "completely undermined" because of the abusive conduct of his general manager and the lack of consultation about his future role following a reorganisation of the business. The Appeal Court disagreed with the tribunal and found there to be insufficient repudiatory conduct to warrant a finding of constructive dismissal. Applying Ld Steyn's test from *Malik v. BCCI SA* 1997 "*whether the employer's conduct so impacted on the employee that viewed objectively the employee could properly conclude that the employer was repudiating the contract*". The court felt that the employer's conduct here while unsettling was not repudiatory.

If it is custom and practice in an organisation to demote an employee where his competence is in issue, this may not constitute a fundamental breach of contract for the purposes of constructive dismissal.

In *Vaid v. Brintel Helicopters Ltd.* 1994 the applicant, a helicopter pilot, who held the rank of senior captain, was demoted to co-pilot for a period of two years following a potentially dangerous incident which reflected on his competence. As a consequence the applicant resigned and complained of constructive unfair dismissal. The EAT agreed with the tribunal that there was an implied term in the applicant's contract which allowed for demotion and in these circumstances no fundamental breach of contract for the purposes of constructive dismissal.

The need to look for a clear breach of contractual term in applying the conduct test has encouraged both tribunals and courts in the absence of relevant express terms to imply terms into a contract of employment. It is the need therefore to accommodate the doctrine of constructive dismissal that has encouraged judicial ingenuity in applying the business efficacy test to find implied obligations in employment contracts. An excellent example is provided by the need to maintain trust and confidence in the employment relationship. In *Courtaulds Northern Textiles Ltd. v. Andrew* 1979 the EAT stated that *"there is an implied term in a contract of employment that the employers will not, without reasonable and proper cause, conduct themselves in a manner calculated or likely to destroy or seriously damage the relationship of confidence and trust between the parties"*. Here a comment made to the complainant by his assistant manager that "you can't do the bloody job anyway" which was not a true expression of his opinion was held to justify the complainant in resigning and treating himself as constructively dismissed. While criticism of a worker's performance would not necessarily amount to repudiatory conduct so as to lead to constructive dismissal, here telling the employee that he could not do his job, when that was not a true expression of opinion, was conduct which was *"likely to destroy the trust relationship which was a necessary element in the relationship between the supervisory employee and his employers"*.

In many cases the employee resigns in response to an act which is the `last straw' and the culmination of a long period of events which have caused the employee distress. In such circumstances it would be perfectly valid for a tribunal to consider whether the events, taken together, constitute a breach of the implied term of trust and confidence, and so justify a finding of constructive dismissal. Certainly it is a breach of the implied obligation of mutual trust and confidence for an employer to fail to treat an allegation of sexual harassment with due seriousness and gravity, and in such a case an employee is entitled to resign and treat herself as constructively dismissed. A good example is provided by *Reed and Bull Information Systems Ltd. v. Sledman* 1999. Here the complainant was a secretary who alleged that she had suffered sexual harassment by her manager and when she was forced to leave her employment as a result, that constituted constructive dismissal and an act of discrimination under s.6(2) of the Sex Discrimination Act 1975. The EAT held that while she had made no formal complaint about the conduct she had complained to her work colleagues and the personnel department were aware of her deteriorating health. By failing to investigate the incident the employer was in breach of the implied term of trust and confidence and when she was forced to leave as a result, this amounted to a constructive dismissal and an act of discrimination within the meaning of s.6(2) of the Sex Discrimination Act.

Similarly, failing to treat an employee fairly in relation to a disciplinary matter could constitute repudiatory conduct for the purposes of constructive dismissal.

In *British Broadcasting Corporation v. Beckett* 1983 the complainant was a scenic carpenter who having been found guilty of an act of negligence which jeopardised the safety of others was dismissed, and then following an internal appeal, demoted. Refusing to accept the offer of a post as maintenance carpenter the complainant resigned, claiming constructive dismissal. The EAT confirmed that the imposition of a *punishment "grossly out of proportion to the offence"* can amount to a repudiation of a contract of service. Here the conduct of the employer amounted to a fundamental breach of his contractual obligations to justify a finding of constructive dismissal which was also unfair.

In *Greenaway Harrison Ltd. v. Wiles* 1994 the EAT held that a telephonist who refused to accept a radical change in her shift pattern and was threatened with dismissal was entitled to leave and regard herself as constructively dismissed. The threat of dismissal constituted an anticipatory breach of contract by the employer.

In *Dryden v. Greater Glasgow Health Board* 1992 the complainant, an auxiliary nurse, was greatly inconvenienced by her employers introduction of a total smoking ban at her place of work. She claimed that the introduction of the ban constituted a material breach of her contract alleging that there was an implied term that she was entitled to smoke. The EAT rejected her claim confirming that there was no basis for implying a term into her contract that she was entitled to smoke or that the employer should provide facilities for smoking.

Employers have a clear duty in relation to the health of non-smokers so that if smoking is allowed at the workplace this could constitute a breach of the employer's duty towards passive smokers.

In *Walton & Morse v. Dorrington* 1997 The EAT held that a secretary who had left her employment because of the affects of smoking at the workplace had been constructively dismissed. There was no requirement to point to a deterioration in her health but rather establish the repudiatory breach of an implied term in relation to maintaining a suitable working environment. Mr Justice Morison referred to the Health and Safety at Work Act to assist in formulating the implied term. *"...It seems to us that a good starting point for the implication of a term of the sort that the tribunal had in mind is s.2 of the Health and Safety at Work Act 1974. It is to be stressed that his case was not concerned with health and safety, in the sense that there was no evidence before the tribunal that being exposed to tobacco smoke is in fact injurious to the health of those who have to endure it. On the other hand, s.2(2)(e) of the 1974 Act is concerned with the employer's duty to provide and maintain a working environment for his employees that is reasonable safe, without risk to health, and is adequate as regards facilities and arrangements for their welfare at work. ...We ourselves would be inclined to the view that the correct implied term to deal with the complaint in this case is that the employer will provide and monitor for his employees, so as is reasonably practicable, a working environment which is reasonably suitable for the performance by them of their contractual duties."*

The failure by an employer to deal promptly and fairly with an employee's grievance by providing and implementing a grievance procedure could amount to a breach of contract.

In *W A Goold (Pearmak) Ltd. v. McConnell* 1995 such as failure led to employees resigning and claiming constructive dismissal. The EAT held that *"it is an implied term in a contract of employment that the employers will reasonably and promptly afford a reasonable opportunity to their employees to obtain redress of any grievance they may have"*. The right to obtain redress of a grievance is fundamental and referred to in the statutory statement of particulars of employment so that the failure to provide a grievance procedure was a breach of a contractual implied term sufficient to justify constructive dismissal.

An employer is of course vicariously responsible for the actions of his employees within the scope of their employment so that if a supervisor in reprimanding an employee does so in a reprehensible manner this can be taken to be *the "employers' conduct"* for the purpose of constructive dismissal.

In *Hilton International Hotels (UK) Ltd. v. Protopapa* 1990 an employee resigned when she was subjected to an officious and insensitive reprimand not justified by her conduct. The industrial tribunal held that she was *"humiliated intimidated and degraded to such an extent that there was breach of trust and confidence which went to the root of the contract"*. The employer nevertheless appealed against the finding of constructive dismissal arguing that the person who had carried out the reprimand, while a supervisor, had no authority to effect a dismissal. This the EAT found was an irrelevant consideration and restated the general principle that an employer is bound by acts done in the course of a supervisory employee's employment. *"Therefore, if the supervisor is doing what he or she is employed to do and in the course of doing it behaves in a way which if done by the employer would constitute a fundamental breach of the contract between the employer and employee, the employer is bound by the supervisor's misdeeds."*

Even where there is a well drafted mobility clause in a contract of employment, for example, 'the bank may from time to time require an employee to be transferred temporarily or permanently to any place of business which the bank may have in the

UK for which a relocation or other allowance may by payable at the discretion of the bank', an employer must act reasonably when relying upon it.

So in *United Bank Ltd. v. Akhtar* 1989 (considered in Chapter 4) the employer was in repudiatory breach of an implied term of the contract of employment requiring reasonable notice when he sought to rely on the above clause to require a junior bank employee to move from the Leeds branch to Birmingham after giving only six days notice. As a consequence the employee who refused to move without more notice could regard himself as being constructively dismissed. Furthermore the employer's conduct in relation to the transfer could also be said to be in breach of the general implied contractual duty of trust and confidence set out by Browne-Wilkinson J in *Woods v. W H Car Services (Peterborough) Ltd.* 1982.

In cases where the employee is threatened with dismissal if he does not resign then a subsequent resignation is taken to be a dismissal. It is the threat of dismissal which causes the resignation.

In *Sheffield v. Oxford Controls Company Ltd.* 1979 however, while such a threat had been made to the employee in question, terms of the resignation emerged which were satisfactory to him and to which he agreed. In such circumstances therefore it is not the threat of dismissal which causes the termination of the employment but rather the fact that the employee is content to resign because of the nature of the terms offered. Here therefore, there was no dismissal in law.

It would be acceptable for an employee to serve notice in a constructive/unfair dismissal scenario, in which case the contract of employment will expire when the notice period runs out.

Having established that an employer has been guilty of repudiatory conduct for the purpose of constructive dismissal, this will normally lead to finding that the dismissal was also unfair. Fairness however, is to be judged by applying different criteria to the circumstances of the case rather than contractual breach and it is still open for an employer to justify the reasons for his conduct and convince a tribunal that he had acted fairly. In *Savoia v. Chiltern Herb Farm* 1982 there was a constructive dismissal when the employee resigned after being moved from one job and offered another but there were background facts which the Court of Appeal held were wholly favourable to the employer and could justify the tribunal finding that the dismissal was in fact a fair one.

In *Durrant and Cheshire v. Clariston Clothing Co. Ltd.* 1974 there was a complaint of unfair constructive dismissal when textile machinists who had been provided with free transport to work by their employer had the service withdrawn on the grounds that it was uneconomical. The withdrawal was held to be the breach of an important term of the contract sufficient to justify constructive dismissal. However the tribunal further held that the dismissals were for some other substantial reason and because of economic considerations, fair.

If there is no dismissal under s.95(1) a contract of employment could nevertheless terminate by operation of the doctrine of frustration, by a clear resignation, or by the mutual agreement of the parties to it. We should examine each in turn.

Frustration

There is no dismissal for the purposes of s.95 if it can be shown that the contract of employment has been brought to an end through the operation of the common law doctrine of frustration. Frustration occurs where, due to a change in circumstances, performance of the contract becomes impossible or radically different than the performance envisaged by the parties when they made the contract. The specified events upon which a claim of frustration could be based are limited generally to long illness, and imprisonment. Certainly the distinction between the termination of a contract of employment by dismissal and termination by frustration is of critical importance. The view of the Court of Appeal in *London Transport Executive v. Clarke* 1981 and subsequently the EAT in *Norris v. Southampton City Council* 1984 was that frustration could arise only where there is no fault by either party. In the latter case, therefore, where the employee's misconduct made him liable to be sentenced to a term of imprisonment, the contract of employment was not frustrated but rather the employee was guilty of a repudiatory breach which, if accepted by the employer, could lead to a dismissal. Such a blatant repudiation of the contract would, of course, normally result in a finding that the dismissal was fair. These cases suggest therefore that frustration should be limited to situations where the employee is prevented through illness or accident from performing the work required of him.

> In *F C Shepherd & Company Ltd. v. Jerrom* 1986 however, the Court of Appeal considered the position of an apprentice plumber who was sentenced to Borstal training for a minimum period of six months. Failure to dismiss him in accordance with standard procedures for apprentices led the tribunal and the EAT to find that he had been constructively dismissed unfairly and so entitled to compensation. The Court of Appeal disagreed however and held that the four year apprenticeship contract had been frustrated by the six month sentence.

While a successful claim for unfair dismissal may have been difficult to swallow in the above case it does seem that the doctrine of frustration was stretched to cover a change in circumstances brought about by the conduct of the employee rather than circumstances over which the parties had no control. The imposition of a prison sentence would normally provide sufficient evidence of misconduct upon which the employer could rely to justify a fair dismissal.

It is difficult in any given case to say whether the circumstances of an illness are such that it is no longer practical to regard the contract of employment as surviving. Obviously the seriousness and length of the illness are crucial factors but generally all the circumstances are relevant, including the nature of the job, the length of employment, the needs of the employer and obligations in relation to replacement, and the conduct of the employer.

> In *Notcutt v. Universal Equipment Company* 1986 the Court of Appeal considered the position of a worker who, two years from retirement and with 27 years' service, suffered an incapacitating heart attack with a medical prognosis that he would never work again. A finding that the contract was terminated by frustration meant that the employee was not entitled to sick pay during his statutory period of notice. The court held that *"there is no reason in principle why a periodic contract of employment determinable by short or relatively short notice should not in appropriate circumstances be held to have been terminated without notice by frustration, according to the accepted and long established doctrine of frustration in the law of contract. The coronary which left the complainant unable to work again was an unexpected occurrence which made his performance of his contractual obligation to work impossible and brought about such a change in the significance of the mutual obligations that the contract if performed would be a different thing from that contracted for."*

We saw in Chapter 4 that if an illness falls within the definition of a disability then under the Disability Discrimination Act 1995 the dismissal of a disabled person may be required to be justified by the employer.

The EAT in *Williams v. Watsons Luxury Coaches* 1990 has now provided guidance to determine whether a contract of employment has been discharged by frustration. In accordance with the House of Lords' decision in *Davies Contractors Ltd. v. Fareham UDC* 1956 the test for whether a contract has been discharged by frustration is whether, if the literal words of the contractual promise were to be enforced in the changed circumstances, performance would involve a fundamental or radical change from the obligations originally undertaken. The EAT approved of the following principles in applying the doctrine of frustration to a contract of employment in the event of dismissal:

- the court must guard against too easy an application of the doctrine of frustration, especially when redundancy occurs and the true situation may be a dismissal by reason of disability;

- although it is not necessary to decide that frustration occurred on a particular date, to decide a date is useful in helping to determine that a true frustration has occurred;

- there are a number of relevant factors which include, the length of previous employment, the length of foreseeable employment, the nature of the job and terms of employment, the nature, length and effect of the illness and prospect of recovery, the employer's need for a replacement, the risk of the employer acquiring statutory obligations to a replacement, the conduct of the employer, whether wages or sick pay has been paid and whether in all the circumstances a reasonable employer could be expected to wait any longer;

- the party alleging frustration should not be allowed to rely on the frustrating event if that event was caused by the default of that party.

If a contract of employment is frustrated by the operation of the common law then no further rights can survive under it.

Sharp v. McMillan 1998 provide further guidance as to the consequences of a frustrated employment contract and whether an employment relationship can exist outside of a contract. The claimant was a joiner who because of a hand injury was unfit for work and was given formal notice that his contract was frustrated because of ill health. Because of potential pension benefits however the company agreed to keep him "on the books". Subsequently the employee claimed a redundancy payment and notice payments from the employer. The EAT held that the applicant's contract of employment had indeed been frustrated by his inability to work and was a consequence at an end by operation of the law. It is possible however to then enter into an arrangement falling short of a contract under the umbrella of employment. The practice of keeping such employees on the books, has been recognised in case-law and in s.212(3)(c) in relation to continuity of employment. As the contract of employment had been terminated by operation of the law then there was no dismissal and consequently no right to notice payments or a redundancy payment.

Resignation

There is no dismissal if the employee expressly terminates the contract of employment by resigning. A resignation will usually be express but could be implied from conduct provided that it is clear and unambiguous.

In *Sothern v. Franks Charlesly* 1981 the Court of Appeal had no difficulty in disagreeing with the EAT's finding that an employee's words "I am resigning" are ambiguous and when relied on by an employer should not be regarded as a dismissal. The EAT held that the words "I am resigning" are not ambiguous. *"They are in the present tense and indicate a present intention of resigning. They have the same meaning as 'I am resigning now' or 'I resign'. The words do not mean I am going to resign in the future. She was not pushed into the decision, not an immature employee and no evidence that the words were spoken in the heat of the moment"*. Resignation by an employee should have normal legal consequences and terminate the employment relationship.

In *Kwik-Fit v. Lineham* 1992 as a direct consequence of issuing a written warning to a depot manager in accordance with the company's disciplinary procedure, he walked out in protest. While the employer took the view that the manager had resigned he nevertheless presents a complaint of unfair dismissal. The EAT held that where words or action of resignation are unambiguous an employer can accept them as such unless there are `special circumstances'. *"Words spoken or action expressed in temper or in the heat of the moment or under extreme pressure, or the intellectual make-up of an employee may be such special circumstances"*. In a case such as this, where there are special circumstances, an employer is required to allow a reasonable period to elapse, perhaps a matter of days, before accepting a resignation to determine an employee's true intention.

The correct question to ask in deciding whether a resignation constitutes a dismissal is *"Who really terminated the contract of employment"*.

In *SAS Service Partners v. Whalley* 1993 the EAT found that an employee who had agreed to resign during an internal appeal against dismissal, rather than have the dismissal confirmed, could nevertheless claim constructive dismissal.

In *Ely v. YKK Fasteners (UK) Ltd.* 1993 the employee had given notice of his intention to resign at some time in the future and such a notice, the Court of Appeal held, was insufficient to bring the contract of employment to an end. When the employer in this case acted upon the notice however, and gave the employee a termination date, despite the fact that the employer was relying on a termination by resignation it was possible for the tribunal to interpret the circumstances as constituting a termination by express dismissal for the purposes of unfair dismissal.

In *BAA plc v. Quinton* 1992 the EAT confirmed that a clear resignation can only be withdrawn with the approval of the employer.

In *Sovereign House Security Services Ltd. v. Savage* 1989 a security officer was told that he was to be suspended pending police investigations into theft of money from his employer's office. The fact that the applicant told his superior that he was "jacking it in" was held by the Court of Appeal to amount to a clear resignation.

There will normally be a contractual provision as to the length of notice to be given and, in addition, there is a statutory minimum period of one week where the employee has at least one month of continuous employment. Failure to comply with notice requirements is a breach of contract for which the employee could be made liable in damages. Employers rarely sue in these cases due mainly to the problem of quantifying their loss which would include the additional cost of advertising for and hiring a replacement during the notice period.

The unilateral act of resigning must be distinguished from the consensual termination of employment which normally involves an exchange of consideration, e.g. a lump sum in return for the loss of the job.

Mutual Termination

It is a fundamental principle of contract law that a contract can be terminated by the parties mutual agreement which constitutes a second contract. Fixed term contracts in particular are most usually terminated by the agreement of the parties. In the world of football management the premature termination of a manager's fixed term contract is often agreed to the mutual satisfaction of the parties involving a sum of compensation to the outgoing manager or his employer by a third party employer.

Considerable support was given by the courts to the view that if the employer and employee mutually agree that the contract of employment should terminate on the happening or non-happening of a specified event, then the contract would terminate automatically on its occurrence, and there would be no dismissal for the purposes of statutory rights. Such agreements were regarded as variations of existing contracts of employment.

In *British Leyland v. Ashraf* 1978 the employee was given five weeks' unpaid leave to return to Pakistan on condition that he expressly agreed that if he failed by a given date to return to work, "your contract of employment will terminate on that date". The EAT held that a failure by the employee to return to work on the due date amounted to a consensual termination of the contract of employment and consequently not a dismissal for the purposes of unfair dismissal.

Some retreat from the somewhat harsh conclusion was evidenced by the later decision in *Tracey v. Zest Equipment* 1982 where the EAT stressed that very clear words are required to constitute such a mutual agreement to terminate a contract of employment. Here the EAT no doubt recognised the pressure placed upon an employee to sign such an agreement as a condition of the grant of a period of leave.

The validity of automatic termination clauses must now be seriously in doubt following the judgment of the Court of Appeal in *Igbo v. Johnson Matthey Chemicals Ltd*. 1986. The case concerned a similar extended leave clause to that in Ashraf with a provision for mutual termination of the contract of employment in the event of non-compliance. Both the tribunal and the EAT, applying *Ashraf* held that there was no dismissal and, therefore, no unfair dismissal rights despite the fact that the employee had a medical certificate to explain her failure to return to work on the due date. Reaching a different conclusion the Court of Appeal held that the tribunal and the EAT were wrong in law and that the Ashraf decision should be overruled. The conclusion was reached by applying s.140(1) of the Employment Protection (Consolidation) Act 1978 (now s.203 ERA 1996) to automatic termination clauses. The section stipulates that any provision in an agreement shall be void *"in so far as it purports ... to limit the operation on of any provision of this Act"*. By limiting the right not to be unfairly dismissed, automatic termination agreements offended s.140(1) and were therefore void. To allow reliance on such clauses would mean that, *"the whole object of the Act could be easily defeated by the inclusion of a term in a contract of employment that if the employee was late for work on any day, no matter for what reason, the contract should automatically terminate. Such a provision would virtually limit the operation of the section, for the right not to be unfairly dismissed would become subject to the condition that the employee was on time for work."*

It should be stressed that the operation of this section will not prevent the parties to an employment contract reaching agreement as to the termination of the contract by mutual consent not contingent upon the happening or non-happening of an event. Accordingly if the parties to a contract of employment, without duress and after taking proper advice, enter into a separate contract, supported by good consideration, with the objective of terminating the employment relationship by mutual consent, the contract will be valid and enforceable.

Such was the case in *Logan Salton v. Durham County Council* 1989. Here the complainant was a social worker who, as a result of disciplinary hearings, had been redeployed by his employer. In a statement to be considered at a further disciplinary hearing the complainant was given notice of a number of complaints against him and a recommendation that he be summarily dismissed. Prior to that meeting his union representative negotiated on his behalf a mutual agreement to terminate his employment with the Council. By that agreement the employment contract was to terminate in seven weeks' time and an outstanding car loan of £2,750 wiped out as a debt. Despite the fact that the agreement was signed by both parties, the complainant subsequently complained to an industrial tribunal that he had been unfairly dismissed. It was argued that a dismissal had occurred in law, for the mutual agreement to terminate was either void as an agreement entered into under duress, or void because its effect was to remove statutory protection, similar to *Igbo v. Johnson Matthey Chemicals Ltd*. Both these arguments were rejected by the industrial tribunal and on appeal by the EAT. The EAT found that this case could be distinguished from Igbo as here there was a separate contract rather than a variation of an existing contract of employment, and the termination of employment did not depend upon the happening of some future event. Furthermore, the fact that the appellant was aware of the employer's recommendation of dismissal did not constitute duress, bearing in mind the financial inducement. *"In the resolution of industrial disputes, it is in the best interests of all concerned that a contract made without duress, for good consideration, preferably after proper and sufficient advice and which has the effect of terminating a contract of employment by mutual agreement (whether at once or at some future date) should be effective between the contracting parties, in which case there probably will not have been a dismissal."*

The fact that an employee signs a document which states that the reason for the termination of employment is mutual consent my not be decisive.

In *Hellyer Brothers Ltd. v. Atkinson and Dickinson* 1994 the Court of Appeal held that mutual consent was not the reason for termination when two trawlermen signed off a crew agreement when their employer's fleet was decommissioned. The court agreed with the tribunal and the EAT and found that despite the express reference to mutual consent it was the employer who effectively brought about the termination of employment by means of a dismissal by reason of redundancy.

In *Birch v. University of Liverpool* 1985 the acceptance of a financial package was held to be a voluntary early retirement rather than redundancy.

A common scenario in employment is the situation where an employee is offered a substantial change in employment or alternatively a severance deal involving a lump sum payment and pension rights.

In *Kirkland v. Mercedes-Benz UK Ltd*. 1993 this was the choice facing the complainant a field service engineer who had 24 years service with his employer. After taking legal advice the complainant wrote to his employer rejecting the change in employment and confirming that he wished to remain employed. He also stated in his letter that the consequence of his decision was that his contract would be terminated and he would be entitled to a severance payment. The company responded by confirming that he had chosen the severance option and set a date for his contractual termination. Subsequently the complainant claimed unfair dismissal and the issue before the tribunal was whether there had been a dismissal. Both the tribunal and the EAT found that there was no dismissal deciding that the complainants letter, while ambiguous, seemed to acknowledge the termination of employment by means of an acceptance of the severance payment. His letter should be treated as a voluntary acceptance of a mutual termination rather than an acknowledgement of dismissal.

Post Contract Terms

There is an issue as to whether certain contractual terms may remain enforceable following the termination of the contract of employment. The best example is the contract in restraint of trade which contains an express term which purports to survive the contract.

Such express terms found in many contracts of employment is a clause which purports to restrict the freedom of the employees, on the termination of employment, from engaging in a competing business or working for a competitor for a specified period. Provided such a clause is inserted to protect a genuine proprietary interest of the employer and is reasonable in extent, the express restraint will be valid and enforceable. A restraint clause which purports to restrict the free choice of an ex-employee as to the employment options open is prima facie void as a contract in restraint of trade. Such a contract is nevertheless valid and enforceable if reasonable in the circumstances because:

(a) *the employer has a genuine proprietary interest worthy of protection such as clientele, confidential information, or trade connection; and*

(b) *the restraint clause is drafted in such a way that it is no wider than is reasonably necessary to achieve the desired objective.*

If the court is satisfied that the purpose of the restraint clause is no more than to prevent healthy competition then it will be declared void and of no legal effect.

> In *Strange v. Mann* 1965 the manager of a bookmakers agreed not to engage in a similar business to that of his employer with in a twelve mile radius on the termination of his employment. In an action to enforce the clause, the court held that, as the bookmaker had little or no influence over the firm's clientele and in fact communicated with them mainly by telephone, the employer had no valid interest to protect. As the primary aim of the clause was simply to prevent competition it was declared void.

The validity of a restraint clause will depend initially upon whether the employer has legitimate trade secrets worthy of protection. In *FSS Travel and Leisure Systems Ltd. v. Johnson* 1998 the Court of Appeal agreed that there was an unreasonable restraint of trade when an employer sought to enforce a restrictive covenant against a computer programmer. The court felt that the covenant was simply an attempt to control a former employee's skill, expertise and knowledge gained during employment.

A distinction must be drawn between an attempt by an employer to prevent his ex-employee revealing trade secrets or lists of clients to competitors and simply preventing an ex-employee putting into practice the knowledge, skills and abilities that he acquired during his period of employment.

> In *Herbert Morris Ltd. v. Saxelby* 1916 a seven year restraint on the employee was held to be void as simply an attempt to prevent the employee making use of the technical skill and knowledge which he acquired with his employer if he took up employment with a rival firm.

> In *Forster and Sons v. Suggett* 1918 on the other hand, a covenant which was aimed at preventing the defendant divulging a secret glass making process to any rival organisation in the United Kingdom, was held to be valid and enforceable.

Having identified a proprietary interest worthy of protection, the next step is to analyse the restraint clause to discover whether it is reasonable in the circumstances. A number of factors are deserving of attention to assist in the analysis, such as the area of the restraint, the length of time it is to run and the nature of the work which the employer is attempting to restrain. The wording of the restraint clause is therefore crucial, for if it is too extensive in the geographical area of protection, or too long in time, it will be unenforceable. Each case turns on its own facts and all the circumstances are considered.

In *Fitch v. Dewes* 1921 a lifetime restraint on a solicitor's clerk from working for another solicitor within a radius of seven miles of Tamworth Town Hall was nevertheless held to be valid. The House of Lords felt that the modest area of the restraint which the employer relied on for his clientele justified even a lifetime restraint.

If a restraint clause is drafted in such a way that it purports to prevent the ex-employer from obtaining non-competitive employment then it will be declared void.

In *Fellows & Sons v. Fisher* 1976 a conveyancing clerk employed by a firm in Walthamstow agreed that for five years after the termination of employment he would not be employed or concerned in the legal profession anywhere within the postal district of Walthamstow and Chingford or solicit any person who had been a client of the firm when he had worked there. Not only was the five year restraint thought to be too long, bearing in mind the large population in the areas identified, but the attempt to exclude any work in the legal profession, which would include legal work in local government and the administration of justice, was also thought to be unreasonable and the restraint was declared void.

In *Mason v. Provident Clothing and Supply Company* 1913 the restraint clause purported to prevent the plaintiff canvasser from competing with the defendants within a twenty-five mile radius of the centre of London. The fact that the plaintiff had only come into contact with her employer's customers in a specified area of London meant that the restraint clause was too extensive in nature and declared by the House of Lords to be void.

In *Commercial Plastics v. Vincent* 1965 the defendant was employed as a plastics technologist to co-ordinate research and development in the production of thin PVC calendering. In that role he had access to secret information so that it was a condition of his contract of employment that he would not seek employment with any of the plaintiff's competitors in the calendering field for one year after leaving employment. The Court of Appeal held that in the circumstances the restraint clause was drafted in such a way that it purported to protect the employer on a world-wide basis when, in fact, the company did not require protection outside the United Kingdom. Accordingly the condition was unreasonable and consequently void and unenforceable.

A different attitude to restraint clauses is illustrated by the decision of the Court of Appeal in *Littlewoods Organisation v. Harris* 1978. Here the defendant was employed as a director by Littlewoods, a large company which competes with Great Universal Stores Ltd. for the major share of the mail order business in the United Kingdom. As a consequence, the defendant agreed in his contract of employment that he would not, for a period of twelve months after its termination, enter into a contract of employment with Great Universal Stores Ltd. or any subsidiary company. Littlewoods, by such a restraint clause was seeking to protect confidential information of which the defendant was aware, relating to the preparation of their mail order catalogue. As Great Universal Stores operated all over the world it was argued that the restraint clause was wider than reasonably necessary to protect Littlewoods' interest in the UK. A majority of the court held however that restraint clauses should be interpreted bearing in mind their object and intention. As a proper construction, the clause was intended to relate to the UK mail order business only and was therefore valid and enforceable.

It is crucial to the validity of a restraint clause that the employer limits its extent to protect the clientele and business locations which apply to the employee's term of employment. It would be unreasonable for an employer to attempt to prevent competition in geographical locations into which it has not yet operated.

In *Greer v. Sketchley Ltd.* 1979 the restraint clause purported to prevent the employer competing nation-wide when in fact the employer's business was limited to the Midlands and London. The argument that an employer is entitled to seek protection in geographical areas in which he intends to expand, was rejected.

In *WAC Ltd. v. Whillock* 1990 the Scottish Court of Session emphasised that restrictive covenants must be construed fairly and it is *"the duty of the Court to give effect to them as they are expressed and not to correct their errors or to supply their omissions"*. Here the clause in question specifically prevented any ex-company-shareholders for two years carrying on business in competition with the company. The clause did not impose any restriction on the right of an employee to be a director or employee of another company which carried on business in competition and so could not prevent the employee/shareholder from becoming a director of a competing company.

In *J A Mont (UK) Ltd. v. Mills* 1993 the Court of Appeal restated the general principle that restrictive covenants which are two wide should be declared void and of no legal effect and the courts should not strive too urgently to find implied limitations on the terms of such covenants to enable them to be enforced.

In *Dentmaster (UK) Ltd. v. Kent* 1997 the High Court felt that a restraint clause was too wide when it purported to restrain the ex-employee from soliciting the trade of any customers of his employer whom he had dealt with during the course of his employment, from its very commencement. On appeal however the Court of Appeal disagreed and said that such a clause is not bound to be found invalid particularly in view of the short restraint period of six months.

If a restraint clause is drafted in such a way that it is reasonable in extent, then provided it does not offend the public interest it will be binding and can be enforced by means of an injunction. In practice such injunctions are rarely granted for the very presence of the clause acts as a sufficient deterrent.

There have also been a few exceptional cases where the courts have determined that part of a restraint clause is unreasonable but other separate parts of the clause are reasonable and would be valid and enforceable. In such circumstances, rather than declare the whole clause to be void and unenforceable, the courts have severed the unreasonable part of the contract and, provided that what remains can stand alone, declared it to be valid and enforceable.

In *Lucas T Company v. Mitchell* 1974 the defendant salesman contracted that he should not for one year after the determination of his employment: solicit orders within his trading area from present customers and those whom his employer supplied during the previous twelve months; and deal in the same or similar goods to those that he sold. In an action for breach of contract, the court found that two obligations were severable so that the second clause against dealing was unreasonable and void but the first clause not to solicit orders was valid and enforceable.

In *Rex Stewart Ltd. v. Parker* 1988 the defendant who was the joint managing director of the plaintiff's advertising agency, moved to an agency which he set up himself. The move was alleged to be in breach of his covenant not to solicit the plaintiff's clients for eighteen months after his employment with them had terminated. The defendant claimed that the plaintiffs had forfeited their right to rely on the covenant by giving him six months salary in lieu of notice rather than the actual notice, and in any case the covenant was unreasonably wide and should be declared void. The Court of Appeal upheld the High Court decision that the payment was not n breach of covenant, and that the covenant was not unreasonably wide after irrelevant prohibitions had been severed.

In *Living Design (Home Improvements) Ltd v. Davidson* 1994 the employer attempted to restrain a promotions manager's employment activities for period of six months on the termination of her *employment "however that comes about whether lawful or not"*. The contract also attempted to deal with the possibility of the restraint being found unreasonable and void by providing for the unlawful content to be severed from the agreement. Such clauses the Court of Session held were in themselves unreasonable and would not be enforced. A wrongful dismissal in breach of contract will always have impact on the validity of a restraint clause. Also it is for the courts to determine the extent to which severance is applicable. *"The court should not strike out words where to do so would alter the scope and intention of the agreement. Moreover, in the case of a covenant by an employee, there should be severance only if the enforceable part is clearly severable and, even then, only where what it struck out is of trivial importance or technical and not part of the main import and substance of the clause."*

Sometimes an employment restraint will be in the form of a tie to operate during the subsistence of the employment arrangement, rather than to commence at the end of it.

This was the position in *Watson v. Prager* 1991. The plaintiff, a boxer, entered into a contract in 1987 with the defendant, better known as the boxing promoter, Mickey Duff. The contract provided for the defendant to act as the plaintiff's manager for three years. The defendant had an option to extend the period for a further three years if the plaintiff won a title. He did so in 1987, taking the Commonwealth Middleweight championship. The defendant then exercised his option to extend the management contract. The plaintiff's claim was that the extended contract was an unreasonable restraint, because the defendant in his capacity as a promoter could arrange a fight for the plaintiff, and in his capacity as a personal manager require the plaintiff to take part in it. This was a conflict of interest, since the defendant's responsibility towards the career interests of the plaintiff could conflict with his personal financial interest in a promotion. The court agreed. The test for a restraint is what could happen within the scope of it. The fact that under this contract a conflict had not yet occurred, and indeed might never occur, was not relevant to the validity of the restraint.

The kind of tie occurring in *Watson v. Prager* is standard practice in the music industry where recording contracts between musicians and their recording companies generally bind the parties to each other for many years, frequently resulting in well publicised disputes when companies refuse to release their artists from the recording deal that had been signed. The musicians argue that these ties restrict their artistic freedom or complain that their companies do not sufficiently promote them. Lawyers for the musicians rely on the claim that long tie clauses are an unreasonable restraint and that the agreements containing them are frequently tainted by undue influence.

In these cases a crucial question will be whether the agreement has been signed after taking independent specialist advice. If it has a court will be far less likely to declare the agreement invalid. Such was the position in *Panayoitou v. Sony Music Entertainment (UK) Ltd.* 1994 where George Michael unsuccessfully sought to extricate himself from a 15 year deal with

Sony. His original contract with the company gave him the opportunity to renegotiate it, and he had used this option to secure superior terms for himself. These terms were renegotiated for him by specialist lawyers. A clause in the renegotiated contract said, *"I am not a minor and I have taken legal advice in relation to this agreement prior to entering into the same."* On this evidence the court was not prepared to declare the agreement invalid.

The argument in *P R Consultants Scotland Ltd. v. Mann* 1996 was that to restrain an ex employee for 12 months after termination of employment from soliciting customers was unenforceable because the restrictive covenant was to apply upon termination of employment *howsoever caused*. This meant that the covenant was to apply even if the employee was dismissed unlawfully as in *Living Design v. Davidson* above. The Court of Session rejected this interpretation and held that the expression *howsoever caused* could be taken to apply only to the many lawful ways a contract of employment could be terminated. On the balance of convenience the court was prepared to grant an order enforcing the covenant and preventing the employee operating the account of an important ex client of his previous employer.

The case of *Provident Financial Group v. Hayward* 1989 is an example of a practice known as 'garden leave' where an employee under notice is not working for his employer but paid in full provided he does not work for anyone else. The employee in question was the financial director of an estate agency business who was seeking to take up employment with a rival agency. The Court of Appeal upheld the High Court's decision to refuse an interlocutory injunction to restrain the employee from working for anyone else while on 'garden leave'. It was within the High Courts judge's legitimate discretion to refuse the injunction because of the level of prospective detriment to the plaintiffs if it were not granted. The director had not been working with sensitive information and the new employer was operating in a different part of the estate agency market. *"The defendant here is to have his full salary, together with his company car and all other benefit until 31 December after which he is free. No starvation. Even considering idleness, per se, as a separate matter, it can hardly arise in this case. The defendant's status as an accountant is one unlikely to atrophy in a period of three months. Nor is he likely to suffer severe withdrawal symptoms from lack of job satisfaction over the period."*

The Court of Appeal in *Credit Suisse Asset Management Ltd. v. Armstrong* 1996 considered the impact of a garden leave clause and indicated that *"by means of such a clause employers are able to obtain protection from competition by people who wish to leave their employment but who may have confidential information or important contacts with customers or clients which the employer wishes to terminate before the end of the period of notice."* Here the court held that a period of six months garden leave could be followed by a legally enforceable six month restraint clause. While the existence of garden leave may be a factor in determining the validity of a restraint clause in this case a period of twelve months protection was not unreasonable.

It now seems that if an employer wishes to have the option of requiring an expressly dismissed employee to take garden leave during the notice period then he should provide for this possibility in the contract of employment. In *William Hill Organisation Ltd. v. Tucker* the Court of Appeal refused to grant an injunction to prevent an ex-employee taking up employment with a competitor and accept salary without work during a six month notice period. The court felt that *"whether there is a right to work is a question of construction of the particular contract in the light of its surrounding circumstances"*. Here the employee had a duty to provide the employee with work during the notice period so as to enable him to exercise his skills as a specialist in the field of spread betting.

An employee may be discharged from obligations arising from a restriction covenant it it is established that there was a wrongful dismissal or a resignation arising from the acceptance of a repudiatory breach of contract by the employer.

The High Court held in *Dairy Crest Ltd. v. Wise* 1994 that the conduct of the employer which led to the employee's resignation, was a breach of the implied duty of trust and confidence and consequently a repudiatory breach of covenant. Accordingly the court refused to grant an injunction to prevent the ex-employee from operating a milk round which would otherwise have been in breach of a restrictive covenant not to solicit ex-customers.

One final issue that may be addressed in relation to restraint clauses and contractual terms generally is the extent to which they remain enforceable when clearly expressed in an original contract of employment but not re-stated on various promotions within the organisation.

In *Marley Tile Co Ltd. v. Johnson* 1982 the defendant's original letter of appointment contained a number of clearly expressed restraint clauses designed to prevent him seeking employment from rival organisations or competing for a period of twelve months after the termination of his employment. On a promotion to area manager some years later, the defendant agreed similar restraint clauses but then, when made a unit defendant resigned and took up employment with a rival firm within one month, his employer sought an interlocutory injunction to enforce the restraint clause. The Court of Appeal held that covenants which form part of the employee's original contract applied to his subsequent appointment as a unit manager, despite the failure to refer to them expressly. Lord Denning MR expressed the position when he said that, *"All that had happened in the present case was that the defendant had been promoted in the same company. Both parties would assume that the original terms of employment, including the restrictive covenants, would continue unless something was said to the contrary".* Stressing this important point in relation to the variation of a contract of employment, Eveleigh L J said that, *"The defendant's appointment as a unit manager was varied. No reference was made in the memorandum and letter of appointment to the motor car which the defendant continued to have, or to telephone expenses, or to lunch and subsistence allowances, all of which were matters dealt with in the previous formal agreement".* In fact the covenants, although part of the contract, were held to be void and unenforceable because they were thought to be too wide in area and extent.

Case Studies

Dalton West plc - Brian's Transfer

Dalton West is a large manufacturer of fork lift trucks with depots and retail outlets situated all over Britain.

Brian Simmonds was employed by Dalton West from 1978 to March 1997 as a HGV driver at their Newcastle-upon-Tyne depot. All the drivers at the Newcastle depot are members of the Fitters and General Workers Union which is recognised by the company as the bargaining agent. Brain, unhappy at the attitude of the FGWU shop steward of the depot, left the union three months ago. Although there is no closed shop at the depot the other drivers threatened to strike if Brian was not sacked or moved elsewhere.

Two months ago the Transport Manager at the company's office in Newcastle-upon-Tyne instructed Brian by letter that he must either rejoin the FGWU or work under similar conditions from the Middlesbrough depot where union membership is not an issue. Brian replied by letter stating that the company had no right to move his place of work, particularly to pacify militant trade unionists, and that he was left with no option but to tender his resignation. Brian's employment terminated at the end of last month and within three weeks the company received notification from the Regional Office of Industrial Tribunals of Brian Simmond's claim for unfair dismissal.

Brinkley Business School - The 'Intellectual Pigmy'

Brinkley Business School was set up last year by merging a number of departments in the University of Brinkley. The Director of the School is Miriam Perot who, with her two deputies, comprise the senior management team of the School. The senior management team is the final arbiter on staffing issues in the School, subject to formal ratification by the academic board of the University.

Last month David Royle, a deputy director of the Business School, despite having eighteen years loyal service walked out of the University after a meeting of the Senior Management Team. In a heated discussion over departmental budgets Miriam had called David an "intellectual pigmy" and he had responded by telling her to *"stuff her job"* and walked out. In the interim there had been no communication between the parties and at the next meeting of the Senior Management Team Miriam had confided in Alice Lawson, the remaining deputy director, that *"she was glad to see the back of him"*. She also indicated that she intended to write to Mr. Royle to confirm his resignation and to *"sort out any payment of salary that was due to him"*.

Chapter 11
Unfair Dismissal

Unfair Dismissal

The introduction of the right not to be dismissed without good reason in the Industrial Relations Act 1971 was a recognition that an employee has a stake in his job which cannot be extinguished simply by serving contractual notice. In the same way that a tenant may in certain circumstances acquire security of tenure in his home and resist the enforcement of a notice to quit unless it is reasonable in the circumstances, an employee, through continuous employment, can acquire security in his job. The right not to be unfairly dismissed is intended to act as a constraint on employers who feel they have the authority to hire and fire as they please. The extent to which the law of unfair dismissal achieves the objective of constraining management prerogative is arguable. Over the last thirty years unfair dismissal has developed into a highly complex area of law recognised as such as early as 1977 by Philips J in *Devis & Sons Ltd. v. Atkins* 1977, when he said, *"the expression 'unfair dismissal' is in no sense a common-sense expression capable of being understood by the man in the street"*. The present unfair dismissal law is contained in the Employment Rights Act 1996 as amended. The right not to be unfairly dismissed is perhaps the most fundamental of all statutory employment rights so that it is inevitable that it is necessary to devote a reasonably lengthy chapter to a consideration of the law.

Under s.94(1) *in every employment to which the section applies, every employee shall have the right not to be unfairly dismissed by his employer.*

An employee is entitled to have a complaint of unfair dismissal heard before an employment tribunal even if the employer offers to pay the maximum compensation recoverable with no admission of unfair dismissal.

> In *Telephone Information Services Ltd. v. Wilkinson* 1991 the EAT held that *"An employee has a right to a claim of unfair dismissal decided by an industrial tribunal. Such a claim is not simply for a monetary award; it is a claim that the dismissal was unfair. The employee is entitled to a finding on that matter and to maintain his claim to the tribunal for that purpose. He cannot be prevented from exercising that right by an offer to meet only the*

monetary part of the claim. If that were so, any employer would be able to evade the provisions of the Act by offering to pay the maximum compensation. If employers wish to compromise a claim, they can do so by admitting it in full but they cannot do so by conceding only part of it."

Having established that a prospective applicant is classified as an employee for the purpose of s.94(1) (see Chapter 3), it is then necessary to determine whether the employee is otherwise qualified to present a claim for unfair dismissal.

Qualifications

The Act identifies the qualifying period and the upper age limit for the purpose of unfair dismissal.

Prior to 1995 a distinction was drawn between full-time and part-time employees and you should be aware that the law did make distinction. Full-time employment means working under a contract of employment which involves work for sixteen hours or more per week and a full-time employee qualified with two years continuous service. An employee who had a contract which provides for employment for between eight and sixteen hours had to work continuously for five years or more to qualify. Significantly this provision was held to be indirectly discriminatory and contrary to European Community Law by the House of Lords in *R v. Secretary of State for Employment ex-parte the EOC* 1994.

> In *Clifford v. Devon County Council* 1994 the EAT considered the case of a local authority employee who claimed unfair dismissal despite the fact that for part of her continuous employment she worked less than eight hours per week. The EAT referred *to R v. Secretary of State for Employment ex parte EOC* which declared that *"the provisions of the EPCA whereby employees who work for fewer than sixteen hours per week are subject to different conditions in respect to the right to compensation for unfair dismissal from those which apply to employees who work for sixteen hours per week or more are incompatible with Council Directive 76/207/EEC 9 February 1976".* The conclusion of the EAT was therefore that *"It appears from the House of Lord's decision that the number of hours per week which are worked is no longer relevant to unfair dismissal compensation or qualification for redundancy pay in the case of public sector employees who have worked for an employer for more than two years".*

While the above case deals with the position of part-time public sector employees the position of private sector employees was left unresolved.

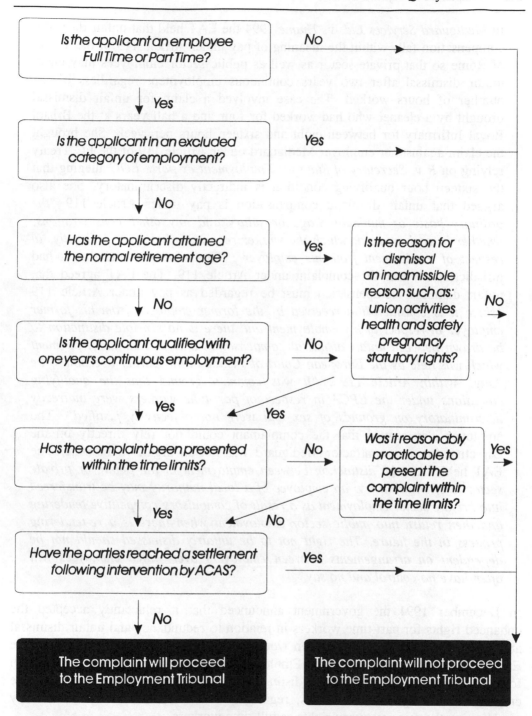

Unfair Dismissal Complaint

In *Mediguard Services Ltd. v. Thame* 1994 the EAT held that unfair dismissal compensation falls within the meaning of pay under Article 119 of the Treaty of Rome so that private sector as well as public sector employees may claim unfair dismissal after two years continuous employment regardless of the number of hours worked. The case involved a claim for unfair dismissal brought by a cleaner who had worked for four and a half years at the Bristol Royal Infirmary for between eight and sixteen hours per week. She brought the claim against her employer Mediguard under Article 119 of the EC Treaty relying on *R v. Secretary of State for Employment ex parte EOC* alleging that the sixteen hour qualifying condition is indirectly discriminatory. She also argued that unfair dismissal compensation is pay under Article 119 *"the ordinary basic or minimum wage or salary and any other considerations, whether in cash or kind, which the worker receives, directly or indirectly, in respect of employment from his employer"*. The tribunal found that it had jurisdiction to hear the complaint under Article 119. The EAT agreed that unfair dismissal compensation must be regarded as pay under Article 119 *"since it is consideration received by the former employee from his former employer in respect of his employment and there is no sensible distinction to be drawn between unfair dismissal compensation and a redundancy payment which was held by the European Court of Justice in the Barber decision to be "pay" within Article 119"*. *"It was common ground that the qualifying conditions under the EPCA in respect of part-time workers were indirectly discriminatory on grounds of sex and were not objectively justified"*. The employer also argued that the complainant could not rely directly on the Directive for as a contractor Mediguard was not an organ of the state. The EAT held that *"the distinction between employment in the public or private sector is often arbitrary: an employee of a local authority may be transferred into private sector employment as a result of compulsory competitive tendering and then return into public sector employment when there is a re-tendering process in the future. The right not to be unfairly dismissed should not be dependent on arrangements between employers over which employees will often have no control and no say"*.

In December 1994 the government announced that it reluctantly accepted the enhanced rights for part-time workers in relation to redundancy and unfair dismissal and accordingly amending legislation would follow. On the 6th February 1995 the Employment Protection (Part-Time Employees) Regulations came into force which formally abolished the thresholds distinguishing between full-time and part-time employment. All part-time workers, regardless of the number of hours that they work, enjoy the same statutory rights as full-time workers.

Continuous Employment

The period of continuous employment for an employee to qualify for unfair dismissal protection is contained in s.108(1).

Under s.108(1) ..., section 94 does not apply to the dismissal of an employee unless he has been continuously employed for a period of not less than one year ending with the effective date of termination.

The qualifying period of continuous employment having been increased to two years in 1985 was reduced to one year in 1999 for dismissals which occur after the 1st of June 1999.

To fall within the provisions of s.94 then an employee had to show continuous employment in a job which is not an excluded category of work. The minimum period of continuous employment is not less than one year ending with the effective date of termination. This is the date that the contract of employment actually comes to an end and if a summary dismissal is unjustified it may be necessary to add the statutory period of notice onto the date of dismissal. If the employee can establish that the reason for dismissal is inadmissible and automatically unfair, for instance pregnancy or trade union activities, then under s.108(3) the period of continuous employment does not apply. (See later in the chapter).

In 1997 a case was taken to the House of Lords, *R. v. Secretary of State for Employment ex parte Seymour-Smith and Perez*, where there was a legal challenge to the qualifying period of continuous employment for unfair dismissal and redundancy on the grounds that it was indirectly discriminatory to women. It was a similar claim to the successful case based upon indirect discrimination against part-time workers. Judgment was not given until 2000 in *R. v. Secretary of State for Employment ex parte Seymour-Smith and Perez (No 2) 2000* because the House of Lords had decided to refer a number of legal issues to the European Court of Justice for ruling. It has been suggested that the case was instrumental in the government's decision to reduce the qualifying period of employment to one year from the 1st June 1999. Also numerous tribunal decisions have been awaiting the outcome of the case. The House of Lords held that:

- the extension of the qualifying period for unfair dismissal to two years in 1985 was indirectly discriminatory against women under article 119 of the Treaty of Rome (now article 141) as it had a considerably greater adverse impact on women in 1991;

- nevertheless this indirect discrimination was objectively justified by reference to the social and economic policy aim of the government in 1985 to encourage fuller employment.

The claim of indirect discrimination therefore failed, the judges being unanimous in the decision but having adopted different legal reasoning.

The courts and tribunals have accepted that an employer may adopt employment practices designed to prevent an employee acquiring sufficient continuity for the purposes of unfair dismissal.

In *Booth v. United States of America* 1999 the applicants were employed by the United States Army under a series of fixed term contracts with a break of at least two weeks between each contract. The breaks were designed to prevent the applicants securing sufficient continuity of employment for the purposes of redundancy and unfair dismissal. The applicants argued that the breaks fell within s.212(3)(c) of the 1996 Act which provides that absence from work by arrangement or action is regarded as continuing of employment. This argument was rejected by the EAT who felt the employee's clearly did not want the employment relationship to continue and there was no evidence to suggest that there was a custom or arrangement that it should continue, merely an expectation that the applicants would be re-employed. *"If by so arranging their affairs, employers lawfully are able to employ people in such a manner that the employees cannot complain of unfair dismissal or seek a redundancy payment, that is a matter for them. It is for the legislators, not the courts, to close any loopholes that might be perceived to exist."*

Unfortunately the EAT failed to consider the substance of the above employment practices and declare them to be devices or shams. The arrangements above were designed to prevent employees acquiring statutory rights and the EAT effectively supported the employees prerogative to achieve that aim.

Retirement Exclusion

A further requirement under s.109(1) is that if on, or before, the effective date of termination, the employee has reached the 'normal retiring age' or, if more than the age of 65 (whether male or female), then there is no right to present a claim. The House of Lords in *Waite v. Government Communication Headquarters* 1983 felt that normal retiring age refers to the age that employees can normally be compelled to retire, unless there is some special reason to apply a different age in a particular case. Most emphasis has to be given to the reasonable expectations of the employees which could show that a contractually agreed retirement age has now been superseded by some different age. In *Hughs v. DHSS* 1985 the House of Lords held that an employer can alter a normal retirement age practice by a simple announcement to that effect.

Certainly the phrase *"normal retiring age"* has been the subject of a great deal of judicial interpretation the culmination of which is guidance given by the Court of Appeal

In *Barclays Bank plc v. O'Brien and others* 1994 the issue was whether a number of bank messengers who had been made redundant by their employer were qualified to present complaints of unfair dismissal. The complainants had worked past the Bank's retirement age of sixty under a practice which enabled them to apply for yearly extensions up to the age of sixty five. The employer argued that since the messengers had attained the normal age of retirement before the effective date of termination of employment the tribunal had no jurisdiction to hear their complaints. Eventually the Court of appeal confirmed that the EAT had correctly held that here there was a normal retiring age of sixty for the employees in question so that they were not qualified to present complaints. The court said that *"the question is whether there is a norm for the retiring age and whether retirement at different ages can be said to constitute an exception which does not destroy that norm"*. Here the fact that there had been exceptions to the norm for a special reason did not destroy the continuation of the normal retiring age of sixty. After reviewing the previous case-law Peter Gibson LJ put forward a number of propositions in relation to determining the normal retiring age.

- *The social policy underlying the section is to secure fair treatment as regards compulsory retirement as between different employees holding the same or a similar 'position'*

- *Where there is a contractual retirement age applicable to all or nearly all the employees in the group there is a presumption that the contractual retiring age is the normal retiring age for the group.*

- *The presumption can be rebutted by evidence that there is in practice some higher age at which employees in the group are regularly retired and which they have reasonably come to regard as their normal retiring age.*

- *The question to be asked by the industrial tribunal is: what, at the effective date of termination of the applicant's employment and on the basis of the facts then known was the age at which employees of all ages in the group could reasonably regard as their normal retiring age?...*

In *Patel v. Nageson* 1995 the Court of Appeal rejected the employer's contention that the employees complaint should be rejected because she had reached the normal retirement age. One of the reasons for the complaint was a response to the employer's attempt to impose on the complainant a contract which reduced the retirement age for employees and it was this imposition that the complainant was resisting.

Later in the chapter we shall discover that certain reasons for dismissal are classified by statute as inadmissible reasons and automatically unfair, such as dismissal for a reason connected with trade union activities, health and safety and pregnancy. Under ss.108(3) and 109(2) above a claim may be presented despite the fact that the employee has insufficient continuous employment or is over age.

In addition to qualifying through service, an employee must not fall within one of the excluded categories of employment.

- Persons employed in the police force.

- Share fishermen e.g. members and crew paid by a share of the profits.

- Employees who work ordinarily outside Great Britain.

  In relation to seamen, *"a person employed to work on board a ship registered in the United Kingdom"*, they are also excluded if *"the employment is wholly outside Great Britain"*.

  In *Wood v. Cunard Line Ltd.* 1990 a seaman was employed under an agreement extended into England, for employment on a British registered ship, but the ship never visited the United Kingdom. The issue was whether he was employed "wholly outside" Great Britain bearing in mind he was employed in England and spent his leave there. The Court of Appeal held that as he only worked on board the ship outside British waters he was employed wholly outside Great Britain and not qualified to bring a complaint of unfair dismissal.

- Employees covered by a designated dismissal procedure agreement.

- Certain registered dock-workers.

- Members of the armed forces. Following the Trade Union Reform and Employment Rights Act 1993 members of the armed forces can claim unfair dismissal if they have exhausted the internal service procedures.

Procedure

The procedure involved in presenting a complaint of unfair dismissal is considered in Chapter 2. An employee must initiate proceedings by submitting an IT1 form to the Central Office of Industrial Tribunals or Regional Office of Industrial Tribunals within three months of the effective date of termination. This is an important requirement and deserving of special attention.

Time Limits

Under s.111(1) A complaint may be presented to an industrial tribunal against an employer by any person (the complainant) that he was unfairly dismissed by the employer.

(2) Subject to subsection (3), an industrial tribunal shall not consider a complaint under this section unless it is presented to the tribunal before the end of the period of three months beginning with the effective date of termination or within such further period as the tribunal considers reasonable in a case where it is satisfied that it was not reasonably practicable for the complaint to be presented before the end of the period of three months

Section 111(2) provides therefore that a tribunal will not have jurisdiction to hear a complaint unless it is presented within three months *"beginning with"* the *"effective date of termination"*.

The phrase "beginning with" was analysed in *University of Cambridge v. Murray* 1993. The tribunal held that if the word *"from"* or *"after"* had been used then the three months would be calculated to the corresponding date of the relevant late month or if no date the last day of the month. As the expression *"beginning with"* is used however the starting date is a day earlier and so ends with the day before the corresponding date of the later relevant month. If the effective date of termination is the 30th April therefore, the three month period expires on the last moment of the 29th July.

It should be emphasised from the outset that time limits in relation to unfair dismissal claims are enforced strictly. Popplewell J in *Foster v. South Glamorgan Health Authority* 1988 expressed the attitude of the EAT when he said *"It has been the practice of industrial tribunals and this appeal tribunal, to apply the limitation periods with very great strictness. They go to jurisdiction. The rather leisurely pace at which proceedings in the High Court and elsewhere are conducted have no place in industrial tribunals or this appeal tribunal".*

A significant feature of unfair dismissal procedure is that under s.111(4) it is possible for an employee who is dismissed with notice to lodge a complaint of unfair dismissal when still employed and serving out the notice period. If following a dismissal with notice and a subsequent complaint, there is a summary dismissal, the Court of Appeal held in *Patel v. Nagesan* 1995 that the original complaint is unaffected. *"Once s.111(4) bites, there is a valid complaint which the tribunal has to consider. There is nothing in the section to suggest that the employer, whether deliberately or not, can invalidate the complaint by proceeding at a later date to dismiss summarily."*

Effective Date of Termination

The expression *"effective date of termination"* means for most purposes the date that the employment actually terminates.

Under s.92(6) the "effective date of termination"

(a)   *in relation to an employee whose contract of employment is terminated by notice, means the date on which the notice expires;*

(b)   *in relation to an employee whose contract of employment is terminated without notice, means the date on which the termination takes effect; and*

(c)   *in relation to an employee under a contract for a fixed term, which expires without being renewed under the same contract, means the date on which that term expires.*

In *McMaster v. Manchester Airport plc* 1998 it was held that the effective date of termination cannot be earlier than the date on which the employee receives the knowledge that he is being dismissed

In a resignation/contructive dismissal scenario the effetive date of termination is the date that the decision to leave the employment is comminicated.

In *Edwards v. Surrey Police* 1999 the Employment Tribunal held that in a constructive dismissal scenario the effective date of termination was the date that the applicant had drafted her letter of resignation, the 17 July 1997. Accordingly when she presented her application alleging unfair dismissal on the 17 October she was time barred. On appeal the EAT held that the tribunal was wrong to decide that the effective date of termination was the date that the applicant had decided she no longer wished to work for the employer and drafted her letter of resignation. For a constructive dismissal the EAT thought that there must be a proper communication, by words or conduct, to the effect that the employment has terminated. Mr Justice Morison said that *"before a contract can be terminated there must have been communication by words, or by conduct, such as to inform the other party to the contract that it is at an end. An employee alleging constructive dismissal therefore must communicate to the employer the fact that they are terminating their employment. It is not an infrequent occurrence that employees find their working life intolerable, walk out in a huff, but do not intend to bring their employment relationship to an end".*

It seems that for a summary dismissal under s.92(6)(b), whether or not in breach of contract, the effective date of termination is the date of dismissal.

In *Stapp v. The Shaftesbury Society* 1982 the Court of Appeal held that the 'effective date of termination' means the actual date of termination of the employment whether or not the employee was wrongfully dismissed. Here the effect of a summary dismissal with wages paid in lieu of one month's notice was to make the effective date of dismissal the date of termination of employment and so the employee had insufficient continuous employment to bring a claim for unfair dismissal.

There is one exception to the rule that the effective date of termination is when the employee actually leaves work.

Under s.92(7) where the contact of employment is terminated by the employer and the notice required by section 86 to be given by the employer would, if duly given on the material date, expire on a date later than the effective date of termination the later date is the effective date of termination.

Section s.92(7) provides therefore that the effective date of termination can be extended beyond the date of dismissal if the employer has been denied his right to the minimum period of statutory notice under s.86. In that case the effective date of termination is the date on which the statutory notice would have expired.

What then is the position when an employee is summarily dismissed for gross misconduct, with wages in lieu of notice? Is that sufficient to preclude the operation of s.92(7) and so extend the effective date of termination by the statutory minimum notice to which the claimant is entitled under s.86.

In *Lanton Leisure Ltd. v. White and Gibson* 1987 the EAT thought not and held that simply to designate a dismissal as one for gross misconduct was not sufficient to prevent a claimant from extending the effective date of termination by the minimum notice period. It is for the tribunal to decide whether the alleged misconduct was sufficient to warrant summary dismissal.

In *Batchelor v. British Railways Board* 1987 the Court of Appeal held that a dismissal expressed to be "with immediate effect" takes effect on that date even if it is in breach of a contractual disciplinary procedure. The effective date of termination is the date that the actual termination of the contract took place whether unlawful or not.

In *Valeo Distribution (UK) Ltd. v. Barber* 1992 the applicant was a warehouseman who was summarily dismissed by his employer for poor time-keeping by a letter he received on the 20 July 1991. Having started work on the 7 August 1989 the first issue before the tribunal, and subsequently the EAT, was whether the applicant met the two year qualification period. The tribunal held that as the letter of dismissal did not allege gross misconduct to trigger summary dismissal the applicant was entitled to notice under s.86. This notice brought the effective date of termination forward so that he had qualified with two years service. On appeal the EAT referred to *Stapp v. Shaftesbury Society* which held that the effective date meant the actual date of termination and similarly held that *"it does not matter whether or not the notice of dismissal or dismissal without notice constituted a breach of contract the section operates irrespective of whether, as a matter of contract, the employer ought to have given some notice or a longer time"*. The letter brought the employment to an end on the 20 July which was the effective date of termination. While s.92(7) allows the effective date of termination to be extended in some cases by the statutory notice period, this would have only added one week to the applicants period of employment so that he would still be unable to qualify to claim unfair dismissal.

Finally it should be mentioned that the effective date of termination can be a date agreed expressly by the parties. In *Lambert v. Croydon College* 1999 the effective date of termination was held to be the agreed date of termination rather than the date of the agreement and as a consequence a subsequent claim for unfair dismissal was time barred.

Claims Out of Time

Section 111(2)(b) further provides that a tribunal may hear a complaint presented outside the time limits if it is satisfied that it was not reasonably practicable to present the claim in time. The exercise of this discretion by tribunals has been the issue in a number of cases. In *Palmer and Saunders v. Southend on Sea Borough Council* 1984 the Court of Appeal held that in construing the expression 'reasonably practicable', the best approach is to read 'practicable' as the equivalent of 'feasible' and to ask *"was it reasonably feasible to present the complaint to the industrial tribunal within the relevant three months"*. Also the court stressed that the issue is one of fact for the industrial tribunal and it is seldom that an appeal from its decision will lie.

In *St. Basil's Centre v. McCrossan* 1991 the application to complain of unfair dismissal was posted in Birmingham on Friday 19 May but did not arrive at the Central Office of Industrial Tribunals in London until Tuesday 23 May which was one day late. The EAT held that the tribunal could decide that it was not reasonably practicable for the complainant to be presented in time as the evidence suggested that the applicant could have expected the complaint to arrive within the time limit. *"Where an unfair dismissal application is posted within the three months time period but arrives after that period has expired, the question to be determined is whether the claimant would reasonably have expected the application to be delivered in time in the ordinary course of the post. This is a question of fact for the industrial tribunal to determine on the evidence".*

The requirement that time limits must be complied with is a stringent one and solicitors representing complainants should take all reasonable steps that applications are presented in time and should *"employ some system of checking that replies which might reasonably be expected within certain periods have in fact been received and that the conduct of business is taking a normal course".* In *Camden & Islington Community Services NHS Trust v. Kennedy* 1996 the cut off date was 27 December. The application was posted by a solicitor on the 19 December and on the 30 January the solicitors enquired by phone and were told the application had not been received. In reversing the tribunal's decision the EAT held that here the conduct of the solicitor was not sufficient to show that he took all steps that were reasonably practicable to comply with the time limits. *"A competent solicitor practising in this field must be taken to appreciate the vital importance of complying with time limits strictly and having in place a system designed to ensure that such limits are complied with at the time they are supposed to be complied with".*

Where illness is used as a ground for not presenting a complaint within the limitation period the courts have suggested that a disabling illness which falls near the end of the period should carry more weight. So held the Court of Appeal in *Schultz v. Esso Petroleum* 1999 which overlooked the fact that the claimant was in a fit state to start proceedings during the earlier part of the limitation period. Usually it is not 'reasonably practicable' to present the complaint prematurely but rather attempt to avoid litigation by pursuing alternative remedies.

In some cases it could be argued that the reason for the delay in presenting the claim was due to the time involved in investigating facts which give rise to the belief that the dismissal is unfair.

In *Churchill v. Yeates & Son Ltd.* 1983 the reason relied on by the employer for dismissal was redundancy, but subsequently the applicant discovered that someone else was doing his old job. In addition to alleging that the process of dismissal was unfair because of lack of consultation or warning, etc., the applicant presented his claim for unfair dismissal out of time when he discovered that someone else had been engaged to do his job. The tribunal ruled that as the claim of unfairness based on the true reason for dismissal was not related to unfairness due to the process of dismissal, it was reasonably practicable for the applicant to present his claim within the time limits. This somewhat harsh decision was reversed by the EAT who held *that "ignorance of a fact, the existence of which is fundamental to the right to claim unfair dismissal, can amount to circumstances which render it not reasonably practicable for a complaint of unfair dismissal to be presented within the three month limit"*. This is the case even if there are other grounds which could have formed the basis of a timely complaint. Here the new factual allegation challenged the honesty and genuineness of the reason for dismissal given by the employer and was fundamental to the success or failure of the claim.

It does seem therefore that if a ground for presenting a complaint for unfair dismissal came to light outside the three month time limit, then provided the complaint is presented within a reasonable period thereafter it will not be time barred. The Court of appeal in *Marley (UK) Ltd. v. Anderson* 1996 confirmed that this is the case even where more than one ground for presenting a complaint is alleged. *"The questions posed by s.111(2)(6), reasonable practicability of presentation within time and the reasonableness of any subsequent period elapsing before presentation, are both matters to be weighed separately, ground by ground and fact by fact, under each head of unfair dismissal upon which a complaint or complaints is or are founded."* New facts emerge which indicate a different reason for dismissal a complaint could still be made but only within a reasonable period and in *James W. Wood Ltd. v. Tipper* 1990 the Court of Appeal said that a delay of four weeks or more once the true facts had emerged should be regarded as longer than a reasonable period.

The fact that an applicant relied on bad advice from a skilled advisor is not an excuse to present a claim out of time.

In *Riley v. Tesco Stores Ltd.* 1980 the reason that the dismissed employee put forward for not presenting an unfair dismissal claim within the three month period was that she had relied on the advice of a skilled advisor. Following a dismissal for alleged theft from her employer, she was advised by the Citizens Advice Bureau that she could not proceed with her complaint of unfair dismissal until after the criminal proceedings had run their course. Almost ten months after the effective date of termination, when she was acquitted of the charge against her, she presented a claim for unfair dismissal which both the tribunal and EAT held could not be heard as it was out of time. Having engaged a *"skilled advisor"* it was reasonably practicable for her to present the claim within the three month time limit. This decision was upheld by the Court of Appeal who found that if a claim is presented out of time due to ignorance of rights it is the role of the tribunal to consider the circumstances of the mistaken belief and any explanation for it, including advice taken, and then ask whether the ignorance or mistake is reasonable. If either the applicant or his skilled advisor was at fault or unreasonable, then it was reasonably practicable to present the claim in time.

In *Dowty Aerospace Ltd. v. Ballinger* 1993 the EAT held that even if there is genuine confusion between the complainant and his trade union advisor as to who would present an application for unfair dismissal this was no excuse for a late application. The tribunal has been wrong therefore to decide that as a result of the "confusion" it had not been reasonably practicable for the complainant to present the complaint in time.

In *Jean Sorelle Ltd. v. Rybak* 1991 the bad advice was given by an employee of the industrial tribunal and the EAT found that as a consequence it was not reasonably practicable for the employee to present the claim within the time limit.

In cases where the claim is not presented in time due to the negligence of an advisor it may be possible for an aggrieved employee to maintain an action in damages against the advisor for the lost opportunity of securing a remedy for unfair dismissal.

In *Siraj-Eldin v. Campbell Middleton Burness & Dickson* 1989 the Court of Session held that to succeed in a claim for damages in negligence against solicitors who failed to present an unfair dismissal claim in time, an employee had to show that the complaint had some substance, and possessed more than nuisance value. If, in examining the complaint, the court feels that no reasonable tribunal could have concluded on the evidence that dismissal was not a reasonable option, then the emsployee will not have suffered loss in being denied the opportunity of presenting his claim.

In *London International v. Sen* 1992 the complainant was one day late with an unfair dismissal complaint after relying on erroneous advice as to time limits from his solicitor and the Central Office of Industrial Tribunals. The EAT held that the complaint should be heard as it was not reasonably practicable to present it in time.

Where redundancy is the reason relied on for dismissal and an employer subsequently appoints a replacement for the job in question, this may provide the complainant with evidence that this was not the true reason for dismissal.

In *Machine Tool Research Association v. Simpson* 1988 the complainant, aware that staff reductions were planned, accepted the decision that she was dismissed by reason of redundancy. Subsequently, however, when she discovered that in fact she had been replaced, she had good reason to doubt that redundancy was the true reason for dismissal and presented a claim for unfair dismissal but, unfortunately, some three days outside the statutory three month time limit. Both the industrial tribunal and the EAT felt that the tribunal had jurisdiction to hear the complaint, as it had not been reasonably practicable for the applicant to present the claim in time. The Court of Appeal agreed and held that it was not reasonably practicable to present a complaint where during the three month limitation period there were crucial or important facts unknown to the applicant which subsequently become known and gives rise to a genuine belief that he may have a claim. To establish that it was not reasonably practicable to present the claim in time, the applicant must satisfy three stages of proof.

- It was reasonable for him not to be aware of the relevant fact which would help establish the claim.

- Knowledge of the fact has been reasonably gained in the circumstances and that knowledge is crucial in promoting the belief that the applicant may have a substantive claim.

- Acquisition of that knowledge must be crucial to the decision to bring a claim.

It does seem that the courts will only accept reasonable practicability when it is established that the employee was unaware of facts necessary to enable him to present a complaint.

In *London Underground Ltd. v. Noel* 1999 the Court of Appeal disagreed with the tribunal and the EAT that there were special facts which justified a finding that it was not reasonably practicable for an employee to present an unfair dismissal complaint within the three month time limit. Both the tribunal and EAT had felt that an offer of re-employment in a new job which was then withdrawn by the employer subsequent to the dismissal was a fact which was fundamental to his right to bring a claim. It was when the offer of re-employment was withdrawn that the technical right to bring a claim of unfair dismissal actually arose. This argument was rejected by the Court of Appeal which held that the offer of re-employment had no impact upon the statutory time limit and the right to present a complaint. *"In the present case every fact which the employee needed to know in order to present a complaint of unfair dismissal was known to him before the expiry of the three month time limit and the offer of re-employment and its subsequent withdrawal did not alter any such fact."* While it is in the interests of the parties to seek an internal solution to a dismissal dispute through a process of appeals and hearings, such a process does not override the requirement under s.171 to present the originating application for unfair dismissal within three months of the effective date of termination.

Conciliation

A copy of the IT1 having been sent to ACAS, a conciliation officer is appointed to get in touch with both parties in an attempt to resolve the conflict and reach an amicable settlement. It should be stressed that in many cases an agreement is reached because of the intervention of the conciliation officer. While he is under a statutory duty to endeavour to promote a voluntary settlement of the complaint by encouraging an agreement to reinstate the employee, or make a payment of compensation, there is no requirement for the parties to co-operate or even communicate with him.

If the employee is resolved to proceed with the complaint, however, then prior to a full hearing by the tribunal, there is a pre-trial assessment at which the details of the claim are presented. At this stage any party to the proceedings could be warned by the tribunal that full costs may be payable if he proceeds to a full hearing. The Secretary of State has power to require that at a pre-trial review a deposit of £150 will have to be paid by a party wishing to continue with the proceedings.

If the complaint proceeds to a full hearing, the burden of proof is on the complainant to show that he has been dismissed unless that is conceded. The various forms of dismissal under s.95 and the alternative means by which a contract of employment may be brought to an end were examined earlier in Chapter 10.

> The EAT in *Hogg v. Dover College* 1990 pointed out that dismissal is defined in terms of the contract being terminated and not necessarily the employment relationship so that if the employee continues in an employment relationship with the same employer under a new contract it is still technically possible to present a complaint of unfair dismissal. Accepting the terms of a new contract from an employer does not necessarily amount to an affirmation, providing the employee makes his non affirmation clear to the employer and states his intention to pursue an unfair dismissal claim.

The principles of the above case have since been applied to the situation where an employee was demoted as a result of disciplinary action.

> In *Joseph v. British Railway Board* 1993 the applicant was demoted following a final appeal in the internal disciplinary process. He could not accept the decision and prepared an originating application to the industrial tribunal. The argument by the employer was that no claim for unfair dismissal could be initiated when the disciplinary procedure gave them the right to demote for

misconduct. This argument was rejected, the tribunal deciding the preliminary issue that there had been a dismissal, with no affirmation by the employee of his new contract.

Having established that a dismissal has occurred, it then falls to the tribunal to determine the reason for dismissal, whether it is a reason categorised in the Employment Rights Act 1996 and, if so, whether the dismissal is fair or unfair and redress where appropriate. To appreciate the process by which a claim of unfair dismissal is determined therefore it is necessary to consider the reason for dismissal, statutory reasons, fairness and remedies.

Reason for Dismissal

To assist the complainant in a claim for unfair dismissal the complainant is entitled to be provided with the reason for dismissal.

> *Under s.92(1) An employee is entitled to be provided by his employer with a written statement giving particulars of the reasons for the employee's dismissal*
>
> *(a) if the employee is given by the employer notice of termination of his contract of employment;*
>
> *(b) if the employee's contract of employment is terminated by the employer without notice; or*
>
> *(c) if the employee is employed under a contract for a fixed term and, that term expires without being renewed under the same contract.*

This right applies therefore when there is an express dismissal or dismissal by reason of the expiration of a fixed term contract. An employee who alleges constructive dismissal is not entitled to be provided with a written statement.

To trigger the right the employee must request the statement which should be provided within fourteen days. Under s.92(4) there is no need to make such a request if the dismissal occurs while the employee is pregnant or after childbirth.

The written statement provided under this section is important evidence of the employer's reason or reasons for dismissal. The period of continuous employment to qualify for this statutory right is under s.92(3) one year. Following the Employment Protection (Part-Time Employees) Regulations 1995 the right applies to part-time employees regardless of their hours of work. If an employer unreasonably fails to comply with a request the employee may present a complaint to the tribunal under s.93(1) which may declare what it finds the reasons for dismissal are and also compensate the employee with an award of two weeks' wages. Originally the section provided that the complainant had to show that the employer also unreasonably refused to provide a statement. This is no longer a requirement following an amendment brought in by the Trade Union Reform and Employment Rights Act 1993.

In *Kent County Council v. Gilham and Others* 1985 the Court of Appeal held that following a request for a statement of the reason for dismissal it is acceptable for an employer to make a response which refers to earlier communications. That is, providing the covering letter specifically refers to the earlier communication, and it does contain the reason or reasons for dismissal.

The purpose of the statutory right to compel the employer to supply the employee with the reason or reasons relied on for dismissal is to enable the employee to scrutinise them in advance of the proceedings and also to tie the employer down to that reason in any subsequent proceedings. The Act requires an employer to state truthfully the reason that he was relying on in dismissing the employee so that the employee does not start with the disadvantage of not knowing the reason for dismissal if he wishes to pursue a claim for unfair dismissal.

In *Harvard Securities plc v. Younghusband* 1990 the EAT held that whether or not the employer is telling the truth in identifying the ground relied upon does not involve an examination of the justification for the dismissal. Here the tribunal had held that as the written reason referred to divulging confidential information, it was untrue under because the information in question could not in any sense be regarded as confidential. This, the EAT decided, was the wrong approach. *"There is no need under the section to embark upon a consideration of whether the reason was intrinsically a good, bad or indifferent one ... whether the employees were correct in describing the information in question as 'confidential' was irrelevant to the identification of the reason upon which they relied for dismissing the employee."*

In *Catherine Haigh Harlequin Hair Design v. Seed* 1990 it was held that an industrial tribunal has no jurisdiction to hear a complaint that the employer has not provided a dismissed employee with a statement of the particulars of the reason for dismissal unless there has been a request by the employee for the particulars.

In *Copeman Hart & Co. Ltd. v. Berzins* 1993 the complainant was dismissed by a letter of the 6th July 1990 and subsequently six weeks later made a written request for the reasons for dismissal to which the employer did not respond. The tribunal upheld a complaint and on appeal the employer argued firstly that the complainants letter did not constitute a request and secondly that they had complied with the requirements of the section in their letter of the 6th July. Both arguments were rejected by the EAT who felt that the complainants letter was a valid request and that the earlier communication could not constitute a sufficient response unless specifically referred to in a written response.

Statutory Reasons for Dismissal

The heart of unfair dismissal law is contained in s.98 and it is to this section we must devote some attention.

Under s.98 (1) In determining for the purposes of this Part whether the dismissal of an employee was fair or unfair, it shall be for the employer to show–

> *(a)   what was the reason or, if there was more than one, the principal reason for the dismissal, and*

> *(b)   that it was a reason falling within subsection (2) or some other substantial reason of a kind such as to justify the dismissal of an employee holding the position which that employee held.*

(2)   In subsection (1)(b) the reference to a reason falling within this subsection is a reference to a reason which–

> *(a)   related to the capability or qualifications of the employee for performing work of the kind which he was employed by the employer to do, or*

> *(b)   related to the conduct of the employee, or*

> *(c)   was that the employee was redundant, or*

> *(d)   was that the employee could not continue to work in the position which he held without contravention (either on his part or on that of his employer) of a duty or restriction imposed by or under an enactment.*

Statutory Reasons for Dismissal

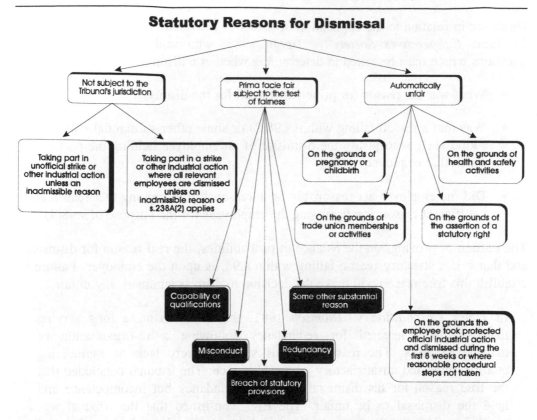

Under the section therefore it clearly states that it is the employer who must show the reason or principal reason for the dismissal, and that the reason falls within one of the four categories of admissible reasons identified in s.98(2) or is a substantial reason under s.98(1) of a kind such as to justify the dismissal of an employee holding the position which that employee held. If the employee establishes the true reason for dismissal, and that it falls within one of the five admissible statutory reasons identified in s.98, then the dismissal is prima facie fair. The final determination of fairness is achieved by applying the test of reasonableness contained in s.98(4).

If the complainant alleges an inadmissible automatically unfair reason for dismissal then if he has less than one years continuous employment he will need to establish the jurisdiction if the tribunal is to hear the complaint. The burden of proof would in those circumstances be on the complainant to establish that the reason for dismissal falls within an inadmissible category such as pregnancy, trade union membership or linked to health and safety etc. Inadmissible reasons for dismissal are considered later in the chapter.

Guidance in relation to the application of s.98 was provided by Lord Bridge in *West Midlands Cooperatives Society v. Tipton* 1986, who said that there are three questions which must be asked in determining whether a dismissal is fair or unfair.

- What was the reason (or principal reason) for the dismissal?

- Was that a reason falling within s.98(2) or some other substantial reason of a kind such as to justify the dismissal of an employee holding the position which that employee held?

- Did the employer act reasonably or unreasonably in treating that reason as a sufficient reason for dismissing the employees for the purpose of s.98(4)?

The burden of proving, on the balance of probabilities, the real reason for dismissal, and that it is a statutory reason falling within s.98, is upon the employer. Failure to establish this true reason will make the decision to dismiss automatically unfair.

In *Timex Corporation v. Thomson* 1981, the complainant, a long serving manager, was selected for redundancy following a re-organisation of managerial posts. The reasons for his selection were lack of engineering qualifications and unsatisfactory job performance. The tribunal concluded that the true reason for his dismissal was not redundancy but incompetence and held the dismissal to be unfair. The EAT confirmed that the tribunal was entitled to find that they were not satisfied that the employer had put forward the true reason for dismissal. *"Even where there is a redundancy situation it is possible for an employer to use such a situation as a pretext for getting rid of an employee he wishes to dismiss. In such circumstances the reason for dismissal will not be redundancy."* Here the employer had not satisfied the burden cast by the section and so the dismissal was consequently unfair.

In *Philip Hodges & Co. v. Kell* 1994 the employer purported to dismiss the complainant a legal secretary, by reason of redundancy while she was on maternity leave. The EAT held that prior to the dismissal there was suitable alternative work available which the complainant should have been offered, so that there was no dismissal by reason of redundancy and as a consequence the dismissal was unfair.

Clearly then if the tribunal is convinced that the reason put forward by the employer is not the true reason that was in his mind at the time of the dismissal, then it is entitled at this stage to decide that the dismissal is unfair.

In *Price v. Gourley* 1973 the complainant worked in a cake shop and, after seven years' service, received top wages for her grade. She was dismissed and when she asked for a reason was told by the manager that it was *"just one of those things"*. At the tribunal the employer alleged that the reason was incompetence, but as he failed to show any deterioration in her work it did seem unreasonable that it was seven years before he took any action. The true reason for dismissal the tribunal held was simply that the employer was attempting to reduce overheads by replacing a well-paid employee with a junior on lower pay. As the alleged reason was not the true reason, and cost cutting was not a reason falling within the statute, the dismissal was consequently unfair.

If an employer decides not to rely on a justifiable reason for dismissal and rather chooses to put forward another reason which proves to be unjustifiable, then the result may be a finding of unfair dismissal. Ironically the fact that the employer could have relied on a valid reason to dismiss will not prevent a tribunal from making an award of compensation if the dismissal is found to be unfair.

In *Trico-Folberth Ltd. v. Devonshire* 1989 the employer decided on compassionate grounds to withdraw a dismissal by reason of poor attendance and substitute instead a dismissal on the grounds of medical unfitness. While the original reason was perfectly justifiable the dismissal on the ground of a medical condition was unfair because of the failure of the employer to investigate and consult. The Court of Appeal confirmed that the dismissal was unfair, and whether or not the employer could have dismissed for another justifiable reason would not affect the amount of compensation awarded.

Having decided the true reason for dismissal it is then necessary for the employer to establish that it falls within one of the four statutory reasons contained in s.98(2) or is some other substantial reason of a kind to justify dismissal under s.98(1). In practice it is rare for an employer to fail to show that the reason is categorised in the Act, so that the reason will in most cases be prima facie fair. The crucial issue is whether the reason relied on satisfies the test of fairness in s.98(4). We will consider the general approach to substantive fairness and their relation to each of the potentially four reasons.

The Test of Fairness

Once the employer has shown that the principal reason for dismissal is prima facie fair it is then necessary for the tribunal to determine the heart of the issue, whether the employer acted reasonably in the circumstances.

The test of fairness is contained in s.98(4) which provides that the determination of the question of whether the dismissal was fair or unfair, having regard to the reason shown by the employer, shall depend on whether in the circumstances (including the size and administrative resources of the employer's undertaking) the employer acted reasonably or unreasonably in treating it as a sufficient reason for dismissing the employee, and that question shall be determined in accordance with equity and the substantial merits of the case.

Substantive Fairness

This important test involves an assessment of the employer's conduct from the viewpoint of substantive fairness and procedural fairness. Here we will consider substantive fairness and deal with procedural fairness later in the chapter. Inevitably the test of fairness has been the subject of judicial interpretation since its introduction in 1971 and you should appreciate that there have been a number of approaches as to how it should be applied.

An important issue in deciding the reasonableness of the employer's conduct is determining the date upon which fairness of the decision to dismiss is to be tested. There is case-law, notably the decision of the House of Lords in *Devis & Sons Ltd. v. Atkins* 1977 which seem to suggest that the reasonableness of the decision to dismiss should be assessed at the date when notice to terminate the employment was given and nothing that happened afterwards could have any effect upon the fairness of the decision to dismiss. While this is acceptable in relation to matters discovered after dismissal by the employer, which could support his decision to dismiss, the fact that in *West Midland Cooperative Society v. Tipton* 1986 the employer refused the employee his contractual right of appeal could be taken into account to decide the fairness of his conduct. Certainly matters which come to light during the appeal process may be taken into account in considering the overall *"equity and substantial merits of the case"*. The House of Lords ruled in the Tipton case that a dismissal is unfair if the employer unreasonably treats the reason as a sufficient reason to dismiss or when he maintains that decision at the conclusion of an appeal process. By totally denying an employee a contractual right to appeal against a decision to dismiss, the dismissal could also be held to be unfair.

> In *Stacy v. Babcock Power Ltd. (Construction Division)* 1986 after an initial warning in November 1983, the applicant was given a notice of redundancy in February 1984 that his contract would terminate on the fourth of May 1984. The decision to dismiss by reason of redundancy was incontestably fair when given, but in April 1984 the employer secured a contract which provided new opportunities for employees to do work of the kind that the applicant had been doing, and at a nearby location. Despite these fresh employment opportunities the applicant's contract was terminated without any offer of re-engagement. On a claim for unfair dismissal the tribunal held that the circumstances which arose after the decision to dismiss in February were irrelevant and the decision to dismiss was consequently fair. On appeal however the EAT

reversed the decision and took the view that the process of dismissal was not complete until the notice had expired and a dismissal which was fair when the notice was given could become unfair by the date of its expiry. Here *"fair industrial practice would have required the respondents to offer the complainant, as a long standing employee, the opportunity of new employment before filling all the vacancies with newly recruited employees"*. Failure to offer fresh employment made the decision to dismiss unfair.

We said that the reason or reasons relied on by the employer to justify a dismissal must be the reason which the employer had in mind at the time of the dismissal. In *Patinson v. March Consulting Ltd*. 1997 the Court of Appeal suggested that the reason given at the time of giving notice to the employee cannot be divorced from the reason relied on when the dismissal actually occurs. This means that it is necessary to take account of circumstances which occur during the notice period including relevant facts or correspondence. In this case the applicant had been told at the time of notice that his position would become redundant because of a possible new post which had yet to be determined. The fact that the new post had been settled during his notice period was a "fact" which could be used to support the reason for dismissal. Sir Iain Glidewell said that *"There is nothing in the statute or the authorities which prevent an employer who is required to give an employee a long period of notice, and who reasonably anticipates that at the end of that period a decision will have been made or facts will exist which will render the employee's services unnecessary, from giving a notice in anticipation of that decision or those facts and giving what he expects to happen on the reason for dismissal"*.

Further support for considering the reason for dismissal in the light of the dismissal process is provided by *Alboni v. Ind Coope Retail Ltd*. [1998] where the Court of Appeal held that a tribunal is not only entitled but is bound to have regard to events between notice of dismissal and the date that dismissal took effect both in determining the reason for dismissal and whether the employers acted reasonably in the circumstances in treating it as a reason for dismissal.

Where there are multiple reasons for dismissal it must be determined which is the principal one for the purposes of applying s.98(4).

As recently as 1989 the Employment Appeal Tribunal in *Post Office Counters Ltd. v. Heavey* 1989 found it necessary to confirm that in an unfair dismissal complaint, while the burden of showing the reason for the dismissal is on the employer, the requirement of acting reasonably is not subject to any burden of proof. It is not for the employer to *show* or for the tribunal to be *satisfied* the employer acted reasonably in dismissing the employee. Rather the burden of proof was made neutral by the Employment Act 1980.

In Boys *and Girls Welfare Society v. McDonald* 1996 the EAT stressed the neutral burden of proof in a complaint of unfair dismissal and confirmed that there is no onus of proof on the employer to satisfy a tribunal as to reasonableness. The tribunal must ask itself whether the dismissal falls within the range of reasonable responses.

'Fairness' then has to be judged by the industrial tribunal acting as an industrial jury applying the words of s.98(4). The tribunal is not an arbitrator and has no jurisdiction to substitute its own views of reasonableness for the employer's but must adjudicate upon what a reasonable employer would have done in the circumstances.

Useful guidelines in relation to the approach to be adopted in applying s.98(4) were provided by the EAT in *Iceland Frozen Foods v. Jones* 1982. Here Brown Wilkinson J. suggested that the approach which should be adopted by tribunals.

- *the starting point should always be the words of the section themselves;*

- *in applying the section an industrial tribunal must consider the reasonableness of the employer's conduct, not simply whether they (the members of the industrial tribunal) consider the dismissal to be fair;*

- *in judging the reasonableness of the employer's conduct an industrial tribunal must not substitute its decision as to what was the right course to adopt for that of the employer;*

- *in many, though not all, cases there is a band of reasonable responses to the employee's conduct within which one employer might reasonably take one view, another quite reasonably take another;*

- *the function of the industrial tribunal, as an industrial jury, is to determine whether in the particular circumstances of each case the decision to dismiss the employee fell within the band of reasonable responses which a reasonable employer might have adopted. If the dismissal falls within the band the dismissal is fair, if the dismissal falls outside the band it is unfair.*

This approach to the application of s.98(4) has been widely adopted.

In *Rentokil v. Mackin and Another* 1989 the EAT in Scotland emphasised that the function of an industrial tribunal in an unfair dismissal case is to act as an industrial jury and determine whether in the circumstances the decision to dismiss falls within the band of reasonable responses which a reasonable employer might have adopted. Such a test does not mean however that such *"a high degree of unreasonableness be shown so that nothing short of a perverse decision to dismiss can be held to be unfair within the section"*. Here the EAT refused to interfere with the decision of an industrial tribunal that an employer had acted unfairly when he dismissed two employees who had admitted helping themselves to a milkshake while working in the kitchen of one of the employer's clients.

In *Conlin v. United Distillers* 1994 the Scottish Court of Session confirmed the principle that while consistency is an important ingredient in taking disciplinary proceedings against employees, each case must be considered on its own merits. The court also stressed the need for industrial tribunals to demonstrate that they are applying the test of fairness. In determining an unfair dismissal complaint *"it is essential that it should be apparent from the tribunal's decision that the correct test has been identified and applied."* Here the EAT were correct to overturn the decision of the tribunal when *"there was nothing in the industrial tribunal's decision to indicate that the question of whether the dismissal of the employee fell within the range of responses of a reasonable employer was ever considered"*.

When deciding under s.98(4) whether the decision to dismiss comes within the band of reasonable responses of a reasonable employer it is possible for a tribunal to find that a dismissal is fair despite the fact that it disagrees with it.

In *Iredale v. Huddersfield Health Authority* 1993 the EAT held that in dismissing a nurse for slapping a mental patient the employer had reached a decision within the band of reasonable responses. As a consequence the dismissal was fair even though the tribunal had expressed the view that it did not believe in the circumstances of the case that the misconduct merited dismissal.

As the test of fairness is based upon the actions of a reasonable employer it is possible to find an employer acting within his contractual authority to be nevertheless acting unfairly for the purposes of unfair dismissal.

In *George v. Plant Breeding International* 1991 a worker was dismissed because he refused to accept Sunday working for a three month period in a year. His work involved seed processing and the three month period covered harvesting time when the company was at its busiest. Working twelve hours a day seven days a week was claimed to be disruptive of family life despite the fact that the worker had fifteen years service with the company. The employer relied on an express contractual term which provided that the employee was "required to work extra hours beyond those mentioned in your letter of appointment at the request of management when the workload made it necessary". The industrial tribunal held that this contractual power did not give the employer the right to demand seven day working for a three month period and it was unfair to dismiss the employee for refusing to obey the instruction to work. The tribunal confirmed that unfair dismissal law is not based on contract and that even if an instruction is lawful it could still be unfair. The justification for the decision was that flexible working arrangements may be challenged on grounds of public policy. *"Unless time is created for members of the family to meet and relate to one another, family life in Britain is likely to show fragmentation of family arrangements."*

If a tribunal finds the facts and applies the relevant law in reaching a decision as to the fairness or otherwise of a decision to dismiss, then it is only in exceptional cases that an appellate body can overturn its decision on the grounds of perversity.

In *County of Hereford and Worcester v. Neale* 1986 the Court of Appeal found that the EAT had been wrong to overturn a decision of the industrial tribunal that a school teacher had been fairly dismissed. The reason for the dismissal was the teacher's unprofessional conduct when invigilating an 'A' level examination and while the decision to dismiss had procedural deficiencies attached to it, the industrial tribunal nevertheless found it to be within the band of reasonable responses open to a reasonable employer. The EAT found however that the decision to dismiss regarded in the round had *"too much haste about it, too much stubbornness and secrecy and too little concern for the appearance of fairness"* and was consequently unfair. The attitude of the Court of Appeal was that the EAT was simply substituting its own view for that of the tribunal and that was insufficient to disturb the tribunal's decision. To overturn a decision of an industrial tribunal its conclusion must offend reason and be one which no reasonable tribunal would have reached. The response of the appellate body to it should be *"My goodness, that was certainly wrong"*.

In *East Berkshire Health Authority v. Matadeen* 1992 the EAT held that it can allow an appeal against the decision of a tribunal if *"first, there is an error of law on the face of the decision, a misdirection or misapplication of the law; secondly, if there is a material finding of fact relied upon by the tribunal in the decision which was unsupported by any evidence or contrary to the evidence before them, and thirdly, if there is a finding of perversity"*. The decision of a tribunal would be perverse if after applying the reasonable response test they reached a conclusion which *"defied logic and ignored generally accepted standards to be maintained in industrial relations"*. Here the complainant was a night charge nurse who having been disciplined by his employer had subsequently admitted making nuisance telephone calls to the hospital where he worked. As a consequence he was dismissed and on a complaint the tribunal found the dismissal to be unfair deciding that there was no gross misconduct and the *"decision to dismiss was not within the band of reasonable responses for these employers in these circumstances"*. The tribunal's decision was reversed by the EAT who substituted a finding that the dismissal was fair. The EAT felt that the tribunal's decision was irrational, deciding that *"the decision to dismiss a senior nurse holding managerial and supervisory responsibility in a mental hospital, for what is plainly calculated and gross misconduct and who has previously received a final warning must fall within the band of reasonable responses of this employer. A decision to the contrary would make absolutely no sense in an industrial relations context. "*

A challenge to the band of reasonable response test

In 1999 Mr Justice Morison, the retiring President of the EAT cast serious doubts about the approach of the courts to assess the validity of a decision to dismiss, particularly in cases of misconduct.

> In *Haddon v. Van Den Bergh Foods* 1999 Mr Justice Morison in the EAT provide a different analysis of the approach to s.98(4). The facts of the case reveal a bizarre management style. The applicant was to receive a good service award after 15 years service where food and drinks would be served. The presentation was to take place over a two hour period during the applicant's shift. He received mixed messages about returning to work after the presentation and on the day having consumed alcohol he decided not to return to work for the one and a half hours necessary to complete his shift. Subsequently the applicant was dismissed for failing to carry out a proper and reasonable instruction, an offence categorised in the company's disciplinary procedure as gross misconduct for which no warning was necessary. Despite believing that many employers would not have dismissed in these circumstances the tribunal held that it could not be said that a reasonable employer would not have done so and held that the dismissal fell within the band of reasonable responses and was consequently fair.

The President of the EAT held that the band of reasonable response test developed as a test to determining fairness under s.98(4) should no longer be applied. He referred to the test as *"an unhelpful gloss on the statute"* stating that the test of fairness should be applied *"without embellishment and without using mantras so favoured by lawyers in the this field"*. The approach signals a return to using employment tribunals as true industrial juries applying their own industrial experience and judgment in deciding the fairness of an employer's decision making. The significant question is still whether a reasonable employer with those resources would have decided to dismiss but in answering it a tribunal is entitled to take account of what it would have done in the circumstances. Mr Justice Morison emphasises that the test of fairness is still an objective one he merely recognises that *"it is neither reasonable not realistic to expect the objective question to be answered without the tribunal members having first asked what they would have done and since the tribunal is composed of people who are chosen to sit as an industrial jury applying their own good sense of judgment, what the tribunal themselves would have done will often coincide with their judgment as to what a reasonable employer would have done".*

If the interpretation of s.98(4) in *Haddon* is followed and tribunals are required to take account of their own view of fairness when considering the reasonableness of the employer's conduct it is unlikely that a decision such as the EATs in *Iredale* above would logically be reached. To disagree with the employer's decision and then uphold it as fair could not be justified if all the words of s.98(4) are applied.

Unqualified approval of Mr Justice Morison's approvals to s.98(4) was provided by the EAT in November 1999 in *Wilson v. Ethicon Ltd.* 2000. The Employment Tribunal had decided that the decision to dismiss an employee for failing to carry out a testing procedure fell within the band of reasonable responses open to an employer after conducting a reasonable inquiry into the misconduct. This test, first enunciated in *British Home Stores v. Burchell,* was not applied by the EAT which adopted the *Haddon* approach and endorsed the statements of Mr Justice Morison. In cases of misconduct dismissal it is essential to address the whole question of reasonableness in terms of s.98(4) and *"stand back from the decision of the employer and assess in the knowledge of what was known to him at the time whether or not the dismissal was reasonable in the circumstances".* Here the nature of the misconduct viewed against the employee's impeccable record should have led the employer to consider alternative remedies such as a written warning.

Certainly a return to emphasising the role of the tribunal as an 'industrial jury' and so using its own knowledge and expertise to judge the actions of the reasonable employer is to be welcomed. Also by failing to apply the words of s.98(4) relating to "equity and substantial merits" tribunals did not always do justice to the applicant employee. Cases such as *Saunders v. Scottish National Camps* (see later) which support management prerogative to take economic decisions at the expense of innocent employees can hardly be regarded as just and equitable.

One of the reasons that Mr Justice Morison accepted the need for a new approach was the belief that the band of reasonable response test had led tribunals to applying almost a perversity test. This was never the original intention and there is case-law authority which rejects that interpretation. In *Rentokil Ltd. v. Machin* 1989 (above) the tribunal held that two employees who had taken milkshakes from the kitchen of the employer's client were unfairly dismissed. The employer appealed arguing that such an act of dishonesty and consequential loss of trust would surely amount to conduct which would lead to a dismissal within the band of reasonable responses. The EAT disagreed and unequivocally rejected the notion of fairness equating with perversity. *"The test of whether an employer's decision to dismiss falls within the band of reasonable responses of a reasonable employer does not mean that such a high degree of unreasonableness be shown so that nothing short of a perverse decision to dismiss can be held to be unfair".*

The new President of the EAT, Lindsay J, was given the opportunity to pronounce on the *Haddon* approach to fairness in *Midland Bank v. Madden* 2000 He was unequivocal in declaring that it is only the Court of Appeal or higher tribunal that can dispense with the *"reasonable response test"*. However a tribunal is free to substitute its own views for those of the employer as to the reasonableness of dismissal as a response to the reason shown for it. In misconduct cases the *Burchell* test should be applied and a tribunal is free to substitute its own views for those of the employer in coming to a view on each of the three parts of the test. It seems therefore that his view was not very different from Morison in *Haddon*.

The controversy over the correct approach to the be taken to assess the fairness of misconduct dismissals now seems to be resolved, firstly by the EAT and secondly by the Court of Appeal itself.

> The EAT in *Beedell v. West Ferry Printers Ltd.* 2000 reasserted the significance of the band of reasonable response test and stressed that an employment tribunal should not put itself in the position of management to decide whether they would have dismissed an employee or not. Here the complainant, who had an impeccable employment record had been dismissed for fighting at work. The tribunal concluded that the employer's response to dismiss in this marginal case was not unreasonable despite the fact that the tribunal would not have dismissed in the circumstances. Reviewing the previous trilogy of cases the EAT held that where they follow earlier binding precedents of the Court of Appeal they add nothing and where they differ they cannot be sustained. Relying on the authorities the EAT is bound to apply the reasonable response test until modified or abandoned by the Court of Appeal.

The test survives

Having reaffirmed the reasonable response test from *Iceland Frozen Foods* the EAT also supported the proposition from that case that the tribunal must not substitute its decision as to the right course of action to adopt for that of the employer. Holding that the tribunal's decision disclosed no error of law the claimant's appeal was dismissed.

> On the 31st July 2000 the Court of Appeal in expedited proceedings handed down judgment on the employer's appeal in *Madden,* now called *Foley v. Post Office HSBC Bank plc* (formerly *Midland Bank plc v. Maddon*) 2000. Upholding the appeal, the court has overruled the decisions of the EAT in both *Madden* and *Haddon* and re-emphasised the primacy of *the "range of reasonable response test"*. Lord Justice Mumery held that the approach in *Iceland Frozen Foods* and *Burchell* was to be applied and that *Haddon* was an unwarranted departure from previous case-law.

The Court of Appeal has for the moment reaffirmed the position pre Haddon but there is no doubt that the approach adopted by Morison J had its supporters and has provoked a constructive debate as to the correct approach to applying s.98(4).

Having considered the general approach to be adopted by tribunals in determining its issue of substantive fairness we can now show how fairness has been applied in relation to the statutory reasons for dismissal. It is then necessary to consider fairness in the light of any disciplinary procedure adopted and applied by the employer

Capability or qualification s.98(2)a

For the purposes of this reason *'capability'* is assessed by reference to skill, aptitude, health or any other physical or mental quality. The majority of cases where capability is the reason relied upon relate to incompetence or ill health. Where an allegation of incompetence is established through evidence, in determining the reasonableness of the employer's decision to dismiss it is also necessary to examine the reasons for the alleged incompetence. This could involve a consideration of the employer's appraisal processes, the amount of training and supervision required, and the extent to which employees are given the opportunity to improve their performance. Obviously there are degrees of incompetence, but even one serious lapse could be sufficient to justify a dismissal.

> In *Taylor v. Alidair Ltd.* 1978 the applicant pilot was dismissed when as a result of an error of judgment, the passenger plane he was flying landed so hard that serious damage was caused to the plane. The Court of Appeal held that *"the company has reasonable grounds for honestly believing that the applicant was not competent"*. As a result of this serious act of incompetence the belief was reasonably held, and the dismissal was consequently a fair one.

If incapability is alleged, due to the ill health of the employee, once again reasonableness of the employer's decision to dismiss must be viewed by the extent to which it is an informed judgment bearing in mind the various options available. Earlier in Chapter 10 we considered the extent to which a long illness can amount to a frustration of the contract of employment.

> In *Links and Co. Ltd. v. Rose* 1991 the reason for dismissal was capability related to ill health. The Court of Session re-emphasised that an employer reaching a decision to dismiss in those circumstances must act reasonably for the dismissal to be fair. *"Therefore, in deciding whether an employer acted fairly or unfairly in dismissing an employee on grounds of ill health, an industrial tribunal must determine as a matter of fact and judgment what*

consultation, if any, was necessary or desirable in the known circumstances of the particular case; and whether or not that consultation process was adequate in all the circumstances. If it was not adequate, the dismissal will be unfair."

If an employee is permanently unfit for work due to a medical condition, provided the employer has carried out a thorough investigation the illness could constitute a fair reason for dismissal.

In *London Fire & Civil Defence Authority v. Betty* 1994 the complainant was retired from the fire service on medical grounds when he suffered a nervous breakdown. The tribunal found that the dismissal was unfair because the reason for the complainant's condition was the treatment he received from his employer. The EAT took a different view however and found the dismissal to be fair. *"An employer does not disable himself from fairly dismissing an employee whom he has injured. The employer's duty to act fairly in dismissing an employee on the grounds of ill health is unaffected by consideration as to who was responsible for the employee's unfitness for work. The question is whether the dismissal was fair having regard to the employee's medical condition and the enquiries and procedures which the employer made and used before deciding to dismiss".*

If the reason for dismissal is related to 'qualifications' of the employee this is taken to mean *"any degree, diploma or other academic, technical or professional qualification relevant to the position which the employee held."*

In *Blackman v. The Post Office* 1974 the employee was recruited for a particular job on an unestablished basis. A collective agreement provided that such employees' employment should only be continued if the employee passed a written aptitude test. Despite showing aptitude for the job, the employee failed the test three times. The tribunal held that either capability or qualification could be a ground relied on for a fair dismissal.

There is no doubt however that *'qualification'* has in mind matters relating to aptitude or ability so that a mere licence permit or authorisation is not such a qualification unless it is substantially concerned with the aptitude or ability of the person to do the job.

In *Tayside Regional Council v. McIntosh* 1982 the loss of a valid driving licence when the employee is contractually obliged to have one was held to be substantially connected with his ability to do the job and fair reason for dismissal.

Misconduct s.98(2)(b)

Misconduct as a reason for dismissal covers a wide range of circumstances including such matters as lateness, absenteeism, insubordination, breach of safety rules and immorality. Of course the gravity of the misconduct, and the steps taken by the employer to address it, are crucial factors in determining whether the decision to dismiss for misconduct is a reasonable one or not. Misconduct at work has been held to include:

- breach of exclusivity and trust and confidence - *Scottish Daily Record and Sunday Mail v. Laird* 1996;

- stealing from the employer - *Trust House Forte Hotels v. Murphy* 1977;

- a breach of safety instructions - *Wilcox v. Humphries & Glasgow* 1976;

- refusal to obey reasonable instructions - *Atkin v. Enfield HMC* 1975;

- immorality - *Wiseman v. Salford City Council* 1981;

- drunkenness - *Connely v. Liverpool City Council* 1974; and

- absenteeism - *Hutchinson v. Enfield Rolling Mills Ltd.* 1981.

If the misconduct of the employee is of a sufficiently serious nature it may be reasonable for the employer to dismiss the employee with immediate effect.

In *Hamilton v. Argyll & Clyde Health Board* 1993 the complainant was a chief hospital technician who was dismissed following an allegation that she had torn up a request card for a respiratory test on a patient so that the test was not carried out. Following an investigation the employer concluded that she had committed the guilty act and dismissed her for gross misconduct. The misconduct complained of, the employer believed, fell within the definition of misconduct set out in the employer's disciplinary procedure as "conduct on the part of the employee which affects the relationship between the employee and the employer to such an extent that the employee can longer reasonably be retained in employment". The finding of a fair dismissal in the tribunal was challenged on appeal on the grounds that the employer had, in response to a union request, considered the employee for employment within some other sphere within the organisation. As the employment relationship had not been destroyed by the misconduct, the misconduct could not be classified as "gross" within the definition. This argument was rejected by the EAT which upheld the tribunal's decision. *"Willingness by an employer to offer re-employment is not inconsistent with a conclusion that an employee has been guilty of gross misconduct. What is gross misconduct must be considered in relation to the particular employment and the particular employee. There is no necessary inference that because an employee has been guilty of something which falls to be regarded as gross misconduct in relation to their actual employment, they must necessarily be considered unsuitable for any employment with the employer whatsoever".*

Even misconduct outside of work could be classified under this head as the reason for dismissal, and provided the misconduct has some impact on the employee's job, the dismissal could be justified.

In *Singh v. London County Bus Service Ltd.* 1976 the applicant who drove a one-man operated bus, was convicted of dishonesty committed outside the course of his employment for which he was dismissed. The EAT held that misconduct does not have to occur in the course of work to justify a dismissal, so long as it would affect the employer when he is doing his work. For the purposes of the job, honesty was a fundamental requirement, so that an employer could fairly dismiss an employee who was found guilty of an offence of dishonesty.

In *Mathewson v. R B Wilson Dental Laboratory Ltd.* (1988) the EAT considered the case of a dental technician who was arrested and charged with being in possession of a small amount of cannabis while on his lunch break. When he returned to his place of work he informed his employers who subsequently dismissed him. The employers sought to justify their decision to dismiss on the grounds that it was not appropriate to employ someone engaged in the skilled work that he did who was using drugs. Additionally his conduct was a bad example to junior staff. The EAT held that the tribunal had not acted unreasonably in dismissing the applicant on the grounds that he had been arrested and charged with a drugs offence. On the information the employer had, particularly the admission of guilt, the decision to dismiss fell within the band of reasonable responses which a reasonable employer might have adopted.

In *P v. Nottinghamshire County Council* 1992 the complainant was dismissed from his job as assistant groundsman when he was convicted of an offence of indecent assault against his own daughter who was a pupil at the school where he worked. The Court of Appeal confirmed that the employer was entitled to take the view that the employee could not continue in employment which brought him into even casual contact with young girls.

Certainly, for private conduct to be used as the reason for dismissal it has to be of exceptional gravity and capable of damaging the employee's business.

In *Bradshaw v. Rugby Portland Cement Company* 1972 the applicant was dismissed following his conviction for incest. As the offence had no bearing on his work as a quarryman, and the relationship that he had with fellow workers had not deteriorated in any way, the tribunal held that a reasonable employer would not have dismissed in the circumstances, so that his dismissal was accordingly unfair.

If the reason for dismissal is connected with the employer's belief in the culpability of an employee, then to act reasonably the employer must have made due investigation and enquiry in order to equip himself with sufficient information to arrive at an *"honest belief"* in the employee's guilt.

In *British Home Stores Ltd. v. Burchell* 1978, Arnold J. set out a threshold test which requires that in a case of dismissal on grounds of misconduct the employers must establish three stages. (1) that they believed that the employee was guilty of the misconduct; (2) that they had reasonable grounds to sustain that belief; and (3) that they had carried out as much investigation into the matter as was reasonable in the circumstances. This test has been subsequently approved by numerous courts and tribunals and still goes to the root of the question as to whether an employer has a sound basis for the allegations of misconduct which have been made. In *Beedell v. West Ferry Printing Ltd.* 2000 the EAT approved the *Burchell* test confirming that stage one related to the reason for dismissal and the employer's belief in it and will satisfy s.98(1) or s.98(2) stages 2 and 3 relate to reasonable grounds for that belief based upon a reasonable investigation and relates to s.98(4), the test of fairness.

In *British Railways Board v. Jackson* 1994 the complainant, a buffet car steward, who had fourteen years service with British Rail, was summarily dismissed when he was discovered to have bread and bacon in his possession at the beginning of his early morning shift without a satisfactory explanation. The reason for dismissal was contravening the BR rule relating to the possession of goods for the purposes of engaging in trade or business for his own benefit. Following a disciplinary hearing the complainant was summarily dismissed for gross misconduct. Both the tribunal and the EAT felt that the employer had *"jumped the gun"* in that the complainant was challenged in the locker room and had not taken the food onto the train. This conclusion was held to be flawed by the Court of Appeal who stated that the *"question which the tribunal had to determine was whether it was reasonable for the employers to find that the employee intended, in breach of the rules, to trade for his own advantage in the goods found in his possession. It was the wrong approach to adopt a legalistic stance and ask whether technically the BR rule had been infringed and conclude: that the employer had 'jumped the gun'."* To determine whether dismissal was a reasonable response the employer was entitled to take into account:

- the prevalence of this type of conduct among stewards;

- the need to deal with it severely as a deterrent;

- the conduct of the employee in not owning up and put forward unconvincing explanations.

Despite the facts that there was no completed act of dishonesty and the complainant had a long period of service with a good record, there was no basis that the tribunal could conclude that the decision to dismiss was not a reasonable response to the misconduct.

The reasoning of the EAT in *Farrant v. The Woodville School* 1998 in a misconduct case is somewhat surprising given the requirements of equity and "substantial merits" in decision making. Here the decision of school management had been to implement a reorganisation by requiring the applicant technician to move from one department to another when he refused to move he was dismissed for gross misconduct. Subsequently it was discovered that the employer was not entitled to move the applicant under the terms of his employment contract. Nevertheless the EAT upheld the tribunal's finding of a fair dismissal and felt that the lawfulness of the instruction to move was not decisive in determining the fairness of the dismissal. A genuine of mistaken belief that the applicant was guilty of from misconduct in refusing the new work was a sufficient ground to act reasonably in dismissing him. *"Although the employers were not entitled under the terms of his contract to require the employee to work to the new job description, it was not unreasonable of them to act on the advice they received as to the lawfulness of that instruction, and that having regard to the compelling need for the reorganisation and the fact that the employee had been given ample warning of the employer's intention and ample time to discuss his concerns with them, on balance the dismissal was fair"*.

The standard of conduct required of an employer will necessarily vary with the circumstances taking account of his status and resources.

In *Ulsterbus Ltd. v. Henderson* 1989, the Northern Ireland Court of Appeal found that the tribunal had expected too much of an employer when faced with an unfair dismissal claim by a bus conductor, who had been dismissed following an allegation that he failed to issue tickets to the value of the fares he collected from the passengers. *"What the tribunal appears to be suggesting is that in certain circumstances it is incumbent on a reasonable employer to carry out a quasi-judicial investigation with a confrontation of witnesses and cross-examination of witnesses"*. Here the tribunal had merely substituted its own view of fairness for that of the employers and its finding of unfair dismissal was as a consequence overturned.

If an employee is dismissed for alleged misconduct the employer is normally obliged to investigate the circumstances and this is the case even where an employee is already under a final written warning.

> In *FMU v. Sutheran* 1993 the complainant, who has already had a final written warning, was dismissed when she became involved in a heated argument on the shop floor. The EAT held that it was wrong to dismiss her without investigating the circumstances but compensation would be reduced by 50% to reflect her contributory conduct.

There have been cases where the employer is aware that at least one of a number of employees is guilty of some act of default but even after a thorough investigation he cannot trace the culprit.

> In *Monie v. Coral Racing Ltd*. 1980 in a case involving alleged dishonesty, the employer was held to have acted fairly when he decided to dismiss both employees when only one of them may have been responsible for the guilty act.

> In *Whitbread & Company plc v. Thomas* 1988 the justifiability of so called 'blanket dismissals' was called in question. Here the employer's off licence, which was staffed by three part-time assistants had been plagued with stock losses for many years. Despite a number of formal warnings and a temporary transfer of all three staff to other shops, when they returned to work at the off-licence in question the losses continued. Without any suggestion of dishonesty the three staff were dismissed for failing to prevent the stock losses. The complaint of unfair dismissal was upheld by the industrial tribunal which felt that dismissal was not a reasonable option open to the employer. The principle relating to blanket dismissals applied in *Monie v. Coral Racing* 1980 did not apply here as the present case did not involve dishonesty. The EAT disagreed however and held that the Monie principle could apply where the reason for dismissal was capability or conduct, although such a case would be exceptional. An employer could dismiss all the members of a group where he cannot identify the individual responsible for the act when three conditions are satisfied.

> - the act must be such that if committed by an identified individual it would justify dismissal, and

> - the tribunal must be satisfied that the act was committed by one or more of the group, and

- the tribunal must be satisfied that there has been a proper investigation by the employer to identify the person or persons responsible for the act.

Here then the decision to dismiss after a thorough investigation was within the band of reasonable responses open to a reasonable employer and accordingly fair.

The approach to be adopted by tribunals in relation to *"blanket dismissals"* was further considered and refined by the EAT in *Parr v. Whitbread plc t/a Thresher Wine Merchants* 1990. The case concerned the theft of £4,600 from an off-licence where the evidence suggested that one of four employees could have been responsible, but the employer had found it impossible to discover the guilty party. All four employees were dismissed and one of them, the branch manager, presented a claim for unfair dismissal. Both the tribunal and the EAT found the dismissal to be fair. The dismissal of a group of employees in such circumstances is justified provided that the employer's beliefs at the date of dismissal are based on solid and sensible grounds and the tribunal is able to find in the evidence that:

- an act had been committed which if committed by an individual would justify dismissal,

- the employer had made a reasonable, sufficiently thorough investigation into the matter and with appropriate procedures,

- as a result of that investigation the employer reasonably believed that more than one person could have committed the act,

- the employer had acted reasonably in identifying the group of employees who could have committed the act and each member of the group was individually capable of doing so,

- as between the members of the group the employer could not reasonably identify the individual perpetrator.

Redundancy s.98(2)(c)

The employer may show that the reason for dismissal was that the employee was redundant. Essentially a redundancy situation arises when an employer closes part or all of his business operation, the purposes for which the employee was employed, or alternatively the requirements of the business for workers of a particular kind have ceased or diminished. The interpretation of the complex definition of redundancy is explored in some depth in Chapter 12 on redundancy payments. For the purposes of unfair dismissal however, not only must the dismissal be by reason of redundancy but the selection of the employee in question must also be fair.

Consequently if in a redundancy selection the employer failed to observe agreed industrial practice, this could render a decision to dismiss on grounds of redundancy unfair.

Guidance in relation to the approach to be adopted by industrial tribunals in determining the fairness of redundancy selections was provided by the Employment Appeal Tribunal in *Williams v. Compair Maxim Ltd*. 1982. Here the complainants had been dismissed for redundancy, the employer having failed to consult with the recognised trade union. Selection had been left to departmental managers, one of whom gave evidence that he had retained those employees whom he considered would be best to retain in the interests of the company in the long run. Length of service was not a factor taken into account. The industrial tribunal's finding of fair dismissal was reversed by the EAT which held the decision to be perverse. Measuring the conduct of the employer in question with that of a reasonable employer, a tribunal taken to be aware of good industrial practice, could not have reached the decision that the dismissals were fair. The employer's decision to dismiss was not within the range of conduct which a reasonable employer could have adopted in these circumstances. While accepting that it was impossible to lay down detailed procedures for a selection process, the EAT felt that reasonable employers would attempt to act in accordance with five basic principles and should depart from them only with good reason.

- As much warning as possible should be given of impending redundancies to enable the union and employees to inform themselves of the facts, seek alternative solutions and find alternative employment.

- The employer will consult with the union as to the best means of achieving the objective as fairly and with as little hardship as possible. Criteria should be agreed to be applied in selection and the selection monitored.

- The criteria agreed should not depend upon subjective opinion of the person selecting but it must be capable of objective scrutiny and include such matters as attendance record, job efficiency, experience or length of service.

- The employer must seek to ensure that the selection is made fairly in accordance with these criteria and consider union representations.

- The employer should examine the possibility of finding suitable alternative employment.

The above principles, the court held, are also reflected in the Trade Union and Labour Relations (Consolidation) Act 1992 which applies where there is a recognised Trade Union. In addition the code of practice on redundancy as an integral part of employment law should also be taken account of by an employer wishing to act fairly. Here the dismissals were carried out *"in blatant contravention of the standards of fair treatment generally accepted by fair employers"* and were consequently unfair.

The approach adopted in Compair Maxim was applied approvingly by the Northern Ireland Court of Appeal in *Robinson v. Carrickfergus Borough Council* 1983. Here a technical officer of the council had been dismissed by reason of redundancy without warning or consultation, but because there was no agreed redundancy procedure which applied to him the tribunal had decided by a majority that his dismissal was fair. This decision was reversed by the Court of Appeal who held that by applying the Compair Maxim principles the decision to dismiss was *"outside the range of conduct which a reasonable employer could have adopted"*.

Also in *Grundy (Teddington) Ltd. v. Plummer* 1983 the EAT held that in deciding to dismiss two managers for redundancy without any warning, adherence to agreed selection criteria, consultation, or seeking alternative employment prospects, the employer had failed to comply with the Compair Maxim principles of good industrial practice and consequently the decisions were unfair. The argument that the EAT in Compair Maxim should not have laid down 'guidelines' as to what would constitute reasonable conduct was rejected. Equally however, a failure to comply with one of the five principles would not necessarily make a decision to dismiss unfair, for they are dealing with what a reasonable employer would seek to do if circumstances permit.

It is not good industrial practice for an employer to abrogate his decision making in relation to redundancy selection.

In *Boulton & Paul Ltd. v. Arnold* 1994 the complaint of unfair dismissal arose from the selection of the complainant for dismissal by reason of redundancy. The selection was made by applying a number of criteria one of which was attendance and the complaint of unfairness arose from the fact that in the complainant's case no distinction had been made between authorised and unauthorised absences. When the complainant appealed against her selection for redundancy the employer offered to retain her but on terms that another employee would be dismissed in her place. The complainant rejected the offer and presented a complaint of unfair dismissal. On appeal the EAT upheld the tribunal's finding of unfair dismissal *"An offer to retain an employee under notice at the expense of another employee cannot be held to prevent a finding of unfair dismissal on the basis that the employee has had the opportunity of staying employed. It is unfair to put the onus on an employee to decide whether she or another employee is to be selected for dismissal. That is effectively an abrogation of the employer's responsibility to manage the business."*

If unfairness in the selection process is alleged then it may be necessary to obtain evidence as to how the selection criteria was applied in other cases to enable comparisons to be drawn. In *FDR v. Holloway* 1995 the complainant claimed that the selection criteria for redundancy had not been applied fairly in his case. He was one of a pool of eight employees who was selected for dismissal by reason of redundancy after applying the selection criteria. Both the tribunal and the EAT agreed that to assist his claim it was right to order discovery of documents and particulars relating to all eight employees so that comparisons could be drawn, and a determination made as to whether the criteria were applied fairly and reasonably in his case.

Certainly the need for consultation in a redundancy situation is one of the fundamentals of fairness and it is only in exceptional cases that a failure to consult can be overlooked.

So said the EAT in *Holden v. Bradville* 1985. Here the employer had argued that both the need for secrecy in a company take-over and the practical difficulties involved in interviewing and consulting up to thirty three employees selected for redundancy meant that the employer could ignore the need for consultation prior to dismissal. This argument was rejected by the EAT who held that in a redundancy situation you should presume that consultation is a prerequisite to fair selection but it was up to an industrial tribunal to decide whether in the particular circumstances of the case before it, even without consultation, the selection is nevertheless fair. This case was not one where consultation was impracticable and nor was there evidence to support the view that consultation would have made no difference to the result. *"There was at least a chance that an employee could have pointed to her good performance record, her experience and her age and seniority as factors in favour of her retention, with sufficient eloquence and force to persuade the management to take her name off the redundancy list and replace it with that of one of her colleagues".*

In *Lloyd v. Taylor Woodrow Construction Ltd.* 1999 the EAT held that a defect in the consultation process in a redundancy situation could be corrected at later appeal hearings and as a consequence the decision to dismiss in this case by reason of redundancy was a fair one.

The Court of Session in *King v. Eaton Ltd.* 1996 set out the law in relation to redundancy consultation, both with a recognised trade union and the individual employee selected. Previously the EAT had held that despite the fact that the employer had failed to carry out individual consultation, the fact that there had been extensive consultation with the unions made the decision to dismiss fair. The Court of Session disagreed and felt that the facts revealed no extensive consultation with the trade unions. Any meetings held with the unions were after the employer's proposals had been formulated and insufficient time was given to consider and respond to them. The criterion for fair and proper consultation set out by Lord Justice Glidewell in *R. v. British Coal Corporation ex parte Price* 1994 was approved. *"Fair consultation means:*

- *consultation when the proposals are still at a formative stage;*

- *adequate information on which to respond;*

- *adequate time in which to respond;*

- *conscientious consideration by an authority of a response to consultation.*

Another way of putting the point more shortly is that fair consultation involves giving the body consulted a fair and proper opportunity to understand fully the matters about which it is being consulted, and to express its views on those subjects, with the consultor thereafter considering those views properly and genuinely."

If there is no consultation between a trade union or relevant employees unless it would be futile consequential dismissals will normally be unfair. The EAT in *Mugford v. Midland Bank Ltd.* 1997 provided further guidance. The EAT stated that *"whether a reasonable employer would or would not consult with an individual employee is essentially a question of fact for the industrial jury directly itself. Individual consultation with the employee before the final decision identifying him as redundant is not a prerequisite for a fair dismissal. On the other hand the obligation to consult is not necessarily discharged if the employer consults with the union where one is recognised. Having regard to the authorities the position is as follows:*

1. *where no consultation about redundancy has taken place... the dismissal will normally be unfair unless... consultation would be futile;*

2. *consultation with the trade union over selection criteria does not of itself release the employer from considering with the employee individually him being identified for redundancy;*

3. *it will be a question whether consultation with the individual and/or his union was so inadequate as to render the dismissal unfair".*

Quite often employees are selected for redundancy on the basis of a points system based on criteria discussed with their union. In *John Brown Engineering Ltd. v. Brown* 1997 the employer argued that once a fair process for selection has been agreed upon with the union and put into practice without objection then there was no need to consult with individual employees or their representatives about the actual marks scored. Both the tribunal and EAT held that it was an unfair selection for redundancy on the basis of a point system in circumstances which individual employees had not been told of their own marks. *"Obviously individual consultation is the easiest way to assert even-handedness on the part of the employer, but we would not wish to suggest that is is necessarily required in every case. On the other hand, a policy decision to withhold all markings in a particular selection process may result in individual unfairness if no opportunity is thereafter given to the individual to know how he has been assessed. We recognise it may be invidious to publish the whole identified 'league tables', but in choosing not to do so the employer must run the risk that he is not acting fairly in respect of individual employees. It also has to be reasserted that it is no part of the industrial tribunal's role, in the context of redundancy, to examine the marking process as a matter of criteria under a microscope; nor to determine whether, intrinsically, it was properly operated. At the end of the day, the only issue is whether or not the employers treated their employees in a fair and even-handed manner."*

Employment in contravention of the law s.98(2)(d)

For the purposes of this limited category it must be shown that it would be illegal to continue to employ the employee in question. A good example is where driving is an integral part of the employee's work and he is disqualified from driving, for example *Fearn v. Tayford Motor Company Ltd.* 1975. As usual the reasonableness of the employer's decision to dismiss must be viewed in the light of the particular circumstance, not least the availability of alternative work.

> In *Gill v. Walls Meat Company Ltd.* 1971 to have continued to employ the complainant, who worked on an open meat counter would have infringed Food Regulations, for he had grown a beard. After refusing to shave it off and also an offer of alternative work, the tribunal held that the decision to dismiss was a fair one.

Some other substantial reason s.98(1)(b)

This final category of reason is used to include reasons for dismissal which do not fall neatly into the previous categories. Of course it is not every *other reason* which will be included within s.98(1) so that the dismissal in *Price v. Gourley* 1973 for a cost cutting exercise was held not to be a reason of a substantial kind to justify the dismissal for the purposes of s.98(1). Nevertheless the approach seems to be that if the employer puts forward a genuine reason, which he honestly believes to be substantial, it will fall in this category. It would be permissible for an employer to require his staff to accept change for economic considerations and this could lead to a dismissal for some other substantial reason.

> A clash of personalities in the office was held to be a substantial reason of a kind to justify dismissal in *Treganowan v. Robert Knee & Company Ltd.* 1975. Here the complainant was dismissed because the atmosphere in the office where she worked had become so hostile that it was seriously affecting the employer's business. The prime cause of the trouble was the complainant, whose constant reference to her private life seriously upset her colleagues who felt that they could not work with her.

If the reason for dismissal is related to unacceptable periods of absence because of illness then s.98(1) may be relied on as the reason for dismissal.

> In *Wharfedale Loudspeakers Ltd. v. Poynton* 1993 the complainant was eventually dismissed after having been given three written warnings in relation to her long periods of absence due to genuine illness. The EAT held that in these circumstances some other substantial reason could be relied on as the reason for dismissal which was potentially fair.

Certainly the refusal of an employee to accept an alteration in terms of employment has been held to fall within this category. *In St. John of God (Care Services) Ltd. v. Brooks* 1992 (considered in Chapter 7) the EAT held that a reorganisation in a hospital which involved offering staff less favourable terms of employment fell within the category of some other substantial reason for dismissal when some staff were dismissed for failing to accept changes in their contracts of employment.

> In *Ellis v. Brighton Cooperative Society* 1976 the applicant was dismissed for refusing to accept a new working system following a reorganisation. The EAT held that *"where there has been a properly consulted-upon reorganisation which, if it is not done, is going to bring the whole business to a standstill, a failure to go along with the new arrangements may constitute "some other substantial reason"*. Here the employer had acted reasonably in requiring that all the staff should co-operate with the change in working methods.

If an employee is employed under a fixed term contract which expires then under s.95 this will constitute a dismissal for the purposes of the Act. A complaint of unfair dismissal could be made if such an employee is unfairly rejected when applying for a new post involving broadly similar duties. In such circumstances it would be wrong to limit the application of s.98(4) to the act of dismissal but rather the fairness of the decision not to select for the new job should also be judged.

In *Oakley v. The Labour Party* 1988 the complainant was told that when her fixed term contract expired it would not be renewed and that following a re-organisation she could apply for a new post, which involved a broadly similar job. She complained of unfair dismissal when she was not selected for the new post. The Court of Appeal held that her interview for the new job was no more than a charade, for the employer had clearly decided beforehand that she should not be appointed. Restructuring was merely a pretext to get rid of the complainant so, inevitably, the employer's conduct was unreasonable and unfair.

If the substantial reason for dismissal relied upon is an economic one then the employer must be able to establish financial difficulties at the time of dismissal. Poor trading conditions were used as a reason for withdrawing the staff christmas bonus in *Selfridge Ltd. v. Wayne and Others* 1995. Of the 1500 staff affected all but 50 accepted the withdrawal of the bonus and they were given three months notice of termination of employment with the offer of new contracts without the bonus when the notice expired. The EAT held that dismissals in these circumstances were unfair for when the notice was given the fact that the majority of staff had accepted the change meant that the risk of financial difficulties had been alleviated so there was no substantial reason for dismissal.

In rare cases the pressure on an employer to dismiss an employee comes from some third party source such as a trade union, customers or clients and even fellow employees. They may claim that the employee has been guilty of some objectionable conduct, that there is an insoluble personality conflict, or that the reason for the pressure is based upon some rational or irrational fear of HIV contagion. In this type of case the employer could rely on some other substantial reason as the reason for dismissal. The issue of fairness of a dismissal in these circumstances will depend largely on the conduct of the employer who should have made practical and genuine efforts to resolve the conflict. The circumstances should be investigated and there should be consultation with the parties concerned with a view to reaching a solution. The employers should consider solutions other than dismissal, for instance, a relocation of work. Dismissal under third party pressure is only fair if after investigation there is a valid and serious complaint or the goodwill of a third party is so important that dismissal is the only sensible commercial decision.

In *Courtaulds Northern Spinning Ltd. v. Sibson* 1988 the third party pressure came from the Transport and General Workers Union who wanted the complainant an HGV driver dismissed, or moved to another depot, when he left the union. The complainant refused the employer's instruction to move to another depot a mile away and resigned, claiming a constructive dismissal which was unfair. Both the tribunal and the EAT found that there was unfair dismissal but the Court of Appeal disagreed deciding that the employer had an implied right to move the complainant from one depot to another, within reasonable commuting distance, and the reason for the move was irrelevant. Accordingly there was no breach of contract by the employer and therefore no constructive dismissal.

A decision to dismiss based purely on economic considerations could constitute *some other substantial reason* and fall within the band of reasonable responses of a reasonable employer.

In *Saunders v. Scottish National Camps* 1980 the complainant, a handyman employed at a children's holiday camp, was dismissed when the employer discovered that he was a homosexual. The reason for dismissal was that the employee indulged in homosexuality and it was unsuitable to employ someone of that tendency in children's camps. Both the industrial tribunal and the EAT found the dismissal to be fair. They decided that a large proportion of employers in this situation would perceive that the employment of a homosexual should be restricted where there is close contact with children. This is despite the fact that such a view may not be rational or supported by evidence which is scientifically sound. There is no doubt however that the continued employment could have proved to be an economic liability for the employer, bearing in mind the views of certain parents.

Procedural Fairness

In addition to determining fairness in relation to the reasons relied upon, the process of determining the reasonableness of the employer's decision to dismiss necessarily involves a consideration of the procedure implemented by the employer in relation to the dismissal. There exists a Code of Practice drawn up by ACAS on *"Disciplinary Practice and Procedures in Employment"*. The Code provides that employees should be fully informed of disciplinary rules and procedures and the likely consequences if the rules are broken. Also the Code identifies the essential features of a disciplinary procedure so that in cases of misconduct, at some point, the employee should be given the opportunity of putting his side of the case accompanied by a representative from a trade union or otherwise. The procedure should have built in a process involving formal and informal, oral and written, first and final warnings. In *Lock v. Cardiff Rail* 1998 the EAT held that the employer's decision to dismiss for a one off act of misconduct was perverse bearing in mind the employer's failure to implement the ACAS Code. The Code forms the basis on which the employee's conduct should be judged. The graver the misconduct the less requirement there would be to implement a system of warnings. Also, where warnings are given for less serious matters they should be recorded but then after a period of satisfactory conduct eventually disregarded. If a dismissal occurs because of the breach of a final written warning the warning must be in force for the employer to place reliance on it.

In *Bevan Ashford v. Malin* 1995 the complainant had been issued with a final
written warning about his work on the 29th January 1992. The warning was to
remain in force for 12 months *"from the date of this letter"* and stated that any
reoccurrence of the behaviour in question would be grounds for dismissal. On
the 29th January 1993 a further behavioural problem arose and at a
disciplinary hearing on the 3rd of February a decision was taken to dismiss
the complainant on the basis that the final written warning was still in force.
This interpretation of the warning the tribunal and EAT believed to be
incorrect. The warning had *"come into effect on 29th January 1992, had
expired at midnight on 28th January 1993 and, accordingly, was not in force
on 29th January 1993 when the incident which led to the dismissal occurred."*

A second source of procedural standards is the increasing tendency of tribunals to
require that the process of dismissal adheres to the rules of natural justice developed
and refined in administrative law.

The need to comply strictly with disciplinary procedures to justify a dismissal as fair
was a feature of the approach of tribunals to reasonableness in the 1970s but by the
end of the decade there was a change in approach.

In *British Labour Pump v. Byrne* 1979 the EAT formulated *the "no difference
principle"* under which procedural defects could be overlooked. If, despite the
non-compliance with a disciplinary procedure, the employer could show that,
on the balance of probabilities, the same course would have been adopted, the
tribunal was entitled to find the decision to dismiss a fair one. The *"no
difference principle"* was subsequently approved by the Court of Appeal in W
& J Wass Ltd. v. Binns 1982.

A change in attitude was expressed by the House of Lords in the important
case of *Polkey v. A E Dayton Services Ltd.* 1987. Here, both of the previous
cases and the 'no difference principle' were overruled. The basic facts of the
case were that the complainant, a van driver, employed by the defendants for
over four years, was without warning or consultation, handed a letter of
redundancy. His claim of unfair dismissal was based on the employer's failure
to observe the statutory code of practice which provides for warning and
consultation in a redundancy situation. Despite there being *a "heartless
disregard"* of the code, the tribunal, EAT and the Court of Appeal all found
that the dismissal was fair. Applying the *"no difference principle"*, if a fair
procedure had been adopted, the employer could still have reasonably decided
to dismiss. This approach was rejected by the House of lords who held that
the employer's decision to dismiss had to be judged by applying the wording
of the test of reasonableness. There was no scope for deciding what the
employer might have done had he adopted a different procedure. Where the
employer fails to observe the code, he will only be acting fairly if the tribunal

is satisfied that *"the employer could reasonably have concluded in the light of circumstances known at the time of dismissal that consultation or warning would be utterly useless"*.

The House of Lords held in Polkey therefore that a failure to follow an agreed procedure in dismissing an employee is likely to result in a finding of unfair dismissal. This is subject to the exception where it is obvious that use of the proper procedure would be futile. The Court of Appeal has recently provided guidance as to when as employer can rely on this exception.

In *Duffy v. Yeomans & Partners Ltd*. 1994 the Court of Appeal held that to come within the Polkey exception there was no need for an employer to have actually considered and rejected the possibility of going through a consultative process required by a disciplinary procedure. Rather the test is an objective one, for the industrial tribunal must ask itself whether an employer acting reasonably could have failed to consult in the circumstances.

It is now established that in assessing the fairness of the employers decision to dismiss or otherwise it is necessary to consider whether the disciplinary code was fully adhered to.

In *Stoker v. Lancashire County Council* 1992 the complainant was employed by the County Council as a laboratory technician at a Polytechnic. His contract of employment incorporated the college's two stage disciplinary procedure involving a hearing and then a possible appeal but in addition he was also entitled to have any decision reached confirmed by a committee of the Council with the possibility of further appeal. A decision to dismiss the complainant because of misconduct was taken following a disciplinary hearing and appeal and this decision was subsequently ratified by the Council disciplinary sub-committee and appeals sub-committee. Rather than allowing a full rehearing of the case as provided for in the disciplinary procedure the Council sub-committee confined itself to a renew of the 'sentence' after hearing from both sides. Both the tribunal and Appeal Tribunal felt that this short-cut was permissible in the circumstances given the fact that the complainant *"had been afforded every reasonable opportunity, and indeed much more than that, both to state his own case and challenge that of the respondents"*. The Court of Appeal disagreed however and felt that the industrial tribunal had *"misinterpreted the contractual disciplinary procedures"*. As the disciplinary procedure required a full rehearing at the two external stages this should have been complied with. *"A reasonable employer can be expected to comply with the full requirements of the appeal procedure in its own disciplinary code"*.

The contemporary view seems to be that even in a case involving a procedural flaw the decision to dismiss an employee may still be regarded as fair and reasonable.

Hussain v. Elonex plc 1999 concerned the dismissal of a computer engineer for allegedly head-butting another employee. Witness statements which had been taken were not disclosed to the complainant at the disciplinary hearing. Both the tribunal and the EAT took the view that the complainant was aware of what he was being accused of and the reasonable investigation and fair procedure adopted made the decision to dismiss a fair one. The Court of Appeal agreed that despite the procedural flaw there was no failure of natural justice because the complainant was aware of the case against him and given a full opportunity to respond to it.

Support for the view that a less stringent approach to procedural requirements is provided by the decision of the EAT in *Lloyd v. Taylor Woodrow Construction* 1999. Here a redundancy decision had been taken in relation to the applicant which was flawed in the sense that ad hoc selection criterion had been used. On internal appeal however the selection criterion were identified and the applicant was given the chance to contest them and then again on further appeal. Despite the failure in the original decision to consult over selection criterion the tribunal rejected the complaint of unfair dismissal. The tribunal and later the EAT confirmed that the defect in procedure had been corrected at later appeal hearings so that the decision to dismiss was fair. *"The general principle that a procedural defect at the dismissal stage maybe cured at the appeal stage, provided that the appeal represents a rehearing and not merely a review of the original decision applies to a failure to consult in the context of a redundancy dismissal"*. The EAT also said that potential for correcting a procedural defect by means of a rehearing also applies to any of the potentially fair reasons for dismissal under s.98.

The need for employers to comply strictly with disciplinary codes has been emphasised.

In *Cobaj v. Westminster City Council* 1996 following the dismissal of a senior computer programmer for poor attendance, the appeal tribunal which considered his appeal against the decision to dismiss, was attended by the Chief Executive of the council and two members, rather than three members required by the disciplinary code. The EAT disagreed with the tribunal and found that this significant error rendered the dismissal unfair. The EAT stated that *"where an employee has a contractual right to have an appeal against dismissal heard and decided by an appeals panel constituted in a particular way, as a matter of law a defect in the composition of such a body is a significant contractual and jurisdictional failure, not simply a matter of procedural error"*. On further appeal the Court of Appeal agreed that in this case there was a contractual right to an appeal tribunal consisting of three members. However the failure to provide such an appeal was not sufficient to make the decision to dismiss a necessarily unfair one. *"Failure by an employer to observe its own contractually enforceable disciplinary procedure does not inevitably require an industrial tribunal to conclude that a dismissal was unfair. The question which the industrial tribunal has to determine under the legislation is not whether the employer acted reasonably in dismissing the employee, but whether the employer acted reasonably or unreasonably in treating the reason shown as a sufficient reason for dismissal. The relevance to that question of failure to entertain an appeal to which the employee was contractually entitled, as Lord Bridge pointed out in West Midlands Co-operative Society v. Tipton, is whether the employee was "thereby" denied the opportunity of showing that the real reason for dismissal was not sufficient. As Lord Mackay and Lord Bridge indicated in Polkey v. A E Dayton Services Ltd, it is also relevant to consider whether the employer acted reasonably if he actually considered or a reasonable employer would have considered at the time of dismissal that to follow the agreed procedure would in the circumstances of the case be futile."*

In *Securicor Guarding Ltd. v. R* 1994 the complainant was dismissed from his post as a security guard with an important customer when his employer discovered that he had been charged with sex offences against children. The decision to dismiss was reached after holding a disciplinary hearing. The employer concluded that the reputation of the business could suffer if they continued to employ the complainant. Both the tribunal and the EAT found the dismissal to be unfair. The EAT held that the tribunal *"was entitled to find that although the employers were unable to carry out any inquiries into the truth of the allegations, before deciding how to deal with the employee, any reasonable employer would have enquired of the customer concerned to see what they thought of the situation and what they wished to be done. The mere fact that an employee in a sensitive position has been charged with an offence will not justify the employer in dismissing him rather than suspending him or moving him away from the sensitive position until the truth of the matter is determined."*

Even if the employer invokes the appropriate disciplinary procedure leading to a dismissal it must be implemented fairly and in accordance with the rules of natural justice.

In *Spink v. Express Foods Group Ltd.* 1990 prior to the dismissal of the complainant sales representative the employer had taken disciplinary proceedings against him which involved holding a disciplinary inquiry. The fact that the employer deliberately decided not to reveal the purpose of the inquiry to the complainant and the allegations against him made the proceedings and the decision to dismiss unfair. The EAT held that *"it is a fundamental part of a fair disciplinary procedure that an employee knows the case against him. Fairness requires that someone accused should know the case to be met; should hear or be told the important parts of the evidence in support of the case; should have an opportunity to criticise or dispute that evidence and adduce his own evidence and argue his case."*

Furthermore in *Louies v. Coventry Hood and Sealing Co. Ltd.* 1990 the complainants dismissal for alleged theft was found by the EAT to be unfair on the grounds that employer's belief in his guilt was based largely on the statement of two witnesses and the complainant was denied access to those documents throughout the disciplinary proceedings. *"Where the essence of the case against an employee is contained in written statement by witnesses, it is contrary to the rules of natural justice and prima facie unfair for an employer to refuse to let the employee see these statements".*

In cases of misconduct an industrial tribunal should still be guided by *British Home Stores Ltd. v. Burchell* 1978 which provides that an employer is required to show a genuine belief in the misconduct with reasonable evidence upon which to formulate that belief. This will normally involve adherence to a reasonable investigation and a process which gives the employee an opportunity, in accordance with the rules of natural justice, to put his side of the case. It is only in rare cases, where perhaps the complainant is *"caught red handed"* that there is no need to adhere to procedures.

In *Sutherland v. Sonat Offshore (UK) Inc.* 1993 the complainant's misconduct of testing positive for drugs while working on an oil rig was held by the EAT to be of such a nature that he could be fairly dismissed without the need for a disciplinary hearing. The procedures adopted by the testing company were *"as near fail-safe as was humanly possible"*.

In *P v. Nottinghamshire County Council* 1992 the complainant, a school groundsman, was dismissed by the respondents after he had been convicted of an offence of indecent assault against his daughter, a pupil at the school at which he worked. On his dismissal the complainant was paid wages in lieu of twelve weeks notice and told that an attempt would be made to redeploy him in other council work but that proved to be unsuccessful. The tribunal decided that because insufficient time had been spent on investigating the circumstances of his offences and the possibility of alternative work before the decision to dismiss was reached, it was an unfair decision. The EAT and then the Court of Appeal reversed this decision as perverse on appeal. In relation to alternative work the Court of Appeal held that *"in an appropriate case, and where the size and administrative resources of the employer's undertaking permit it may be unfair first considering whether the employee can be offered some other job notwithstanding that it may be clear that he cannot be allowed to continue in his original job. There is nothing in the section to suggest that the question of alternative employment must be investigated before the giving of notice to dismiss".* As far as investigating the circumstances of the offence is concerned the Court stated that *"when an employee has pleaded guilty to an offence or has been found guilty by the decision of a Court or the verdict of a jury it is reasonable for an employer to believe that the offence has been committed by the employee. Any other conclusion would be ridiculous".*

The effect of an unjustifiable delay in carrying out disciplinary proceedings could make a decision to dismiss unfair which would otherwise have been held to be fair. This would be the case even where it is shown that the complainant suffered no prejudice as a result of the delay.

This was the decision of the EAT *in The Royal Society for the Prevent of Cruelty to Animals v. Cruden* 1986. Despite the gravity of the complainant's gross misjudgment and idleness, in this case the protracted delay in implementing disciplinary proceedings against him rendered the decision to dismiss unfair. The Act *"is concerned with whether the employer had acted fairly and not whether the employee had suffered an injustice."* In an attempt to do justice in the case however the EAT reduced both the basic award and the compensatory award to nil to reflect the complainant's grave neglect and the fact that the employer would be failing in his duty if he failed to dismiss in these circumstances.

In *Slater v. Leicestershire Health Authority* 1989 the Court of Appeal held that the fact that a manager had carried out a preliminary investigation of the applicant's misconduct and had then conducted a disciplinary hearing leading to a decision to dismiss did not of itself render the dismissal unfair. While a breach of the rules of natural justice is clearly a matter to take account in determining reasonableness, it is possible for the same person to conduct an investigation and still carry out a fair inquiry.

Automatic Unfair Dismissal

Under the Employment Rights Act 1996 certain reasons for dismissal are classified as inadmissible and automatically unfair and under s.108(3) there is no qualifying period of continuous employment. In recent years there has been a steady increase in the number of categories of automatically unfair dismissal. They are dismissals where the reason is connected with

* pregnancy or childbirth s.99(1)

* health and safety s.100(1)

- trade union activities TULR(C) A

- the assertion of a statutory right s.104(1)

- making a protected disclosure

- non compliance with the Working Time Regulations s.101A

- non compliance with the National Minimum Wage s.104A

- participation in official industrial action s.238A(2)

- for a reason connected with a business transfer TUPE Reg 8 TULR(C)A.

To each of these cases the onus is on the complainant to establish the reason for dismissal with the inadmissible category and is therefore automatically unfair.

Dismissal on the grounds of pregnancy or childbirth

It is automatically unfair to dismiss an employee because she is pregnant or has given birth or has taken maternity leave. This is contained in s.99 of the Employment Rights Act 1996 and it applies regardless of the length of service. A decision to dismiss by reason of pregnancy therefore will also constitute direct discrimination and given that the maximum level of compensation has been removed in sex discrimination cases it could provide a more significant remedy than unfair dismissal. The law relating to pregnancy dismissals is examined in Chapter 6 on Equal Opportunities at the Workplace.

Dismissal in connection with union activities

For dismissals in relation to trade union activities there is no requirement for the complainant to show continuous employment to qualify to present a claim or be within the prescribed age limits.

Under s.152 of the Trade Union and Labour Relations (Consolidation) Act 1992 a dismissal shall be regarded as unfair if the reason for it was that the employee:

(a) was, or proposed to become, a member of an independent trade union, or

(b) had taken part, or proposed to take part, in the activities of an independent trade union at an appropriate time, or

(c)   *was not a member of any trade union, or of a particular trade union, or of one of a number of particular trade unions, or had refused or proposed to refuse to become or remain a member.*

Previously a dismissal for non-membership of a trade union could, in certain circumstances, be fair if it was to prevent the contravention of a closed shop agreement supported by a ballot. Following the Employment Act 1988, all dismissals for non-membership of a trade union are automatically unfair irrespective of whether there is a closed shop agreement. Section 152 then is concerned with dismissals connected with membership or non-membership of trade union or for taking part in trade union activities. For claims based on membership, the union in question must be independent and so not under the control or domination of an employer or a group of employers. A certificate of independence may have been issued by the Certification Officer.

Discount Tobacco and Confectionery Ltd. v. Armitage 1990 provides a good example of how the section may be applied in practice. Here the complainant was a shop manageress who, having enlisted the help of her union official to secure a written contract of employment from her employer, was determined to raise a number of discrepancies between the written terms and those originally proposed to her. Not wishing to engage in such a dialogue the employer dismissed her giving the reason as lack of suitability or capability. The employer claimed that she had been dismissed because of her trade union membership, so that despite the fact that she only had a short period of continuous employment with the company, she was entitled to claim unfair dismissal. The industrial tribunal upheld her complaint and she was awarded compensation. On appeal the EAT upheld the decision confirming that the section was applicable when an employee is dismissed for making use of her union membership to confirm the terms and conditions of her employment. *"For the purpose of the section there is no genuine distinction between membership of a union on the one hand and making use of the essential services of a union officer on the other. The activity of a trade union officer in elucidating and negotiating terms of employment is an important incident of union membership and the outward and visible manifestation of it. To construe the section so narrowly as to apply only to the fact that a person was a member of the union without regard to the consequences of that membership would be to emasculate the provision altogether.*

In *Overprint Ltd. v. Malcolm* 1992 the complainant employee having joined a trade union was required by his employer to sign a written contract of employment. After taking union advice he refused to do so and was promptly dismissed. He alleged that his dismissal was automatically unfair by virtue of s.152 TULR(C)A 1992. The tribunal found the reason for dismissal was not the complainant's membership of the union but rather the fact that as a consequence of his membership he might make demands on the employer. Applying *Discount Tobacco* (above) the tribunal held that the dismissal was automatically unfair under s.152 and ordered his reinstatement. The EAT agreed deciding that there was no requirement for the tribunal to find any substance to the employer's apprehensions about union membership for s.152 to apply. Even if the consequences of membership were nothing more than considerations operating in the mind of the person who decided to dismiss, the reason for dismissal remained union membership.

The EAT in *Dundon v. GPT Ltd.* 1995 made it clear that for s.152 to apply an employer does not have to be motivated by malice or be shown to have deliberately intended to get rid of a trade union activist.

For claims based on 'union activities' carried on at an *'appropriate time'*, further guidance is needed to determine whether a dismissal falls within this category. The Act deals with the question of *'appropriate time'* by limiting it to a time outside working hours or within working hours with the employer's consent.

> In *Marley Tile v. Shaw* 1980, the Court of Appeal confirmed that in a proper case the consent of an employer to trade union activities could be implied. Here however, where a union meeting was held without express permission, causing more than *"a mere trifling inconvenience"*, to the employer's business, it was not carried out at an *"appropriate time"*, for it was carried out during working hours and was not in accordance with arrangements made or consent given.

The expression *'union activities'* is not defined in the Act and so we must rely exclusively on case-law to provide us with guidance.

> In *Brennan v. Ellward* 1976 it was held that to determine trade union activities it is necessary to summarise all the acts and facts relied on a constituting *"activities"* including as an element whether any employee involved is a representative or not, and then decide as a matter of common sense whether such acts constitute activities of an independent trade union.

> In *Bass Taverns v. Burgess* 1995 the complainant shop steward was dismissed from the trainer manager part of his job following a presentation he made at an induction course for trainee managers. The employer's contention that the presentation was biased ultimately led to the complainant's resignation and complaint of unfair constructive dismissal. Disagreeing with the tribunal the EAT and subsequently the Court of Appeal held that at the time of dismissal the applicant was taking part in trade union activities at an appropriate time and so under s.152 this meant that the dismissal was automatically unfair. The Court of Appeal made the point that the employer had consented to the

meeting being used on a recruitment forum and that consent could not be subject to an implied limitation that the union recruiter would not criticise the company *"A consent to recruitment must include a consent to underline the services which the union can provide and that may reasonably involve a submission to prospective members that in some respects the union will provide a service which the company does not."*

It seems that distributing union material, recruiting and advising members and attending meetings are all types of conduct which could be described as trade union *activities*.

The section confers protection on an employee who is proposing to take part in union activities and dismissed as a result.

In *Fitzpatrick v. British Railways Board* 1991 an employee with a reputation as a union activist was dismissed because it was felt she would be a disruptive influence. This dismissal was unfair as contrary to the section. This case is considered in more depth in Chapter 5.

Dismissal in connection with health and safety

Under s.100(1) of the Employment Rights Act 1996 all employees, irrespective of hours and service have the right not to be dismissed or subjected to any detriment for engaging in activities such as:

(a)   acting as a safety representative;

(b)   bringing a health and safety matter to the employer's attention where the employee reasonably believed there was potential harm;

(c)   carrying out designated activities in connection with preventing or reducing risks to health and safety;

(d)   leaving or refusing to return to the place of work because of a reasonable belief in a serious or imminent danger;

(e)   in circumstances of danger taking steps to protect himself or other persons from danger.

This section emphasises the significance of health and safety at the workplace so that if an employee is dismissed for raising safety issues, or complaining about safety equipment or the working environment the dismissal should be automatically unfair. The limit on the compensatory award for this type of dismissal was removed by the

Employment Relations Act 1999. Two contemporary examples of a liberal interpretation of s.100 dismissals are shown below.

In *Masiak v. City Restaurants (UK) Ltd.* 1999 the complainant chef who had worked for his employers for just over a month, left the premises after refusing to cook food which he considered was a potential hazard to public health. In a complaint of unfair dismissal the chef relied on s.100(1)(e) but this was rejected by the tribunal who felt that the expression *'other persons'* in the section referred exclusively to work colleagues rather than members of the public. On appeal however the EAT disagreed and held the expression 'other persons' in s.100(1)(e) extends to protection of members of the public from danger. The complainant was also entitled to damages for breach of his common law right to reasonable notice an implied term in every contract of employment.

In *Harvest Press Ltd. v. McCaffery* 1999 the complainant was a machine minder who walked out of his workplace after less than three months service because of the abusive behaviour of a work colleague. When he failed to obtain assurance about his safety the complainant claimed unfair dismissal relying on s.100(1)(d). The question faced by the EAT was whether the expression *'in circumstances of danger'* which the employee believed to be imminent, was restricted to dangers generated by the workplace. The EAT held that the word danger was intended to cover any circumstances and would cover abusive behaviour of fellow employees.

Dismissal in connection with statutory rights

Under s.104 of the 1996 Act it is automatically unfair to dismiss an employee for alleging that the employer had infringed a statutory right or for bringing proceedings to enforce such a right. Once again employees are entitled to make a complaint regardless of their length of service

In *Mennell v. Newell & Wright (Transport Contractors) Ltd.* 1996 the complainant Mr Mennell an HGV driver, refused to sign a new contract of employment because one of the clauses in the draft contract provided that the employers would recover certain training costs by way of a deduction from payment of final salary due to the employee on termination of employment. He maintained that any such deduction from his wages would amount to a breach of the Wages Act. Eventually Mr Mennell was dismissed and he claimed that he had been dismissed for asserting a statutory right. The industrial tribunal, accepted the employers argument that because no deduction had in fact been made from Mr Mennell's wages, there had been no infringement of any right under the Wages Act in respect of which a complaint could be made to an industrial tribunal and, therefore, no infringement of a relevant statutory right. The Employment Appeal Tribunal held that the industrial tribunal had wrongly interpreted the section. *"A threat of dismissal in order to impose a variation of the contract of employment so as to enable the employer to make deductions from wages may amount to an infringement, at the time the threat is made, of the employee's statutory right under the Wages Act not to have deductions made from wages without his freely given written consent."*

In *Lopez v. Maison Bouquillon Ltd* 1996 the complainant, a counter assistant in a cake shop, left her workplace and complained to the police that she had been assaulted by the chef who was married to the shop manageress. Subsequently the complainant was told by her employer that she no longer worked for the company. Claiming unfair dismissal she said that the reason she was dismissed was that she left the workplace, but in the circumstances that was perfectly reasonable, given the assault. The tribunal found that the dismissal was unfair. In this type of scenario a complainant who can show that a dismissal is related to the fact that she raised health and safety issues or had taken appropriate steps to protect herself from imminent danger can rely on section 100(1) ERA 1996. A dismissal in these circumstances is automatically unfair and no qualifying period of employment is required.

Dismissal for making a protected disclosure under s.103A. An employee is protected if dismissed for making a protected disclosure under the Public Interest Disclosure Act 1998. (See Chapter 9) The Employment Relations Act 1999 removed the limit on the compensatory award for this type of dismissal and in July 2000 an applicant was awarded £200,000.

Dismissal for non compliance with the working time regulations. Section 101A protects employees who are dismissed for refusing to accept a requirement imposed by the employer in contravention of the Working Time Regulations 1998. (See Chapter 9)

Dismissal for non compliance with minimum wage. Section 104A is designed to protect employees who are dismissed in connection with taking action to secure the national minimum wage under the 1998 Act. (See Chapter 9)

Dismissal for participating in official industrial action. A dismissal in these circumstances is considered under the heading Unfair Dismissal and Industrial Action later in the chapter.

Dismissal for a reason connected with a business transfer. Such a dismissal is automatically unfair under the Transfer of Undertaking (Protection of Employment) Regulations 1981 reg 8 and considered next

Dismissal in connection with business transfer

The Transfer of Undertakings (Protection of Employment) Regulations 1981 provides some degree of protection to employees who are dismissed on the transfer of a business undertaking. Under the regulations it is provided that the dismissal of an employee before or after a relevant transfer is to be regarded as unfair if the reason is connected with the transfer. The dismissal is prima facie fair however, under reg 8(2), if it is for an *'economic, technical or organisational reason'* entailing change in the workforce and so regarded as *'some other substantial reason'* for the purpose of s.98(1). If the decision to dismiss is regarded as reasonable it is fair.

Guidance in relation to the interpretation of economic, technical or organisational reason was provided by the EAT in *Wheeler v. Patel & J. Golding Group of Companies* 1987. Here the unfair dismissal claim by a sales assistant against the purchaser of the shop where she worked was rejected because she had been dismissed before the contractual date set for completion of the sale. In relation to the phrase an *"economic reason"* for dismissal the EAT felt that like technical or organisational reasons *"it must be a reason which relates to the conduct of the business"*. A desire to obtain an enhanced price for the business or to achieve a sale is not a reason relating to the conduct of the business. This limited meaning given to the *phrase "economic reason"* reflects the fact that if a broad literal interpretation were given to it, the majority of dismissals by transfers in such circumstances would be regarded as for an *"economic reason"*. Here the dismissal, in order to comply with the requirement of an intending purchaser, was not for *an "economic reason"*, for it did not relate to the conduct of the business, rather the vendor's desire to sell. As the vendor had not shown that the dismissal was for an economic technical or organisational reason, the unfair dismissal claim against the vendor was upheld.

The Court of Appeal in *Whitehouse v. Chas A Blatchford & Sons* 1999 agreed with the EAT in *Wheeler* above and found that the words *"economic, technical or organisational reason entailing changes in the workforce"* clearly means that the reason must be connected with the future conduct of the business as a going concern. Here the transferee business needed to reduce the number of technicians to secure the award of a contract as so the complaints dismissal could be categorised as for an economic or organisational reason within the meaning of reg 8(2) end the employee had a defence to the complaint.

A dismissal caused by or connected with the transfer of a business for the purpose of the regulations will be fair if the reason for dismissal is an *"organisational one"* entailing changes in the workforce.

The changes imposed upon the complainant in *Crawford v. Swinton Insurance Brokers* 1990 on the transfer of business were held to be so radical that when she resigned as a result of them she could regard herself as constructively dismissed. From a clerk/typist who worked mainly at home, she was offered other work, with the changed function of selling insurance. The tribunal further held however that the changes imposed were dictated by the new employer's organisational requirements, and to offer new standard conditions to existing staff was a *"change of the workforce"* for the purpose of the regulations . Such a finding was approved by the EAT which held that there can be a *"change in the workforce"* if the same people are kept on but given different jobs. In the case of a constructive dismissal following an organisational change however, it is the tribunal's function to *"identify the principal reason for the conduct of the employer which entitled the employee to terminate the contract and then determine whether the reason is an economic, technical or organisational one entailing changes in the workforce"*.

An important transformation of the law relating to liability for dismissals on a business transfer was brought about by the House of Lords' decision in *Lister v. Forth Dry Dock and Engineering Company Ltd.* 1989. Here the Lords held that liability for a dismissal by the vendor prior to the transfer, will pass to the purchaser, if the employee has been unfairly dismissed for a reason connected with the transfer. In order to give effect to the EEC Employee Rights on Transfer of Business Directive, Regulation 5(3) which provides that liability is to be transferred only where the employee is *"employed immediately before the transfer"* is to have the words added *"or would have been so employed if he had not been dismissed"* in the circumstances described in the regulation. The effect of this change is that an employee who is dismissed solely because of a transfer is automatically passed to the transferee but if the employee is dismissed for an economic, technical or organisational reason then liability will not pass unless the employee was still employed at the time of transfer. Without such an interpretation, employees in cases like this would be left with *"worthless claims for unfair dismissal"* against an insolvent employer.

In cases where there is a relevant transfer for the purposes of regulations and a dismissal before the transfer by the transferor it was thought that under regulation

5(2) the act of dismissal was deemed to have been done by the transferee who would be responsible for the dismissal.

> In *Allen v. Stirling DC* 1994 the EAT indicated that regulation 5(2) while imposing liability on the transferee does not necessarily remove it from the transferor. The EAT held that *"there are no words which can be said to exclude the transferor's liability apart from the word 'transferred' itself and some addition or qualification such as the word 'instead' or an equivalent had to be added to that word for liability to go to the transferee instead of the transferor".*

Further guidance as to the operation of regulations 8 and 5 was provided by the EAT in *Kerry Food Ltd. v. Creber* 2000. The applicant's employer went into receivership and eventually the business was purchased by Kerry Food Ltd. who acquired the company's brand name and goodwill. None of the remaining staff were employed by Kerry but applying the Court of Appeal's decision in *Elm (Vehicle Delivery Service) v. Cox* 2000 the EAT nevertheless held that a transfer had occurred, the employment of staff being only one of the relevant factors to take account of. Further guidance provided by the EAT included:

- any dismissal by a transferor due to an impending transfer is automatically unfair and the employee should proceed against the transferee. Issues about economic, technical or organisational reasons(ETO) do not arise if the transfer was the principal reason for the dismissal;

- if the main reason for the dismissal by the transferor is an ETO reason the employee can claim unfair dismissal against the transferor;

- if the transferee dismisses the employee he can claim automatic unfair dismissal against the transferee if the dismissal was connected with the transfer or unfair dismissal against the transferee for an (ETO) reason.

Newly inserted Arts 5(4A) and 5(4B) of the TUPE regulations effectively remove unfair dismissal rights from an employee who would normally have his contract transferred to a new owner and objects to becoming employed by the transferee. The transfer will terminate his employment with the transferor and such termination cannot be regarded as a dismissal.

The Trade Union Reform and Employment Rights Act 1993 amended the transfer regulations so that they apply to all relevant transfers rather than simply where the undertaking is *"in the nature of a commercial venture"* (see Chapter 9).

Unfair Dismissal and Industrial Action

If an employee is dismissed while taking part in industrial action such as a strike, work to rule, go slow or even an overtime ban which may not be even a breach of contract, the law provides limited protection. Following recommendations in the Fairness at Work White Paper published in May 1998 and the consultation that followed it, the government took the view that employees who are dismissed for taking part in lawfully organised official industrial action should have the right to complain of unfair dismissal to a tribunal. Under s.16 and Schedule 5 of the Employment Relations Act 1999 it is automatically unfair to dismiss employees for the first eight weeks of their participation in official and "protected" industrial action and this right is inserted as s.238A of the Trade Union and Labour Relations (Consolidation) Act 1992. This important statutory right must be viewed in the light of existing provision of TULR(C)A 1992 which are still relevant and can still remove tribunal jurisdiction in relation to unfair dismissal during industrial action. An important distinction is drawn between official and unofficial industrial action. Official action must have been lawfully sanctioned by the relevant trade union under s.237(2). Participation in unofficial industrial action effectively removes the tribunal's jurisdiction in relation to unfair dismissal.

It seems therefore that if the action is unofficial then an employer is protected even if he selectively dismisses particular employees, for there is no prospect of unfair dismissal claims.

The right to present a claim for unfair dismissal is also restricted if at the time of dismissal the employee in question was engaged in official industrial action. Under s.238 of the Trade Union and Labour Relations (Consolidation) Act 1992 (previously s.62 EPCA 1978) the jurisdiction of a tribunal to hear a complaint may also be removed.

Under s.238(1) this section applies in relation to an employee who has a right to complain of unfair dismissal (the "complainant") and who claims to have been unfairly dismissed, where at the date of the dismissal:

(a)   the employer was conducting or instituting a lock-out, or

(b)   the complainant was taking part in a strike or other industrial action.

(2)   In such a case an industrial tribunal shall not determine whether the dismissal was fair or unfair unless it is shown:

(a)   that one or more relevant employees of the same employer have not been dismissed, or

(b) *that a relevant employee has before the expiry of the period of three months beginning with the date of his dismissal been offered re-engagement and that the complainant has not been offered re-engagement.*

Provided that an employer does not discriminate between those he dismisses and those he re-engages within the minimum periods, the section effectively removes the right to present a claim if an employer decides to dismiss all those workers, who, at a given time, are engaged in a strike or other industrial action. The right to present a claim will arise once again, however, if the employer re-engages any striking workers within three months of the date of the complainant's dismissal. For this reason the complainant has a time limit of six months from the date of dismissal to present a claim.

For the purposes of the section it can be a difficult question to determine whether an employee is taking part in a strike or other industrial action.

In *Glenrose (Fish Merchants) v. Chapman* 1990 the EAT said that it is for the employer to prove on the balance of probabilities that employees were participating in industrial action and that either s.238 or s.237 applies. Here some fish filleters had refused to do an extra hour filleting on one day as a protest against the re-introduction by management of compulsory overtime. They were dismissed the following day, at which point the overtime ban had been lifted, so the tribunal did have jurisdiction to hear their complaint.

In *Coates v. Modern Methods and Materials* 1982 the Court of Appeal held that for the purposes of the section, an employee who stops work when a strike is called, and does not openly disagree with it, while he may be an unwilling participant, he is nevertheless taking part in the industrial action. Here the employee's fear of crossing the picket line and subsequent certified illness during the period of the strike were insufficient reasons to rebut the presumption that she was taking part in industrial action.

In *McKenzie v. Crosville Motor Services Ltd.* 1989 an employee and TGWU member, who had worked during a strike by TGWU members, then failed to report to work during a subsequent dispute without reason. When he was dismissed on the grounds that he was on strike, the industrial tribunal refused to entertain his claim of unfair dismissal deciding that it was the employee's obligation to make it clear to the employer that he was not participating in the strike, and that there was some other reasonable explanation for his absence. On appeal the EAT agreed with the tribunal's decision, *"where an employee absents himself from work, it is incumbent upon him, as an implied contractual obligation, to provide his employer with information and a reason for his so doing. Where strike action is taking place, in addition to this normal obligation it falls to the employee to maintain contact with the employer so as to establish that he is not away from work as a result of withholding his labour".* The burden of disassociation, therefore, is entirely on the employee.

"Relevant employees" under s.238(2) are defined as those employees at the establishment who were taking part in the strike at the date of the complainant's dismissal. It does not include, therefore, those employees who have participated in the strike and then returned to work before that date, so the fact that they are not dismissed does not entitle the dismissed employees to present a claim.

In *Crosville Wales Ltd. v. Tracey and others* 1993 it was held that the term "offer of re-engagement" for the purposes of s.238 does not cover the situation where the employer is merely advertising vacancies and subsequently makes job offers to those participating in the industrial action.

In deciding whether a tribunal has jurisdiction to entertain a complaint of unfair dismissal, the time at which it has to be shown that one or more employees who took part in a strike were not dismissed, is the conclusion of the relevant hearing at which the tribunal determines whether it had jurisdiction. So held the Court of Appeal in *P & O European Ferries (Dover) Ltd.. v. Byrne* 1989. Consequently if the identities of the strikers who had not been dismissed are revealed during the proceedings, an employer can absolve himself of liability by simply dismissing them. An employer who, by mistake, fails to dismiss all the strikers in these circumstances will still be able to shelter behind the section, therefore, if the mistake is revealed before the conclusion of the proceedings and those strikers employed are summarily dismissed.

There is a difference between the definition of *"relevant employees"* at the date of dismissal where the employer is conducting a lock out as opposed to dismissing during a strike or other industrial action. If an employer dismisses strikers then for the purposes of s.238 *"relevant employees"* exclude those who have returned to work at the date of dismissal. If however at the date of dismissal the employer is operating a lock out *"relevant employees"* are defined in s.238(3)(a) as employees directly interested in the dispute in contemplation or furtherance of which the lock out occurred. This means that an employee who has been locked out, but who had already returned to work at the time of dismissal could still be a relevant employee. In the famous 1993 industrial dispute between the Timex Electronics Corporation and its employees at its Dundee factory, the staff overwhelmingly rejected the company's offer of radically less favourable terms and conditions of employment. The subsequent strike was followed by an attempted return to work under protest and a management lock out. The employers strategy was to recruit a replacement workforce and dismissal notices were issued to existing staff. To retain the protection of s.238 and so removing the threat of unfair dismissal claims the company also dismissed seventeen workers who had returned to work. These workers could still have been classified as *"relevant employees"* under s.238

The full impact of section 238 was demonstrated by the Court of Appeal in *Power Packing Casemakers Ltd. v. Faust and others* 1983. Here the employees had been operating a voluntary overtime ban in pursuance of wage negotiations. When threatened with dismissal, all except three employees agreed to work overtime. The three were promptly dismissed and their complaint of unfair dismissal was upheld by an industrial tribunal. This was despite the fact that they were taking industrial action, for the tribunal felt that the section was inapplicable as the men were not in breach of their employment contracts. The EAT disagreed however, stating that the tribunal had no jurisdiction to hear the complaint as the men were taking part in *"other industrial action"* within the meaning of the section. The Court of Appeal held on further appeal, that industrial action whether in breach of contract or not, if it has the object of applying pressure or disrupting the employer's business, must remove the jurisdiction of the tribunal, unless the employees could show that they had been subject to discriminatory treatment.

By pursuing a form of industrial action which does not constitute a breach of employment contracts, the employees in the above case were nevertheless effectively stripped of their statutory right to present a claim for unfair dismissal.

In *TNT Express (UK) Ltd. v. Downes and others* 1993 following the dismissal of employees who participated in a one-hour long strike, claims for unfair dismissal were presented when within days of the strike there was selective re-engagement of two of the strikers who were long standing employees. Under s.238 the tribunal had jurisdiction to hear the complaint and awarded compensation for unfair dismissal and refused to reduce the amount or account of the employees conduct in participating in the industrial action. The EAT disagreed however and held that all the circumstances should be considered in assessing compensation, including the industrial action. In doing so the EAT departed from its previous decision in *Courtaulds Northern Spinning v. Moosa* 1984.

In cases where an individual worker is dismissed for misconduct during a period of industrial action, then it is only by applying the basic principles of unfair dismissal law that the fairness of the decision to dismiss can be determined.

In *McClaren v. National Coal Board* 1988 following an alleged assault by the complainant on a working miner, his employer decided to report the matter to the police rather than implement the normal disciplinary procedure at the colliery. When convicted of an offence, the decision was taken to dismiss the complainant. On a complaint of unfair dismissal, the tribunal found that normally the failure to give the complainant a chance to put his side of the case would render the dismissal unfair but not so in the circumstances of industrial warfare. Both the EAT and the Court of Appeal disagreed however, and held that *"standards of fairness are immutable"*. *"No amount of heat in industrial warfare can justify failing to give an employee the opportunity of offering an explanation".*

The legal position in relation to official industrial action and dismissal has been substantially amended by the Employment Relations Act 1999 and the insertion of s.238A into TULR(C) 1992.

> *Under s.238A(2) an employee who is dismissed shall be regarded as unfairly dismissed if*
>
> > (a) the reason for the dismissal is that the employee took protected industrial action and
> >
> > (b) subsection (3), (4) or (5) applies to the dismissal.
>
> (3) *This subsection applies to a dismissal if it takes place within the period of eight weeks beginning on the day on which the employee started to take protected industrial action.*
>
> (4) *This subsection applies to a dismissal if*
>
> > (a) *it takes place after the end of that period, and*
> >
> > (b) *the employee had stopped taking protected industrial action before the end of that period.*
>
> (5) *This subsection applies to a dismissal if*
>
> > (a) *it takes place after the end of that period*
> >
> > (b) *the employee had not stopped taking protected industrial action before the end of that period and*
> >
> > (c) *the employer had not taken such procedural steps as would have been reasonable for the purposed of resolving the dispute to which the protected industrial action relates.*

For the purpose of the section therefore the dismissal must take place within an eight week period beginning with the day on which the employee started to take the protected industrial action. Alternatively the dismissal took place after the end of the eight week period but the employee had stopped taking protected industrial action before the end of that period. It is also automatically unfair to dismiss after the end of the eight week period when the employee has continued to take protected industrial action and the employer had not taken *"such procedural steps as would have been reasonable for the purposes of resolving the dispute to which the protected industrial action relates".* If a collective agreement established a procedure for the resolution of a dispute that will be deemed to be the appropriate procedure for these purposes it would be tempting to presume that the new s.238A would make s.238 redundant however this is not the case. For s.238A to be triggered the industrial action taken must be official and protected which effectively means sanctioned by the relevant trade union and lawfully confirmed through balloting. Section 238 is relevant if the industrial action is official and satisfies s.237(2) but is not protected because of a failure in the balloting process. Also s.238 is relevant where there are selective dismissals outside the eight week period and the employer has nevertheless taken the appropriate procedural steps to bring the dispute to an end.

Remedies for Unfair Dismissal

The diagram on the next page shows the various remedies which may be awarded by a tribunal on a finding of unfair dismissal.

Reinstatement or Re-engagement

If a complaint of unfair dismissal is successful, the tribunal has authority to make an order for reinstatement or re-engagement or make an award of compensation. Irrespective of whether he has requested the remedies on his IT1, the tribunal is obliged to explain the remedies of reinstatement and re-engagement to a successful complainant and discover whether he wishes to apply for such an order.

Under s.114(1) An order for reinstatement is an order that the employer shall treat the complainant in all respects as if he had not been dismissed, (2) on making such an order the tribunal shall specify–

(a) *any amount payable by the employer in respect of any benefit which the complainant might reasonably be expected to have had but for the dismissal, including arrears of pay, for the period between the date of termination of employment and the date of reinstatement;*

(b) *any rights and privileges, including seniority and pension rights, which must be restored to the employee; and*

(c) *the date by which the order must be complied with.*

An order for reinstatement therefore requires the employer to treat the complainant in all respects as if he had not been dismissed. By such an order, the employer would be required to make good any arrears of pay or any rights or privileges which would have accrued but for the dismissal. If the employee would have benefited from improvements in terms and conditions but for the dismissal, then the order must reflect the improvement from the date it was agreed. In exercising its discretion to make an order of reinstatement the tribunal must take account of:

- the wishes of the complainant;

- whether it is practicable for an employer to comply with such an order; and

- whether the complainant contributed to the dismissal and whether it would be just to make such an order.

If the tribunal decides not to make an order for reinstatement it must then consider the possibility of re-engagement.

Under s.115(1) An order for re-engagement is an order on such terms as the tribunal may decide, that the complainant be engaged by the employer, or by a successor of the employer or by an associated employer, in employment comparable to that from which he was dismissed or other suitable employment.

(2) On making an order for re-engagement the tribunal shall specify the terms on which re-engagement is to take place, including

(a) the identity of the employer;

(b) the nature of the employment;

(c) the remuneration for the employment;

(d) any amount payable by the employer in respect of any benefit which the complainant might reasonably be expected to have had but for the dismissal, including arrears of pay, for the period between the date of termination of employment and the date of re-engagement;

(e) any rights and privileges, including seniority and pension rights, which must be restored to the employee; and

(f) the date by which the order must be complied with.

For re-engagement the tribunal must take account of the following considerations:

- the wishes of the employee;

- whether it is practicable for the employer to comply with an order for re-engagement; and

- where the employee contributed to some extent to the dismissal and whether it would be just to order re-engagement and if so, on what terms.

In *Nairne v. Highland & Islands Fire Brigade* 1989 the complainant was found to be unfairly dismissed because of a procedural irregularity, in that the purpose of a disciplinary interview had not been made clear to him, and he was never warned that he could be dismissed. This was despite the fact that the reason for dismissal was justifiable. The employee in question was a fire officer, who for the second time had been found guilty of a drink/driving offence and as a result had been disqualified from driving for three years. It was a contractual requirement of his job that he was able to drive and it was unreasonable to employ a substitute driver for a three year period. The finding of unfair dismissal was affirmed on appeal and the extent of the employee's contributory fault increased from 25% to 75%. Such a high degree of contributory fault and the fact that there was no suitable alternative job available made this an unsuitable case to order re-engagement.

In *Port of London Authority v. Payne* 1994 the industrial tribunal found that 17 shop stewards had been selected for redundancy because of their trade union activities and accordingly that their dismissals were unfair. The tribunal ordered re-engagement but this was reversed by the EAT on the grounds that the tribunal had failed to make a final determination as to practicability. The Court of Appeal offered some guidance on the issue of practicability. *"Before an order for re-engagement is made, an industrial tribunal must make a determination or assessment on the evidence before it whether it is practicable for the employer to comply with such an order. But the determination at this first stage is of necessity provisional. The final conclusion as to practicability is made when the employer finds whether he can comply with the order in the period prescribed. At this second stage, where an order for re-engagement is made but not complied with by the employer and the size of the special award is being considered, the burden of proof rests firmly on the employer".* In determining the issue of practicability at this second stage an employer is *"entitled to say what in his commercial judgment is in the best interests of his business and provided that the decision or judgment of the employer is within ... reasonable brackets ... it should be respected."*

In *Wood Group Heavy Industrial Tribunal v. Grossan* 1998 despite a finding of unfair dismissal the EAT was convinced that there was a breakdown of trust and confidence given that the employer substantially believed the allegations made against the employee. As a consequence the tribunal felt that re-engagement was an inappropriate remedy for it would be unlikely to repair the breakdown in confidence between the employer and the employee

The EAT in *Stena Houlder Ltd. v. Keenan* 1993 confirmed that when making a re-engagement order the tribunal must set out the terms of employment as specified in the section and an order which left the exact nature of the work and the rate of pay subject to agreement was insufficiently specific. Also in *Rank Xerox (UK) Ltd. v. Stryczeh* 1995 following a finding of unfair dismissal the tribunal ordered that the complainant should be re-engaged in a vacant position which had a higher salary and increased benefit. On appeal against the decision the EAT held that it is generally undesirable for a tribunal to order re-engagement in respect of a specific job rather than identifying the nature of the proposed employment. *"As a matter of law, an industrial tribunal cannot order that an employee be re-engaged on significantly more favourable terms than he would have enjoyed if he had been reinstated in his former job".*

If a tribunal decides not to make either order it must make an award of compensation. But even if either order is made, a tribunal has no power to ensure that it is complied with. Failure to comply or fully comply with an order of reinstatement or re-engagement can only lead to an award of compensation subject to the maximum limit.

> In *Artisan Press v. Strawley and Parker* 1986 after finding that the complainants had been unfairly dismissed from their jobs on security staff because of membership of an independent trade union, the tribunal ordered that they should be reinstated. The employer purported to re-employ them, but in fact their job duties differed significantly and rather than security, the new jobs involved cleaning with minor security functions. A further complaint of non-compliance with the reinstatement order was upheld, the tribunal awarding sums of £18,367 and £20,080 respectively. On an appeal against the amount of the additional awards, the EAT refused to accept the employer's argument that a distinction should be drawn between non-compliance with an order of reinstatement and failing to comply fully with such an order. Here the amount of the awards would not be interfered with.

> In *O'Laoire v. Jackel International Ltd.* 1990 the Court of Appeal held that if a reinstatement order is not complied with, whether wholly or in part, the complainant's only remedy is to apply to the tribunal for an award of compensation. The earlier decision of the EAT in *Conoco (UK) Ltd. v. Neal* 1989, that the monetary provisions of a reinstatement order were enforceable through a separate cause of action in the County Court was wrong and would be overruled.

Regardless of the loss which could include substantial arrears of wages, if the employer refuses to re-employ, the complainant's compensation was limited to the statutory compensation in force at the time, the basic compensatory and additional awards. Now following the Trade Union Reform and Employment Rights Act 1993 there is no longer a limit on the extent of compensation for non compliance with an order.

Compensation

The most common form of redress for unfair dismissal is compensation.

An order for compensation as redress for unfair dismissal may consist of a basic award, a compensatory award, an additional award and where the dismissal related to the membership or non-membership of a trade union, a special award.

Basic award

The basic award is payable in all cases of unfair dismissal irrespective of loss and is calculated under s.119(1) with reference to the complainant's continuous employment and average week's wage. It should be noted however that if it can be shown that the complainant contributed to the dismissal through his own fault, or has unreasonably refused an offer of reinstatement, the amount of the basic award can be reduced by a just and equitable proportion. The computation of the basic award is the same as for a redundancy payment, so the present maximum is £6,900.

The amount of the basic award is calculated by reference to the period the employee has been continuously employed, ending with the effective date of termination. By reckoning backwards from the effective date of termination the number of years employment can be determined allowing:

> *one and a half weeks' pay for each year of employment in which the employee was not below 41 years of age;*

> *one week's pay for each year the employee was not below 22 years of age;*

> *a half week's pay for each year of employment between 18 and 21 years of age.*

To calculate the basic award therefore it is necessary to determine the employee's gross pay up to a maximum of £230, his length of service up to a maximum of 20 years and his age. The maximum award payable therefore is for an employee who is dismissed after 20 years' service, over the age of 41, with a gross wage in excess of £230. He will be entitled to a basic award of 20 x 1½ x £230 = £6,900.

In many cases the employee's period of continuous service will cover more than one age rate barrier. In such circumstances it is necessary to calculate the entitlement at the relevant rate, e.g. for an employee who is made redundant at the age of 44 who, after 15 years' service has a gross wage of £160, is entitled to:

3 years x 1½ x £160   £ 720

plus

12 years x 1 x £160   £1,920

£2,640

A disturbing rule under s.119(4) for employees close to retirement is that on the effective date of termination, for each month that an employee is over the age of sixty four, the amount of the basic award is reduced by one-twelfth for each complete month worked. The justification for this is that the point of the basic award is to compensate the employee for the loss of accrued redundancy rights which, of course, are not payable on retirement.

Under s.122(4) of the employee is entitled to a redundancy payment because of an unfair dismissal by reason of redundancy, the basic award is reduced by the amount of the redundancy payment. Since both awards are calculated in the same way, in most cases the redundancy payment will reduce the basic award to nil. In *Bowman v. Allmakes Ltd.* 1995 the Court of Appeal held that the basic award should be reduced by the amount of a statutory redundancy payment only where the true reason for dismissal is redundancy. *"It is not enough that an employer made a payment to an employee which was expressed as being on the ground that the dismissal was by reason of redundancy, even if the employee accepted that description at the time"*. This means that if the tribunal determines that the dismissal in question is not one of redundancy then s.122(4) is irrelevant and the basic award in a finding of unfair dismissal is payable.

Finally under s.120 there is one case where there is a minimum basic award payable regardless of the calculation and that is where the dismissal is connected with redundancy, with trade union representation under s.103 or health and safety under s.100. The minimum payment is £2,900 but even that sum could be reduced because of contributory fault.

Compensatory award

In assessing the amount of the compensatory award, under s.123, a tribunal must have regard to the loss sustained by the complainant in consequence of the dismissal. A significant increase in the maximum compensatory award to £50,000 was introduced by the Employment Relations Act 1999 and in force from 25 October 1999.

Under s.123(1) the amount of the compensatory award shall be such an amount as the tribunal considers just and equitable in all circumstances having regard to the loss sustained by the complainant in consequence of the dismissal in so far as that loss is attributable to action taken by the employer

(2)   The said loss shall be taken to include

> *(a)   any expenses reasonably incurred by the complainant in consequence of the dismissal, and*

> *(b)   subject to subsection (3) any loss of any benefit which he might reasonably be expected to have had but for the dismissal.*

If there is no loss, then no compensatory award is payable.

Such was the position in *Isleworth Studios Ltd. v. Richard* 1988 where the complainant was unfairly dismissed when his fixed term contract was prematurely brought to an end. The fact that during the unexpired term of the contract the complainant went on to earn £10,000 in excess of what he would have earned in his former employment meant that he had suffered no loss.

The amount of a compensatory award should under s.123(4) take account of any failure by the employee to mitigate his loss, for instance by refusing an offer of suitable alternative employment. The Court of Appeal held in *Babcock Fata v. Addison* 1987 that any money paid in lieu of notice should be deducted from a compensatory award as should any ex gratia payment made. Heads of compensation that are assessable include the loss of fringe benefits attached to the job, expense incurred in seeking alternative work, net wages lost up to the hearing, estimated future earnings, the termination of continuous employment which necessarily limits future rights and the loss of pension rights.

It should have been stressed that the compensatory award is not equivalent to an award of damages under the common law. Section 123 is a statutory provision constituting its own code for the assessment of compensation and *the "just and equitable"* criterion confers a degree of flexibility on the industrial tribunal in deciding whether state benefit should be deducted from an award. In *Rubenstein and Roskin v. McGloughlin* 1996 the EAT held that *"In determining whether benefits received by the employee should be deducted from the compensatory award, it is legitimate to have regard to the fact that for a number of social security benefits, including invalidity benefit, there are statutory provisions affecting the damages recoverable for personal injury which mitigate the extremity of the common law by adopting solutions which involve treating employer and employee equally, either by dividing the value of the benefits between them by the device of half deduction or by removing it from both by requiring recoupment."* The EAT decided that in the case of invalidity benefit to which the claimant had contributed, but which is not in the category of pure "insurance monies", fully funded by the employee, it was just and equitable to deduct one half of the benefit received by the employee from the compensatory award.

As a general rule the compensatory award is limited to financial loss and cannot extend to hurt feelings. Although unfair dismissal may be traumatic, no damages are available for the distress caused by the employer's action. It would be possible however to compensate for financial loss resulting from the manner of the dismissal, rather than injury to feelings, particularly when it affects future prospects of employment. Injury to feelings are recognised for the purposes of compensation in discrimination legislation so that if a dismissal is proved to be sex or race discrimination then the distress suffered by the applicant can be compensated.

In *Hilton International Hotels (UK) Ltd. v. Faraji* 1994 it was held that an unfairly dismissed employee was still entitled to a compensatory award for loss of earnings notwithstanding that he was in receipt of invalidity benefit during the relevant period. *"It does not inexorably follow that because invalidity benefit is being paid that a person has no earning potential over the relevant period and so cannot have suffered loss in terms of the section". Invalidity benefit can properly be characterised as an insurance type of benefit and as such does not fall to be deducted from unfair dismissal compensation".*

In *Devine v. Designer Flowers Wholesale Florist Sundries Ltd.* 1993 the EAT found that the complainant, who had been unfairly dismissed was entitled to a compensatory award which reflected the fact that as a result of her dismissal she suffered from anxiety and reactive depression which meant that she was unfit to look for work. *"An employee who has become unfit for work wholly or partly as a result of an unfair dismissal is entitled to a compensation for loss of earnings at least for a reasonable period following the dismissal, until she might reasonably have been expected to find other employment. The industrial tribunal must have regard to the loss sustained by the employee, consider how far it is attributable to action taken by the employer, and arrive at a sum which it considers just and equitable. There is no reason why the personal circumstances of the employee, including the effect of dismissal on her health, should not be taken into account in ascertaining the appropriate amount of compensation."*

The compensatory award, like the basic award, may, under s.123(6), be reduced because of the complainant's contributory fault.

In *The Post Office v. Ramkisson* 1993 an employee with a long unblemished service record was dismissed for a serious incident of misconduct involving the falsification of a medical certificate in order to obtain a further week's sick pay. Both the tribunal and the EAT felt that given his service record, the decision to dismiss, rather than opt for some other course of action was not open to a reasonable employer applying the proper principles of industrial relations. It was also decided however that as the complainant had contributed to his dismissal by 90% his compensation should be reduced by this percentage to reflect his contributory fault.

In *Soros and Soros v. Davison and Davison* 1994 the EAT held that in assessing the compensatory award for unfair dismissal it is not permissible to take account of post-dismissal conduct of the employee. Here it was argued that the alleged misconduct of ex employees in selling information about their employer to a national newspaper, after the finding of unfair dismissal, constituted a breach of duty which was relevant to the issue of redress. The EAT said that *"The section is concerned with events which have existed during the contract of employment, not subsequent to it. That is the plain meaning of the language of the subsection. The proposition that any misconduct even if committed after the employee was dismissed should be brought into the scales when assessing compensation was not supported by the decision of the House of Lords in W. Devis & Sons Ltd. v. Atkins 1977".*

In *Gosling v. Ford Motor Co. Ltd.* 1992 the applicant was dismissed for misconduct the employer alleging that he was guilty of disruptive behaviour in inciting unofficial industrial action. This complaint of unfair dismissal alleged trade union activities as the reason for dismissal. The EAT found that the true reason for dismissal was misconduct but that the dismissal was unfair due to procedural irregularities. The EAT agreed with the tribunal that his compensatory award could be reduced to reflect his contributory fault (75%). While in *Courtaulds Northern Spinning Ltd. v. Moosa* 1984 the EAT had ruled that tribunals could not apply contributory fault when employees were dismissed for taking part in industrial action this did not apply when the alleged misconduct was incitement to take unofficial industrial action.

In unfair dismissal cases by reason of discrimination there is always the possibility of additional liability under the Sex Discrimination Act or the Race Relations Act. In such circumstances if there is potential compensation under unfair dismissal and discrimination legislation under s.126(1) a tribunal should not award double compensation for the same loss.

Under a new s.127A if the tribunal finds that the employer provided a procedure for appealing against a dismissal and the employee was given written notification of that fact but did not use it, then the tribunal must reduce the award by a sum which it considers just and equitable. Alternatively if the employer prevents the applicant from using the procedure then the tribunal should make a supplementary award.

Under the Industrial Tribunals (Interest) Order 1990 provision is made for interest to be payable on any sums *"payable by virtue of a relevant decision of a tribunal"* with effect from *"a calculation day"* which is defined as *"the day immediately following the expiry of the period of forty two days beginning with the relevant decision day"*. In *Hilton International Hotels (UK) Ltd. v. Faraji* 1994 the EAT held that as invalidity benefit is dependent upon the payment of national insurance contributions it should not be deducted when assessing the level of a compensatory award.

In *O'Laoire v. Jackel International Ltd.* 1991 the Court of Appeal held that an award of the maximum compensatory award for unfair dismissal should not be deducted from a separate award of damages under the common law for wrongful dismissal.

In *Rushton v. Harcos Timber and Building Supplies Ltd.* 1993 the EAT held that on a finding of unfair dismissal no compensation is payable when an ex gratia redundancy payment has been made.

Additional award

The additional award is payable under s.117 where an employer does not comply with an order of reinstatement or re-engagement and fails to establish that it was not reasonably practicable to comply with the order. The amount of the award is not less than 26 nor more than 52 weeks pay. Following the Employment Relations Act 1999 the special award for dismissals relating to trade union membership or the activities of safety representatives has been abolished.

Interim relief

If the dismissal is in connection with trade union membership or participating in trade union activities, or health and safety an application may be made under s.128(1) for interim relief within seven days of the dismissal, supported by a signed certificate from a trade union official that there are reasonable grounds to believe that this is the true reason for dismissal. A tribunal satisfied that there are reasonable grounds can order that the employment should continue until the final hearing.

In *Alexander v. Standard Telephones and Cables Ltd. and Wall* 1990 the common law rule that the courts will not grant an injunction which will have the effect of compelling specific performance was re-emphasised, the High Court indicating a solitary exception where it can be shown that the employer has not lost confidence in the employee in question. Since this will rarely be the case in a dismissal situation, the prospect of an injunction to restrain a dismissal must now be highly unlikely.

Case Studies

Dalton West plc - The Blanket Dismissal

Dalton West is a large manufacturer of fork lift trucks with depots and retail outlets situated all over Britain. David, Jim and Frank are all employed as storekeepers by Dalton West at the company's Darlington depot. David and Jim both have six years service with the company while Frank has been employed for the past eighteen months. Between them they man the store on a shift system eighteen hours a day, six days a week. For some time the store at its Darlington depot has been plagued by serious stock losses and despite extensive efforts to identify the cause or the culprits the management have been unable to do so. All three storekeepers have received both oral and written warnings and earlier in the year were temporarily transferred to other depots in the North of England for a six week period. During that period there was no evidence of losses at any depot including Darlington. Now that David, Jim and Frank have returned to Darlington the stock losses are more serious than ever. Two months ago Frank was summarily dismissed with wages paid in lieu of notice. When further losses were identified subsequently David was dismissed summarily last month with wages in lieu of notice and Jim walked out of the job in sympathy. Frank believes that he was chosen for dismissal because he is a shop steward of the Fitters and General Workers Union and Dalton West do not encourage union membership.

Dalton West plc - Irrational Fears

Dalton West is a large manufacturer of fork lift trucks with depots and retail outlets situated all over Britain. A problem has emerged at the monthly meeting of management and shop stewards of the Fitters and General Workers Union at the Coventry factory. During a heated debate relating to health and safety the stewards raised an issue about Peter Armitage, a machine fitter who had been employed by the company for the past eighteen months. The stewards stated that they have been informed by a reliable source that Peter has contracted the human immunedeficiency virus (HIV) which is almost unanimously agreed to be the causative organism of the acquired immunedeficiency syndrome (AIDS). Furthermore they have received complaints from a number of Peter's workmates, who, aware of the rumours about him have expressed a genuine fear of contagion. The view of the stewards is that it would be in the best interests of the company to *"sack"* Peter, *"perhaps by making him redundant"*. This is despite the fact that management point out at the meeting that the fear of infection is hardly rational given that HIV infection is not readily transmitted and seems to require a mixture of body fluids, which is a very rare event in most workplaces. At a subsequent meeting of personnel and Peter he denies that he has contracted the virus and claims that the rumours are based solely on the fact that he is a homosexual. He also claims that he has been discriminated against because of his sexuality and that the FGWU stewards *"have got it in for him"* because *"he won't join their bloody union"*.

Case Studies

Major Homes

Major Homes Ltd. is a large construction company specialising in residential housing development, mainly in the north of England. On March 15 the company's personnel manager for the North East reported to senior management that Andrew, the site manager on a development in Durham, has been charged with assault occasioning actual bodily harm for which he is to be prosecuted in the near future. It is alleged that following a heated argument between Andrew and Barry, a labourer, Andrew attacked Barry and physically assaulted him. The argument concerned Barry's entitlement to overtime pay.

Foreseeing the possibility of further conflict, the management decide to transfer Andrew to a new site in Birmingham. They inform him of their decision on March 20, and require him to start work on the new site on April 1. Andrew objects to the proposed transfer almost immediately, stating that there is no mobility clause in his contract. He subsequently fails to report for work in Birmingham on April 1, despite having nine years of loyal, unbroken service with Major Homes.

On April 14 Andrew's requests for an internal hearing was rejected by the company on the grounds that the appeal procedure only applied to dismissals and not to a resignation. Despite Andrew's conviction for the lesser offence of common assault in early June he now wishes to "take the company to the tribunal" to secure legal redress.

Chapter 12
Redundancy

Redundancy Payments

The concept of redundancy owes part of its complexity to the various contexts in which the term appears.

For the purpose of a redundancy payment redundancy occurs under the legal definition when an employee is dismissed because an employer has closed his business or the business is closed in the place the employee works. Alternatively there is redundancy if the employer no longer requires or has a reduced requirement for employees to carry out work of a particular kind. In both cases there must be no suitable alternative employment. As far as unfair dismissal is concerned a dismissal by reason of redundancy is a statutory reason for dismissal and provided the employer consults when he need to and adopts rational criterion for selection, such a dismissal may be classified as fair. There is also the layman view of redundancy as a term used by employers and employees whenever a business decides to shed some of its staff.

The right to a redundancy payment for workers dismissed because there is no longer a demand for their services was first introduced in 1965 under the Redundancy Payments Act. The 1965 Act represented a major statutory intervention in the individual employment relationship, for while redundancy/severance payments have always been contractually agreed, the Act made the State redundancy payment a statutory requirement for qualifying employees. It was the first example of any State provision for compensation for workers who lost their jobs through no fault of their own. The complex provisions of the Act are now found in the Employment Rights Act 1996. It should be stressed from the outset that redundancy payments are now dwarfed by potential unfair dismissal compensation so that their significance has greatly diminished over the years.

The object of redundancy provision is to compensate a worker for the loss of a long term stake he has in his job. In the mid 1960s it was thought that the provision of lump sum severance payments to redundant employees would encourage a shake out of underemployed labour in industry generally, with less risk of industrial action. It was also thought that such payments would encourage mobility of labour to accommodate technological advances. Under the original scheme every employer made contributions to the Redundancy Fund and received a rebate of 35% for every payment made. In 1986 the rebate was abolished except for those employers who employ less than ten employees and payments can still be made by the State on an employer's insolvency. Employment tribunals have jurisdiction over disputes relating to entitlement and the amount of any redundancy payment and also where the complaint is one of unfair dismissal due to unfair selection for redundancy. It should be recognised that between 1965 and 1971 disputes in relation to redundancy provided the main work of industrial tribunals in industrial conflict. When the right not to be unfairly dismissed was introduced in 1971 however, employees were more likely to argue that they had been dismissed unfairly rather than redundant and so entitled to increased compensation. To qualify for the right to a redundancy payment an employee must establish under s.155 with the same employer. For an unfair dismissal claim of course the qualifying period has been reduced to one year.

Qualifying Workers

Originally to qualify for the right to a redundancy payment it was necessary to establish two years continuous employment with the same employer as a full-time employee over the age of eighteen. Now part-time employees regardless of their hours can also qualify for a payment with two years continuous employment. This right is contained in the Employment Protection (Part-time Employees) Regulations 1995. For the moment redundancy payments are only available to employees so that status as a worker or an independent contractor would not qualify.

It is not unusual for controlling shareholders of small companies to claim that as they work under a contract of employment they should be entitled to a payment when the company goes into liquidation. Over the years there have been conflicting decisions as whether controlling shareholders can qualify as employees. Recently the Court of Appeal in *Secretary of State for Trade and Industry v. Bottrill* 1999 considered the position of a managing director of a small UK company who had been engaged under a contract of employment and did not receive directors fees. He had intended his shareholding to be purchased by an American company but prior to that, his company got into financial difficulties and he was dismissed by the receiver. The Court of Appeal held that there was a genuine employment relationship between the shareholder and his company and he could be classified as an employee.

To qualify the period of employment must be continuous and continuity of employment is examined in Chapter 9. For the purposes of redundancy however s.213(3)(c) is significant for it provides that breaks will not affect continuity:

(a) *if some kind of arrangement was made whereby employment is to be treated as continuing, or*

(b) *established custom and practice dictates that the break does not affect continuity of employment.*

However following *Booth and others v. United States* 1999 (see Chapter 9) it seems that if the break in employment is clearly intended by the employer and is designed to defeat the effect of redundancy and/or unfair dismissal then s.213(3) will not apply. Certainly the practice of employing staff on a series of fixed term contracts, with breaks in continuity for the purpose of removing statutory rights, should encourage legislators to implement the provisions of the Directive on Fixed Term Employment.

Under s.135(1) An employer shall pay a redundancy payment to any employee of his if the employee:

(a) *is dismissed by the employer by reason of redundancy, or*

(b) *is eligible for a redundancy payment by reason of being laid off or kept on short-time.*

For the purpose of the section therefore it is necessary to consider what would constitute a dismissal, and whether it is attributable to redundancy.

Certain categories of employees are also excluded from making a claim:

- Persons who have attained retirement age which under the Employment Act 1989 is 65 for both men and women.

- Persons employed under a fixed term contract of two years or more who agree in writing to exclude their rights to a payment provided they do so before the expiration of the term under s.197(3).

- Persons ordinarily employed outside Great Britain unless on the date of dismissal for redundancy they are in Great Britain following the employer's instructions.

- Persons who are covered by a redundancy agreement approved by the Secretary of State.

- "Office holders" who are not employees.

- Domestic servants in a private household who are close relatives of the employer.

To qualify to make a claim for a redundancy payment, an employee must have been dismissed by reason of redundancy, laid off or kept on short time. The definition of dismissal for this purpose is set out in s.136(1) of the Employment Rights Act 1996 in broadly similar terms to the definition of dismissal under s.95 for the purposes of unfair dismissal.

Dismissal

Dismissal for the purposes of redundancy will normally be express under s.136(1)(a) but it could also occur on the expiration of a fixed term contract under s.136(1)(b) or even be a constructive dismissal under s.136(1)c).

In *Bass Leisure Ltd. v. Thomas* 1994 the applicant claimed a redundancy payment when she left her job after the employer had tried to move her to an unsuitable job location. As the express or implied terms of the contract did not authorise the move, it was a fundamental breach of contract and constituted a constructive dismissal by reason of redundancy.

A decision of the EAT in 1996 in two cases involving part-time lecturing staff, *Pfaffinger v. City of Liverpool College and Muller v. Amersham & Wycombe College*, confirmed that part-time employees employed on a succession of fixed term lecturing contracts are dismissed for redundancy on the expiration of each contract. That is the combined effect of the definition of dismissal and the definition of redundancy under the Employment Rights Act 1996. *"Thus, a college lecturer with three fixed-term contracts during the academic year may be dismissed three times during that year for redundancy. In such a case, the college's need for employees to carry out the function of lecturing ceases or diminishes from the beginning of the vacation until the start of the new term. There is no teaching during that period and therefore no need for teachers. That is a redundancy situation."*

It should be noted that s.197(3) provides that under a fixed term contract of two years or more an employee may agree to waive his rights to a redundancy payment on its expiration. The Employment Relations Act 1999 removed the right to waive unfair dismissal rights but not the right to a redundancy payment which in a fixed term contract scenario is not envisaged by the contract.

The Act further provides under s.136(5) that there is a deemed dismissal because of the employer's act or some event affecting him, for example the employer's death, dissolution of a partnership, or winding up of a company.

In *Brown v. Knowsley BC* 1986 the applicant having been employed in a college of further education under a number of fixed term contracts was offered a one year temporary contract from 1 September 1983, stipulated to last as long as funds from the Manpower Services Commission were provided for the course she taught. On 3 August 1984 she was given written notice that as the MSC funding had ceased, her employment terminated on 31 August 1984. The applicant's claim for a redundancy payment was rejected by the tribunal who found there to be no dismissal but rather a discharge of the contract by performance. The EAT agreed that there had been no dismissal, and held that the contract was terminable on the happening or non-happening of a future event, in this case the withdrawal of funding by the MSC.

If an employee leaves prematurely in a redundancy situation without waiting to be dismissed, then this will prejudice the success of a claim.

In *Morton Sundour Fabrics v. Shaw* 1966 the employee in question, having been warned of the possibility of redundancy, left to take other employment. The court held that as he had not been dismissed, he was therefore not entitled to a redundancy payment.

Even when notice of dismissal by reason of redundancy has been served, if employees subsequently accept an offer of voluntary early retirement, as an alternative to redundancy, they would not be entitled to a redundancy payment.

This was the controversial decision of the EAT *in Scott v. Coalite Fuels and Chemicals Ltd.* 1988. By reaching an agreement as to a voluntary termination of employment, the nature of an earlier notice of dismissal was consequently changed so that the tribunal was entitled to find that there had been no dismissal for the purpose of redundancy.

In *Mowlem Northern Ltd. v. Watson* 1990 a foreman employee was given notice that his employment would terminate by reason of redundancy on a given date when his contract came to an end. Without prejudicing his right to a redundancy payment the employee was offered the chance to work temporarily beyond the date that the redundancy notice expired in the hopes that this would lead to an offer of further permanent employment. The employee took up the offer but after a few months resigned and claimed the redundancy payment. The employer's decision to withhold the payment was upheld by the industrial tribunal who felt that the subsequent termination of employment was not by reason of redundancy. On appeal however the EAT held that *"there is nothing in statute to preclude the employer and employee from postponing the date by mutual agreement until the happening of an agreed event"*. The idea of offering temporary employment in the hope that something permanent might arise was *"a thoroughly sensible arrangement and there was nothing in law preventing it"*. An employee should in such circumstances retain the right to a redundancy payment.

If an employee succumbs to pressure to resign in a redundancy situation, the resignation could still be treated as a dismissal for the purposes of redundancy.

In *Caledonian Mining Co Ltd. v. Bassett* 1987 a sympathetic approach was taken by the EAT to employees who in a redundancy situation had written to their employer terminating their employment. The men had originally been told that manpower on their site would be reduced, and asked whether they would be interested in alternative employment. Despite an expression of interest by the men, the employer did not respond and failed to offer alternative work. The men did receive an offer from the National Coal Board which they accepted. This led to the letter of termination which the employer argued constituted a resignation, and as there had been no dismissal in law there was no right to a redundancy payment. The EAT agreed with the tribunal however and held that the men had been encouraged to resign and take another job with the intention of avoiding redundancy payments. The true position here was that the employer had caused the men to resign, and in reality the employer was terminating the contract. Accordingly the employees were dismissed in law and entitled to a redundancy payment.

In *Hellyer Brothers Ltd. v. Atkinson and Dickinson* 1993 the Court of Appeal held that despite the fact that two seamen had signed a document showing the reason for contractual termination as 'mutual consent' the tribunal and the EAT were entitled to decide that the true reason for termination was dismissal by reason of redundancy.

The Act recognises that it may be in the employee's interest to leave prematurely in a redundancy situation and still qualify for a payment. If an employee has already received notice of dismissal, he may, during the obligatory period of that notice, serve his own notice to terminate the contract earlier than the employer's notice. Provided the employee's notice is served during the obligatory period which is the minimum period of notice required by statute, basically one week for each year's employment up to twelve, then the employee will not lose his right to a redundancy payment. If the employee's notice is served outside the obligatory period it will be interpreted as a resignation and no redundancy claim can be made. Also, as a response to the employee's notice, the employer can, serve a second notice requiring the employee to withdraw his notice. Failure to comply could lead to an employee losing the right to the whole or part of the payment.

Under s.136(1)(c) a unilateral variation of the contract of employment to which the employee does not assent could constitute a repudiatory breach and entitle an employee to leave and regard himself as constructively dismissed.

In *Marriott v. Oxford District Coop Society Ltd.* 1969 a foreman supervisor was told by his employer that the position of foreman was no longer required and that his wage would be reduced by £1 per week to reflect his loss of status. The employee continued to work under protest for three weeks before terminating his employment by notice, claiming redundancy. The Court of Appeal held that there had been no true consent to the contractual variation, and the contract of employment had been terminated by reason of redundancy so that the employee was entitled to a redundancy payment.

In Chapter 7 the fluid nature of the contract of employment was discussed, particularly in relation to contractual variation. While the express terms of the contract of employment could provide for a change in contractual duties, there is also a degree of managerial discretion or prerogative to effect changes in work patterns. It could be therefore that a reorganisation of the working day, a requirement to adapt to new working methods or a change in the place of employment, even without express authorisation in the contract of employment, could nevertheless be justified on the grounds of efficiency, and so would not constitute a breach of the contract of employment.

Lay Off and Short-time

In cases where there is a cessation or diminution in work requirements the employer may respond by laying off staff or putting them on to short-time. In the absence of a contractual right to do so, such action could of course, constitute a breach of contract enabling the employee to regard himself as constructively dismissed and so entitled to claim redundancy or unfair dismissal. For a lay off or short-time of four consecutive weeks or an aggregate of six or more weeks in a period of thirteen weeks, s.148 provides that an employee can serve notice that he intends to make a claim for a payment. For this purpose "lay off" occurs where no work and no wages are provided and short-time means that an employee earns less than one half his wages in any given week. In such a situation an employee could then serve notice to terminate the contractual relationship altogether and so qualify for a redundancy payment. This is subject to the employer's right to serve a counter notice within the time limits, which will defeat the claim if the employer can show that there is a reasonable prospect of work in not later than four weeks time, for at least thirteen weeks, without the possibility of lay off or short-time working. The onus is on the employer to establish through evidence the likelihood of the period of employment, and failure to do so will mean that the employee is entitled to a redundancy payment.

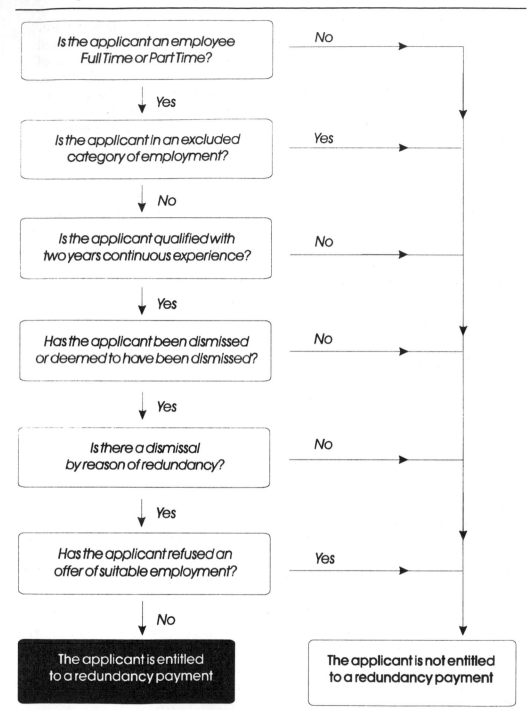

Entitlement to a Redundancy Payment

Redundancy Dismissal

The right to a redundancy payment arises when a qualifying employee has been dismissed by reason of redundancy or is laid off or kept on shot-time for the purposes of s.148. The reason for dismissal must therefore be redundancy, a presumption of which arises in favour of the applicant unless the contrary is proved under s.163(2). It is for the employer to rebut the presumption of redundancy on the balance of probabilities by showing that the dismissal was for some reason other than redundancy.

Before we analyse the complex definition of redundancy and the different approaches to its interpretation by the courts you should appreciate that the definition serves different purposes. In the years before the introduction of unfair dismissal in 1971 it is the employee exclusively who would seek to establish a redundancy dismissal in order to qualify for a redundancy payment. Post unfair dismissal the employee may still attempt to establish the right to a payment but a redundancy is a potentially fair reason for dismissal and an employer may have an interest in asserting that redundancy is the reason for dismissal which is potentially fair. An employer alleging a fair redundancy dismissal is more likely today bearing in mind the potential £50,000 compensatory award for unfair dismissal. Using the statutory definition for different purposes has inevitably caused confusion in the approach of the courts and tribunals to its interpretation.

In s.139(1) the Act provides that there is a dismissal by reason of redundancy if it is *attributable wholly or mainly to:*

(a)   *the fact that his employer has ceased or intends to cease, (i) to carry on the business for the purposes of which the employee was employed by him, or (ii) to carry on that business in the place where the employee was so employed, or*

(b)   *the fact that the requirements of that business (i) for employees to carry out work of a particular kind, or (ii) for employees to carry out work of a particular kind in the place where the employee was employed by his employer, have ceased or diminished or are expected to cease or diminish.*

Business closure

This is the more straightforward part of the definition.

Redundancy could occur under s.139(1)(a) because the business is closed or it is intended that it will be. Such a closure could relate to the whole business or just a part of it and be permanent or temporary. In addition redundancy could arise if the business is closed in the place where the employee works. If, however, the employee's contract provides that he could be required to move to a new work location, and the employer attempts to trigger the clause, this could prevent redundancy. Even without an express clause there is an implied term in the contract of employment that the employee may be moved to a new work location within reasonable commuting distance from home. Consider however the following case.

In *High Table Ltd. v. Horst* 1997 the Court of Appeal considered the position of silver service waitresses who all worked for one particular client in the City of London but who following a reorganisation were no longer required at that place of work. Their contracts of employment contained a mobility clause which authorised the employer to move them to other work locations. Applying s.139(1)(a) the issue was whether the women were redundant because they were no longer required at their usual client or whether the mobility clause extended their place of work to any potential work location. The Court of Appeal disagreed with the EAT and rejected the contractual approach to place of work stating that *"if an employee has worked in only one location under his contract of employment for the purposes of the employer's business, it defies common sense to widen the extent of the place where he was employed merely because of the existence of a mobility clause"*. Here the place where the employee worked was the particular client and there was a redundancy situation there which caused their dismissals.

In *High Table* the Court of Appeal is recognising that an employer could easily use the device of a wide mobility clause to defeat a finding of redundancy. In such circumstances the courts should concentrate on the factual circumstances which obtained rather than apply a contractual test to determine redundancy.

Diminution in requirements

There is also a redundancy situation where the requirements of the business for employees to carry out work of a particular kind have ceased or diminished or expected to do so under s.139(b).

There were two different approaches to this definition which have been rejected by the House of Lords. You should nevertheless appreciate that each approach has its supporters. The job function test attempts to identify redundancy in terms of economic requirements of the employer for the work to be done so that if the job function still exists there is no redundancy. The alternative approach called the contracts test is to consider whether the requirements of the business have diminished by reference to all the contractual duties of the employee. An issue of contention is when the definition refers to a diminution for employees to carry out work of a particular kind does that refer to the work of a dismissed employee or is it sufficient that a reduction in work has caused the dismissal.

The term 'bumping' has been used to explain the situation where a reduction in requirements has led to an employee being replaced and dismissed. A good example was used in *Safeway Stores plc v. Burrell* 1997. Where the EAT held that the principle of bumped redundancies is statutorily correct. *"For example, if a fork-lift truck driver, delivering material to six production machines on the shop floor, each with its own operator, is selected for dismissal on the basis of last in first out within the department following the employer's decision that only five machines are needed, and one machine operator with longer service is transferred to driving the fork-lift truck the truck driver is dismissed by reason of redundancy. Although under both the contract and the function test he is employed as a fork-lift truck driver. There is no diminution in the requirements for the fork-lift drivers, nevertheless there is a diminution in the request for employees to carry out the machine operator's work and that has caused the driver's dismissal".*

The fact that the dismissed employee has been replaced by another employee will not normally lead to a finding of redundancy for it cannot be said that the requirements of the business for an employee have ceased or diminished. There would be a redundancy, however, if it could be shown that the replacement employee was moved because of a reduction in requirements. Here an employee is being dismissed to make way for an employee who would otherwise be surplus to requirements and so the dismissed employee is entitled to a redundancy payment.

Would there be a redundancy dismissal under s.139 if a part-time secretary was replaced by a full-time secretary. This was the issue facing the EAT in *Barnes v. Gilmartin Associates* 1998 when the part-time secretary was replaced by a full-time worker and dismissed. Having decided that the secretarial job existed but in a different form, the EAT then concluded that there was no cessation or diminution for employees to carry out work of the particular kind so that the applicant was not redundant. In *Johnson v. Nottingham Combined Police Authority* 1974 the Court of Appeal had held that a change from regular hours to shifts was not redundancy stressing that it was the work not the hours which were relevant for deciding *"work of a particular kind".* Here the business reorganisation was a substantial reason of the kind to justify a dismissal under s.98(1).

The requirements of the business for employees of a particular kind will have ceased if they are replaced by independent contractors. To replace an employee with a self-employed person will be a dismissal by reason of redundancy and the dismissed employee will be entitled to a payment. This will also be the case where it is the employee himself who is being reinstated on self-employed status. Liability to make redundancy payments could be one of the costs of an employer transferring work from employees to independent contractors, but it may be that there are financial benefits in the long run. Such benefits would include the loss of future rights to redundancy payments and possible unfair dismissal rights and lower National Insurance contributions.

In situations where the employee's skills have become outdated because of changes in working methods to which he cannot or is not prepared to adapt, there have been conflicting views as to whether, if he is dismissed, it is by reason of redundancy or incapability.

In the history of the law of redundancy there are early examples of the courts being called upon to draw a distinction between diminishing requirements for an employee because of a reduction in a particular kind of work carried on, and diminishing requirements for an employee due to his failure to adapt to new working methods.

In *North Riding Garages Ltd. v. Butterwick* 1967 a workshop manager with thirty years experience was dismissed following a take-over and reorganisation of the business. The manager found it difficult to adapt to new methods which had been introduced, in particular coping with costs estimates. The repair side of the workshop for which he had been responsible was deliberately run down and the sales side increased. Following his dismissal a new workshop manager was engaged. The tribunal upheld the employee's claim for a redundancy payment deciding that the presumption of redundancy had not been rebutted. On appeal, however, it was held that there had been no change in the requirements of the business to carry out a particular kind of work, for there was still a need for a workshop manager. It was the employee's personal deficiencies which caused the dismissal rather than redundancy. *"An employee remaining in the same kind of work was expected to adapt to new methods and higher standards of efficiency, unless the nature of the work he was required to do was thereby altered so that no requirement remained for employees to do work of the particular kind which was superseded."*

"Personal deficiencies" was again the reason put forward by the employer for dismissal in *Hindle v. Percival Boats* 1969. The claimant, a highly skilled woodworker with twenty years boat-building experience was dismissed for being *"too good and too slow"* when fibreglass became the main material for boat-building rather than wood. He claimed a redundancy payment on the grounds that his dismissal was attributable wholly or mainly to a reduction in the employer's requirements for woodworkers. A majority of the Court of Appeal held that there was no dismissal by reason of redundancy, for the true reason for dismissal was that the claimant was too slow and his continued employment uneconomical. In the dissenting judgment, however, Lord Denning, M R, placed great emphasis on the statutory presumption of

redundancy. *"Redundancy payment is compensation to a man for the loss of the job; and a man should not be deprived of it merely because the employer thinks or believes that he is being dismissed for a reason other than redundancy."*

The approach to change seemed to be that so long as the job function remains, there is no redundancy. If an employee is given a very wide job function, that is likely to mean where there are technological or social changes in the way that a job is performed, that does not make it a different kind of work for the purposes of redundancy. In cases where an employee has an express flexibility clause in his contract that would not prevent a finding of redundancy where there is a clear reduction in requirements for him to carry out his primary job function. In *Johnson v. Peabody Trust* 1996 the claimant was employed for a number of years as a roofer by a housing association however a term in his contract provided for flexibility in that if there was no roofing work he could be redeployed on other building operations such as plastering. In 1993 the claimant was, along with others, selected for redundancy due to a down turn in roofing work. The tribunal felt that the claimant was employed as a roofer and the fact that the employers requirements for roofing work had diminished meant that he was redundant. On appeal it was argued that under the contract test, as the claimant could be required to carry out multi trade operations, which had not diminished, he could not be classified as redundant. The EAT rejected this argument and held that here there was a fair dismissal by reason of redundancy despite the flexibility clause in the roofer's contract. The essential nature of the claimant's contract was that of a skilled roofer and the fact that he could be required to do other work did not alter that fact. In applying the contract test the EAT said that *"the contract should not be read in an over-technical or legalistic way but should be looked at in a common-sense manner in order ascertain the basic task which the employee is contracted to perform. Where, as here, an employee is employed to perform a particular, well recognised and well defined category of skilled trade, namely roofing work, in our judgment it is that basic obligation which has to be looked at when deciding whether the employer's requirements for work of a particular kind have or have not ceased or diminished. Were it otherwise an employer could in practice never establish that any skilled tradesman, employed as such, who had accepted a flexibility clause of the kind in this case, had become redundant without establishing that a redundancy situation existed in every single other trade encompassed within the ambit of such a flexibility clause."*

Earlier we mentioned *Safeway Stores Plc v. Burrell* 1997 where the EAT moved away from the contract and job function test. The EAT held that the correct test for determining a redundancy dismissal involves three stages. Firstly was the employee dismissed? Secondly was this a diminution or cessation in the requirement of the employers business for employees to carry out work of a particular kind, or an expectation of such in the future. Thirdly was the dismissal of the employee caused wholly or mainly by that state of affairs. The EAT confirmed that there maybe a number of underlying causes of a redundancy situation. There could be a need for economies, a reorganisation, a reduction in production requirements or unilateral changes in employment terms. Such factors must be considered in deciding whether they have led to a diminution or cessation in the requirements. If that is the case the question then is whether the dismissal was attributable wholly or mainly to redundancy.

An important ruling of the House of Lords in 1999 seems to signal a new more simplistic approach to the definition of redundancy.

In *Murray v. Foyle Meats Ltd.* 1999 the House of Lords considered the statutory definition of redundancy describing it as *"simplicity itself"*. The case involved meat plant operatives who normally worked in the slaughter hall but whose contract of employment provided that they would be required to work anywhere in the factory. When a reorganisation of the factory resulted in a reduction in the need for skilled slaughterers the applicants were selected for redundancy. Both the tribunal and the Northern Ireland Court of Appeal felt that as the requirements of the employer for the employees to carry out work of a particular kind, the slaughtering, had ceased or diminished, the applicants had been made redundant. On appeal to the House of Lords however it was argued that work of a particular kind means contractually engaged work of a particular kind and as all the factory workers were on similar flexible contracts it was wrong to limit the redundancy situation to the slaughtermen. The House of Lords stressed that the key word in the statutory definition was *"attributable"* and both the contract test and the function test miss the point. Irrespective of the terms of an individuals' contract or the function he performs the issue is simply whether there is a diminution in requirements and if so whether the dismissal of the applicant is attributable to it. It is an issue of fact and one for the tribunal whether there is a causal connection between the reduction or needs and the applicant's dismissal.

The House of Lords by emphasising the word *"attributable"* in s.139 is giving redundancy a wide definition so that there is no reason why the dismissal of an employee should not be attributable to a reduction in requirements irrespective of contractual terms or the job functions he performs. The two questions are *"is there an economic state of affairs involving a diminution of requirements and if so is the dismissal attributable to it"*. Applying the new test a bumped redundancy would certainly be covered by the definition.

While the potential to qualify for redundancy payments are consequently increased as a result of this interpretation of the definition in Murray the opportunity for employers to use redundancy as a fair reason for dismissal are also greater.

In cases where the reason for dismissal is redundancy, but the employer was entitled to terminate the contract by reason of the employee's misconduct, the right to a redundancy payment will be lost. Obviously if the reason for dismissal is misconduct then the question of a redundancy payment does not arise. If the employee has already served notice of the "obligatory period" for redundancy, and the employee is dismissed for gross misconduct during that period, the employee can still apply to the tribunal which can award all or part of the redundancy payment. Furthermore, if the misconduct takes the form of strike action during the "obligatory period" any dismissal for that form of "misconduct" will not operate to disqualify the redundancy payment. If, however, the strike takes place before the notice of dismissal for redundancy, and the employee participates, that would be classed as misconduct so as to disqualify a redundancy claim.

> In *Bonner v. H Gilbert Ltd.* 1989 the applicant was given notice that his employment would terminate on 13 February 1987 for redundancy, but in fact he was dismissed on 13 January 1987 for alleged dishonesty. The issue was whether the employer was entitled to terminate the contract because of the employee's conduct. The EAT held that the tribunal was wrong in applying the unfair dismissal test of reasonableness to the employer's decision to dismiss for misconduct. Rather, the contractual approach adopted for the purposes of constructive dismissal should be applied. The employer's burden was "to show that the employee was guilty of conduct which was a significant breach going to the root of the contract or which showed that the employee no longer intended to be bound by one or more of the essential terms of the contract".

As we noted earlier, due to the fact that the possible compensation payable for unfair dismissal is well in excess of the State redundancy payment it may be that an applicant is more likely to pursue a claim for unfair dismissal rather than a redundancy payment. Redundancy is of course one of the specific reasons identified as a prima facie fair ground for dismissal. If redundancy proves not to be the true reason relied on for dismissal then a tribunal is entitled to find that the dismissal is unfair.

> In *Timex Corporation v. Thomson* 1981 the applicant, one of three managers, who, after fourteen years of employment with the company, was dismissed when the three management posts were re-organised into two. The two new posts required engineering qualifications which the applicant lacked, but it was also alleged that he was not selected because of his poor job performance. The EAT agreed with the tribunal and held that even though there was a redundancy situation they were not convinced that the reason for the applicant's dismissal was redundancy. Here the evidence of the applicant's incapability seemed to suggest that redundancy was used as a pretext for

dismissal. The tribunal were entitled to hold that they were not satisfied as to the employer's true reason for dismissal, which was unfair.

Suitable Alternative Employment

Under s.138 if before the employment terminates, the employer makes the employee an offer either to renew the contract of employment or re-engage the employee under a new contract which constitutes suitable alternative employment, then provided the new contract is to commence within four weeks of the previous one terminating, an unreasonable refusal to accept such an offer will mean that the employee will not be entitled to make a claim for a redundancy payment. Failure to take up an offer of a new contract on identical terms and conditions of employment therefore would normally constitute an unreasonable refusal to accept re-engagement and, as a consequence, an employer will lose the right to make a claim for payment. If the offer is of alternative employment, it is necessary to determine its suitability in relation to the previous employment. For the new employment to be 'suitable' it must be substantially similar to the previous job and not employment of an entirely different nature at the same salary. The question is one of fact and degree and one which the tribunal must examine in the light of the particular circumstances of the case including such matters as the nature of the work, the rates of pay, the place of work, the new status, and fringe benefits. Personal factors affecting the employee may also be considered such as social and family links, accommodation, and the children's education.

> In *Devonald v. J D Insulating Company Ltd.* 1972 the applicant was required to move from a factory in Bootle to another in Blackburn. He refused, and on his claim for redundancy the tribunal held that suitable alternative employment had been offered as he was already required under his present employment to do outside contract work.

Additional factors identified in *Thomas Wragg & Sons Ltd. v. Wood* 1976 included the fact that the offer of alternative employment was made late in the redundancy process when the employee had accepted alternative work and the fact that it was a declining industry.

In practice the question as to whether the alternative employment is suitable or not will be considered at the same time as the issue as to whether it is reasonable to refuse it or not.

> In *Fuller v. Stephanie Bowman Ltd.* 1977 the applicant typist refused to move from Mayfair to a new office in Soho. She found the move distasteful, particularly as the new office was above a sex shop. The tribunal found that

the refusal to move was unreasonable in the circumstances, as it was based on undue sensitivity and the claim for redundancy consequently failed.

The headmaster in *Taylor v. Kent County Council* 1969 was not insensitive when he refused to accept work as a supply teacher, given his previous status.

Even if there is an offer of suitable alternative employment it may still be reasonable to refuse it.

In *Cambridge & District Co-operative Society Ltd. v. Ruse* 1993 the complainant and manager of a butcher's shop was transferred to manage a butchery department in a large store when his shop was closed down. Having less responsibility and in his mind status in his new position he gave notice and claimed a redundancy payment. The employer claimed that the transfer was within the terms of a mobility clause in his contract which provided "you may be required to pursue your employment at any of the establishments comprising the food division". The EAT agreed with the tribunal and held that there was no unreasonable refusal of an offer of suitable alternative employment. The tribunal was entitled to find that the employee's perceived loss of status in the job offered made it reasonable for him to refuse it, notwithstanding the tribunal's unanimous conclusion that the offer was of suitable alternative employment.

The decision of the EAT in *Gloucestershire County Council v. Spencer* 1985 supports the view that it is for management to set the appropriate standard of work to be achieved. Here the number of cleaners at a school had been reduced from five to four and the hours of work of the remaining employees cut by forty five minutes. The employer recognised that standards would drop, but maintained nevertheless, that the new terms constituted an offer of suitable alternative employment. This offer was rejected by the remaining cleaners on the grounds that they felt they could not continue to do a satisfactory job. The industrial tribunal agreed and found that while the alternative jobs were 'suitable' within the meaning of the section, the employees' refusal to accept the new terms was not unreasonable as they could not do the new jobs adequately in the time allotted. The EAT held that the tribunal was in error, for the standard of work set by the management, cannot be reasonably objected to by employees as a ground for refusing to work. Accordingly the offer of suitable alternative employment had been unreasonably rejected and the applicants were not entitled to redundancy payments.

If an employee accepts an offer of alternative employment on different terms and conditions, he is entitled to a trial period under s.138. The length of the period is four weeks, but if the new job requires retraining, the parties can specify a longer trial period in writing. If, for any reason, during the trial period the employee gives notice to terminate his employment, or the employer terminates for a reason connected with the change to the new job, then the employee is treated as dismissed from the date that the previous contract terminated. To determine his rights to a redundancy payment it is then necessary to examine the original reason for dismissal, whether the offer of alternative work was suitable, and whether the termination by the employer reasonable. In cases where the offer of new employment involves changes in employment terms, which would otherwise constitute a repudiatory breach, then under the common law, an employee who nevertheless accepts the new job for a period could still change his mind and resign claiming constructive dismissal. In such circumstances therefore, there is a common law trial period which on its expiration, can be extended further by the statutory trial period under s.138.

Redundancy on a Business Transfer

To secure the right to a redundancy payment where an employee is dismissed on the transfer of a business undertaking the employee must establish that he is qualified to claim and that he is dismissed by reason of redundancy within the definition. For transfers of a commercial venture covered by the Transfer of Undertakings (Protection of Employment) Regulations 1981 an employee's contract is automatically preserved with the transferee employer so that rights in relation to redundancy are preserved with the new employer.

The effect of the Regulations is that where a relevant transfer is made the employee's contract continues with the new employer so that there is no dismissal and consequently no redundancy. Regulation 5(3) of the 1981 Regulations states that a transfer of liability to the transferee employer will only occur where the employee was employed in the undertaking *"immediately before the transfer"*. If an employee is dismissed because of the transfer then liability in relation to him is passed automatically to the new employer. If however an employee is dismissed because of an organisational economic or technical reason under regulation 8(1) then liability will not pass unless he was still employed at the time of the transfer.

In *Warner v. Adnet* 1998 a company accountant lost his job when his employer went into receivership and when the staff were re-employed by a new company on a business transfer he was not included. The Court of Appeal held that the dismissal was for a reason connected with the transfer of the undertaking but under reg 8(1) it was not automatically unfair as it was for an economic reason falling within the ETO defence. Also the normal requirement to consult could be overlooked because it would not have made a difference.

Those employees who are subsequently dismissed by the transferee employer will have the right to a redundancy payment if the dismissal is by reason of redundancy.

Dismissal could even be constructive, as for instance where the transfer employer unilaterally attempts to impose radical changes in terms and conditions of employment on the employee. It is still open to the employer of course to make an offer of suitable alternative employment to the employees which, if unreasonable refused will prejudice his right to a payment.

If an employee is made an offer of alternative employment by the new employer which is suitable but unreasonably refused then under s.141 the employee may lose the right to a payment. Where alternative employment is offered either by the old employer or the new employer then the employee is entitled to have a trial period of four weeks (or longer if agreed) in the new job. The employee has then the option of either accepting the new employment, or terminating the contract in which case he will be regarded as having been dismissed on the date the previous contract came to an end for the reason which applied then. It may then be necessary, for the purpose of redundancy entitlement, to decide whether the new employment was in fact an offer of suitable alternative work.

Redundancy Procedure

The Trade Union and Labour Relations (Consolidation) Act 1992 contains a number of rules relating to the procedure to be invoked in a redundancy situation where an independent trade union is recognised in relation to the class of employees involved. In *Commission of the European Communities v. United Kingdom of Great Britain and Northern Ireland* 1994, the European Court of Justice has ruled that by failing to ensure worker representation in the work place where there is no recognised trade union the UK has failed to comply with Community law obligations to ensure that workers representatives are informed and consulted on collective redundancies. It seems that the UK government will respond by providing for worker representation in future legislation. The primary duty imposed on the employer is to consult with trade union representatives.

Under s.188(1) where an employer is proposing to dismiss as redundant 20 or more employees at one establishment within a period of 90 days or less, the employer shall consult about the dismissals all the persons who are appropriate representatives of any of the employees who may be affected by the proposed dismissals.

(1A) The consultation shall begin in good time and in any event:

(a)   *where the employer is proposing to dismiss 100 or more employees at one establishment at least 90 days and;*

(b)   *otherwise at least 30 days before the first of those dismissals takes effect.*

(4)   *For the purposes of the consultation the employer shall disclose in writing to the trade union representatives:*

(a)   *the reasons for his proposals,*

(b)   *the numbers and descriptions of employees whom it is proposed to dismiss as redundant,*

(c)   *the total number of employees of any such description employed by the employer at the establishment in question,*

(d)   *the proposed method of selecting the employees who may be dismissed, and*

(e)   *the proposed method of carrying out the dismissals, with due regard to any agreed procedure, including the period over which the dismissals are to take effect [and*

(f)   *the proposed method of calculating the amount of any redundancy payments to be made (otherwise than in compliance with an obligation imposed by or by virtue of any enactment) to employees who may be dismissed].*

In *R v. British Coal Corporation and Secretary of State for Trade and Industry ex parte Price and others* 1994 the High Court gave some guidance as to the practicalities of consultation in a redundancy situation stating that:

* a proper opportunity must be given to the union to understand fully the matters about which it is being consulted and to express views on those subjects;

* the employer must consider those views properly and genuinely;

* where possible the consultation should take place when the proposals are at a formative stage;

* adequate information must be given and adequate time to respond.

In *MSF v. GEC Ferranti (Defence Systems) Ltd. No2* 1994 the EAT considered the statutory requirements of an employer to provide information to a recognised trade union over proposed redundancies to enable meaningful consultations to take place the tribunal stated that *"whether a union has been provided with information which is adequate to permit meaningful consultation to commence is a question of facts and circumstances. There is no rule that full and specific information under each of the heads listed in s.188(4) TULR(C)A) must be provided before the consultation period can begin"*. The issue in the case before the EAT was whether sufficient information had been given to the union about *"the number and descriptions of employees who it is proposed to dismiss as redundant"* to trigger the consultation period. The EAT held that here it was insufficient to merely give the total number of redundancies broken down into job categories and more precise details were necessary, in particular relating to the divisions of the company which would be affected by the redundancies.

The Trade Union Reform and Employment Rights Act 1993 amended the redundancy consultation procedures to bring the UK in line with the EC Collective Redundancies Directive. Under the Act the information to be given to union representatives when redundancies are proposed is expanded to include the proposed method of calculating payments. The consultation should consider how redundancy dismissals may be avoided and how the consequences of dismissal may be mitigated.

If an employer fails to comply with the consultation requirements then the trade union could seek a remedy by presenting a complaint to an employment tribunal. The tribunal can make a declaration as to non-compliance and also make a protective award requiring the employer to pay the specified employees their wages for the "protected period", specified not to exceed the consultation period to which they were entitled. An employer who fails to comply with a protective award can be required to do so on an individual complaint to a tribunal by an employee.

The duty to consult under s.188 is an obligation which must be complied with even where it is obvious that nothing can be achieved.

In *Sovereign Distribution Services Ltd. v. Transport & General Workers Union* 1989 the EAT found that the industrial tribunal had rightly made a protective award against an employer who had failed to consult the recognised trade union over redundancies as required by the section. The purpose of the section is to ensure consultation takes place even where the employer thinks that to consult will achieve nothing. *"The statutory duty to consult in many cases provides the only opportunity for employees through their recognised trade unions, to be able to seek to influence the redundancy situation and to put forward other ideas and other considerations, not only as to the overall decision but also as to the individuals who should be made redundant and other material aspects."*

In *Rowell v. Hubbard Group Services Ltd.* 1995 it was held that consultation must amount to more than a warning of redundancy and be fair and genuine giving those consulted a proper opportunity to appreciate the consequences. See also *Mugford v. Midland Bank plc* 1997 in Chapter 11.

Finally, mention should also be made of the fact that an employee with two years' service who is given notice of dismissal by reason of redundancy has the right, during the notice period, to be given reasonable time off during working hours, to look for new employment or make arrangements for future training. The employee is also entitled to be paid at the appropriate rate during the period of absence and can present a claim to a tribunal if his rights are denied.

Redundancy Calculation

If an employee believes that as a qualifying worker he has been dismissed by reason of redundancy, the onus is upon him to make a claim to his employer for a redundancy payment. If the employer denies the claim or simply refuses to make a payment, the remedy of the employee is by way of complaint to an industrial tribunal. If a redundancy payment is made (otherwise than in compliance with an order of the tribunal specifying the amount), then an employer is guilty of an offence if he fails without reasonable excuse to give the employee a written statement indicating how the payment was calculated. The sum is calculated in the same way as a basic award by reference to the age of the claimant, the length of continuous employment and the weekly pay of the claimant.

Amount of the payment

Age (inclusive)	Amount of week's pay for each year of employment
18 – 21	½
22 – 40	1
41 – 65	1½

Given that the aim of the payment is to provide a lump sum for the employee while he is seeking new employment, the fact that he will soon qualify for state retirement pension is also a factor in calculating the amount. Accordingly, for each month that the claimant is over sixty-four at the relevant date, the amount is reduced by one twelfth.

The Employment Act 1989 equalised the age at which men and women cease to be entitled to a statutory redundancy payment and in so doing brings the age limits on entitlement to redundancy payment into line with those on the right to claim unfair dismissal. The tapering provision which previously started at 64 for men and 59 for women and which had the effect of reducing the redundancy payment by one twelfth for each month of employment beyond those ages, will in future apply to both men and to women. An employee will be excluded from the redundancy payment scheme where there is a normal retiring age of below 65 for employees holding the position which he held, applicable to both men and women alike, and the employee has reached that age. If the normal retiring age is over 65, or is different for men and women, or there is no normal retiring age, the age limit for entitlement will be 65.

Another feature of the calculation is the fact that each year the maximum week's pay is adjusted to reflect the current average wage which is presently £210. Consequently the maximum redundancy payment is 20 years x 1½ (for employment between the ages of 41-65) x £230 = £6,900. For employees on a weekly fixed rate then the contractual rate is the current average wage. In cases where the wage does vary, however, a week's pay is calculated by reference to the average hourly rate of remuneration over the last twelve weeks of employment.

> In a complex decision relating to the calculation of an average week's wage for the purpose of redundancy entitlement, the House of Lords held in *British Coal Corporation v. Cheesebrough* 1990 that in calculating an employee's average rate of remuneration, work in overtime hours must be treated as if they had been done in normal working hours and the remuneration reduced accordingly. Where however an employee's contract provides for bonus payment only for work done during normal working hours, the overtime hours worked should not be treated as if they would attract bonus payments.

While the payment is made by the employer, originally he was entitled to claim a rebate from the Redundancy Fund financed by weekly levies from employers. Under the Employment Act *1988* the Redundancy Fund was abolished.

Case Study

Brinkley Business School - The Redundancy Situation

Brinkley Business School was set up last year by merging a number of departments in the University of Brinkley. The Director of the School is Miriam Perot who, with her two deputies, comprise the senior management team of the School. The senior management team is the final arbiter on staffing issues in the School, subject to formal ratification by the academic board of the University.

A difficult issue has arisen in relation to three lecturers in the Business School who were originally recruited by the University as specialists in economic and social history. Following the reorganisation of the University they found themselves deployed in the Business School in the economics section. Unfortunately while there is a call for a historical perspective in some areas of the Business School, the subject of economic history no longer features as part of the curriculum in any of the courses within the Business School. The three members of staff affected by the closure have been interviewed by the Director of the Business School and various suggestions have been made in relation to their future.

1.   *Michael Johnstone is fifty seven a senior lecturer in economic history who has worked at the University for twenty seven years. He has been offered early retirement with a lump sum and pension relating to his years of service and a sum equivalent to treble the state redundancy payment. Michael's present salary is £24,728 per annum.*

2.   *William James is thirty seven, a lecturer in economic and social history, who has worked at the University for eleven years. Foreseeing the diminution in his area of work the Director of the Business School decided to relocate William last year in the management section of the Business School. William agreed in his meeting with the Director to "give it a go for a term". William resigned last month stating that despite retraining he found it "difficult to cope as a lecturer in management".*

3.   *Alex Grey is thirty one, a part-time lecturer in economic history who has worked at the University for the last four years on average between five and seven hours per week over a thirty six week academic year. He has been told by the Director that his services will no longer be required.*

Index

THE OXFORD ILLUSTRATED HISTORY OF THE
Royal Navy

J. R. Hill served for over 40 years in the Royal Navy in sea and Whitehall appointments, ending his career in 1983 as a Rear-Admiral. He has since been Under-Treasurer of the Middle Temple, retiring in 1994, and since 1980 has written nine books on maritime warfare, strategy, history, and arms control. He has lectured and given conference papers, worldwide, on similar subjects. He is editor of *The Naval Review* and was Chairman of the Society for Nautical Research from 1994 to 1999.

The late **Bryan Ranft** was formerly Professor of History at the Royal Naval College, Greenwich, Visiting Professor and subsequently Senior Research Fellow in War Studies at King's College London. He was the author (with Geoffrey Till) of *The Sea in Soviet Strategy* and editor of *The Beatty Papers. Selections from the Private and Official Correspondence and Papers of Admiral of the Fleet Earl Beatty, 1902–1927*.